MENTALIZING IN THE DEVELOPMENT AND TREATMENT OF ATTACHMENT TRAUMA

Developments in Psychoanalysis Series

Series Editors: Peter Fonagy, Mary Target, and Liz Allison

Other titles in the series:

Developmental Science and Psychoanalysis: Integration and Innovation
  Edited by Linda Mayes, Peter Fonagy and Mary Target

Mentalizing in Child Therapy: Guidelines for Clinical Practitioners
  Edited by Annelies J. E. Verheugt-Pleiter, Jolien Zevalkink
  and Marcel G. J. Schmeets

*Taboo or not Taboo? Forbidden Thoughts, Forbidden Acts in Psychoanalysis
and Psychotherapy*
  Edited by Brent Willock, Rebecca C. Curtis and Lori C. Bohm

*Destructiveness, Intersubjectivity, and Trauma: The Identity Crisis of Modern
Psychoanalysis*
  Werner Bohleber

*Early Development and its Disturbances: Clinical, Conceptual, and Empirical
Research on ADHD and other Psychopathologies and its Epistemological Reflections*
  Edited by Marianne Leuzinger-Bohleber, Jorge Canestri and Mary Target

MENTALIZING IN THE DEVELOPMENT AND TREATMENT OF ATTACHMENT TRAUMA

Jon G. Allen

KARNAC

First published in 2013 by
Karnac Books Ltd
118 Finchley Road
London NW3 5HT

British Library Cataloguing in Publication Data

A C.I.P. for this book is available from the British Library

ISBN-13: 978-1-78049-091-5

Typeset by V Publishing Solutions (P) Ltd., Chennai, India

www.karnacbooks.com

To Esther and Dick, in Memory

CONTENTS

ABOUT THE AUTHOR

Jon G. Allen is a Senior Staff Psychologist and holds the Helen Malsin Palley Chair in Mental Health Research at The Menninger Clinic. He is Professor of Psychiatry in the Menninger Department of Psychiatry and Behavioral Sciences at the Baylor College of Medicine and an adjunct faculty member of the Houston-Galveston Psychoanalytic Institute and the Institute for Spirituality and Health in the Texas Medical Center. Dr. Allen received his B.A. degree in psychology at the University of Connecticut and his Ph.D. degree in clinical psychology at the University of Rochester. He completed postdoctoral training in clinical psychology at The Menninger Clinic. He conducts psychotherapy, diagnostic consultations, psychoeducational programs, and research, specializing in trauma-related disorders and treatment outcomes. He has taught extensively at the undergraduate, graduate, and postdoctoral levels. He is past editor of the *Bulletin of the Menninger Clinic,* associate editor of the *Journal of Trauma and Dissociation,* and a member of the editorial boards of *Psychological Trauma: Theory, Research, Practice, and Policy* and *Psychiatry: Interpersonal and Biological Processes.* His books include *Coping with Trauma: Hope through Understanding, Coping with Depression: From Catch-22 to Hope,* and coauthored with Peter Fonagy and Anthony Bateman, *Mentalizing in Clinical Practice,* all published by American

Psychiatric Publishing, Inc. He is also author of *Traumatic Relationships and Serious Mental Disorders,* and coeditor with Peter Fonagy of *Handbook of Mentalization-Based Treatment,* both published by John Wiley and Sons. He has authored and coauthored numerous professional articles and book chapters on trauma-related problems, psychotherapy, the therapeutic alliance, hospital treatment, and psychological assessment.

DEVELOPMENTS IN PSYCHOANALYSIS: SERIES FOREWORD

Peter Fonagy, Mary Target and Liz Allison

After the first hundred years of its history, psychoanalysis has matured into a serious, independent intellectual tradition, which has notably retained its capacity to challenge established truths in most areas of our culture. Above all, psychoanalytic ideas have given rise to an approach to the treatment of mental disorders and character problems, psychodynamic psychotherapy, which has become a thriving tradition in most countries, at least in the Western world. With an ever expanding evidence base, based on randomized controlled trials as well as investigations of brain function, psychodynamic psychotherapy can aspire to legitimacy in the world of science, yet retains a unique perspective on human subjectivity, which continues to justify its place in the world of humanities and all spheres where human culture is systematically studied.

The biological psychiatrist of today is called to task by psychoanalysis, as much as was the specialist in nervous diseases of Freud's time, in turn of the century Vienna. Today's cultural commentators, whether for or against psychoanalytic ideas, are obliged to pay attention to considerations of unconscious motivation, defences, the formative impact of early childhood experience, and the myriad other discoveries which psychoanalysts brought to twentieth-century culture. Twenty-first century thought implicitly incorporates much of what was discovered by psychoanalysis in the last century. Critics who try to pick holes in or even demolish the psychoanalytic edifice are often doing this from ramparts constructed on psychoanalytic foundations. A good example of this would be the recent attacks by some cognitive behavior therapists on psychodynamic approaches. Vehement as these are, they have to give credit to psychoanalysis for its contribution to cognitive therapeutic theory and technique. These authors point to the advances they have made in relation to classical ideas, but rarely acknowledge that the psychodynamic approach has also advanced. An unfortunate feature of such debates is that often attacks on psychoanalysis are addressed to where the discipline was fifty or even seventy-five years ago.

Both the epistemology and the conceptual and clinical claims of psychoanalysis are often passionately disputed. We see this as a sign that psychoanalysis may be unique in its capacity to challenge and provoke. Why should this be? Psychoanalysis is unrivalled in the depth of its questioning of human motivation, and whether its answers are right or wrong, the epistemology of psychoanalysis allows it to confront the most difficult problems of human experience. When else is the motivation of both victim and perpetrator of sexual abuse going to be simultaneously considered? What other discipline will take the subjectivity of a newborn, or in fact, an in-utero infant as a serious topic for study? The discipline, which has found meaning in dreams, continues to search for understanding in relation to acts of the greatest humanity and inhumanity. It remains committed to attempting to understand the most subtle aspects of the intersubjective interplay that can occur between two individuals, one struggling to overcome the barriers that another has elected to create in the path of their own progress through the world. Paradoxically, our new understanding of the physical basis of our existence—our genes, nervous systems, and endocrine functioning—rather than finally displacing psychoanalysis, has created a pressing need for a complementary discipline which considers the memories, desires, and meanings that are beginning to be recognized as influencing human adaptation even at the biological level. How else, other than through the study of subjective experience, will we understand the expression of the individual's biological destiny within the social environment?

It is not surprising, then, that psychoanalysis continues to attract some of the liveliest intellects in our culture. These individuals are by no means all psychoanalytic clinicians, or psychotherapists. They are distinguished scholars in an almost bewildering range of disciplines, from the study of mental disorders with their biological determinants to the disciplines of literature, art, philosophy, and history. There will always be a need to explicate the meaning of experience. Psychoanalysis, with its commitment to understanding subjectivity, is in a leading position to fulfill this intellectual destiny. We are not surprised at the upsurge of interest in psychoanalytic studies in universities in many countries, which is driven by the limitations of understanding that modern science, including modern social science, all too often provide. The courageous accounts of psychoanalysts meet a fundamental human need for discovering the meaning behind actions, and meet this need head on. While some may consider psychoanalytic accounts speculative, we mustn't forget that in relation to many descriptions of action, feeling, and cognition the explorations based in the consulting room have proved to be profound and readily generalizable. No one now doubts the reality of childhood sexuality; no one believes the conscious mind, in any sense, to represent the boundaries of subjectivity. Non-conscious conflict, defense, the mental structures that encode the quality of early relationships into later interpersonal functioning, and the motivation to become attached and to look after represent early psychoanalytic discoveries that have become an inalienable part of twenty-first century culture. The books in this series aim to address the same intellectual curiosity that has made these educational projects so successful.

The theme of our series is a focus on advances in psychoanalysis and hence our series title "Developments in Psychoanalysis". In our view, while psychoanalysis has a glorious and rich history, it also has an exciting future with dramatic changes and shifts as our understanding of the mind is informed by scientific, philosophical, and literary enquiry. Our commitment is to no specific orientation, to no particular professional group, but to the intellectual challenge to explore questions of meaning and interpretation systematically, and in a scholarly way. Nevertheless, we would be glad if this series particularly spoke to the psychotherapeutic community, to those individuals who use their own minds and humanity to help others in distress.

Nothing could give the editors more satisfaction than to welcome this book into our successful series as it serves as a template for almost all other volumes that have been part of this imprint. Jon Allen is a remarkable, creative integrator of ideas, who over the years has provided psychodynamic thinkers with an exceptionally powerful synthesis of attachment theory and clinical, empirical, and neuroscientific observations. His books on trauma have changed the thinking of many of those working psychotherapeutically with individuals with a history of severe adversity. He has found a combination of techniques and theoretical ideas that stand as a powerful testament to the value of committed scholarship, thoughtful reading, and crystal clear communication. Allen makes accessible to every clinician the remarkable advances in the neuroscientific understanding of attachment relationships and how these advances can be translated into therapeutic techniques in the best interest of our patients. He has succeeded in distilling the common elements of diverse, successful approaches that have been taken with traumatized individuals over the past decades. This book leaves us better clinicians on its last page than we were when reading the first, as long as we carefully read the ones in-between, as carefully as Jon Allen has done in his reading of a century's work on this subject.

The aim of this series is to convey the excitement the editors feel in relation to teaching and practicing psychodynamic ideas. This volume fulfills this goal and more, and will fulfill our ambition for the series in making accessible psychoanalytic ideas to an even larger group of students, scholars, and practitioners worldwide.

Peter Fonagy, Mary Target, and Liz Allison
University College London

PREFACE

I was fortunate to work with a group of colleagues at The Menninger Clinic in the late 1980s and early 1990s in developing specialized inpatient treatment for trauma, which we called the Trauma Recovery Program. We worked with patients who had been admitted for treatment of complex and chronic psychiatric disorders to which trauma in early attachment relationships had made a substantial contribution. I developed a psychoeducational group as a core component of this program, meeting with the patients twice weekly in a seminar-like format. Some staff members and trainees joined in. I taught and we all brainstormed. Without setting out to do so, I discovered that teaching patients was the best way to learn. I was gratified that, with the enthusiasm of numerous colleagues, this trauma education program spread throughout the clinic, not only to all the adult hospital programs as well as the adolescent treatment program but also to the partial hospital and outpatient programs. We all learned together, and I learned how to teach.

As I set out on this educational venture, I discovered attachment theory somewhat fortuitously. I had not learned anything about Bowlby's work in any of my education or training. Somewhat by happenstance, I came across his concise book, *A Secure Base*. At the time, I was working with a particularly challenging patient with severe dissociative disturbance; nothing I had ever read seemed to pinpoint her problems as well as attachment theory. I was hooked. Accordingly, I used attachment theory as a foundation in my first book, *Coping with Trauma*.

As I continued working on understanding trauma, I had a second stroke of good fortune: coincident with the publication of my first book, Peter Fonagy was invited to the clinic to reshape research with a focus on developmental psychopathology. Working with Peter and several of his close colleagues over many years, I gradually began to acquire a proper education in attachment theory. In the process, I also became hooked on one of Peter's main interests, mentalizing: the natural human capacity to apprehend and interpret behavior as related to mental states. What could be more interesting than trying to fathom how the mind comes into being in attachment relationships? And what could be more crucial to clinical work than the ways in which this process becomes derailed in attachment relationships? As I eventually came to appreciate fully, derailed mentalizing is the crux of attachment trauma.

In several previous books, I continued to include attachment theory and mentalizing as a foundation for understanding trauma and related disorders. With Peter's encouragement, I wrote this entire book about that foundation and added a chapter about treatment. My enthusiasm (and perhaps egocentrism) is unbridled: I aspire to explicate what I think we all need to know about attachment, which includes a thorough understanding of mentalizing. And my intended audience is not restricted to professionals. I have found that patients also are keen on learning about attachment theory and research; they readily appreciate its pertinence to their struggles, just as I did when I started reading Bowlby's work. Accordingly, consistent with my background in patient education, I have written this book in a conversational style so that it will be accessible to inquisitive laypersons.

I could not have written this book outside the setting of The Menninger Clinic, which provided a rare combination of devotion to clinical work and scholarly activity, all in the context of long-term inpatient and outpatient treatment. This long-term treatment setting was vital to conducting the ambitious and thoroughgoing educational work with patients that has kept me grounded in developing a common language—now including "mentalizing"—that all can understand.

In the past several years, concomitant with our changing practice patterns, my clinical work has focused on intensive inpatient treatment of several weeks' duration—long compared to customary inpatient stays in the United States of a few days' length. We no longer maintain the specialty program but rather treat trauma throughout the hospital. I include several clinical examples from this more recent practice in the past decade. To maintain patients' confidentially, I have disguised identifying details and intermingled aspects of the clinical presentation from different individuals.

I am grateful to Dick Munich, our former Chief of Staff, who enticed me to make the move when the clinic relocated from Topeka, Kansas to Houston, Texas to forge a partnership with the Baylor College of Medicine. Dick carved out a position for me that enabled me to continue the writing that has culminated in this book. And I am grateful to our current Chief of Staff, John Oldham, as well as to Ian Aitken, Sue Hardesty, and Tom Ellis, whose administrative support has been vital in allowing me the space to continue this work. I also thank several colleagues who have read and critiqued the material in this book as I have been developing it: Chris Fowler, Tom Ellis, John Hart, Liz Newlin, Ramiro Salas, Lane Strathearn, and Roger Verdon. I am grateful to Steve Herrera for his help in obtaining references. Last, I thank my wife, Susan, not only for her considerable forbearance with my preoccupation while writing this book but also for reading the entire manuscript to maximize the likelihood that all of it is understandable.

INTRODUCTION

I believe that understanding lies at the heart of treating trauma. Therapists must understand patients' experience; patients must feel known; and this experience of understanding must occur at an emotional level. I wrote this book to enrich therapists' and patients' understanding of trauma in attachment relationships. In its prototypical form, attachment trauma consists of childhood maltreatment—abuse and neglect. Yet more subtle and pervasive failures of emotional attunement in early attachment relationships also can have long-term adverse effects on development, and it is crucial that we all understand the full spectrum of these traumatic experiences.

Attachment theory and research has established a substantial niche in the huge literature on childhood maltreatment, with good reason. If the trouble lies in attachment relationships, attachment theory goes straight to the heart of the matter. In the wake of discovering the strong relations between maltreatment, profoundly insecure infant attachment, and subsequent developmental psychopathology, trauma has been a central concern of attachment researchers over the past two decades. Therapists and patients have much to learn from this research, because it points directly to the means of healing: restoring a feeling of psychological and emotional connection in a trusting relationship that provides a feeling of safety and security in relation to painful emotional experience. As I will explain at length, the lack of psychological connection with painful experience is the basis of traumatic attachments.

I intend this book to have broad applicability to psychotherapy, as my approach to treatment applies to a wide range of psychiatric disorders and can be employed by therapists working from a number of different theoretical perspectives. Moreover, although my main subject is attachment trauma, knowledge of attachment theory and research is pertinent to the full range of psychological stress, simply because secure attachment relationships provide our best means of ameliorating emotional distress—as John Bowlby put it, from the cradle to the grave. Even more broadly, I hope this book will justify my bold claim that attachment theory and research provides our best way of understanding therapeutic relationships, given its deep roots in understanding their forerunners: parent-child relationships.

For readers who are minimally acquainted with attachment theory, this book will provide a comprehensive foundation, and no specialized knowledge is needed to understand it. For those who are already knowledgeable, this book will provide an update with a focus on trauma. Even for specialists, keeping up with the burgeoning literature on attachment is a daunting task. For example, Jude Cassidy and Phil Shaver's second edition of the *Handbook of Attachment* published in 2008 consists of forty chapters and 1,000 pages of double-column print. These chapters are mere summaries of a huge body of literature, and this literature continues to bloom. I aspire to offer a readable synthesis useful to clinicians and patients as it pertains to treating trauma, broadly construed. Long as this book might be, it is a mere snapshot that might entice readers to stay abreast of this rapidly evolving field.

Overview

The first chapter on attachment in childhood provides solid footing in attachment theory, starting at the beginning with the origins of the theory as well as its basic language and concepts. Consistent with the central topic of this book, I will emphasize continually the role of attachment relationships in regulating emotional distress. I describe the basic patterns of secure and insecure attachment as they are clearly evident by twelve months of age, and I include consideration of many influences on these patterns—not only caregiving but also child temperament and the broader environmental context. Over the course of development, these influences contribute to a balance of stability and change in attachment patterns. The developmental advantages of attachment security have been well demonstrated from childhood onward, and these advantages justify our attention to fostering attachment security throughout life, in psychotherapy and in other attachment relationships.

The second chapter on attachment in adulthood begins by linking attachment to romantic relationships, the closest counterparts to childhood attachments. Remarkably, albeit with innumerable modifications, the basic secure and insecure attachment patterns evident at one year of age show striking parallels in adult attachment relationships. For similar reasons, these adult attachment patterns also show a balance of stability and change. The marriage of childhood and adulthood attachment research has given rise to a profoundly important discovery: the intergenerational transmission of attachment security and insecurity. Understanding this intergenerational process points the way toward intervention; the possibility of interrupting this intergenerational transmission process is one of the most heartening stories in attachment research.

The third chapter introduces what I consider the fulcrum for understanding the development of attachment relationships and the means by which our therapeutic efforts might improve attachment security and emotion regulation: mentalizing, that is, attunement to mental states in self and others. To put it simply, mentalizing in relationships entails a meeting of minds—and, more poetically, a meeting of hearts. Mentalizing is the means by which we establish attachment relationships, and mentalizing distinguishes human attachment relationships from those of our animal kin. In this third chapter, I also take pains to explicate the complex relations between mindfulness and mentalizing, in part because mindfulness is more familiar and liable to be confused with mentalizing. Pulling these two strands of research and clinical practice together, I propose that mindful attention to mental states is a necessary foundation for mentalizing.

With the first three chapters providing the needed background, the fourth chapter addresses downright traumatic attachment relationships. Attachment trauma was discovered somewhat belatedly in attachment research, evident in anomalous infant attachment behavior that came to be classified as *disorganized*. This discovery led to research on the intergenerational transmission of trauma that linked parents' histories of childhood attachment trauma to disorganized attachment in their infants. In conjunction with disorganized attachment, we are now beginning to appreciate the cardinal role of mentalizing impairments in the intergenerational transmission of attachment trauma. Thus this chapter includes consideration of the ways in which mentalizing impairments are associated with different forms of childhood maltreatment as well as noting the parallels between childhood and adulthood forms of attachment trauma.

I include a fifth chapter on neurobiological perspectives merely to explicate some links between current trends in neuroscience and the central concerns of this book: attachment, mindfulness, and mentalizing. I am not keen on the idea that we must see a psychological phenomenon on a brain image to view it as "real." The full reality of attachment disturbance as reviewed in the preceding chapters will be all too evident to patients and therapists. But understanding something about the physiological basis of attachment trauma helps us take the developmental research even more seriously. Doing so, however, presents us with a double-edged sword: the emerging evidence that enduring problems in emotion regulation stemming from attachment trauma have a basis in altered physiology underscores not only the reality of these problems but also the difficulties in overcoming them. All in all, I find it best to face the reality: ideally, patients can be more compassionate toward themselves for the difficulty they experience in overcoming trauma, and therapists can be more compassionate toward themselves in relation to the sheer difficulty of their therapeutic endeavors. Above all, we must remain hopeful, and hope must be predicated not on wishful thinking but rather on realistic expectations. Readers should be forewarned that this fifth chapter is an exception to the rule of this book: I have written the book to be accessible to a broad audience, but this chapter narrows that field somewhat; it will be easier going with some very basic knowledge of brain anatomy. Nonetheless, understanding something about your brain can help you understand more about your mind, and I have written the chapter with that aim in mind.

You might sense an imbalance in this book, with several chapters devoted to understanding the problem and only one to treatment. As I stated in the introduction to this Introduction, understanding *is* the treatment. I make some brief links to treatment implications in the earlier chapters simply to help readers keep treatment in mind throughout. I include this last chapter to explicate the connections more fully.

I summarize the range of psychiatric disorders that trauma treatment must address, and I review briefly a number of existing treatment methods. This discussion of psychopathology and treatment sets the stage for conveying my view of the mentalizing approach as a distinctive style of therapy and illustrating how this style of therapy applies to treating attachment trauma. I employ only one technique: conversation. I have only one main aspiration, moment to moment: mentalizing and engaging the patient in doing the same. And I aim toward one main treatment outcome: enhancing the patient's capacity to establish and maintain increasingly secure attachment relationships. I do not mean to imply that these intentions are all that is on my mind; hardly so. But these overarching goals comprise the heart of the therapeutic process as I understand it. I find extensive support for this broad focus in attachment research, and I need a solid foundation to keep me oriented and grounded in what is inevitably an emotionally challenging process in which it is all too easy to lose my footing, if not my mind.

CHAPTER ONE

Attachment in childhood

When I educate adult patients about psychiatric disorders, I use a stress-pileup model to advocate a developmental perspective. While acknowledging the role of genetic risk and temperament, the model predicates childhood adversity as promoting vulnerability to disorder in the face of adulthood stress. Yet, taking the devil's advocate position, I preface this presentation by posing the question: Why should you care how you got into difficulty? Why not just concentrate on how to get out of it? Patients readily assert that knowing how they got into difficulty can help them get out and stay out of it. My focus on attachment and mentalizing in development and treatment provides the substance for their assertion. I add that adopting a developmental perspective fosters compassionate understanding, particularly for patients who fail to acknowledge their history of adversity and its impact on their development. Then they berate themselves (as their family members also might do): "I have so much going for me—I have no reason to be so anxious and depressed!" Such patients minimize the seriousness of their illness and the significance of their early experience.

I start this book by giving childhood its due, with my transparent bias that attachment theory and research provides the most solid foundation for psychotherapeutic treatment of trauma. The connections from development to treatment are so direct that we need no translation—merely a bit of explication that I will provide throughout.

I launch this developmental project by anchoring attachment theory in the broader domain of personality development, relying on Sidney Blatt's (2008) influential theory of personality organization, which revolves around two fundamental developmental lines: relatedness and self-definition. Blatt's approach to personality development dovetails beautifully with attachment theory. I find this overarching framework to be commonsensical and elegant, and it is thoroughly grounded in research. I will interweave these two perspectives throughout this book.

Attachment theory and research has a long developmental history, and awareness of this history prepares the ground for a summary of basic concepts and an overview of the ways in which attachment relationships evolve over the course of childhood. All this groundwork sets the stage for reviewing the typical patterns of secure and insecure attachment that orient the conduct of psychotherapy. I have a considerable way to go before getting to traumatic attachments, but these more ordinary patterns of secure and insecure attachment remain crucial, because traumatic attachments invariably are intermingled with and superimposed on them. Moreover, a solid understanding of secure attachment guides trauma treatment in which the attainment of greater security is paramount.

Attachment theory, like its progenitor, psychoanalysis, runs the risk of blaming mothers (as well as fathers and other caregivers) for psychological problems and psychiatric disorders. No doubt, some egregious parenting practices are blameworthy, and a focus on trauma highlights these. Nonetheless, to reiterate the point of taking a developmental perspective, my aim is compassionate understanding, and this includes compassionate understanding of the challenges parents face in the context of *their* developmental history and adult life circumstances. A blaming perspective is a gross oversimplification as well as a disservice to parents (Sroufe, Egeland, Carlson & Collins, 2005). Attachment develops in a partnership, and my review of secure and insecure patterns will be followed by a consideration of the child's contribution to attachment relationships, although research suggests that child temperamental characteristics play a surprisingly limited role. In contrast, the broader family and social context influences attachment relationships in a powerful way that contributes to continuity and change in attachment patterns over the course of development. The chapter concludes with a summary of the impact of secure and insecure attachment on adjustment in childhood.

Two lines of personality development

We can understand best the profound significance of early attachment relationships by viewing them as embedded in our lifelong quest for psychological maturity. Based on decades of clinical experience and scholarly research, Blatt's (2008) book, *Polarities of Experience,* identifies the need for each of us to develop and integrate two fundamental poles of experience over our lifetime, relatedness and self-definition. The self-definition pole is associated with autonomy, and I will use these terms somewhat interchangeably. Blatt summarizes:

> Every person throughout life confronts two fundamental psycho-logical developmental challenges: (a) to establish and maintain reciprocal, meaningful, and personally satisfying interpersonal relationships and (b) to establish and maintain a coherent, realis-tic, differentiated, integrated, essentially positive sense of self .... the articulation of these two most fundamental of psychological dimensions—the development of interpersonal relatedness and of self-definition—provides a comprehensive theoretical matrix that facilitates the integration of concepts of personality development, personality organization, psychopathology, and mechanisms of therapeutic change into a unified model. (p. 3)

In tandem with attachment theory, I will use Blatt's framework through-out this book to help us see the forest for the trees. While we all must balance and integrate our need for relatedness and self-definition, we all tend to tilt in one direction or the other by virtue of our basic temper-ament and life experience. As Blatt explicates, these two poles of experi-ence also are encouraged in different ways by different cultures, and there are conspicuous gender differences as well. Western industrialized soci-eties place greater emphasis on self-definition, a stereotypically mascu-line quest. Traits consistent with an emphasis on self-definition include independence, autonomy, self-reliance, agency, competition, achieve-ment, dominance, power, and separateness. When the emphasis on self-definition becomes defensively exaggerated to the exclusion of relatedness, maladaptive traits become evident, including envy, entitlement, narcissism, self-critical perfectionism, aggression, isolation, and alienation. Such imbalanced individuals are liable to undermine their relationships by being aloof, domineering, critical, judgmental, and hostile.

In contrast, Eastern collectivist societies place a greater emphasis on relatedness, a stereotypically feminine quest. Traits consistent with an emphasis on relatedness include dependency, cooperation, collaboration, communion, mutuality, reciprocity, altruism, empathy, affection, and intimacy. When the emphasis on relatedness becomes defensively exaggerated to the exclusion of self-definition, maladaptive traits become evident, including excessive dependency or neediness, submissiveness, passivity, self-sacrifice, and exquisite sensitivity to neglect or abandonment.

Over the course of development, we need to cultivate our capacities for relatedness and self-definition while also coordinating and integrating them: as Blatt puts it, "normal personality development involves simultaneously and mutually facilitating dialectical interaction between the two primary developmental dimensions of interpersonal relatedness and self-definition" (p. 104). These two poles are synergistic; when they are in reasonable balance, the development of each facilitates the development of the other. We come to know ourselves and define ourselves in the context of being known by others; and our sense of identity and self-worth allows us to enter into intimate relationships with others while maintaining personal boundaries and autonomy. This integration typically reaches a point of consolidation in adolescence:

> Although these two developmental lines interact throughout the life cycle, they also develop relatively independently through the early developmental years until adolescence, at which time the developmental task is to integrate more mature expressions of these two developmental dimensions into the comprehensive structure Erikson called 'self-identity.' (p. 104)

To foreshadow the ensuing discussion, secure attachment exemplifies the achievement of a balance between relatedness and self-definition, a balance that is evident directly in using attachment as a safe haven and secure base as well as developing an internal sense of security in relating to yourself. Exaggerated reliance on one developmental pole or the other is evident in the two main patterns of insecure attachment: avoidant attachment is associated with greater concern with self-definition and autonomy to the exclusion of close relationships, whereas ambivalent attachment is associated with an exaggerated effort to maintain close relationships to the exclusion of the development of self-identity. This organizing framework for understanding development and the challenges of treatment now seems so obvious that we can overlook the brilliant clinical observations and research that led to the attainment of the framework. In the following historical sketch, I will quote liberally from the progenitors of attachment theory to underscore the contemporary relevance of their original insights.

The early development of attachment theory and research

To provide a general orientation to attachment theory, we can take four findings as fundamental (van Ijzendoorn & Sagi-Schwartz, 2008): (1) Given any opportunity, and barring extreme neurobiological impairments, all infants form attachments with one or more caregivers—including abusive and neglectful caregivers. (2) The majority of infants become securely attached. (3) Infants are more likely to be securely attached to caregivers who are sensitive and responsive to the infant's needs. (4) Attachment security contributes positively to children's emotional, interpersonal, and cognitive competence. These findings justify our attention to attachment when coupled with one final principle:

> attachment behaviour ... is characteristic of human nature through-out our lives—*from the cradle to the grave*. Admittedly it is usually less intense and less demanding in adolescents and adults than it is in earlier years. Yet an urgent desire for love and care is natural enough when a person is anxious and distressed. (Bowlby, 1988, p. 82, emphasis added)

It seems fitting that attachment theory and research has a father, John Bowlby, and a mother, Mary Ainsworth. In his captivating book, *Becoming Attached*, Robert Karen (Karen, 1998) summarized their pioneering work, the social controversies and professional politics in which it was embedded, and the subsequent evolution of attachment research. I hit some highlights here.

John Bowlby

For the past century and a half since its inception, the field of early life trauma has been fraught with controversy (Dorahy, van der Hart & Middleton, 2010). Bowlby, a psychiatrist and psychoanalyst in London, worked his way into the controversy and contributed to it. Peter Fonagy (Fonagy, 2001), also a psychoanalyst and attachment theorist, began his book integrating these two fields with the following declaration: "There is bad blood between psychoanalysis and attachment theory" (p. 1). In the ensuing years since this declaration, however, owing to Fonagy's and others' efforts at rapprochement (Fonagy, Gergely & Target, 2008), the bad blood has, at the very least, diminished considerably (Eagle & Wolitzky, 2009). How did it come to be in the first place? To over-simplify a long and controversial story, Bowlby differed from Freud about trauma in the context of Freud having differed from himself. The outlines of this story are well known, but the story bears repeating to underscore Bowlby's radicalism.

Early in his career as a therapist, Freud aspired to understand the childhood origins of a wide range of symptoms in his adult patients; these symptoms included anxiety, depression, suicide attempts, painful physical sensations, and eruptions of intense emotions associated with images of hallucinatory vividness—the welter of symptoms we continue to face in conjunction with traumatic childhood relationships. Having worked with eighteen patients, Freud concluded in 1896, "At the bottom of every case … there are one or more occurrences of premature sexual experience, which occurrences belong to the earliest years of childhood but which can be reproduced through the work of psycho-analysis in spite of the intervening decades" (Freud, 1896/1962, p. 203). By 1897, he changed his mind, writing in a letter to his colleague, William Fleiss, "there was the astonishing thing that in every case … blame was laid on perverse acts by the father" but then concluded that "it was hardly credible that perverted acts against children were so general" (Freud, 1954, pp. 215–216). Decades later, in 1933 he wrote about this early turning point: "almost all my women patients told me that they had been seduced by their father. I was driven to recognize in the end that these reports were untrue and so came to understand that … symptoms are derived from phantasies and not from real occurrences" (Freud, 1964, p. 120). Freud never doubted the potentially damaging impact of early childhood trauma, or sexual abuse in particular; but he had come to doubt its sheer pervasiveness. Thus he began to interpret his patients' symptoms as stemming from forbidden childhood sexual desires and conflicts about them rather than from actual traumatic experience. Accordingly, without denying the impact of traumatic realities, he shifted his *emphasis* from external reality to internal and unconscious conflicts stemming from powerful and forbidden sexual and aggressive drives.

At the start of his career in the 1930s, while training in psychoanalysis, Bowlby became interested in the relation between maternal deprivation and psychological disorders. He focused mainly on children's experience of being separated from their mother, but he also was concerned about the impact of mothers' emotional attitudes toward their children. Thus Bowlby's attention to the external world of the child put him at odds with his psychoanalytic colleagues' focus on the internal world. Consider the dramatic contrast between Bowlby's orientation and that of his psychoanalyst, Joan Riviere, who wrote:

> Psychoanalysis is … not concerned with the real world, nor with the child's or the adult's adaptation to the real world, not with sickness or health, nor virtue or vice. It is concerned simply and solely with the imaginings of the childish mind, the fantasied pleasures and the dreaded retributions. (quoted in Fonagy, 2001, p. 90)

The "bad blood" to which Fonagy refers also was fueled by psychoanalysts oversimplifying Bowlby's work and vice versa (Fonagy, 2001). Integrating psychoanalysis and attachment theory remains a work in progress (Fonagy, Gergely & Target, 2008) but, in principle, there is no contradiction: traumatic events exert their influence on the basis of the way they are subjectively experienced; in understanding trauma, we always must take into account external and internal reality. Moreover, although controversy is endemic to the field of trauma (van der Kolk, 2007), we now have extensive evidence about the frequency of occurrence of various forms of childhood trauma (Koenen et al., 2008) and their adverse long-term impact (Felitti & Anda, 2010).

Throughout this book, from the review of development to the discussion of psychotherapy, I am sticking with Bowlby's focus on separation. Notably, Bowlby was following in Freud's (1936) footsteps. In *The Problem of Anxiety*, Freud asserted that the fundamental dangers in infancy—instanced by being left alone, in the dark, or with a stranger— are "all reducible to a single situation, that of feeling the loss of the loved (longed for) person" (p. 75). Freud emphasized the infant's helplessness in the face of unmet needs: "The situation which the infant appraises as 'danger,' and against which it desires reassurance, is therefore one of not being gratified, of an *increase of tension arising from non-gratification of its needs*—a situation against which it is powerless" (p. 76, emphasis in original). Following Bowlby and in contrast to Freud, I will emphasize the sense of *psychological connection* as the fundamental need: the feeling of safety and meeting other needs hinges on psychological connection—mentalizing, to put it technically. Thus I will follow Bowlby's original interest in separation with the proviso that I am compressing the time frame from prolonged separations and permanent losses to home in on repeated and brief—even momentary—separations that leave the child psychologically alone in states of extreme distress. Such states constitute the essence of trauma, explicated with increasing clarity over the course of decades by Freud, Bowlby, and Fonagy.

In the 1940s, Bowlby (1944) published the results of his first research project, which was an intensive study of the early origins of juvenile delinquency—thieving in particular. Bowlby was particularly struck by the role of prolonged separations from the mother after twelve months of age in a subgroup of delinquent children he labeled "affectionless characters." In his words, these children were hardboiled and indifferent, unable to form loving relationships. He viewed their attitudes toward relationships as a self-protective strategy: "not to risk again the disappointment and the resulting rages and longings which wanting someone very much and not getting them involves. If we are indifferent to others or dislike them we disarm them of any power to hurt us" (p. 20). Although Bowlby emphasized prolonged separations in these individuals' lives, these children also were subjected to various forms of maltreatment, which were evident in the histories he presented (Follan & Minnis, 2010). Given his growing expertise, the World Health Organization employed Bowlby to summarize worldwide professional knowledge about the effects of homelessness on children. As a result of this investigation, Bowlby (1951) wrote an influential monograph on maternal care and mental health, and he became recognized as a world expert on the subject.

There were many reasons for maternal deprivation, including prolonged institutionalization, lengthy hospitalizations, and children being shunted from one foster home placement to another. All these separations had the potential to be detrimental to children's mental health. In the 1950s, Bowlby teamed up with a social worker, James Robertson, who made careful observations of the emotional impact of long-term hospitalization on very young children who were thus separated from their parents. Robertson observed a typical sequence of responses: initial *protest* (e.g., crying and clinging), followed by *despair* (e.g., listlessness and loss of hope for the parent's return), ultimately leading to *detachment* (e.g., apparent indifference to the parent on reunion). Professionals generally had minimized the emotional impact of such separations, such that Bowlby and Robertson's work met with considerable resistance. With Bowlby's collaboration, Robertson made a poignant film portraying the child's response to separation, but Bowlby and Robertson continued to fight an uphill battle with pediatricians, nurses, and hospital administrators, who tended to dismiss the significance of their observations. Ultimately, of course, their findings contributed significantly to open parental visitation in hospitals, which we now take for granted.

In giving priority to the external world, Bowlby had made one break with psychoanalysis at the beginning of his career. Soon thereafter, he made another break with psychoanalysis in marrying attachment with his interest in evolutionary theory and ethology—the scientific study of animal behavior. As many of us have observed, for example, ducklings become attached to the first moving object they see—typically their mother—and they follow the object thereafter. Bowlby (1958) proposed that, in a wide range of species, the process of mother-infant bonding evolved to ensure that infants stay close to their mother so as to remain safe, most notably, from predators. Thus mothers are naturally motivated to remain close to their infants, as infants are motivated to stay close to their mother. For example, being separated leads infants of many species to emit a distress cry, which serves as a signal to the mother to reestablish contact with her infant. Bowlby's interest in ethology, coupled with his criticism of the psychoanalytic emphasis on nourishment (and orality) as the biological basis of the mother-infant relationship, earned him the enmity of his psychoanalytic colleagues, one of whom quipped, "An infant can't follow its mother; it isn't a duckling" and "What's the use to psychoanalyze a goose?" (Karen, 1998, p. 107).

With his eye on evolutionary function and ethologists' observations, Bowlby construed physical proximity for the sake of physical protection as a paramount function of attachment:

> It is my thesis that, as in the young of other species, there matures
> in the early months of life of the human infant a complex and nicely
> balanced equipment of instinctual responses, the function of which

is to ensure that he obtains parental care *sufficient for his survival.* To this end the equipment includes responses which promote his close proximity to a parent and responses which evoke parental activity. (Bowlby, 1958, p. 364, emphasis added)

But Bowlby (1958) also recognized the emotional function of attachment in humans: when frightened, the infant seeks proximity to the caregiver as a "haven of safety" (p. 370). We should keep this bedrock principle in mind: when threatened, endangered, distressed, or ill, the child is inclined to make contact with the mother to restore a feeling of safety, security, and wellbeing. The mother is motivated in a complementary way to protect the infant from harm and to relieve the infant's distress. Yet Bowlby also proposed that our need for attachment security goes far beyond infancy and childhood; it remains crucial throughout life for the same reason: restoring security and providing comfort in the face of danger and distress.

Mary Ainsworth

Around the time Bowlby started taking an interest in maternal depriva-tion, Mary Ainsworth was working on her psychology doctoral disser-tation at the University of Toronto on "security theory." A decade later, after establishing herself as an expert in psychological diagnosis and research, Ainsworth moved to London with her husband and, quite for-tuitously, took a position assisting Bowlby with his attachment research. After a few years working directly with Bowlby, she moved with her husband to Uganda where he had taken a teaching position; there she began charting what proved to be the foundation of attachment research: studying the mother-infant attachment relationship in the home envi-ronment (Ainsworth, 1963). In so doing, she made a monumental shift in time frames: whereas Bowlby had been investigating the effects of major (i.e., prolonged) separations, Ainsworth began studying the com-monplace brief separations and reunions in daily life. Crucially, she also examined attachment behavior in relation to the emotional quality of the mother-infant relationship. Thus she made room for psychological disconnection in the context of attachment interactions, which is my primary concern.

In Uganda, Ainsworth (1963) and her assistants conducted many hours of home observations for twenty-eight infants over a period of nine months. From this initial research, she was able to distinguish among different patterns of secure and insecure attachment. Reminiscent of her earlier work in security theory at the University of Toronto, Ainsworth observed what came to be another cornerstone of attachment (coupled with Bowlby's idea of the safe haven): attachment provides a *secure base* for exploration. For example, she noticed that the infants would make brief exploratory excursions away from their mother, while checking periodically on her whereabouts and making brief contacts with her to ensure her availability.

Ainsworth moved back to the United States in 1956 to join the faculty at Johns Hopkins University and, resuming her collaboration with Bowlby in the 1960s, she conducted a series of home observations of mother-infant interactions in Baltimore. There she found essentially the same patterns of secure and insecure attachment that she had observed in Uganda. Ainsworth had established the foundations of attachment research with her naturalistic home observations but, in a stroke of genius, she took a major step forward in designing a brief laboratory procedure to assess attachment security, which she called the "Strange Situation." This procedure, to be discussed later in this chapter in conjunction with secure and insecure attachment patterns in infancy, addresses Bowlby's initial concern, the impact of being separated from the mother and the importance of reestablishing contact with the mother to restore a feeling of security (Ainsworth, Blehar, Waters & Wall, 1978). Yet Ainsworth's shift in time frame redirected attention from the extraordinary (prolonged separations and loss) to the ordinary, and more recent attachment research has shown that the ordinary ubiquitous psychological disconnections can be traumatic.

As will become evident later in this chapter and beyond that, Ainsworth's talent in research made an inestimable contribution not only to attachment theory but also to our understanding of child development more broadly. Following Bowlby's lead, she was putting psychoanalytic ideas to a systematic test. Psychoanalytic theory initially was based on adults' memories of childhood attachment relationships, and adults' memories of childhood remain important in attachment research. But there is no substitute for direct observation. No doubt, many child psychoanalysts—not least, Sigmund Freud's daughter, Anna—made extremely important observations, many of which were consistent with Bowlby's views (Fonagy, 2001). And Daniel Stern's (1985) monumental contribution to establishing empirical foundations for developmental thinking in psychoanalysis must be acknowledged. (I still remember the moment decades ago when my colleague, Marty Leichtman, burst into a classroom declaring that we must read *The Interpersonal World of the Infant*—one of the most important books he had ever read; being highly suggestible, I read Stern's book right away, and doing so paved the way for my appreciation of Bowlby.) Yet Ainsworth's systematic home and laboratory observations put attachment theory on a solid developmental research foundation that has led to the construction of an elaborate edifice in the ensuing decades (Cassidy & Shaver, 2008).

Basic concepts

Although this book might not convey it, there is much more to life than attachment. Attachment theory construes attachment as being one among several "behavioral systems," the others being fear, caregiving, exploratory, and sociable. In this section, I will convey how these systems are intertwined and discuss two other core concepts, affectional bonds and internal working models. Embedded in this section is a major reason for giving attachment central stage in relation to trauma, namely, the role of attachment relationships in emotion regulation. The section concludes with an aspiration for traumatized patients: establishing psychological security.

Attachment-caregiving partnerships

We say of an individual that he or she is securely or insecurely attached to another individual, as the infant is attached to the mother. Yet attachment forms and takes shape in the crucible of a relationship, interaction by interaction, over the course of the relationship. Every attachment has a history.

The infant is predisposed to display attachment behavior and the mother is predisposed to develop complementary caregiving behavior. The relationship ultimately evolves into what Bowlby (1982) termed a *goal-corrected partnership* in which each individual has a sense of the other's goals and the two adapt to each other accordingly—in effect, negotiating to meet their conjoint needs. Ideally, these needs converge: "What is believed to be essential for mental health is that the infant and young child should experience a warm, intimate and continuous relationship with his mother (or permanent mother-substitute) in which *both* find satisfaction and enjoyment" (Bowlby, 1982, pp. xi–xii, emphasis added). From a physiological point of view, this satisfying partnership contributes to mutual homeostasis (Churchland, 2011). Of course, the infant's and mother's needs invariably will run into conflict with each other, some of the time if not much of the time. In extreme cases, such conflict is a source of trauma.

Compared to other animals, we humans are exceptional in needing an extraordinarily prolonged period of parental care. Thus infants are highly dependent, but they are not passive; on the contrary, they are active in meeting their needs. Regarding her home observations in Uganda, Ainsworth (1963) commented,

> One feature of attachment behaviour that struck me especially was the extent to which the infant himself takes the initiative in seeking an interaction. At least from two months of age onwards, and increasingly through the first year of life, these infants were not so much passive and recipient as active in seeking interaction. (p. 101)

As Bowlby (1958) put it, the human infant comes equipped with "complex and nicely balanced equipment of instinctual responses, the function of which is to ensure that he obtains parental care sufficient for his survival." (p. 364). More specifically, Bowlby identified five instinctive attachment behaviors that promote proximity to the parent and evoke caregiving: sucking, smiling, crying, clinging, and following. Bowlby made it clear that we should not view sucking as merely a route to nourishment; ideally, nursing is social, a form of mutually soothing and pleasurable contact and interaction. Smiling, a quintessentially social behavior, also serves to cement attachment. As Bowlby posed, "Can we doubt that the more and better an infant smiles the better he is loved and cared for? It is fortunate for their survival that babies are so designed by Nature that they beguile and enslave mothers" (pp. 367–368). More recently, Sarah Hrdy (2009) elaborated the significance of infants' beguiling capacities in the evolutionary context of communal caregiving. As Bowlby observed, in times of distress, crying draws caregivers close, and clinging serves to maintain proximity. As infants become more mobile, they can forestall separation and maintain proximity by following: crawling and then toddling. Bowlby acknowledged that this quintet of attachment behaviors reaches a zenith in infancy and then declines. But none disappears and, "Furthermore, some of them, particularly crying and clinging, revert to an earlier state of activity in situations of danger, sickness, and incapacity. In these roles, they are performing a natural and healthy function" (p. 371).

Attachment is one of several behavioral systems, and caregiving is a complementary behavioral system (George & Solomon, 2008). Becoming a caregiver entails a significant developmental transition, namely making "a shift away from *seeking protection and proximate care from attachment* figures ... to *providing protection, comfort, and care for a child*" (George & Solomon, 2008, p. 834, emphasis in original). Jude Cassidy defined the caregiving system as

> a subset of parental behaviors—only those behaviors designed to promote proximity and comfort when the parent perceives that the child is in real or potential danger. The chief behavior within this system is retrieval ... others include calling, reaching, grasping, restraining, following, soothing, and rocking. (Cassidy, 2008, p. 10)

The attachment and caregiving behavioral systems are reciprocal in the sense that, when caregiving is activated, attachment can be deactivated and vice versa: when the mother is striving to maintain closeness, the infant need not do so; when the mother's caregiving system is inactive and the infant is in distress, the infant will activate attachment behavior to reengage caregiving. Hence, as Bowlby (1973) made plain, separation is a prime mover of distress and attachment behavior. Moreover, just as the child's fear activates attachment, the mother's fear (e.g., if the child is endangered) activates caregiving (Cassidy, 2008). Ainsworth summarized succinctly the conditions that activate the infant's attachment system:

> Among the various environmental conditions that may activate attachment behavior in a young child who has already become attached to a specific figure are absence of or distance from that figure, the figure's departing or returning after an absence, rebuff by or lack of responsiveness of that figure or of others, and alarming events of all kinds, including unfamiliar situations and strangers. Among the various internal conditions are illness, hunger, pain, cold, and the like. In addition, whether in early infancy or

in later years, it seems apparent that attachment behavior may be
activated, sustained, or intensified by other less intense conditions.
(Ainsworth, Blehar, Waters & Wall, 1978, p. 7)

Plainly, we cannot consider attachment apart from caregiving. Just as
attachment remains significant from the cradle to the grave, so does
caregiving—not just in parenting but also in providing emotional comfort and security to us adults, for example, in romantic relationships,
close friendships, and therapy relationships. Hence, in tandem with
attachment, the quality of caregiving will concern us throughout this
book.

Affectional bonds

Given Bowlby's focus on proximity, it is not surprising that the concept
of *bonding* came to be used alongside attachment. The meanings of *bond*
range from adhesiveness and being tied together to being shackled in
chains, as in bondage. Sadly, this latter sense also applies to attachment
relationships, exemplified by traumatic bonding.

In the context of attachment theory, "bond" is used metaphorically to
refer to an emotional bond—a "psychological tether" (Sroufe & Waters,
1977, p. 3). Ainsworth (1989, p. 711) defined an affectional bond as a
"relatively long-enduring tie in which the partner is important as a
unique individual and is interchangeable with none other." Further,
affectional bonds are characterized by "a need to maintain proximity,
distress upon inexplicable separation, pleasure or joy upon reunion,
and grief at loss." Affectional bonds are not exclusive to attachment
relationships; the criterion for attachment is "the experience of *security
and comfort* obtained from the relationship with the partner" (emphasis
added). Noting that not all attachments are secure, Ainsworth added
the caveat that attachment implies "a seeking of the closeness that, if
found, would result in feeling secure and comfortable in relation to the
partner." She added further that mothers and fathers develop a bond
with their children, but this is *not* an attachment, because the parent
does not normally depend on the relationship with the child for his or
her security. In short, children attach to their parents whereas parents
bond with their children. In this context, Bowlby (1982) observed that
role reversal in which children serve as attachment figures for parents
"is almost always not only a sign of pathology in the parent but a cause

of it in the child" (p. 377). Of course, this role reversal naturally and appropriately comes into play in relationships between aging parents and their children (Magai, 2008).

Internal working models

As Bowlby's interest in ethology attests, attachment behavior and reciprocal caregiving behavior are evident in a wide range of species. Yet attachment takes a radically psychological turn in humans, which will occupy our attention throughout this book. While Bowlby parted company from his fellow psychoanalysts to some degree in placing greater emphasis on the external world of the child, he remained true to psychoanalysis in giving due weight to the child's internal world. Based on their experience in the world, children develop *internal working models* of attachment relationships along with models of other experience. Here is how Bowlby (1982) characterized the development of working models:

> Starting, we may suppose, toward the end of his first year, and probably especially actively during his second and third when he acquires the powerful and extraordinary gift of language, a child is busy constructing working models of how the physical world may be expected to behave, how his mother and other significant persons may be expected to behave, how he himself may be expected to behave, and how each interacts with all the others. Within the framework of these working models he evaluates his situation and makes his plans. And within the framework of the working models of his mother and himself he evaluates special aspects of his situation and makes his attachment plans. (p. 354)

Bowlby proposed that internal working models are *mental representations* of reality, as a map is a representation of the actual terrain. Like maps, mental representations can be more or less accurate, more or less valid or distorted. Perhaps modern painting provides a better analogy than map making. Painters differ from one another in the degree of correspondence between their paintings and their subjects. Edward Hopper's paintings are directly representational, yet punctuated with quirky distortions and noted for the mood they evoke. Vincent Van Gogh's swirling colors infuse landscapes with emotion. And Salvador Dali's surrealistic distortions twist ordinary objects out of shape. Like painters and like us adults, children actively interpret their experience and represent it more or less accurately in their mind, their speech, their drawings, and their play. The external world and the internal world, subjectivity and objectivity, intermingle. Yet, whereas early psychoanalysts gravitated toward fantasy, Bowlby (1973) kept his eye on reality: "the varied expectations of the accessibility and responsiveness of attachment figures that different individuals develop during the years of immaturity are *tolerably accurate* reflections of the experiences those individual have actually had" (p. 202, emphasis added).

Granted Bowlby's claim for tolerable accuracy, we all are vulnerable to distorted perceptions and interpretations of present relationships viewed through the lens of the past; tolerably accurate models of the past might be a poor fit for present relationships. This potential for distortion, earlier or later, applies to models of the self that are developed in the context of attachment relationships as well as models of others. As Bowlby (1973) put it, "in the working model of the self that anyone builds, a key feature is his notion of how acceptable or unacceptable he himself is in the eyes of his attachment figures" (p. 203). Like maps, internal working models of self and others must be updated continually to fit the present terrain. Traumatic early attachment relationships interfere with this essential capacity to update older working models so as to match current relationships.

Inge Bretherton, whose undergraduate education included a course on developmental psychology taught by Mary Ainsworth, has written extensively about internal working models (Bretherton, 2005; Bretherton & Munholland, 2008). She makes a crucial distinction between implicit and explicit models. We employ our *implicit* models habitually and nonconsciously, that is, without awareness that they are shaping our experience. These implicit models are based on memories that guide our behavior, memories that become automatic procedures for interacting. Think of riding a bicycle: you do not need to remember consciously how to ride it; having learned, you just hop on and ride. Of course, these implicit models also must be updated as you move from a tricycle to a two-wheeler and then to a racing bike. To take an example of an implicit working model, consider a child who was relentlessly criticized for any decision that turned out badly, no matter how trivial (e.g., not going out with a raincoat on a cloudy day). Applying this implicit model of being harshly criticized for being incompetent, the adult may respond reflexively with defensiveness and anger to a well-meaning query about the reason for a decision (e.g., "How was it that you took my car to work today, instead of yours?").

By comparison, explicit working models are conscious and thus can be explicated—thought about and talked about. Ideally, this process of explication begins early in life when "parents perform a positive role in helping a child construct and revise working models through emotionally open dialogue" (Bretherton & Munholland, 2008, p. 107). Such explication is essential for updating out-of-date working models of self and others, as we do in psychotherapy. Over time, for example, the patient may come to experience the therapist's questions about the reasons for puzzling actions as indications of caring interest rather than harbingers of harsh condemnation. We should not lose sight of the fact that attachment relationships shape working models of the self as well as working models of others. Crucially, a child who is loved feels lovable; a child who is cared for feels worthy. Thus it is not surprising that securely attached children show high self-esteem (Thompson, 2008).

I hope it is now obvious that our development and ongoing adaptation depends on the construction and reconstruction of internal working models, implicit (procedural) and explicit (narrative). To sum up, in Bretherton's (2005) words, internal working models of attachment serve the purpose of rendering "the relational world more predictable, shareable, and meaningful" (p. 36). But we should not lose sight of the fact that, being representations, these working models profoundly shape our experience of the world, for better or for worse: "representational processes and the resulting working models of self, close relationships, and the world are important, not only because they are reality-reflecting, but because they *create* different realities for self and relationship partners" (p. 39, emphasis in original). The world we create in our mind influences the outer world: the child who has been criticized endlessly at home and sees others as hostile and carries a chip on his shoulder in a way that alienates his peers and teachers at school. Then the outer world comes to mirror the inner world. Such self-fulfilling prophecies borne of pernicious internal working models are grist for the psychotherapeutic mill.

Emotion regulation

With evolution and animal behavior in mind, Bowlby (1982) proposed, "protection from predators is by far the most likely function of attachment behavior" (p. 226). Accordingly, he did not mince words about the significance of attachment: "Unless there are powerful in-built responses which ensure that the infant evokes maternal care and remains in close proximity to his mother throughout the years of child-hood he will die" (Bowlby, 1958, p. 369).

We can be grateful for civilization in at least one respect: rarely are human infants eaten by tigers. If the function of attachment were con-fined to protection from predators, its applicability to psychological trauma would be limited—although it would remain pertinent enough, given our lifelong vulnerability to predators among our fellow humans. But, to reiterate a point from the earlier discussion, Bowlby (1958) also recognized that proximity to an attachment figure not only assures pro-tection but also provides an *emotional refuge* for the infant:

> No matter for what reason he is crying—cold, hunger, fear, or plain loneliness—his crying is usually terminated through the agency of the mother. Again, when he wants to cling or follow or to find a *haven of safety* when he is frightened, she is the figure who com-monly provides the needed object. It is for this reason that the mother becomes so central a figure in the infant's life. (pp. 369–370, emphasis added)

The safe haven of attachment provides protection from all sorts of dan-ger beyond predation; hence the attachment system is active in tandem with another behavioral system, the fear system: when afraid, the infant seeks proximity to the mother. Similarly, when the mother is afraid for the infant, she retrieves the infant. When contact and safety is reestab-lished, the fear system is deactivated for mother and infant.

More generally, the availability of the attachment figure decreases the infant's *susceptibility* to fear. Ainsworth (Ainsworth, Blehar, Waters & Wall, 1978) expressed this point simply in a way we all can easily imagine, echoing Bowlby in emphasizing "how crucial it is in a potentially fear-arousing situation to be with a trusted companion, for with such a companion fear of all kinds of situation diminishes, whereas when alone fear is magnified" (p. 20). As I will emphasize repeatedly, the prototype of traumatizing experience is being afraid and psycho-logically alone.

Accordingly, Bowlby (1982) maintained, "No form of behaviour is accompanied by stronger feeling than is attachment behavior" (p. 209).

Hence, when attachment is working well, proximity to an attachment figure provides a *feeling of security*. We are wise to follow Alan Sroufe and Everett Waters (1977) in giving priority to the feeling of security over physical proximity as the goal of attachment behavior. Proximity is one means of establishing a feeling of security; establishing confidence in the availability of the attachment figure is another. Of course, in the case of extreme distress at any age, physical contact is likely to be the most potent route to a feeling of security (Ainsworth, Blehar, Waters & Wall, 1978). Thus, while casting the emotional state of felt security as the primary role of attachment, we should not give short shrift to the importance of proximity as a means to this goal throughout life:

> inner representations cannot entirely supplant literal proximity and contact, nor can they provide more than minimal comfort in the case of inexplicable and/or permanent loss of an attachment figure—neither for a young child nor for a mature adult. When people are attached to another, they want to be with their loved one. They may be content for a while to be apart in the pursuit of other interests and activities, but *the attachment is not worthy of the name if they do not want to spend a substantial amount of time with their attachment figures*—that is to say, in proximity and interaction with them. Indeed, even an older child or adult will sometimes want to be in close bodily contact with a loved one, and certainly this will be the case when attachment behavior is intensely activated—say, by disaster, intense anxiety, or severe illness. (Ainsworth, Blehar, Waters & Wall, 1978, p. 14, emphasis added)

Yet, physical proximity is no guarantee of felt security; contact with an emotionally remote caregiver will not provide comfort. Accordingly, as Bowlby and Ainsworth demonstrated throughout their work, the *quality of the relationship* is the key to the feeling of security associated with proximity or availability. Proximity to an abusive or indifferent caregiver does not provide an unalloyed feeling of security. Herein lies the main justification for giving so much weight to attachment in relation to trauma: *secure attachment is the mainstay of emotion regulation* and thus our primary means of learning to cope with distress, traumatic stress being an extreme case. Thanks to extensive developmental research with animals as well as human infants we now know a great deal about the way in which attachment relationships mediate physiological regulation and development in tandem with emotion regulation; much of this work focuses on the relation between attachment and the secretion of stress hormones (Polan & Hofer, 2008; Suomi, 2008).

My focus on attachment is predicated not only on its benefits but also on its obvious downside: attachment relationships comprise a paramount source of traumatic stress. Presaging Bowlby, Freud (1929/1961) sagely averred, "We are never so defenceless against suffering as when we love, never so hopelessly unhappy as when we have lost our love object or its love" (p. 33). Unfortunately, loss is only part of the problem: attachment relationships can be traumatic in being downright frightening. Then we face the paradox of needing attachment to regulate the fear engendered by the attachment relationship.

Later in this chapter, I will begin to address variations in emotion regulation associated with the more typical patterns of secure and insecure attachment. I will take up later in the book how attachment relationships can undermine emotion regulation and engender fear. Next, however, I will consider another behavioral system besides caregiving that is thoroughly intertwined with attachment: the exploratory behavioral system.

Exploration and psychological security

When we think of attachment, the safe haven comes to mind: the distressed child seeks contact with the mother to obtain comfort and a feeling of security. Yet, as she had observed in mother-infant interactions in Uganda homes, Ainsworth (1963) highlighted infants' use of their mother as a secure base for exploration:

> Now that the baby is able to crawl, he does not always keep close to his mother, bur rather makes little excursions away from her, exploring other objects and people, but he returns to her from time to time. He may even go outside the room altogether, if he is permitted to do so. His confidence in leaving the secure base is in remarkable contrast to his distress if the secure base gets up and moves off on her own initiative. (pp. 78–79)

The pairing of the safe haven and secure base gives an attachment relationship enormous power to shape a relationship and to influence the course of development. I have just reviewed the prominent role of the safe haven in emotion regulation; the secure base serves an equally important function, promoting autonomy and a sense of security in exploring the world. In Bowlby's (1988) view, "No concept within the attachment framework is more central to developmental psychiatry than that of the secure base" (pp. 163–164). Ainsworth (1963) underscored the developmental significance of the secure base in enabling children "to explore the world, developing skills and knowledge, and to expand their interpersonal horizons to include attachments to figures other than the mother" (p. 104). Thus, crucially, the secure base promotes exploration and learning not only in the physical world but also the social world; hence, the exploratory system can be activated in tandem with the sociable system that promotes affectional bonds and affiliation with peers. Accordingly, the exploratory system promotes learning not only about the external world but also about the internal world of the mind, such as we do in psychotherapy.

Klaus and Karen Grossman and their colleagues made a significant contribution to our understanding of the exploratory system (K. Grossman, Grossman, Kindler & Zimmerman, 2008). They define secure exploration as "confident, attentive, eager, and resourceful exploration of materials or tasks, especially in the face of disappointment. Secure exploration implies a social orientation, particularly when help is needed" (p. 873). The attachment, fear, and exploratory systems interact with each other: fear activates attachment needs and deactivates exploration. This balance is captured elegantly in the concept of a Circle of Security (Marvin, Cooper, Hoffman & Powell, 2002). Picture a toddler on a playground. Feeling secure in the presence of attachment, the toddler toddles off to explore the playground, periodically checking back to make contact with mother, father, nanny, or older sister. Then the toddler falls, scrapes his knee, feels scared, and starts crying. Time to return to the safe haven of attachment to restore a feeling of security. Adequately cared for and comforted, the toddler can return to play— circling to and from in relation to the caregiver as needed.

Attachment research shows that fathers as well as mothers serve as attachment figures insofar as both engage in caregiving. That is, fathers as well as mothers provide a safe haven and promote exploration by providing a secure base. Yet, albeit a matter of degree, the Grossmans also have observed significant role differentiation: fathers tend more to engage in exploratory play with their children, specializing to some degree in the secure base side of attachment. Thus, while the mother provides comfort and relaxation, "the father provides security in the context of monitored, controlled excitement, through sensitive and challenging support when the child's exploratory system is aroused" (K. Grossman, Grossman, Kindler & Zimmerman, 2008, p. 861).

The Circle of Security highlights the importance of a dual sense of safety: safety in attachment and safety in exploration. The Grossmans capture this ideal state of affairs tidily in their concept of *psychological security:*

> We propose that security eventually depends on both attachment security and safe familiarity with the real world. Finding a large number of studies that provide support for this broader view, we advocate the concept of 'psychological security,' which includes both security of attachment and security of exploration, as emerging from sensitive support from both mother and father. (p. 873)

To bring Blatt's developmental polarities back to mind, this concept of psychological security exemplifies the mutually facilitating balance between relatedness and autonomy.

The development of attachment

You maintain attachment through the organization and integration of a complex set of behaviors, and the behaviors you employ vary from situation to situation and from one developmental period to the next (Sroufe & Waters, 1977). As an infant, you cling to your mother's skirt; as an adolescent, you send her a text message.

You are born equipped for social engagement, but attachment comes into being step-by-step over the course of the first year. Bowlby (1982) identified four phases with fuzzy boundaries in the development of attachment and, with gradual development in mind, he concluded, "It is of course entirely arbitrary to say by what phase a child can be said to have become attached. Plainly he is not attached in Phase 1, whereas equally plainly he is so in Phase 3" (p. 268). Hence, in Bowlby's scheme, Phase 2 is a transitional phase, and Phase 4 (typically achieved by age 4) is the gold standard of attachment. Beyond age four your fundamental capacity for attachment remains unchanged, although it is extensively refined and elaborated into adulthood. In this section, I will sketch the four phases and summarize further developments in middle childhood and adolescence. My overview rests heavily on Robert Marvin and Preston Britner's (2008) masterful extension of Bowlby's initial work, based on subsequent research.

Phase 1: Zero to three months

By the time they have reached full-term status, fetuses show preference for their mother's voice and, in the early weeks of life, newborns show a preference for the human face. Newborns are attuned to social stimuli and adept at eliciting caregiving. When the caregiver's responses are well attuned to the baby's behavior and the two are in sync, stable patterns of interaction develop. These synchronized interactions gradually minimize crying and elicit visual orientation and smiling.

Phase 2: Three to six to nine months

The hallmark of phase 2, which makes it transitional to attachment, is the infant's ability to discriminate among caregivers and others. In Bowlby's (Bowlby, 1982) words, "During this phase an infant continues to behave toward people in the same friendly way as in Phase 1, but he does so in more marked fashion towards his mother-figure than towards others" (p. 266). Marvin and Britner (2008) identify several infant behaviors shown distinctly in relation to one or a few main caregivers: crying when the caregiver leaves, ceasing to cry in the caregiver's presence, smiling, vocalizing, orienting, and greeting, as well as climbing and exploring. As Ainsworth fully appreciated and this list of behaviors attests, this second phase is characterized by the infant's growing activity and initiative in the attachment-caregiving partnership.

Phase 3: Six to nine months to two to three years

In tandem with the infant's newfound capacities for locomotion and signaling, Phase 3 is marked by clear-cut safe-haven and secure-base behavior. The infant shows wariness of strangers and, when afraid for any reason, seeks contact with his mother. The infant follows his mother when she departs and greets her when she returns. The infant also makes exploratory excursions away from his mother while maintaining periodic contact. Note that, by eighteen months, most infants have a small network of attachment figures, but one such figure (often the mother) is primary: "attachment behavior tends, especially when an infant is distressed, hungry, tired, or ill, to be focused on a particular person when both that person and other attachment figures are available" (Marvin & Britner, 2008, p. 280). Often enough, this remains true in adulthood as one attachment figure remains primary—typically, a romantic partner.

Phase 4: Toddlers and preschoolers

Toddlers continue to display attachment behavior at the same intensity and frequency as infants, although they make increasingly distant excursions, and they are more likely to rely on calling and searching than crying when they are separated. Beginning between three and four years of age, however, a sea change in attachment relationships develops in tandem with young children's *psychological* development. The crux of this change is their burgeoning capacity to understand behavior as based on mental states such as desires, thoughts, and feelings—in short, their mentalizing capacity.

A full-fledged, goal-corrected partnership develops when children are able to understand their caregiver's goals and intentions, to communicate their own goals and intentions, and to recognize the differences between their goals and intentions and those of the caregiver. At this point in development, the child's mental representations become more explicit as feelings and thoughts about the self and the caregiver can be put into words. Thus, in this partnership, the child and caregiver can adapt to each other and negotiate when their goals are in conflict. As Ainsworth observed, when mental representations of attachment figures are consolidated, "the child becomes able to sustain his relationship with that figure over increasingly longer periods of absence and without significant distress—provided that the separations are agreed to willingly and the reasons for them understood" (Ainsworth, Blehar, Waters & Wall, 1978, p. 13). This principle, established by age four, remains true throughout life. Thus four-year-old children will be less distressed by brief separations when they have a shared plan with their caregiver who might say, "I'm going to get some ice cream and will be right back. Jane will be here while I'm gone. OK?"

Marvin and Britner (2008) enumerate five skills that are associated with increasingly sophisticated internal working models of attachment: the ability to recognize the attachment figure's internal mental states such as feelings and goals; the ability to distinguish between the child's and attachment figure's mental states (e.g., desires); the ability to infer what factors influence the attachment figure's goals and plans (e.g., the needs of a sibling); the ability to assess the degree of agreement versus conflict in goals; and the ability to exert influence over the attachment figure's goals, plans, and actions. Plainly, all these abilities come into play in attachment relationships in adulthood, based on refinements of the basic psychological skills that take root around age four.

Middle childhood

As a consequence of the shift into reliance on flexible mental representation in the late preschool years, older children and adults are far less dependent on physical proximity and more reliant on expectations of availability in case of need. In explaining attachment security to patients, I emphasize *confidence* in the availability and responsiveness of persons to whom they are attached. Such confidence is the basis of psychological security, and confidence diminishes the need for continual reassuring contact. As Ainsworth (1989) put it, "It is the capacity of humans to form representational models of another and of themselves in relationship to the other that enables them to sustain a bond across time and distance" (p. 714). Thus, the *psychological connection* becomes paramount, and this connection depends on open lines of communication, which then remain critical to attachment security throughout life. Of course, a key function of open communication is to ensure that physical proximity and contact can be established readily in times of need—neither older children and adolescents nor adults ever outgrow the need for face-to-face contact and physical comfort in the face of intense distress.

Buttressed by their mental capacities, with increasing age and a wider network of interpersonal support, children rely less on primary attachment relationships for protection. With greater physical separation from their parents, they take on greater responsibility for their own protection and rely on other children and adults for help, including older siblings, extended family members, neighbors, teachers, and coaches. Many such relationships involve affectional bonds, and they blur into attachment relationships depending on the extent to which they provide comfort and a feeling of security, to use Ainsworth's (1989) criterion.

Adolescence

Adolescents, like adults, remain attached to their parents. Yet Joseph Allen (J. P. Allen, 2008) highlighted the major transition in attachment that takes place over the course of adolescence: "it is a period of profound transformation in emotional, cognitive, and behavioral systems surrounding attachment relationships, as the adolescent evolves from being a receiver of care to becoming a self-sufficient adult and potential caregiver to peers, romantic partners, and offspring" (p. 419).

Allen enumerated several more specific transformations of attachment in adolescence. The balance between attachment and exploration shifts dramatically in adolescence, although adolescents continue to return to the parental safe haven in times of significant distress. With increased space and objectivity, coupled with increased cognitive capacities, adolescents have a greater capacity to reflect on their various attachment relationships and to compare these relationships with one another. Accordingly, they are in a position to re-evaluate their internal working models (e.g., moving from more idealized views of parents to more realistic views or, on the other hand, becoming more tolerant and forgiving of parents' flaws and failures) and to develop more integrated and generalized attitudes toward attachment (e.g., becoming more generally trusting or distrusting). Perhaps most significantly, adolescents develop increasing capacity for intimacy and support and thus begin transferring their primary attachments from parents to peers; hence peer relationships (e.g., romantic relationships) develop in the direction of full-blown attachment relationships.

Secure attachment

In reviewing some fundamental transitions in attachment behavior and relationships from birth to adolescence, I have been focusing on normative development, with attachment security in mind. In this and the following sections, I will begin focusing on individual differences in attachment security, that is, distinguishing secure attachment from different types of insecure attachment. I devote the next chapter to adulthood counterparts to these childhood prototypes, but I invite you to anticipate these parallels by imagining adult versions as you read about infancy.

A model of secure attachment guides our therapeutic work significantly particularly as we strive to help patients who have been traumatized in attachment relationships develop more secure attachments—ideally, a network of relationships, including the psychotherapy relationship. In this section, I will continue to expand the concept of secure attachment, focusing on infancy as a vivid prototype. This presentation makes use of extensive research employing observations of mother-infant interactions in the home and the laboratory, the latter being the Strange Situation that Ainsworth designed. I will first consider infants' attachment behavior and then describe the associated pattern of caregiving behavior. A clear picture of normative development sets the stage for appreciating insecure attachment behavior and the patterns of caregiving conducive to learning insecure attachment strategies. This research demonstrates infants' precocity in social learning as they adapt their attachment behavior to different variants of caregiving in their first year of life.

Ainsworth designed the Strange Situation to be moderately stressful to the infant by imposing brief separations in an unfamiliar environment. Here is the scenario, composed of eight episodes:

1. the infant and the mother are brought into an unfamiliar but comfortable room filled with toys;
2. the infant is given the opportunity to play with the toys, potentially with the mother's assistance;
3. a stranger enters the room and plays with the infant;
4. the mother departs, leaving the infant with the stranger and the toys;
5. the mother returns, pausing to give the infant a chance to respond to her return, and the stranger leaves the room;
6. the mother leaves the infant alone in the room;
7. the stranger comes back into the room and interacts with the infant as needed;
8. then the mother returns, and the stranger leaves the room.

Although the infant's reaction to the mother's two departures is important in assessing the infant's security, the most crucial observations relate to the two reunions: How do the mother and her distressed infant interact when the mother returns, and how does this interaction affect the infant's distress? Therein lies the difference between secure and insecure attachment as observed in the home and in the lab.

Infant behavior

Compared with insecure infants, Ainsworth (Ainsworth, 1963; Ainsworth, Blehar, Waters & Wall, 1978) characterized secure infants' behavior at home as having several features: securely attached infants cry relatively little; confident in the attachment, they experience relatively little distress in response to brief separations; they are less anxious; they enjoy close bodily contact with their mother; and they are more cooperative and compliant with their mother's requests. Given that they are relatively unperturbed by routine separations, some of the most solidly attached infants in Uganda displayed relatively little separation anxiety "but rather showed the strength of their attachment to the mother through their readiness to use her as a secure base from which they could both explore the world and expand their horizons to include other attachments" (Ainsworth, 1963, p. 103). Accordingly, secure infants are more outgoing and comfortable with other adults as well as more enthusiastic and less easily frustrated in play and problem-solving tasks.

The same pattern of behavior is evident in the Strange Situation, which, as described earlier, includes two separation and reunion episodes: in the first separation, the infant is left with the stranger in the playroom full of toys; in the second, the infant is left alone. This ingeniously crafted laboratory situation activates several behavioral systems: attachment, fear, exploration, sociability, and—in the parent—caregiving. Introduced to the playroom with his mother available, the secure infant shows relatively little attachment behavior and explores the toys, becoming engaged in play, potentially with the assistance of the mother and sometimes in interaction with the stranger. Given confidence in his mother, he might not protest her first departure, although the activation of his attachment system is likely to be evident in diminished play. He might rely on the stranger for comfort to some degree, but invariably prefers comfort from his mother when he has a choice. The mother's second departure, during which the infant is left alone in the room, is likely to activate attachment more intensely, evoking protest, following, and crying. Regardless of the infant's behavior in response to the separations, the reunions clearly show the activation of attachment, as the secure infant seeks close proximity to his mother and is likely to desire close bodily contact. Their mother's comforting and reassuring behavior quickly soothes secure infants and, when settled, they return to exploration and play. In Blatt's terms, with secure attachment, they benefit from the best of both worlds: relatedness and autonomy.

Caregiver behavior

Ainsworth (1963) summed up her initial conclusions about maternal behavior that promotes infant security as follows:

> those infants whose mothers spend most time with them, whose mothers are most interested in the details of their behaviour and development, and whose mothers enjoy breast-feeding, are those infants who seem most likely to develop a strong attachment to the mother—an attachment which is secure enough to enable them to use it as a base form which to explore the world, developing skills and knowledge, and to expand their interpersonal horizons to include attachments to figures other than the mother. (p. 104)

Ainsworth's characterization of caregiving conducive to secure attachment can be summed up as *sensitive responsiveness*, and extensive research has confirmed this association (Belsky & Fearon, 2008; Sroufe, Egeland, Carlson & Collins, 2005; Weinfield, Sroufe, Egeland & Carlson, 2008). To elaborate, this sensitively responsive caregiver behavior includes warmth and affection; sensitivity to the infant's signals, evident in interpreting them accurately and responding promptly and appropriately, especially in relation to the infant's states of distress; and being actively engaged and involved in the infant's activities in a way that shows cooperativeness and synchrony in the sense of fitting one's actions smoothly into the infant's interests, activity, and mood without interrupting the infant's goal-directed behavior. Importantly, this capacity for sensitive responsiveness hinges on the parent's psychological understanding of the infant, which Sroufe and colleagues (Sroufe, Egeland, Carlson & Collins, 2005) construed as "psychological complexity," entailing "the caregiver's understanding of the infant as an autonomous being, separate but also very much in need of care," a factor that "proved to be potent in all of our analyses of quality of care in infancy" (p. 91). I will have much more to say about this factor later in the book under the rubric of mentalizing. Notably, the mother's psychological attunement to the infant is essential to providing not only a safe haven but also a secure base with attendant sensitive encouragement for exploration and play.

A clever experiment illustrates how implicit internal working models of attachment reflect twelve-month-old infants' expectations of caregiver responsiveness (S. M. Johnson, Dweck & Chen, 2007). One bit of background: infants will look longer at a visual scene that violates their expectations—as if they are puzzled and trying to make sense of what is happening. This experiment was conducted with infants whose attachment security had been assessed in the Strange Situation; one group was securely attached, and the other group insecurely attached. These infants were shown scenes with animated geometric characters, that is, two ellipses, one large (intuitively to the infant, the "mother") and one small (the "child"). Both appear first at the bottom of an incline, and then the "mother" travels halfway up the incline to a small plateau and comes to rest there, and the "child" at the bottom pulsates and bounces, accompanied by an infant crying sound. Then one of two things happens: the mother either travels back to the bottom, restoring proximity to the child (the "responsive mother"); or the mother keeps on traveling up the incline, away from the child (the "unresponsive mother"). Here is the interesting result: in contrast to the insecurely attached infants, the securely attached infants looked longer at the "unresponsive mother" who continued up the hill. This behavior violated their expectations, based on their earlier experience of sensitive responsiveness (as inferred from their security in the Strange Situation). They find her unresponsiveness downright perplexing.

This is the proper juncture to head off a problematic misconception that sensitive caregiving entails an exceptionally high level of caregiver-infant synchrony or contingent responsiveness. On the contrary, as Beatrice Beebe and colleagues (Beebe et al., 2010) have documented, a *moderate level* of contingent responsiveness promotes secure attachment: "A number of macro- and microanalytic studies now converge on an 'optimum midrange model' of interactive contingency for attachment and social outcomes, in which both higher and lower degrees of contingent coordination are problematic" (p. 23). An excessively high level of responsive engagement can be intrusive and overstimulating, whereas an excessively low level of engagement is depriving. A moderate level of responsiveness balances the needs for relatedness and autonomy, providing psychological connection while also allowing psychological space that promotes autonomy and self-regulation. Disruptions and repairs of psychological connections characterize secure relationships. Perfect attunement in parenting or psychotherapy not only is an unrealizable aspiration; it is downright harmful for development.

Ambivalent-resistant attachment

Ambivalently attached infants wear their insecurity on their sleeve. They fail to circle in the Circle of Security; they remain glued to the (not quite) safe haven. Ambivalence is manifested by the simultaneous desire for closeness and comfort, on the one hand, and the frustrated resistance to care and comfort, on the other hand. In Blatt's terms, with ambivalent attachment, relatedness trumps self-definition and autonomy, and this imbalance also is evident in adulthood with more or less subtlety. Like their child counterparts, ambivalent patients are hard to help.

Infant behavior

Ainsworth (1963) described an infant's behavior with his mother in her Uganda study as follows: "He demanded to be in her arms; the minute she put him down he would howl till she picked him up again. She would hold him till he fell asleep, and then put him down, but he would wake immediately and cry" (p. 90). Clinging anxiously to their mother, these insecure infants are not inclined to explore; their mother does not serve as a secure base. Moreover, these infants are ambivalent toward their mother and resistant to comforting: they seek contact and then angrily resist it, for example, demanding to be picked up and then pushing away. Accordingly, while showing a high level of distress, these ambivalent infants are inconsolable.

In her later home and laboratory studies, Ainsworth observed that, compared to secure infants, ambivalent infants cry more, show more separation anxiety, and do not appear to have confidence in their mother's accessibility and responsiveness. In the Strange Situation, they are unique in being distressed by the unfamiliar situation, even with their mother present; they stay close to her and do not engage in play. They are especially wary of the stranger, seeking proximity to their mother when the stranger enters. They respond to their mother's departure with immediate and intense distress; as Ainsworth noted, "their attachment behavior has a low threshold for high-intensity activation" (Ainsworth, Blehar, Waters & Wall, 1978, p. 315).

These insecure infants' angry ambivalence is blatantly observable in the home and in the Strange Situation. As Ainsworth observed, they protest angrily "if the mother's pick-up is badly timed; but they especially protest if they are not picked up when they want to be, or if they are put down when they still want to be held" (p. 315). Resisting exploration, they are angry if the mother attempts to play with them rather than picking them up. At the same time, however, they are slower to be soothed and "even when they are picked up, the accumulated frustration of attachment behavior activated by separation at a high level of intensity may lead them to mingle angry resistance with clinging" (p. 315). For the purpose of classifying attachment behavior in the Strange Situation, Ainsworth provided the following description:

> This variable deals with the intensity and frequency or duration of resistant behavior evoked by the person who comes into contact with or proximity to the baby, or who attempts to initiate interaction or to involve him in play. The mood is angry—pouting, petulance, cranky fussing, angry distress, or full-blown temper tantrums. The relevant behaviors are: pushing away, throwing away, dropping, batting away, hitting, kicking, squirming to be put down, jerking away, stepping angrily, and resistance to being picked up or moved or restrained. More diffuse manifestations are: angry screaming, throwing self about, throwing self down, kicking the floor, pouting, cranky fussing and petulance. These behaviors may alternate with active efforts to achieve or maintain contact with (or proximity to) the person who is being rejected. (Ainsworth, Blehar, Waters & Wall, 1978, p. 350).

Caregiver Behavior

Ainsworth (Ainsworth, Blehar, Waters & Wall, 1978) identified the core problem in ambivalent attachment as consisting of high-intensity activation of attachment coupled with frustration in relieving attachment needs. Such frustration ensues from the caregiver's chronically unresponsive or inconsistently responsive behavior. The infant's angry protest can be viewed as punishing the caregiver as a strategy to elicit more responsiveness. In her Uganda study, Ainsworth (1963, pp. 88–89) painted a poignant portrait of the mother of one ambivalent infant, Muhamidi: "she was an unhappy woman with serious worries; she gave us the impression of having stored up many troubles." Her four-year-old child had died and her five-year old suffered from sickle-cell anemia. Moreover, her marriage was unhappy as her husband "expected her not only to grow the food, but to help him harvest his cash crop of coffee, and she had no help with her two completely helpless children." In short, "She seemed to feel that her world was falling apart." Adding insult to injury, when Muhamidi was seven-months old, his mother left her husband to live with her father in a polygamous household with several young wives and numerous children: "Her own mother now lived elsewhere, and, although she was sure of her father's affection, he was busy, his wives were jealous of her, and she felt there was no real place for her in this household."

Plainly, such stark childrearing conditions are not conducive to sensitive responsiveness. This example underscores the crucial contribution of the environmental context of care to sensitive responsiveness. Muhamidi's mother was distressed, unhappy, and overburdened—feeling neglected: "There were other people there who could help her, but no one really did" (Ainsworth, 1963, p. 89). Broadly, ambivalent attachment is associated with an "unresponsive, underinvolved approach to caregiving" (Belsky & Fearon, 2008). Yet ambivalence also develops in relation to inconsistent responsiveness, which includes intrusiveness that interferes with the infant's autonomy, exemplified by a *chase-and-dodge* pattern wherein the mother's need for contact prompts her to loom into the infant's space, and the infant copes by orienting away from the mother (e.g., averting gaze). Thus the infant is caught in ambivalence, needing to be vigilant to the mother's behavior while avoiding her intrusiveness (Beebe et al., 2010). Consistent with this intermingling of unresponsiveness and intrusiveness, Sroufe and colleagues observed that infants showing this insecure pattern had "the least psychologically aware group of mothers" (Sroufe, Egeland, Carlson & Collins, 2005, p. 98).

The erratic pattern of caregiving associated with ambivalence can have another effect on infant behavior. Ainsworth noted that there are significant individual differences within this ambivalent group of infants, most notably, a group distinguished not by angry protest but rather by pervasive and deeply rooted passivity. She made the following connection between lack of sensitive responsiveness and passivity: "An infant whose mother almost never responds contingently to his signals must have a profound lack of confidence in his ability to have any effective control of what happens to him" (Ainsworth, Blehar, Waters & Wall, 1978, pp. 315–316).

Avoidant attachment

The insecurity of ambivalent-resistant infants is transparent, in contrast to that of avoidant infants, who can appear to be precociously independent. In her Uganda study, Ainsworth (1963) considered the infants in this group to be "non-attached," whereas her subsequent research led her to see them, paradoxically, as attached in an avoidant manner. In Blatt's terms, with avoidant attachment, autonomy trumps relatedness, potentially into adulthood. Like their child counterparts, avoidant adults are hard to reach.

Infant behavior

Here is Ainsworth's (1963) description of a "non-attached" infant in Uganda: "As soon as she could crawl, she wanted to take off to explore the world, and the last thing she seemed to want was to be held close by her mother or by anyone else" (p. 92). In the Strange Situation, the avoidant infant's behavior is the polar opposite of the ambivalent infant, especially in the reunion episodes when the mother returns and provides the infant with an opportunity to relieve the distress of separation: the avoidant infant ignores the mother. Throughout the procedure, the infant is oriented more toward the toys than the mother—exploration takes precedence over attachment. Yet, in contrast to the secure infant's engagement in exploration, which often entails pleasurable interaction with the mother, the avoidant infant is immersed in solitary play. But the reunions are most telling; Ainsworth epitomized avoidance as follows:

> The baby does not greet the mother upon her return in a reunion episode … neither with a smile nor with a protest. He pays little or no attention to her for an extended period *despite the mother's efforts to attract his attention.* He ignores her, and may turn his back to her.

> If his mother nevertheless picks him up, he remains unresponsive
> to her while she holds him, looking around, seemingly interested in
> other things. (Ainsworth, Blehar, Waters & Wall, 1978, pp. 353–354,
> emphasis in original)

The fact that these avoidant infants are insecurely attached rather than
exceptionally secure is evident in the contrast between their behavior
at home and their behavior in the Strange Situation. At home, in contrast to secure infants, avoidant infants cry more and show more distress in response to everyday separations; plainly, they are anxious and
insecure. Nonetheless, in the Strange Situation, they do not use their
mother as a safe haven; on the contrary, they avoid contact. Ainsworth
found their behavior in the Strange Situation to be reminiscent of the
"detachment" that Robertson and Bowlby had observed in infants who
were reunited with their mother after major separations, as described
earlier in this chapter. Ainsworth gradually came to understand this
paradoxical pattern of attachment as serving a defensive function in
relation to more or less subtle emotional rejection on the part of the caregiver, in effect, continual psychological separations on a briefer time
scale.

Caregiver behavior

Ainsworth (1963) portrayed the Ugandan mothers of two non-attached
infants as follows:

> Both of these ladies … practiced what they believed to be accept-
> able European methods of infant care. Both babies were fed by
> schedule. Each baby had her own crib, in the room of her respec-
> tive mother, and she was kept there most of the day, taken out for
> feeding and bathing, and produced in her very best clothes when
> visitors came. These mothers did not believe that a baby should
> be picked up when it cries, and these babies were allowed to cry
> for long hours, unattended. Eventually, they stopped crying. These
> mothers were both very sociable and liked visiting …. When we
> visited, the mothers dressed their babies in their finery and sat with
> them on their laps, seeming warm and affectionate to them. But
> they were most concerned with the role of hostess to the European
> visitor. (pp. 91–92)

In her subsequent observations of mothers of infants observed to be avoidant in the Strange Situation, Ainsworth (Ainsworth, Blehar, Waters & Wall, 1978) commented on their aversion to close bodily contact and their inclination to rebuff their infant's desire for such contact. Such rebuff, of course, heightens the infant's attachment needs. Ainsworth also found these mothers to be irritated by their infant but striving to suppress their anger. They tended to be unemotional, indeed, "characteristically rigid and compulsive," a trait which "is likely to activate anger when the baby's demands interrupt the mother's ongoing activities or when he does not instantly do what she wants him to do" (p. 317). Similarly, Sroufe and colleagues (Sroufe, Egeland, Carlson & Collins, 2005) enumerated several characteristics of mothers of avoidant infants: they had negative feelings about motherhood, were tense and irritable, were less responsive to infant crying, avoided physical contact, and showed a lack of interest, thus providing care in a perfunctory manner. Belsky (Belsky, 2005; Belsky & Fearon, 2008) observed another caregiving pattern conducive to avoidant attachment, namely, intrusive, overstimulating, and controlling behavior that would prompt the child to turn away from the mother. Thus, in the context of distancing, such intrusiveness might further reinforce avoidance.

Secure and insecure attachment: summary

Sensitively responsive caregiving promotes psychological security, that is, a sense of security in attachment and security in the world of exploration. Securely attached children flexibly and confidently traverse the Circle of Security according to their fluctuating needs and interests. Ambivalent-resistant infants, by contrast, are unsure of their caregiver's responsiveness, and thus they are stuck clinging to the (potentially) safe haven at the expense of exploring the world. At the opposite end of the spectrum, anticipating that their attachment needs will be rebuffed, avoidant infants stay at the outer edge of the Circle of Security, stuck in exploration, albeit without the confidence and enthusiasm of secure children. A young woman struggling with psychotic symptoms whom I worked with in psychotherapy heard a lecture I gave on the Circle of Security; she recognized her lifelong pattern and declared that she was so avoidant she had remained *outside* the circle.

Ambivalent and avoidant attachment are opposite strategies for regulating emotional distress. Ambivalent infants have learned to *hyper-activate* their attachment needs, remaining close to the caregiver and turning up the dial on their emotional distress while protesting inconsistent care to maximize the likelihood of evoking a response. Yet the conflict-laden expression of attachment needs leads to continually frustrating and emotionally stormy interactions, perpetuating insecurity. By contrast, anticipating consistent emotional rebuff, avoidant infants have learned to *deactivate* their attachment needs, in effect, turning down the dial on their expression of painful emotions when presented with an opportunity for comforting. The avoidant infant has learned not to be "a bother" to his mother by staying at the outer edge of the circle. Like ambivalence, this strategy is self-perpetuating: keeping emotional distance precludes comforting. Paradoxically, not bothering the mother too much serves to *maintain* the attachment—at a distance—by forestalling further ire and rejection.

This attachment research attests to the social cleverness of infants. By twelve months of age, they have learned to adapt to the contingencies of the attachment-caregiving partnership. Sroufe and colleagues expressed their respect for children's intuitive wisdom, while also recognizing the potentially maladaptive later consequences of initially adaptive behavior:

> in our view, all children at each age make the best adaptation possible in light of available personal resources, environmental resources, and the challenges they are facing. In some circumstances, not seeking close contact from a parent, or being highly demanding, can be the most functional thing for a child to do in an effort to meet his or her immediate needs. Sometimes, staying clear of a parent is necessary. Other times, being demanding is the only way to get any attention. But if these become the core of established patterns, they may be maladaptive in the long run because of experiences they compromise at the time and reactions they garner from others later. (Sroufe, Egeland, Carlson & Collins, 2005, p. 17)

Child temperament

Any parent who has raised more than one child can attest to the role of the child's "nature" in development. Notwithstanding much genetic and environmental overlap, siblings often show dramatic differences from one another. Of course, despite their being in the same family, each sibling has much distinct experience—technically speaking, their non-shared environment. This non-shared environment includes parent-child relationships, which differ to varying degrees for each child as a result of ever-changing family circumstances. But each child's nature—inborn characteristics—also contributes to these individual differences in parental responsiveness. Here I am referring to something we all take for granted: the conjoint role of "nature" and "nurture" (or lack of nurture) in development. Often enough, in thinking about an individual's behavior, such as rebelliousness or friendliness, we are inclined to give more weight to nature or nurture. We also may do so when we think about our own characteristics.

> Aaron sought intensive hospital treatment in his junior year of college after becoming increasingly incapacitated by anxiety, depression, and alcohol abuse. He quickly expressed gratitude for his parents' steadfast understanding and support throughout his lifetime, despite his lifelong moodiness. Thus Aaron presented a compelling case for nature over nurture in his development. He learned from his parents that he had been extremely difficult to soothe as a baby; he would not easily go to sleep or stay asleep; he was a fussy eater; and he cried a great deal. He exemplified the "terrible twos," having recurrent tantrums in childhood that his parents struggled to manage. When he entered school, his "bad temper" created conflicts with peers and teachers. He came to feel like an outcast.
>
> Although Aaron's home and supportive parents provided a vital refuge, he was keenly aware of his parents' distress and recurrent frustration with him, which introduced a substantial degree of instability in these attachments, especially with his father, whom Aaron remembered as frequently losing his temper and occasionally "blowing up in a rage." At such times, his mother became extremely distraught and argued with his father while Aaron watched in fear, feeling "on the outs" and afraid. Although punctuating a generally stable and supportive home, this history of disruptions left Aaron with a legacy of insecurity in himself and in his relationships. He said he could not depend on himself, that is, his own emotional stability. As a result, his relationships also were emotionally stormy. For example, he maintained one enduring friendship through his early school years, but repeated blow-ups rendered that friendship unstable. He felt lonely at best and—in

the aftermath of emotional storms—all alone at worst, even in the midst of his family. Aptly enough, in psychotherapy he described himself as having struggled with "emotional hurricanes" as long as he could remember. As he grew older, he resorted to alcohol to combat the hurricanes, but alcohol only further eroded his emotional control and worsened his depression.

The attachment research I have reviewed in this chapter quite literally emphasizes nurture over nature—the mother's (or other caregiver's) contribution to the child's attachment security. Intuitively, it seems obvious that the infant's individual characteristics also would play a major role in attachment security, consistent with the way Aaron described his own development. As many parents know all too well, some infants are far more difficult to soothe than others. Apart from significant medical disorders, the infant's potential contribution to early attachment relationships comes under the heading of *temperament*, which refers broadly to a range of biologically based personality characteristics, all partly rooted in genetic makeup. Temperamental differences in impulsivity, activity level, and sociability are evident not only in us humans but also in nonhuman primates and other mammals (Buss, 1992). Behavioral inhibition—an indication of proneness to anxiety—is another facet of temperament that is highly pertinent to attachment. Jerome Kagan (2003) observed that about 20% of children are relatively anxious and inhibited, whereas 40% are at the other end of the spectrum, that is, uninhibited. For example, on the first day of nursery school, the inhibited child is likely to sit alone and observe before cautiously becoming engaged, whereas the uninhibited child will plunge eagerly into play with others. It stands to reason that the distress-prone, inhibited infant or child would be more likely to develop insecure attachment.

Could attachment security be determined by temperament rather than parenting? Is insecure attachment merely a manifestation of inborn anxiety proneness or a "difficult" temperament—a genetically based predisposition to emotional hurricanes? Such questions have not been posed with an attitude of idle curiosity. The role of temperament in attachment relationships became a major bone of contention between attachment researchers and more biologically oriented developmentalists (Karen, 1998). This contention was fueled, in part, by the ever-present concern that attachment theory blames mothers (and other caregivers) for children's problems. Of course, blaming children is hardly a desirable alternative.

Bowlby (1982) weighed in on this debate by acknowledging explicitly the potential importance of child temperament while maintaining his focus on the attachment-caregiving partnership and asserting the primary role of caregiving in this partnership:

> An easy newborn may assist an uncertain mother to develop a favourable pattern of care. Conversely, a difficult unpredictable newborn may tip the balance the other way. Yet all the evidence shows that a potentially easy baby is still likely to develop unfavourably if given unfavourable care and also, more fortunately, that with only few exceptions a potentially difficult baby can develop favourably if given sensitive care .... The capacity of a sensitive mother to adapt to even a difficult unpredictable baby and thereby enable him to develop favourably is perhaps the most heartening of all recent findings in this field. (p. 368)

I add to Bowlby's last point the additionally heartening finding that mothers who are struggling with difficult babies can be helped by parent-infant therapies to be more sensitive and thus to improve their infant's attachment security (Berlin, Zeanah & Lieberman, 2008).

Not surprisingly, fueled by the controversy surrounding it, the contribution of infant temperament to attachment security has been studied extensively by attachment researchers. Given well-demonstrated individual differences in temperament, coupled with the intuitively sensible notion that infant and child characteristics will play a major role in security, the research results are surprising: the environment of care exerts a far stronger influence on the development of attachment security than child temperament or genetic factors. But we need to go beyond this broad conclusion to appreciate fully the conjoint role of temperament and attachment—as well as their interaction—in development. Brian Vaughn and his colleagues have summarized this complex line of research (Vaughn, Bost & van Ijzendoorn, 2008), and I will highlight some key conclusions here.

Back to our starting point: temperament refers to individual differences based on biological makeup, that is, inherited neuroanatomical and physiological characteristics. Temperament plays a significant role in two aspects of emotionality that will concern us throughout this book: emotional *reactivity* and emotion *regulation*. Although emotional reactivity includes the propensity for excitement and pleasure, I am primarily concerned with distressing emotions. Aaron's experience illustrates the combination of high emotional reactivity and poor emotion regulation; by adolescence, he had resorted to alcohol to regulate his mood—unwittingly undermining his already limited capacity to manage his emotions. I described earlier in this chapter how a primary function of attachment—in infancy and beyond—is emotion regulation. As he was just quoted, Bowlby made the point that attachment relationships, in conjunction with temperament, influence the child's emotionality— for better or for worse. Ideally, secure attachment buffers reactivity, and the development of psychological security lowers distress.

Temperament and attachment theories share a concern with emotion, but they are fundamentally different. Temperament focuses on the child's internal characteristics whereas attachment is embedded in interpersonal relationships and thus inherently subject to environmental influence. Yet we should not be misled on this point; temperament is *not* an unchanging inborn characteristic. Obviously, neuroanatomy and physiology develop and change over the lifetime, and change is especially rapid and profound early in life. Temperamental reactivity shows only modest stability in the first few years of life and becomes more stable thereafter. What is the basis of this change? Importantly, *temperament is subject to environmental influence*—including the influence of attachment. We now know that the environment—including traumatic stress—exerts an influence on gene expression. For example, through its influence on gene activity, caregiving influences development at the level of neuroanatomy and physiology (Weaver et al., 2004). Thus, as I have been considering all along, attachment affects emotional reactivity and regulation, core aspects of temperament. Bowlby was ahead of his time in appreciating the biological basis of attachment; we now see what Bowlby could not: the influence of attachment extends to the level of molecular biology.

To return to the Strange Situation: given its contribution to emotional reactivity, temperament will play a role in the extent of distress the infant shows in response to separation, that is, the mother's leaving the playroom. Temperamental proneness to distress will be evident, for example, in crying and fussing. Yet the deciding factor in security of attachment is not the infant's distress but rather the extent to which the mother-infant interaction during the reunion calms the infant's distress. However, when attachment fails to regulate distress, the infant's temperament might influence the *type* of insecurity. For example, children with anxious-inhibited temperament are more likely to show ambivalent than avoidant attachment: they are more likely to cling to their mother than to explore the playroom. Moreover, in contrast to secure attachment, ambivalent attachment is likely to fuel anxiety and distress, creating a vicious circle that increases the likelihood of later anxiety problems (Stevenson-Hinde, 2005). Sroufe and colleagues (Sroufe, Egeland, Carlson & Collins, 2005) also noted this interaction of temperament and attachment in predisposition to later anxiety problems: those at greatest risk were newborns with a greater propensity to startle and who subsequently were classified as ambivalent-resistant at twelve to eighteen months.

To recap, caregiving exerts an overriding influence on attachment but, as Bowlby and others since have recognized, child temperament exerts an influence on caregiving behavior. Here is a new wrinkle in this complex relation: *temperament also may influence the child's response to caregiving*. To back up, attachment research consistently demonstrates a relation between parenting behavior and infant attachment patterns. Yet this parental influence is a matter of degree: there is a significant but *modest* correlation between sensitively responsive caregiving and attachment security. Jay Belsky and Pasco Fearon (2008) proposed an intriguing basis for this modest correlation: by temperament, some children are more susceptible than others to parental influence. That is, if all children were highly susceptible to influence, the relation between maternal sensitivity and attachment security would be even stronger; if no children were susceptible, there would be no correlation. As it is, the two groups are intermingled in research. Specifically, these authors distinguish children who are *fixed* strategists, whose development is determined primarily by biological makeup, from those who are *plastic* strategists, whose development is open to environmental influence, that is, childrearing practices. Thus, for better or for worse, there will be a greater correspondence between caregiving and attachment security for children who are genetically predisposed to be more responsive to parenting (i.e., the plastic strategists). This differential susceptibility to parental influence is an instance of a more general principle of gene-environment interaction, namely, genetic control of sensitivity to the environment (Flint, Greenspan & Kendler, 2010).

To sum up, we now understand that the child's temperament influences caregiving and vice versa. By virtue of temperament, some children will be more challenging to parent in a sensitively responsive manner, and some children may be less responsive to caregiving—sensitive or insensitive. For those who are more responsive, caregiving exerts an influence on temperament, for better or for worse. As Vaughn and colleagues concluded, "both attachment and the physiological mechanisms underlying temperamental differences are tuned by the social environment associated with the behavior patterns of significant caregivers" (Vaughn, Bost & van Ijzendoorn, 2008, p. 210). Finally, both temperament and attachment play a significant role in development, for example, influencing physiological reactivity, emotionality, and relationship quality.

I will have more to say about the influence of attachment security on adjustment at the end of this chapter, but next I will consider factors beyond temperament that influence caregiving; there are many. Sensitive responsiveness is not a fixed behavior pattern in the caregiver, and attachment security is not a fixed characteristic of the child; both are subject to numerous outside influences.

The environmental context of caregiving

Caregiving does not occur in a vacuum but rather in an environmental context that influences the caregiver's capacity to provide care—in Ainsworth's (1963) terms, the capacity to be available and sensitively responsive to the child's signals and needs. To take an extreme case, will a mother be sensitively responsive to her infant's fussiness when the house is on fire? Back to the more mundane: will the mother be sensitively responsive when she is in the midst of a fight with her husband; or in the aftermath of her father's death; or when she is depressed, intoxicated, or dissociatively detached? Recall Ainsworth's description of Muhamidi's mother's troubled circumstances, which included the death of an earlier child, caring for another chronically ill child, marital conflict, jealousy among members of a complex household, and her feeling of being neglected by her family members. To state the obvious, parents face innumerable obstacles to availability and responsiveness. All parents face such obstacles some of the time, and many parents face them much of the time. A multitude of factors influence attachment and caregiving: parental age, education, and socioeconomic status; parental mental health; stressful life events; being a single mother; the quality of the marital relationship; and other sources of social support for the mother (Belsky & Fearon, 2008; Bifulco & Thomas, in press; Sroufe, Egeland, Carlson & Collins, 2005).

Broadening our horizons, Belsky (2005) advocated an ecological perspective on attachment, drawing attention to the "fact that the parent-child dyad is embedded in a family system … which is itself embedded in a community, a cultural, and even a historical context" (p. 80). As he stated, we must look beyond mothering and temperament. He reasoned that an accumulation of multiple vulnerabilities, such as an infant with a difficult temperament reared by a mother embroiled in marital conflict, would be most likely to undermine caregiving. Infant security is embedded in an attachment-caregiver partnership; ideally, caregiving also is embedded in a partnership. In their review of the caregiving system, Carol George and Judith Solomon (2008) point out that "the mother's partner can enhance or compete directly with the mother's ability or desire to be caregiver," and they give particular importance to "each parent's ability to work together in a coparenting relationship and to buffer the child from insensitivity in the other parent" (p. 840).

Taking a wide view, Belsky (2005) and his colleagues studied multiple factors that might influence attachment security at one year of age: the mother's own childrearing history, her personality, changes in infant temperament between three and nine months, change in marital quality between pregnancy and nine months postpartum, and social support for the mother, namely, the friendliness and helpfulness of neighbors. The findings are clear: "the more the family ecology could be described as well resourced (i.e., positive maternal personality, positive change in infant temperament, less marital deterioration), the more likely the child was to develop a secure attachment to mother" (p. 81). Moreover, these researchers found similar results for father-infant attachment. Belsky's overall conclusion neatly weaves together the interacting influences of parent personality, infant temperament, and environmental context:

> secure infant-parent relationships were more likely to develop when parents had personalities of the kind likely to foster sensitive parenting, when infants had temperamental dispositions that either made sensitive care easier to provide or had been fostered by such sensitive care, and when extrafamilial sources of support operated in a manner likely to enhance parental sensitivity. (p. 82)

Taking an even wider ecological view, Belsky (Belsky, 2005; Simpson & Belsky, 2008) proposed a theory to account for the adaptive function of *insecure* attachment from an evolutionary point of view. Recall that Bowlby (1958) first emphasized the survival value of attachment in promoting infant-caregiver proximity that would afford protection from predators. But Bowlby and others came to appreciate the emotional value of attachment in promoting a feeling of security in the face of danger and stress. Belsky (2005) thus distinguishes the evolutionary value of secure attachment from its mental health benefits. Accordingly, he proposes that insecure attachment may have evolved to adapt individuals to a harsh environment with limited resources. In effect, a harsh childhood environment (as the child experiences it in the family) forecasts a harsh adulthood environment, and insecure attachment will be an adaptive coping strategy that will serve the child well into the future. In contrast to secure attachment, which is well adapted to a resource-rich environment, Belsky (2005) raises a speculative question about insecure attachment:

> In contrast, might insecure attachment represent a similarly evolved psychological mechanism, also responsive to caregiving conditions, that conveys to the child the developing understanding that others cannot be trusted; that close, affectional bonds are unlikely to be enduring; and that it makes more sense to participate in opportunistic, self-severing relationships rather than mutually beneficial ones? In consequence, does a child who develops such a psychological orientation, in response to the caregiving he or she has received, which itself has been fostered by the less rather than the more supportive conditions that his or her parents have confronted, become inclined to mate earlier and more frequently, perhaps producing more offspring who are poorly cared for, because this approach to optimizing reproductive fitness makes more sense in the world as it is understood to be than by adopting the strategy more characteristic of those who have developed secure attachments? (pp. 91–92)

I bring in this ecological perspective to highlight the fact that secure and insecure attachment patterns are adaptive to caregiving, which, in turn, is adapted to the wider social and environmental context. Understanding this point is crucial for appreciating stability and change in attachment security, which, in turn, reflects stability and change in caregiving and its wider context.

Stability and change in attachment security

By this point, you should appreciate the absurdity of the following belief: attachment patterns are fixed once and forever in infancy; if you were securely attached to your mother at twelve months of age, you are home free; if you were insecurely attached, you are doomed to a life of insecurity. Two basic research findings on infant attachment show the fallibility of this simplistic view: the same infant may be secure with one parent and insecure with the other (Steele, Steele & Fonagy, 1996), and some infants change in their pattern of security—for better or for worse—in the short span between twelve and eighteen months of age (Sroufe, Egeland, Carlson & Collins, 2005). Research demonstrates a middle ground between stability and change. If there were no stability in attachment—if security varied widely from interaction to interaction—we would have nothing to study or to address in psychotherapy. On the other hand, if there were no possibility of change, improving parenting practices or conducting psychotherapy would be pointless.

There are two broad reasons for this intermingling of continuity and discontinuity in attachment security. First, as reviewed in the last section, attachment is embedded in caregiving, and caregiving is embedded in a broader environmental context. If the environment is stable, and caregiving is stable, attachment will be stable—for better or for worse. On the other hand, changes in the environmental context that affect caregiving also will be conducive to changes in attachment (e.g., if the mother of a securely attached infant is divorced, must find full-time employment, and is unable to find adequate childcare). Second, the combination of continuity and discontinuity can be understood in relation to internal working models of attachment relationships, which contribute to stability but also remain open to revision on the basis of new experiences (Bretherton & Munholland, 2008). As noted earlier, these models are built up from a cumulative history of interactions, and they serve to predict the future from the past. These models are the products of a history of interpersonal learning, without which we would not know how to interact with each other. Yet they are *working* models, open to revision on the basis of new experience, revision that depends on self-awareness and open mindedness.

This section will review the middle ground, summarizing the evidence for stability and change. We are now fortunate to have a range of long-term longitudinal studies (K. E. Grossman, Grossman & Waters, 2005) that show impressive continuity as well as predictable discontinuity (Sroufe, Egeland, Carlson & Collins, 2005; Thompson, 2008). Longitudinal studies of stability in attachment classification have covered a range of time spans (e.g., from twelve months to eighteen, twenty-four, and sixty months, as well as from infancy to adolescence and early adulthood); as the foregoing discussion implies, the results are best described as "mixed" as they range from minimal to high stability (Solomon & George, 2008).

Evidence for stability

Imagine that a psychologist tells you that she is going to put a twelve-month-old infant in a laboratory situation for twenty minutes and, on the basis of her observations, she is going to predict something about the infant's future relationships in young adulthood. If you were another psychologist, you would likely tell her that she is deluding herself. Being a psychologist, I find it nothing short of amazing that there is *any* relation—no matter how modest—between attachment in infancy and attachment in adulthood. Indeed, given the effort involved, it is amazing that researchers have been able to keep participants engaged in ambitious research efforts over more than two decades. Yet several fine longitudinal studies of attachment have been conducted (K. E. Grossman, Grossman & Waters, 2005). A number of these studies relate infant behavior in the Strange Situation to the Adult Attachment Interview (AAI; Hesse, 2008) in which participants are asked about their early attachment relationships such that the adulthood classifications of attachment security parallel the infant classifications. These interviews also are suitable for older adolescents.

Not surprisingly, studies of the relation between infant and adult attachment find higher agreement for the more general secure versus insecure classifications than for specific subtypes of insecurity (Bretherton & Munholland, 2008). A few such studies illustrate. Mary Main and colleagues (Main, Hesse & Kaplan, 2005) found a significant match between Strange Situation classifications at twelve months and AAI classifications at nineteen years. Notably, the probability of insecure infants being classified as secure at age nineteen was extremely low. Moreover, the agreement between age periods was higher when participants with intervening trauma were removed from the sample; as we might expect, trauma alters attachment security. Similarly Judith Crowell and Everett Waters (2005) found significant three-way agreement (i.e., secure, ambivalent, and avoidant) between infant attachment and adult interviews administered at age twenty-one to twenty-two (i.e., 64%), and they found even greater agreement between two-way (i.e., secure versus insecure) classifications (i.e., 72%). By contrast, Sroufe and colleagues (Sroufe, Egeland, Carlson & Collins, 2005) failed to find significant correspondence between infant attachment and adult interviews administered at age nineteen. Yet the correspondence between infant and adult attachment measured at age twenty-six was greater, resulting primarily from the specific correspondence between infant and adult security. Notably, infant security—when coupled with quality of parental care, ongoing parental support and positive peer relationships—also predicted the quality of early adult romantic relationships.

Evidence for change

As noted earlier, although it was the exception rather than the rule, Sroufe and colleagues (Sroufe, Egeland, Carlson & Collins, 2005) observed changes in Strange Situation attachment classifications between twelve and eighteen months. This finding exemplifies what has been called *lawful discontinuity* in attachment: the changes were associated with changes in the quality of care, including maternal skill, as well as with changes in the broader environment (e.g., life stress and the mother's relationship status). These authors also found changes from infancy to early childhood to be associated with changes in quality of care, for better or for worse. This study and others (Crowell & Waters, 2005; Main, Hesse & Kaplan, 2005; Weinfield, Sroufe, Egeland & Carlson, 2008) have found many intervening factors to be associated with changes in security from infancy to adulthood: family functioning, stressful life events, social support, divorce, parental death, and serious illnesses in parents or the child.

Discontinuities across development attest to the flexibility of attachment (and working models), as well as to the potential value of professional intervention. Treatment is predicated on such capacity for change over the lifetime (Mikulincer & Shaver, 2007a). Sroufe and colleagues

(Sroufe, Egeland, Carlson & Collins, 2005) found psychotherapy to be one contributor to positive change as well as being associated with breaking the cycle of abuse from childhood to parenthood. The effectiveness of parent-infant interventions designed to promote more sensitive care provides a compelling experimental demonstration of the relation between maternal sensitivity and security of infant attachment (Belsky & Fearon, 2008).

This chapter concludes with a broad look at the relation between attachment and adjustment, and it is important to keep in mind that the many factors beyond caregiving that contribute to attachment also influence adjustment. Accordingly, stability and change in these factors will influence the relation between attachment and adjustment over the course of development.

Attachment security and adjustment

The safe haven and secure base associated with secure attachment are conducive to better adjustment in infancy and beyond. In Blatt's (2008) terms, attachment security is part and parcel of optimal development, which entails a synergy between relatedness and autonomy. Yet, as just discussed, we should keep in mind that secure attachment is intermingled with a host of positive environmental circumstances that contribute to it, and these favorable circumstances also contribute to adjustment. Broadly, secure attachment is a protective factor in the context of environmental risk factors. For example, secure attachment may buffer a child from the ill effects of family stress.

The avoidant and ambivalent patterns of attachment insecurity fall short of ideal; yet they are within the normal range of functioning, as contrasted with more profoundly insecure attachment that I will discuss in the context of traumatic relationships. Accordingly, unlike traumatic early attachments, avoidant and ambivalent attachment typically do not forecast psychiatric disorders in childhood or adulthood. Nonetheless, these insecure adaptations are associated with adjustment problems in childhood and, in worst-case scenarios, they can set up a complex developmental trajectory that ultimately can lead to psychiatric disorders. That is, insecure attachment in infancy and beyond increases the *risk* of maladaptation, but it is the child's cumulative history that leads to disorder. As Sroufe and colleagues (Sroufe, Egeland, Carlson & Collins, 2005) summarize: "disturbance is the outgrowth of patterns of maladaptation interacting with ongoing challenging circumstances in the absence of adequate support" (p. 239). Here I am reiterating the point that, while focusing our attention on attachment, we must not lose sight of the broader family and environmental context. Childhood maladjustment is most likely when there is an *accumulation of risk factors*, for example, when insecure attachment is combined with difficult temperament, ineffective parenting, and a high level of family stress (Deklyen & Greenberg, 2008).

Next I will present a capsule summary of research on the relation between secure attachment and adjustment in childhood to set the stage for appreciating common childhood adjustment problems associated with insecure attachment.

Early developmental benefits of secure attachment

The benefits of secure attachment in childhood are legion (Berlin, Cassidy & Appleyard, 2008; Sroufe, Egeland, Carlson & Collins, 2005; Thompson, 2008; Weinfield, Sroufe, Egeland & Carlson, 2008). In comparison with their insecure counterparts, securely attached children are more capable of regulating emotion with the help of caregivers and then on their own; hence they are relatively easygoing and display positive emotions. They are more socially competent, empathic, and nurturing; in addition, they are relatively skilled at social problem solving, and they also show more advanced conscience development. In ambiguous social situations, they are more likely to see their peers as having benign than hostile intentions. Thus they are more successful in maintaining close relationships and, more generally, they form relatively positive relationships with siblings, peers, friends, and teachers. Given their broad *psychological security*—that is, security in attachment and security in exploration—they are relatively curious and enthusiastic as well as more persistent and competent in problem solving; but, balancing autonomy and relatedness, they also are able to seek help when they need it. Accordingly, their self-confidence and social competence promote cognitive development and learning in school.

A few examples from Sroufe and colleagues' Minnesota longitudinal study (Sroufe, Egeland, Carlson & Collins, 2005) will illustrate the advantages that accrue to children with a history of secure attachment in infancy—contingent on stability in the environmental context of care.

- *Toddlers* (age two) and their caregiver (usually their mother) participated in a laboratory session during which the toddler was presented with a series of problem-solving tasks (e.g., obtaining a reward from a tube using sticks). The mother was instructed to let the toddler work on the problem independently before providing help. The securely attached toddlers showed more enthusiasm and positive emotion in working on the problems. They also were able to tolerate frustration; they not only persisted on their own in the face of difficulty but also were able to use help from their mother when they needed it. Accordingly, they displayed self-confidence and enjoyed a feeling of success in the session.
- *Preschoolers* were assessed in a number of ways. (a) At age three and a half, without their mother present, they were presented with a Barrier Box. This box was full of attractive toys, but it was virtually impossible to open; only after ten minutes did the experimenter open it for them. The securely attached children made considerable effort to open the box and tried different approaches; they stayed focused and did not give up; they were emotionally controlled; and, in all, they were involved, purposeful, and confident. (b) At age four and a half to five, children were given a complicated contraption (the Curiosity Box) to explore and play with as they wished. Again, the securely attached children showed more positive emotion and involvement as well as less frustration and anger. (c) Preschool teachers also evaluated children on social competence and social skills. The securely attached children showed more positive emotion; they initiated contacts with their peers; and they responded to others' initiations with positive emotion. They also showed high levels of empathy and consideration for other children while being less aggressive and fussy than their insecure counterparts.
- Extensive assessments for *middle childhood* included summer camp counselors' evaluations (for children ages nine to ten) as well as elementary school teachers' evaluations, year-by-year. (a) Camp counselors participating in the longitudinal research project made careful observations of children's close friendships, a hallmark of social functioning in middle childhood. Securely attached children were more likely than their insecure counterparts to develop such friendships, and they spent more time at camp in the company of their best friend. (b) Two broad evaluations of several research variables by elementary school teachers were associated with secure attachment and

with both poles of self-definition and relatedness. Securely attached children were rated high in Emotional Health and Self-Esteem; thus they were viewed as confident and self-assured as well as eager to take on challenges. They also were rated high on Competence with Peers, reflecting their social skills, popularity, and leadership qualities. Notably, securely attached children also showed better academic performance in some domains, likely owing to their motivation, persistence, and self-confidence as well as their social adjustment.

As these findings attest, the benefits of secure attachment in infancy are impressive. Yet we must keep in mind the fact that attachment security does not operate in a vacuum. Although infant attachment security alone forecasts this broad pattern of positive functioning, not only the quality of early care but also consistency in later care as well as ongoing family supports and stability make a combined contribution to adaptation throughout childhood.

Dependence

The core of attachment security lies in comfort with depending on others. For many patients, grasping this point requires something akin to a change in worldview. In conducting educational groups, I often surprise patients by making the claim dependence is a good thing. This claim runs counter to the prevailing view in our culture that independence is to be prized. Immediately, however, I qualify this claim: secure attachment is associated with *effective* dependence; moreover, effective dependence promotes effective independence (Weinfield, Sroufe, Egeland & Carlson, 2008). Here I am merely restating the principle of the Circle of Security: securely attached children are able to depend on the safe haven of emotional support and protection when they need it, and thus they are able to engage in independent exploration and problem solving when they have the benefit of the secure base. In short, psychological security is associated with an optimal balance of dependence and self-reliance, relatedness and self-definition.

Infants displaying avoidant attachment give the *appearance* of independence in the Strange Situation, because they do not rely on their caregiver when they are distressed. In contrast, ambivalent infants are blatantly dependent in their clinging to their mother, notwithstanding their angry resistance to comforting. In contrast to the effective dependence of those who are secure, however, *both* avoidant and ambivalent children show problems with dependence: avoidant children are *ineffectively independent*, such that they are somewhat more dependent than secure children by default; conversely, ambivalent children are *ineffectively dependent*; they are particularly likely to become entangled with their mother in frustrating efforts to get help with problems. Accordingly, in school, both groups are more reliant on teachers at the expense of their peer relationships (Sroufe, Egeland, Carlson & Collins, 2005; Weinfield, Sroufe, Egeland & Carlson, 2008).

Given the differences just described, Sroufe and colleagues' Minnesota study found that ambivalent-resistant and avoidant children expressed their dependence on their teachers in different ways. The behavior of one avoidant child, ET, illustrates not only an indirect strategy of depending on the teacher but also a common failing of the avoidant strategy, which collapses under stress:

> children with histories of avoidance were not as direct in expressing their dependency needs as those with resistant histories. Thus, while members of neither of these groups were self-reliant, they showed their dependency in different ways. Whenever children in the resistant group were upset, disappointed, or anxious, all of which happened easily and often, they went right to a teacher. They 'wore their hearts on their sleeves.' Those with avoidant histories tended to seek contact obliquely, as did ET upon entry into the classroom. He walked in a series of angles, like a sailboat tacking into the wind. By approximations, he eventually wound up near the teacher; then, turning his back toward her, he would wait for her to contact him. In keeping with their history of rebuff when needy, these children generally would explicitly *not* go to the teachers when they were injured or acutely upset. For example, one day, when ET bumped and obviously hurt his head, he went off into a corner by himself. Another child sat by himself on the last day of class, until a teacher came, put her arm around him, and suggested he was feeling bad; then he burst into tears. (Sroufe, Egeland, Carlson & Collins, 2005, p. 138, emphasis in original)

Social and emotional functioning

Attachment relationships provide for the social regulation of emotion. As Sroufe and colleagues (Sroufe, Egeland, Carlson & Collins, 2005) summarized, "variations in attachment may be thought of as variations in dyadic regulation of emotion and behavior. Such patterns of regulation promote *to the extent possible* closeness with a particular caregiver and in that sense are the best adaptations possible" (p. 245, emphasis in original). Yet they go on to point out that, "While in an important way serviceable early on, patterns of regulation of the anxiously attached groups seriously compromise later functioning," and they elaborate by contrasting the two insecure groups. Regarding the avoidant pattern: "Blunting one's feelings so as not to express needs, isolating oneself, feeling alienated from others, and failing to turn to them when stressed, make life very difficult, especially in the social arena." By contrast, regarding the ambivalent pattern, they note: "Chronic vigilance, apprehension, and worry about needs being met take a toll" (p. 245).

As these contrasts in emotion regulation strategies imply, not only do insecurely attached children differ from their secure counterparts in the quality of peer relationships, but also avoidant and ambivalently attached children also differ markedly from each other (Berlin, Cassidy & Appleyard, 2008; Sroufe, Egeland, Carlson & Collins, 2005; Weinfield, Sroufe, Egeland & Carlson, 2008). Although I will be focusing on maladaptation here, we also should keep in mind Sroufe and colleagues' (Sroufe, Egeland, Carlson & Collins, 2005) point that these insecure patterns can be positive adaptations in the right contexts: "One may observe, for example, a child with an avoidant history playing contentedly with Legos for a sustained period, or a child with a resistant history sitting quietly on a teacher's lap and looking at a book" (p. 137). Yet the Minnesota study (Sroufe, Egeland, Carlson & Collins, 2005) also revealed significant problems in preschool with each adaptive pattern.

Ambivalent (resistant) children showed the following characteristics: emotionally, they tended to be hyper, tense, anxious, and easily frustrated; socially, they were passive, helpless, dependent, and more teacher-oriented than peer-oriented. Their ineffective independence was conspicuous in highly stimulating and novel situations that involved cognitive challenge and called for mastery; in such situations, they performed more poorly than avoidant as well as secure children. In addition, their relative immaturity and passivity hampered their social functioning, although they were not as socially isolated as avoidant children. Yet, while somewhat oriented toward peers, they had difficulty maintaining one-to-one interactions, for example, hovering near a group while not being fully engaged. In peer nominations of popularity, the ambivalent children tended to be neglected—neither liked nor disliked.

Avoidant children showed the following characteristics: emotionally, they tended to be hostile and aggressive as well as emotionally insulated; socially, they were isolated and unaware, and some showed behavior problems beyond aggression, such being devious, lying, and stealing. Accordingly, avoidant children are likely to be victimizers and engaged in bullying, whereas ambivalent children are liable to be victimized and bullied by them. In contrast to ambivalent children, who were overlooked by their peers in popularity nominations, avoidant children were singled out as being disliked for being mean or aggressive. They also were at risk for being singled out by teachers; unfortunately, the pattern of rejection that avoidant children experienced at home was reenacted in the classroom:

> children in this group were the only ones observed to elicit anger. When one saw a teacher so upset with a child that she wanted to remove him from the classroom, the child was an [avoidant] (who, without exception, had done something very hurtful to another child). The history of rejection experienced by these children was to a degree recapitulated by our teachers, even though they were incredibly compassionate individuals. (Sroufe, Egeland, Carlson & Collins, 2005, p. 145)

Last, in contrast to their securely attached counterparts, insecure children are vulnerable to loneliness and depression as a consequence of their failed social engagement, albeit for different reasons. The ambivalent children are somewhat isolated and neglected by virtue of their passivity and helplessness; whereas the avoidant children are isolated and alienated by virtue of their emotional detachment and hostility.

Without significant changes in environmental circumstances and patterns of care, which might include professional help, these insecure adaptations are liable to continue throughout childhood and adolescence (Sroufe, Egeland, Carlson & Collins, 2005). As I will describe in the next chapter, all these patterns of security and insecurity are templates for emotion regulation and social relationships with clear-cut adult counterparts.

Clinical implications

I hope to have conveyed some of the richness of the childhood attachment literature to provide a solid foundation for understanding attachment trauma and applying that understanding to treatment. Ideally, attachment-caregiving partnerships provide and promote emotion regulation; as I will continue to elaborate, secure attachments are regulating and also foster the capacity for self-regulation—the crux of trauma treatment. I have used the foundational research on secure and insecure attachment patterns and associated caregiving behaviors to cement conceptual templates for attachment behavior—and caregiving potentials—in psychotherapy.

Traumatized patients typically enter into treatment with some amalgam of ambivalent and avoidant proclivities; childhood attachment research attests to the parallel amalgam of stability and openness to change in attachment strategies as well as the influence of subsequent attachment relationships as the fulcrum for change—for better or for worse. Given its embedding in the development of capacities for relatedness and self-definition, the developmental advantages of attachment security are manifold. Regardless of our point of intervention—from infancy to adulthood—we psychotherapists are engaged in a growth-promoting developmental endeavor that will entail addressing ambivalence and avoidance to promote greater security. The means by which we accomplish this aim are akin to those by which caregivers in childhood do so—the raison d'être for this chapter, which paves the way for considering the adulthood counterparts of childhood attachments.

CHAPTER TWO

Attachment in adulthood

Following Bowlby and Ainsworth, I have been taking it for granted that attachment is as applicable to adulthood as it is to infancy. Yet not all researchers agree; attachment theorists have had to make a case for this extension from childhood to adulthood, and I start there. The strongest case can be made for full-fledged attachment in intimate or romantic relationships, although other relationships such as close friendships can meet attachment needs to some degree.

This background sets the stage for adulthood versions of the main attachment patterns as evident in romantic relationships: secure, ambivalent, and avoidant. I also will consider various matches and mismatches between two adult partners' attachment patterns as well as the balance between stability and change in adult attachment. The entire review prepares the ground for one of the most significant discoveries in attachment research: the transmission of attachment security and insecurity from parents to infants. Research on intergenerational transmission enriches our understanding of the three prototypical attachment patterns as they are manifested in adults' discourse about their childhood attachment experiences. On the heels of the stark infant attachment prototypes, these two perspectives on adult attachment patterns—current romantic relationships and recollected childhood attachments—provide a rich tapestry that renders the patterns easily identifiable in psychotherapeutic work.

Having taken pains to elucidate the major attachment prototypes, I will address the limitations of this categorical way of thinking. I will conclude by taking stock of the clinical implications of these first two chapters on attachment as a prelude to homing in on the profound role of impaired mentalizing in attachment trauma in the next two chapters.

Attachment in romantic relationships

Your network of attachment relationships expands dramatically after infancy such that a variety of relationships can serve the primary function of attachment: providing you with a feeling of security when you feel threatened and distressed. Nonetheless, throughout life, you are likely to rely most on a primary attachment figure. In childhood, primary caregivers—your parents most commonly, and your mother in particular—typically serve as your main attachment figures. Beginning in adolescence, you transfer your primary attachment from your parents to your peers, and typically, to a romantic partner (Zeifman & Hazan, 2008). Although you shift among attachment figures throughout life to varying degrees, the essential nature of these relationships endures from infancy through adulthood. Consider Ainsworth's (1989) characterization of attachment relationships while keeping infancy, childhood, adolescence, and adulthood all in mind:

> In attachments, as in other affectional bonds, there is a need to maintain proximity, distress upon inexplicable separation, pleasure or joy upon reunion, and grief at loss. There is, however, one criterion of attachment that is not necessarily present in other affectional bonds. This is the experience of security and comfort obtained from the relationship with the partner, and yet the ability to move off from the secure base provided by the partner, with the confidence to engage in other activities. (p. 711)

In this section, I continue my book-length campaign to persuade you of the crucial role of attachment throughout your lifetime. Is adult attachment *really* attachment? To answer this question I start with the evolutionary function of attachment in adulthood; attachment does far more than provide physical protection in the service of survival. Then I will show how the core characteristics of attachments in childhood also pertain to attachments in adulthood. I will take account of the fact that attachments take time to develop in adulthood, as they do in childhood. Acknowledging the complexity of romantic relationships, I will discuss the ways in which attachment is intertwined with love, sex, and caregiving. These matters lay the foundation for my review of our primary clinical concern, individual differences in adult attachment, as evident in the counterparts to childhood attachment security and insecurity.

Evolutionary functions

The parallel between childhood and adulthood attachment has been criticized on evolutionary grounds (Zeifman & Hazan, 2008). Bowlby (1958) initially emphasized that proximity to the caregiver promoted survival by protecting the infant from predators and other dangers. Thankfully, adult attachment generally does not have the same survival value, although sometimes it does: an adult attachment figure might indeed protect you from a predator, more likely human than otherwise. The adaptive value of childhood attachment goes far beyond physical protection to provide emotional wellbeing (a safe haven) and developmental competence (a secure base). Accordingly, attachment makes a significant contribution to *survival and reproductive fitness* in adulthood, both of which are essential to evolution.

Attachment not only is essential for infants and children to survive and thrive but also is essential for the caregiver to provide optimal caregiving. For example, a mother's capacity to care for her infant is enhanced when she has the support of a secure attachment relationship with her husband. In contrast to other animals, human infants require an extraordinarily long period of caregiving; thus long-term bonds that support caregiving are essential. Debra Zeifman and Cindy Hazan (2008) note that humans "already had available a well-designed, specialized, flexible, but reliable mechanism for ensuring that two individuals would be highly motivated to stay together and vigorously resist being separated. The mechanism was attachment" (p. 446). Accordingly, they concluded that, from an evolutionary standpoint, attachment serves the same basic function in adulthood as it does in infancy; to reiterate, "It cements an enduring emotional bond between individuals that translates ... into differential survival and reproductive success" (p. 447).

Core characteristics of adult attachments

Ainsworth (1989) observed that many relationships have affectional bonds, and this fact implies that the line between attachment relationships and other close relationships is somewhat fuzzy. As she stated, attachment relationships are distinguished from other affectionate relationships by providing comfort and a feeling of security in times of distress. Plainly, close friendships and other relationships that involve emotional confiding meet attachment needs to some extent. We might think of such relationships as *secondary* attachment relationships—that is, secondary to *primary* attachments, which we most commonly form with our parents and then with romantic partners.

Zeifman and Hazan (2008) developed an interview to assess the four core characteristics of attachment relationships: seeking proximity when distressed, feeling distress when separated, relying on the relationship as a safe haven for comfort, and using the relationship as a secure base for exploration. These researchers interviewed children and adolescents ranging in age from six to seventeen years old. Whereas children showed clear-cut attachment to parents, only in the older group (fifteen to seventeen-year olds) did the researchers find full-blown attachments to peers, that is, peer relationships that had all four characteristics. Moreover, these full-blown attachments almost invariably involved a boyfriend or girlfriend. Zeifman and Hazan carried this work further in interviewing adults ranging from eighteen to eighty-two years old while separating them into three groups: (a) those who were not in a romantic relationship; (b) those who had been in a romantic relationship for less than two years; and (c) those who had been in a romantic relationship for more than two years. For these adults, full-blown attachments were most characteristic of romantic relationships lasting two years or more. Hence, in this technical sense of meeting all four criteria for attachment, most of the adolescents and adults were not (fully) attached to friends. Most commonly, therefore, attachment occurs in the context of long-term relationships with affectional bonds—with parents in childhood and romantic partners in adulthood.

The fact that adult romantic relationships are *bona fide* attachment relationships should not obscure several key differences from childhood attachment relationships (Zeifman & Hazan, 2008). First, these adult relationships are reciprocal; each partner relies on the other to meet attachment needs, and thus each partner also is a caregiver to the other. Second, proximity seeking is motivated not only by attachment needs but also by sexual desire. Third, unlike biological parents and their children, members of adult romantic partnerships are not genetically related. Accordingly, these relationships are not necessarily as durable as are parent-child attachments.

Development of adult attachment relationships

Attachment relationships do not spring forth full-blown from the moment of birth. These relationships have a predictable developmental course over the first years of life from budding social engagement in infancy to a true partnership in which each individual takes the other's needs and goals into account in early childhood. Similarly, as just stated, full-fledged attachment relationships typically develop over a couple of years in adulthood.

Zeifman and Hazan (2008) find rather direct parallels between childhood and adulthood in proposing four stages in the development of attachment:

1. The first stage of *acquaintanceship* involves playful and potentially flirtatious, sexually charged interactions. This initial phase is an exploratory venture that engages the sociability behavioral system. Here potential mate selection comes into play, and there is cross-cultural evidence that—on the surface—men tend to focus on physical attractiveness, whereas women tend to focus on social status and earning power. Yet Zeifman and Hazan review evidence that, in choosing potential reproductive partners, men and women alike put the primary value on finding mates who are kind, responsive, competent, and familiar. Notably, these are precisely the characteristics of parents that are conducive to secure attachment in infancy.
2. The second stage of *romantic infatuation* includes prolonged mutual gazing, cuddling, nuzzling, and kissing as well as baby talk. Again, all these are characteristic of infancy as well. The tidy combination of "time, togetherness, and touch" is central in the development of emotional bonds (L. Diamond, 2003, p. 174).

3. The adulthood counterpart of the third stage of *clear-cut attachment* in infancy brings together all the four core facets of attachment (i.e., proximity seeking, separation·distress, safe haven, and secure base) in relation to the partner as a primary attachment figure.

4. As Zeifman and Hazan construe it, the goal-corrected partnership of adult attachment capitalizes on the secure base, "emboldening the individual to explore his or her environment with a greater sense of security" (p. 449). Thus, to repeat a key point, like attachment in childhood, attachment in adulthood reinforces *psychological security:* security in attachment and security in exploration—effective reliance on others balanced with self-reliance or, in Blatt's terms, relatedness and autonomy.

To return to the starting point of this section, psychological security also plays a significant role in caregiving, and I will address the crucial process of intergenerational transmission of attachment in the last section of this chapter.

Love, sex, caregiving, and attachment

As we all know, there is far more to romantic relationships than attachment. With their fondness for ethology, attachment theorists refer to these relationships as "pair bonds," technically put, "selective social attachments between males and females ... which provide a social matrix for reproductive behaviors including sexual behavior and parenting" (Carter et al., 1999, p. 169). From an attachment-theory perspective, such pair bonds or enduring love relationships integrate three *behavioral systems:* sexual mating, attachment, and caregiving (Hazan & Shaver, 1987; Zeifman & Hazan, 2008). In contrast to childhood attachment relationships, adult attachments potentially involve caregiving in two senses: caregiving for the adult partner as well as caregiving for children. To state the obvious, these relationships also involve romantic love as well as sociability and affiliation, that is, companionship and friendship.

To return to evolution for a moment, a behavioral system is "a species-universal, biologically evolved neural program that organizes behavior in ways that increase the chances of an individual's survival and reproduction, despite inevitable environmental dangers and demands" (Mikulincer & Shaver, 2007a, p. 10). As the concept of pair bonding implies, all these behavioral systems often are intertwined in adult relationships characterized by romantic love. Yet the concept of behavioral system, also borrowed from ethology, implies distinctness; such systems can operate independently. To take an obvious example, you can have sex without attachment and caregiving—and without love or even companionship. One implication of this separateness is that monogamy, while generally characteristic of our species, is a matter of degree. Plainly, there are wide individual differences in monogamy, and these variations in monogamy from person to person are partly related to individual differences in attachment security.

Distinguishing love, sex, caregiving, and attachment enables us to free ourselves from stereotypes and thus to appreciate and understand the enormous diversity in adult romantic relationships, including same-sex as well as heterosexual relationships. We can start, as Lisa Diamond (2003) does instructively, with defining *infatuation* (passionate love):

> intense desires for proximity and physical contact, resistance to separation, feelings of excitement and euphoria when receiving attention and affection from the partner, fascination with the partner's behavior and appearance, extreme sensitivity to his or her moods and signs of interest, and intrusive thoughts of the partner. (p. 176)

As Diamond states, infatuation and frequent physical contact are conspicuous in the initial phase of a relationship. If the relationship endures beyond this initial phase, infatuation wanes whereas providing emotional security and comfort (i.e., attachment) becomes more prominent. Although infatuation and sex commonly go together, they do not necessarily do so. Children of all ages report intense infatuations; moreover, a majority of women and a substantial minority of men report experiencing infatuations without any sexual desire. We can become infatuated with partners of either gender, independent of our sexual orientation. For example, Diamond gives examples of "unusually intimate, passionate, platonic same-gender friendships among otherwise heterosexual individuals" (p. 177). Such relationships are more common among women than men, perhaps because of cultural norms regarding heterosexual masculinity that inhibit establishing affectionate bonds.

Given the importance of time, togetherness, and touch, Diamond proposes that such infatuations are most likely to develop in the context of heightened proximity or physical contact over prolonged periods—such as might occur in gender-segregated environments, boarding schools, on the battlefield, and in fraternal organizations. Of course, with time, such passionate friendships also might develop into attachment relationships.

Conventional wisdom has it that sexual desire and love develop in one direction: we feel sexual desire and then we fall in love. Diamond argues against this conventional wisdom: it is not uncommon to develop an emotional infatuation within which physical closeness develops, and which subsequently evokes sexual desire: time, togetherness, and touch can lead to sex. Consequently, sexual desires might evolve in a specific relationship (i.e., close friendship) in a way that contradicts the individual's predominant sexual orientation—often to the surprise and chagrin of the individual. For example, as Diamond observed, some women report that their "first (and sometimes only) experiences of same-gender desire were restricted to specific female friends with whom they had developed unusually intense emotional bonds" (p. 183).

> Betsy had started dating in high school, but her relationships never became serious; she considered most of her dates to be "self-centered jocks." She fell in love in her first year of college, however, when she met a young man who shared her artistic interests and with whom she said she "bonded." But she was devastated when she discovered that he had slept with another woman. Although he tried to excuse it as a one-night stand when he'd had too much to drink, Betsy felt betrayed and refused to see him again.
>
> Betsy vowed to remain "celibate" after the breakup and turned to her best friend, Christie, for consolation. Feeling lonely, she spent many evenings at Christie's apartment, lounging on the couch, drinking wine, listening to music, and watching movies. They also spent weekends together, studying and just hanging out.
>
> Betsy said she could share her innermost feelings and secrets with Christie, and she felt more comfortable and safe with Christie than she had with anyone else in her life. Sometimes when they were together on the couch, Betsy put her head in Christie's lap, and Christie stroked her hair. Sometimes when they were walking, they held hands. After a few months of this "intense togetherness," Betsy would not want to go back to her dorm at night and

occasionally spent the night at Christie's apartment, sleeping on the couch. One night, after more wine than usual, Christie invited Betsy to sleep in her bed, and they began a sexual relationship.

Betsy was extremely confused by this shift in their relationship; she felt guilty and ashamed and yet experienced a kind of tenderness that she treasured. Christie reassured Betsy, but Betsy said she was not "gay" and that she had always wanted to marry and have children. After several months of internal conflict, Betsy started dating men and spent less time with Christie. After many ups and downs, including some tearful and frustrating arguments, Betsy put an end to her physical relationship with Christie and they resumed their friendship, although it was somewhat strained.

Looking back on her relationship with Christie after establishing a stable romantic relationship with Dan, Betsy made peace with her sexuality. She said she valued the "special intimacy" she'd experienced with Christie and she believed that she had grown from the relationship in a way that enabled her to become comfortably intimate with Dan.

As Betsy's experience illustrates, Diamond observed that some women who had formed lesbian partnerships had gone back to identifying themselves as heterosexual. Diamond also observed that some lesbians reported having become sexually involved with close male friends with whom they had fallen in love. Naturally, any of these enduring ties might develop into attachment relationships.

From the evolutionary standpoint of maximizing survival and reproductive fitness, the integration of love, sex, attachment, and caregiving in an enduring adult romantic relationship makes great sense. But who behaves with evolution in mind? Evolution is no straightjacket for us, and diversity is the norm: adult relationships involve only some parts of the complete package. For example, enduring same-sex romantic relationships become attachment relationships and they are similar to enduring heterosexual relationships in this regard. As Jonathan Mohr (2008) stated, there is "no reason to assume that same-sex romantic attachments operate according to a set of different principles … from those operating in heterosexual attachments." As he also commented, "Perhaps the most remarkable feature of the modern same-sex romantic partnership is its resilience in the face of widespread societal condemnation" (p. 487).

As Mohr reviewed, partners in same-sex romantic relationships are generally as satisfied and well adjusted as those in heterosexual relationships. Same-sex relationships show the same patterns of secure, ambivalent, and avoidant attachment as those in heterosexual relationships—and in the same proportions. Many persons in same-sex relationships have children and, as it does in heterosexual couples, partner support plays a significant role in capacity for caregiving. Of course, same-sex relationships pose challenges that impinge on attachment. That is, social discrimination, parental disapproval, internalization of negative attitudes, and secrecy all have the potential to amplify insecure attachment while also heightening attachment needs for comfort and security. The process of coming out may lead to changes in attachment security with parents—for better (in the context of acceptance and enhanced closeness) or for worse (in the context of rejection). In addition, many same-sex partners have been affected by the AIDS epidemic, most extremely, those who are not only bereaved but also HIV+ and facing their own death; sadly, this plight only further escalates attachment needs in the aftermath of loss.

I have reviewed the non-attachment aspects of adult relationships mainly to illustrate the diversity of relationship contexts in which attachment needs develop. This review also underscores the distinct quality of attachment as merely one facet of relationships—even emotionally close relationships. Attachment merits our primary interest, however, because trauma evokes unbearable emotional states, and attachment serves to regulate distress. The effectiveness of this distress-regulation process, however, depends on the quality of the attachment.

Individual differences in attachment security

Cindy Hazan and Phil Shaver (Hazan & Shaver, 1987; Hazan & Shaver, 1994) launched a prolific line of research on attachment when they sought to conceptualize romantic love in relation to attachment and to apply Ainsworth's (Ainsworth, Blehar, Waters & Wall, 1978) classification of individual differences in attachment security to these relationships. They started their research by publishing a "love quiz" in a local newspaper and asking readers to mail in their answers (Hazan & Shaver, 1987). The love quiz included brief descriptions of the three basic attachment patterns (secure, ambivalent, and avoidant) as well as numerous questions about the one relationship the reader considered most important. In effect, the first part of this quiz was a do-it-yourself method of attachment classification. Given your acquaintance with Ainsworth's infant prototypes, these descriptions of their adult coun-terparts should have a familiar ring, and now you can take the main part of the quiz by choosing the description that best fits your romantic relationships.

- *Secure:* "I find it relatively easy to get close to others and am comfort-able depending on them and having them depend on me. I don't often worry about being abandoned or about someone getting too close to me."
- *Ambivalent:* "I find that others are reluctant to get as close as I would like. I often worry that my partner doesn't really love me or won't want to stay with me. I want to merge completely with another per-son, and this desire sometimes scares people away."
- *Avoidant:* "I am somewhat uncomfortable being close to others; I find it difficult to trust them completely, difficult to allow myself to depend on them. I am nervous when anyone gets too close, and often, love partners want me to be more intimate than I feel comfort-able being." (Hazan & Shaver, 1987, p. 515)

With his colleague, Mario Mikulincer, Phil Shaver integrated these three attachment patterns into the following model of attachment behavior (Mikulincer & Shaver, 2007a). When you feel threatened or distressed, and your attachment system is therefore activated, your automatic—instinctive—response is to seek proximity to an attachment figure (i.e., go to someone you love). This is your *primary attachment strategy*, hard-wired by evolution. When you have a secure attachment relationship with a partner who is available and responsive, proximity provides comfort and a feeling of security. By contrast, if your relationship is not secure, you will fall back on one of two *secondary strategies:* (a) the *ambivalent* strategy of anxiously expressing and drawing attention to your attachment needs or (b) the *avoidant* strategy of suppressing your attachment needs and managing as best as you can on your own.

The initial research on attachment in adult romantic relationships revealed not only the same patterns of attachment as in infancy but also about the same proportions of each in adulthood as in childhood: 55% secure, 20% ambivalent, and 25% avoidant (Hazan & Shaver, 1994). But keep in mind that finding the same patterns in the same proportions does not mean that you have merely continued the same attachment pattern from your infancy into your adulthood. On the contrary, in childhood, development is marked by a balance of stability and change, both of which depend on a host of environmental circumstances. The same remains true in adulthood.

In the next few sections of this chapter, I will summarize key findings of adult attachment research for each of the three main prototypes. These three prototypes are powerful models for our close relationships, in adulthood as they were in childhood. I am hitting the highlights by providing prototypical character sketches, and readers are referred to more extensive reviews for the details (Feeney, 2008; Hazan & Shaver, 1994; Mikulincer & Shaver, 2007a, 2008). Be warned: elucidating prototypes as I will do runs the risk of stereotyping; we lose individual richness in these idealizations. Yet ample research provides support for these generalizations and, once thoroughly understood, the patterns stand out in clinical practice, wherein we must go beyond typologies to elucidate individuality.

In much of these sections on secure and insecure attachment, I will be addressing readers directly as "you," indifferent to the distinction between patients and therapists. I am convinced that all of us struggle with insecurity, patients and therapists alike. Thoroughgoing security is an ideal, but adequate security certainly is achievable. I do not think I am unique among therapists in continuing to wrestle with longstanding insecurities, and doing the research for this book has been humbling in making me more keenly aware of them. If my own experience is any guide, as it is for the patients I work with, security is always a work in progress. With acknowledgement of varying degrees of security and insecurity, I use "you" to encourage readers to identify with all patterns, secure and insecure. To put it differently, I think we all have the *capacity*—or at least the potential—to relate in secure, ambivalent, and avoidant ways. By using "you" throughout, I will encourage you to try them all on, at least imaginatively.

Secure attachment

In adulthood as in childhood, the essence of secure attachment is confidence that, when you are in distress, the person to whom you are attached will be available and emotionally responsive to your needs. In this section, I will review the quality of secure attachment relationships in more detail and then discuss the internal working models that support secure attachment, that is, your expectations regarding relationships based on your past experiences. With trauma in mind, I will conclude with a discussion of the reason for making attachment the focus of this book: the role of secure attachment in emotion regulation in adulthood.

Thus it is important for therapists and patients to have a clear image of secure attachment in mind as an ideal, albeit realized only in approximation. In my view, increasing attachment security in emotionally close relationships is a primary goal of trauma treatment, simply because trauma entails such extreme emotional pain. Psychotherapy can be of considerable help here to the extent that the development of increasing security in the patient-therapist relationship can provide a model of secure attachment that you can extend to other relationships. My focus in the following, however, will be on the model of secure romantic relationships—ideally, emotionally close and intimate partnerships that provide a safe haven and secure base.

Relationships

There are no surprises in the findings of research on the quality of secure attachment relationships in adulthood. When you are securely attached, your relationships are characterized by trust and commitment; a high level of self-disclosure and expression of emotion that makes for open communication; as well as a sense of equality and give-and-take that promotes cooperation and interdependence. Accordingly, if married, you are likely to report a high level of marital satisfaction. A relatively high level of stability also characterizes your relationships as evident, for example, in relatively low likelihood of divorce.

This stability is consistent with you and your partner trusting each other with your feelings, which enables you to address problems and conflicts openly and to work together to solve them. This is a crucial point: although secure attachment relationships are relatively positive and stable, they are not free of conflict; no close relationship is conflict free. But the emotional trust facilitates a repair process wherein you can address and resolve problems. Thus I believe that it is not the absence of conflict but rather the partners' confidence that conflicts can be resolved that accounts for stability. Your confidence is supported by the fact that you and your partner tend to assume that each other's intentions are good, and you also are forgiving. Of course, secure attachment provides no absolute immunity to break-ups and loss. Nonetheless, when this happens, you are better able to rebound: secure attachment serves to buffer emotional stress and also enables you to make better use of emotional support in other relationships.

As discussed at the beginning of this chapter, romantic relationships are multifaceted, such that sexuality and attachment are separable aspects of these relationships. Yet the quality of secure relationships just described suggests that attachment security would facilitate healthy sexuality, and research is consistent with this expectation. Secure attachment provides a secure base for exploration, and this includes sexual exploration. Thus, if you are securely attached, you will find it relatively easy to communicate about your sexual desires and preferences and to sustain mutual sexual intimacy and enjoyment. Being secure does not necessarily entail monogamy insofar as it entails comfort with exploration; yet, sexual relationships are more likely to be enduring in the context of secure attachment.

Just as sex and attachment are separable, so are caregiving and attachment. In adulthood, caregiving is not only associated with raising children but also with providing a safe haven and secure base for your adult partner. In adulthood as in childhood, if you are securely attached you are likely to be empathic; you are able to understand emotions and you have a relatively high tolerance for distressing emotion. Your empathy will promote emotional availability and caregiving, evident in your concern about the welfare of others and your willingness to provide care to those who are suffering. Beyond romantic relationships, you are likely to be compassionate and altruistic more generally. In short, if you have received such care, you are more easily able to provide it, based on the models you have had and your emotional learning in these secure attachment-caregiving partnerships.

As I have noted, attachment theory distinguishes sex, love, exploration, caregiving, and attachment. Yet, distinct as all these are, your attachment security helps to glue them together, *integrating* love with sex, caregiving, and support for exploration. But the glue of attachment takes hold gradually over time, in adulthood as well as childhood—as mentioned earlier, over a period of at least a couple of years. At any point in life, you will forge solid trust only from extensive experience with a trustworthy partner.

Internal working models

If you have been traumatized in an attachment relationship, you face a fundamental paradox: to heal and flourish, you must develop trusting relationships. Yet your well-founded distrust constitutes a major barrier to doing so. Trust and distrust stem from your internal working models of relationships. These working models have two sides, namely, models of yourself as worthy of care (or not) and models of others as being emotionally dependable (or not). The concept of *working* models neatly captures a balance between stability and openness to change. You use your working models to form expectations in relationships and thus to guide your behavior, and you can revise and update these models based on new experiences. What is true in childhood remains so in adulthood: depending on your experience—for example, with trustworthiness versus betrayal—you can revise your models in the direction of more or less security.

If you are securely attached, you maintain working models of others as trustworthy, and these models are likely to be embedded in a relatively generalized positive view of human nature that also applies to your close relationships. You view others as benevolent and as having good intentions. You see partners as dependable and supportive. When your partner's behavior violates these expectations, you are likely to be open to forgiving explanations, attributing hostile intent only when you have clear evidence for it. Thus, as noted earlier, when problems arise, you and your partner operate on the assumption that they can be addressed and resolved. Your positive working models of others are based on earlier models: securely attached, you are likely to characterize your parents as having been warm, affectionate, responsive, respectful, caring, accepting, and warmly related to each other.

In childhood and beyond, secure attachment relationships foster a working model of yourself as being valuable, worthy, and loveable. This foundation in positive feelings about yourself has the advantage of making room for criticism from others as well as for self-criticism. The point is obvious: you are more likely to tolerate and benefit from criticism in an overall climate of acceptance; and you will make better use of self-criticism if you are generally self-accepting. Thus secure attachment is associated with a balanced view of yourself, a capacity to see and tolerate the negative as well as the positive. Accordingly, you are likely to be open to others' influence and to be able to change accordingly—as contrasted with being defensive and rigid and thus less open to change if you were more insecure.

The secure base of attachment also supports your sense of competence and capacity for self-reliance and autonomy—security in exploration (J. Holmes, 2010). Thus, securely attached, you maintain a feeling of *self-efficacy*, that is, feeling effective in influencing how things go and making active efforts to exert your influence—as contrasted with feeling helpless, out of control, and passive if you were more insecurely attached. Your self-efficacy includes being able to cope with challenges and to master problems, including interpersonal problem solving: you feel competent in being able to influence others' thinking and behavior, and this includes confidence in eliciting help and caring from others when you need it. Your self-confidence supports curiosity and openness to new experience; indeed, it supports courage, that is, enabling you to go forward in the face of anxiety and fear.

Emotion regulation

Now to the crux of attachment in relation to trauma: security is associated with *emotional* confidence and competence. That is, with security, you are open to your emotions as well as confident that you can manage distressing emotions—to some extent by yourself and also with the help of others. You are likely to be aware of your emotions, able to identify your feelings, to understand them, and to find meaning in them—as contrasted with blocking awareness of them being blindsided and confused by them if you were more insecure. Not surprisingly, given your generally positive feelings about others and yourself, you are more likely to experience positive emotions and moods—interest, excitement, pleasure, joy, and contentment. You see the world—including the interpersonal world—as generally safe rather than threatening or dangerous. Thus you are relatively calm and confident when facing challenges and threats. Not fearing being overwhelmed by your emotions, and confident in the emotional support of others, you can allow yourself to be emotionally vulnerable, that is, to experience and express your distress so as to obtain help and comfort from others. In this sense, your capacity for emotional vulnerability is not a weakness but rather strength—a kind of growth-promoting emotional resourcefulness.

Internal secure base

Sometimes I start a psychoeducational group by asking patients to list the characteristics of an ideal relationship. Naturally, they respond with a number of attributes of secure attachment: trust, caring, compassion, empathy, acceptance, dependability, love, companionship, honesty, and so forth. Then I ask: "What would it be like to have this kind of *relationship with yourself?*" The idea of a relationship with yourself might seem a bit jarring at first, but consider this: if you're like me and most people I ask, you are in a relatively continual dialogue with yourself. And, if you're like me and most people I ask, sometimes you even talk to yourself out loud. I do it when I'm frazzled and need to keep myself on track. Often enough, this dialogue is emotional. Often enough, it is infused with negative emotions: you might berate yourself with criticism when you're in the throes of depression—or as a matter of habit. At worst, your relationship with yourself might be one of self-contempt or self-loathing.

When I was reading a book by New Zealand philosopher, Christine Swanton (2003), entitled *Virtue Ethics*, I realized suddenly that secure attachment provides a model for the ideal relationship with yourself (Allen, 2005). Swanton made the case that self-love is a virtue and one that entails *bonding* with yourself. "Bonding" naturally led me to think of attachment. Jeremy Holmes (2001) aptly termed this kind of secure attachment relationship with yourself as having an *internal secure base*. With an internal secure base, you relate to yourself in a caring mental dialogue that includes both facets of security: You provide a safe haven for yourself when you empathize compassionately with your distress, as evident in your internal dialogue; "It's natural to feel anxious when an argument might erupt." And you provide yourself with a secure base for exploration when you're facing a challenge and encourage yourself; "Hard as it was, I've done it before, and I can do it again."

As Holmes proposes, a solid internal secure base is evident not only in comforting and supportive mental dialogue but also in activities of self-care—*doing* something to soothe yourself in states of distress, such as walking in a park, taking a hot bath, listening to music, or any other relaxing activity. As these examples illustrate, you develop an internal secure base from secure attachment relationships; you learn to do for yourself what others have done for you, in conversations and in actions.

Mikulincer and Shaver (2004, 2007a) demonstrated experimentally the potential power of an internal secure base. They propose that activating mental representations of secure attachment relationships—merely remembering, imagining or thinking about them—can serve a parallel function to interactions with attachment figures, namely, evoking a *feeling of security* that provides a buffer from stress. Their research

(Mikulincer & Shaver, 2004) has shown that, when threatened, persons who are securely attached bring to mind their relationships with their attachment figures along with the positive self-characteristics associated with these relationships. Consequently, they are less emotionally distressed when they are threatened (e.g., in an experimental situation, being confronted with a failure to perform well). As these authors put it, for persons who are inclined to be securely attached,

> activation of the attachment system during times of need can evoke (1) mental representations of oneself (including traits and feelings) derived from interactions with previously available and responsive attachment figures (*self-in-relation-with-a-security-enhancing-attachment figure*) and (2) mental representations of oneself derived from identifying with … features and traits of one or more caring, supportive attachment figures (*self-caregiving representations*). (Mikulincer & Shaver, 2007a, p. 35, emphasis in original)

Remarkably, secure attachment representations can be evoked non-consciously through subliminal *security priming* (e.g., by exposing participants for about one-fiftieth of a second to a drawing of a mother cradling an infant or to words such as "caring" or "love"). Moreover, such subliminal security priming influences persons who are insecurely attached to behave more like those who are securely attached, at least temporarily (Cassidy, Shaver, Mikulincer & Lavy, 2009). Although psychotherapy is inherently anxiety provoking, a therapeutic relationship also provides ample opportunity for extended security priming, at conscious and nonconscious (implicit) levels.

To reiterate, you learn to do for yourself, in your own mind, what others have done for you. In my view, Mikulincer and Shaver's (2004) research has made a substantial contribution to our understanding of how secure attachment promotes exploration and self-dependence. As they put it, "a well-treated child incorporates the protecting, soothing, approving, encouraging, and coaching functions originally performed by a security-enhancing attachment figure into his or her own mental processes" (Mikulincer & Shaver, 2007a, p. 152). Thus thinking about or evoking a visual image of someone to whom you are securely attached, or remembering comforting interactions with this person, provides you with a feeling of security and reinforces your sense of worth and competence. Thus we therapists should strive to bring to mind patients' positive relationships as well as their troubled relationships. As Alicia Lieberman and colleagues (Lieberman, Padron, Van Horn & Harris, 2005) put it, we must be mindful of the angels in the nursery along with the ghosts.

Extending the concept of the internal secure base somewhat, I think of self-worth and self-esteem not as something you *have* but rather something you *do*: you value or esteem yourself, based on the experience of being valued and esteemed. With an internal secure base, you are able to value yourself even when your self-esteem is threatened (Mikulincer & Shaver, 2004). Yet accepting yourself and being compassionate toward yourself is likely to be more valuable in promoting a feeling of security than esteeming yourself (Neff, 2009). As with all else, you can learn to be attentive and compassionate toward yourself more fully and more often. As Mikulincer and Shaver (2007a) summarize, "secure individuals can *mobilize caring qualities within themselves*, qualities modeled on those of their attachment figures, as well as representations of being loved and valued by such figures, and these representations provide genuine comfort and relief during times of stress" (p. 162, emphasis added). Their experimental research bears out these hypotheses: activating these secure mental images leads to positive emotions and alleviates stress. Furthermore, they have shown that activating your internal secure base also disposes you to be more caring toward others.

When I bring up in educational groups the prospect of relating compassionately to your emotional pain, many patients reveal that they cannot relate to the experience and have no idea how to do so. A common therapeutic strategy entails imagining how you would comfort a friend in distress and then relating to yourself in this way. Some therapists advocate writing a caring letter to yourself along the lines of a letter to a friend. A patient in an educational group stated that he had great difficulty composing such a letter but, once he had done so, he found it relatively easy to read and, ultimately, to internalize.

I advocate amending the broad concept of *psychological security* (K. Grossman, Grossman, Kindler & Zimmerman, 2008) to include not only security of attachment and security in exploration but also an internal secure base—a feeling of security with yourself. Unfortunately, although I have not seen it proposed formally, I easily imagine an *internal insecure base* as a counterpart, based on the activation of insecure attachment representations. Just as you can care for yourself when you are hurting, you can criticize and punish yourself. Just as you can encourage yourself when challenged, you can discourage yourself. At worst, you can maintain an emotionally abusive relationship with yourself—a relationship that is especially difficult to escape. Moreover, just as you can be attentive to your emotional distress, you can be emotionally neglectful—ignoring yourself or belittling your distress ("Quit being a baby!"), just as the parent of an avoidant child might do. In the face of relentless internal abuse or neglect, you may not want to be with yourself—a rather untenable prospect. With an internal insecure base that fuels anxiety, resentment, guilt, and shame, some persons attempt to escape through alcohol or drugs. At worst, suicide can be viewed as the ultimate way to escape from a unendingly painful relationship with yourself (Baumeister, 1990).

The concept of an internal secure base reinforces the seeming paradox of attachment theory: secure attachment promotes self-reliance. When you can rely on your internal secure base to regulate your distress, you are less dependent on external sources of security. Of course, being securely attached also enables you to rely on others for comfort and security when you need to do so—the best of both worlds. And internal security enables you to rely on others in an optimal way, that is, without being unduly dependent. Thus the internal secure base is a fine example of the ways in which relatedness and autonomy enhance each other (Blatt, 2008). Your internal secure base and the self-reliance that stem from your secure attachments also enable you provide a secure base for your partner's exploration and thus to promote your partner's self-reliance and autonomy. Thus secure attachment entails two people balancing the safe haven and secure base in the Circle of Security—supporting each other's effective dependence and effective independence.

Ambivalent attachment

Charlene was born eighteen months after her brother, Matthew, who was diagnosed with autism and who suffered a host of childhood illnesses. As she looked back on her childhood from the vantage point of early adulthood, Charlene viewed her mother as a "saint" and a "martyr" in the way she cared for Matthew; she described her as "world weary," continually on the verge of exhaustion. She treasured her relationship with her father, feeling that she was "precious" to him; yet he was the "high-powered, executive type" who was rarely around. In his presence, she felt the "sun was shining" on her; in his more pervasive absence, "the world went dark."

Charlene remembered in her early school years feeling neglected and resentful as well as jealous of Matthew. She said she was "sullen" in school and "shunned" by her peers, with the exception of Nate, a boy in the neighborhood who was, equally, "an outcast." She found some satisfaction in comforting him and in feeling needed by him. She remembered periodic episodes of illness during which she was able to stay home from school; then she was "coddled like Matthew" by her beleaguered mother. She recalled most vividly a seminal event: the funeral of a classmate who killed himself. She confessed relishing the guilt expressed by some of the mourners for not being more attentive to this classmate's pain.

In her later school years and then at the university, Charlene gravitated toward men with whom she became "co-dependent." As she had done with Nate, she sought satisfaction in mothering, while recognizing that her ostensible care served to ensure that they would depend on her and not leave her. Naturally, the opposite happened in a series of conflict-ridden relationships with men whom she described as being "needy" and "unstable." Oscar, her most recent and longstanding boyfriend, seemed helpless and unable to manage his life; Charlene "took over," but he resented and rebuffed her "smothering" behavior, and she resented him for being an "ingrate." Charlene's berating response to Oscar's lack of gratitude only drove him further away, and she became "enraged" when he showed interest in other women.

Charlene discovered that she could draw Oscar back by putting herself in danger. She engaged in a pattern of reckless drinking and barhopping, which culminated in her being raped after a late-night binge. She remembered Oscar as having been "unbelievably caring" after the rape, but this emotional reunion was short-lived, and she quickly felt neglected, unappreciated, and resentful. Charlene began a pattern of overdosing—"flirting with suicide," as she put it. Initially, Oscar responded by being more attentive, which Charlene realized was fueled by his anxiety about losing her role as his "life manager," notwithstanding his resentment and the fact that her capacity to manage her own life was deteriorating. Ultimately, the relationship "blew up," and Charlene was devastated. To make matters worse, Charlene had become alienated from her parents, not only owing to her chronic resentment about her mother's neglect but also because her father had become critical and controlling as her behavior deteriorated; she was ashamed of disappointing him and came to feel intimidated by him.

Charlene sought hospital treatment in the face of escalating depression and substance abuse that led her parents to step in and come to her rescue. She started psychotherapy stating that she needed "an overhaul." She thrived with the support of her peers, benefitting from confiding in two women who had similar problems as well as hearing the perspectives of young men who were foundering in their romantic relationships. Helpfully, she began slipping into her well-established pattern of resentful smothering with a fellow patient, and she used psychotherapy to identify the pattern as it was unfolding and to establish what she learned to identify as "healthy boundaries." She also experienced and expressed the chronically painful loneliness and shame from which she had sought refuge in her frustrating and depriving romantic relationships. Moreover, she recognized her own profound sense of helplessness, which she had combated unsuccessfully by taking over for her helpless boyfriends.

Through family therapy, Charlene was able to achieve more balance in her relationships with her parents, acknowledging long-standing anger toward her formerly idealized father for his merely "fleeting" attentiveness and appreciating her mother's dependability in a crisis. She came to appreciate her mother's capacity for "devotion," albeit directed largely toward her brother, and she also recognized her own capacity for devotion and caring as was evident in her relationships with her peers—"best in moderation," as she put it. Regaining sobriety also contributed significantly to restored self-respect. She concluded that she no longer needed a complete overhaul but rather was embarking on a long course of "fine tuning."

You might find it more or less easy to identify with Charlene's experience. I will continue to use "you" as a form of address, on the assumption that you are not a complete stranger to this form of insecurity, and to draw your empathic attention to it.

In adulthood as in childhood, your ambivalent attachment is associated with obvious insecurity. To repeat, ambivalence is a hyperactivating pattern—turning up the dial on your attachment needs, making your distress blatantly evident, with the hope that doing so is the most likely way to elicit responsiveness and care. Unfortunately, as Charlene's experience exemplifies, this pattern is liable to elicit responsiveness and care in the short run and undermine them in the long run. Whereas secure attachment exemplifies effective dependence, ambivalent attachment exemplifies ineffective (or inconsistently effective) dependence. In the Circle of Security model, the balance is tilted toward attachment at the expense of exploration, grasping the safe haven without a secure base.

Relationships

If you are ambivalently attached, you are liable to enter into intimate relationships at a fast pace: falling in love quickly and passionately, at worst, indiscriminately. The obsessive preoccupation that characterizes passionate love is especially evident in this attachment context. You might idealize your partner, for example, as the perfect love—setting yourself up for disillusionment. You overestimate your similarity to your partner while overlooking or minimizing the differences. For example, you might see your partner as a fellow wounded soul, based on limited shared experience. Part of the fast pace is intimate self-disclosure; you tell too much too soon.

Your insecurity in ambivalent attachment is evident in a high level of anxiety connected with your sensitivity to rejection as well as your fear of separation, abandonment, and loss. Being anxious, you seek reassurance to excess, and yet you are not easily reassured. Your reassurance seeking backfires by frustrating your partner's efforts: unwittingly, you are rejecting the reassurance you seek. Feeling rejected and helpless, your partner may withdraw, perhaps only after redoubling efforts to reassure you. Your adult behavior mirrors the childhood pattern: your attachment strategy is designed to keep your partner close, but you engage in behavior that is liable to push your partner away. Moreover, fearful of abandonment, you are reluctant to grant your partner autonomy, not giving your partner adequate space. Thus, on the one hand, your fear of abandonment can lead you to be submissive and compliant as you give in to avoid conflict. Yet, on the other hand, your fear can lead to controlling behavior, such as demanding that your partner be more affectionate or not go out so much. In addition, in an effort to ensure continued support, you might downplay your competence and problem-solving ability while proclaiming helplessness; this strategy is based on fear that, if you show your competence, your partner will withdraw support. At worst, this strategy blocks you from developing greater competence and self-reliance, which keeps you in a frustratingly dependent position.

As it is in infancy, ambivalence is a recipe for conflict. In our educational groups, my colleague, Helen Stein, referred to ambivalence as the "kick and cling" pattern of attachment, a vivid way of characterizing what we also call *hostile dependency* because of the infusion of anger into the relationship. To empathize with the angry side of the ambivalence, I emphasize the *frustration* involved. Frustration stems from feelings of deprivation—unsatisfied longings for more reliable attentive and affectionate care. Your anger is wrapped up in a major conflict: you suppress your anger for fear that expressing it will lead to rejection and abandonment; yet your frustration and resentment builds, leading to episodic eruptions. Hence your relationships tend to be emotionally stormy and unstable—at the extreme, characterized by repeated breakups and efforts at reconciliation.

In the context of ambivalent attachment, you can use sex as a way of fulfilling your needs for love and security—potentially, as a way of inducing your partner to be more available and loving. You may value holding and caressing, which are associated with attachment more than sex. Indeed, you might put up with sex for the sake of affectionate physical contact. You also might employ sex as a barometer of the quality of your relationship. Thus you can infuse sex with anxiety: anxiety about your attractiveness, worries about your performance, and concerns about rejection and disapproval. You might rely on drugs and alcohol to assuage these anxieties. Your fear of rejection also can lead you to submit and sacrifice your emotional needs in deference to your partner's preferences. This submissiveness and deference can be associated with unsafe sex. Sexual concerns also might be a fulcrum for jealousy, although your jealousy might focus more on emotional than sexual infidelity. In sum, in contrast to secure attachment, which supports sexual satisfaction in the context of balancing various needs, ambivalent attachment tends to override sexuality, undermining confident exploration and enjoyment of sex.

Ambivalent attachment also interferes with caregiving. A high level of anxiety and distress can lead to emotional contagion, leaving you feeling overwhelmed by your partner's distress. Lacking confidence, you can be anxious and self-critical about your efforts to help. In addition, as Charlene's behavior illustrates, your caregiving can become intrusive; you might be caught up in a compulsive need to help for the sake of gaining approval and keeping your partner close. Your anxieties and conflicts can lead to over-involvement and loss of distance and thus are liable to undermine your empathy, which requires a balance of emotional involvement with a capacity to recognize your partner's separateness.

Internal working models

Your ambivalent attachment is founded on working models of caregivers as being potentially capable of emotional responsiveness but unreliable in providing it—an intermingling of trust and distrust, high hopes with disappointments. Your frustration and feelings of deprivation will stem from the erratic and contradictory expectations resulting from viewing your partner alternately as loving and rejecting. Your anxiety is associated with hypervigilance—you are always on the lookout for signs of inconsistency or betrayal. Likely, you will see what you look for. When the inevitable disappointments occur, they confirm your conviction of untrustworthiness: "I knew it would come to this!" Accordingly, in contrast to relationships in which you feel secure, you will find conflicts and ruptures in ambivalent relationships more difficult to repair.

Also in contrast to secure attachment, your working model of yourself in ambivalent attachment is highly negative: a self-critical feeling of being unloved and unlovable, weak, and helpless. Your self-critical inclination also can be associated with a thin-skinned sensitivity to criticism from others. In an effort to overcome such negative and self-critical feelings, you might go to extreme lengths to gain approval, which only reinforces your feelings of dependency and weakness. Thus, at best, your self-esteem is extremely precarious in being contingent on others' responsiveness. Sadly, as in childhood, your need to stay close to the safe haven of attachment and your lack of a secure base interferes with exploration; you are blocked from developing competence and the feeling of self-reliance you need to develop a more positive working model of yourself.

Emotion regulation

Ambivalent attachment is associated with transparent emotion-regulation problems evident in high proneness to distress, driven by persistently activated attachment needs. In ambivalent attachment relationships, you turn up the dial on your distress so your signals do not go unheard. Your anxiety directs your attention toward potential threats—not only external threats such as your partner's suspected insincerity but also internal threats, such as body sensations that might signal anxiety. This anxiety sensitivity tends to escalate your distress. The more you pay attention to signs of anxiety, the more anxious you become. At worst, anxiety sensitivity can escalate into panic.

In ambivalent attachment, distressing emotions predominate over pleasurable emotions. Your high level of emotional reactivity can be coupled with a low level of ability to regulate emotional distress, either on your own or with the help of others. Consequently, you are liable to feel overwhelmed or to be flooded with emotion. When flooded, you will have difficulty identifying your emotions or understanding the reasons for them. You might feel generally "upset" without knowing why. In contrast to secure attachment, where the mere presence of your partner can assuage your emotional distress, your ambivalent relationship conflicts can lead to the opposite: your partner's presence can *increase* rather than decrease your emotional stress. Frustration and feelings of deprivation override comfort.

I do not want to overplay the negative side of ambivalence. The positive side makes the pattern adaptive in a crucial respect: you don't give up on attachment relationships as a way of providing comfort and security. You persist because, in past and present, you have had positive as well as frustrating experience with attachment. Accordingly, your ambivalence is an expression of hope. Indeed, protest is a sign of hope—what Bowlby (1973) called the "anger of hope" (p. 246). Thus you keep working at attachment such that your ambivalence can be a pathway to security.

Avoidant attachment

At least on the surface, avoidant attachment is the polar opposite of ambivalent attachment: in the Circle of Security model, you have tilted the balance in favor of exploration and distance at the expense of attachment. In contrast to the hyperactivating pattern, you adopt a deactivating pattern, turning down the dial on your attachment needs.

Doug sought hospitalization after being blindsided by his first episode of severe depression that culminated in a dangerous weekend cocaine binge. Doug prided himself on his "fierce independence," which he traced back to childhood. As he put it, "Like father, like son." His father was a factory foreman, whom Doug characterized as being "tough and respected." His father was the boss at home as well as at work; if the household was not operating like a "well-run factory," there would be "hell to pay." Acknowledging that his father could act like a "ruthless tyrant" toward him and his mother, Doug nonetheless admired him. Doug said he'd been somewhat wild as a child and benefited from his father's discipline. And he said his mother was "hopelessly disorganized" and the household would have been utterly chaotic if his father had not "kept her in line." Illustrating the ways in which his father was "all business," Doug recounted the loss of the beloved family dog. Their dog suffered from hip dysplasia and became increasingly crippled. His father simply announced one Saturday that he was taking the dog to the vet to "put her out of her misery." When Doug burst into tears, his father scoffed: "Quit your bawling. You knew this was coming. We'll pick up another dog next weekend." Doug remembered his out-of-character protest: "Yea, we'll just go to the dog factory and get another!" His father merely stormed out.

There was nothing unpredictable about Doug's marriage. He picked Penny because she was attractive and admiring. She let him know forthrightly that she was attracted to "strong men," expressing contempt for her father, whom she derided as a "sentimental fool" who "couldn't hold his booze." Penny also made it plain that she was partial to men who were ambitious, and she was attracted by Doug's drive to go to medical school. Doug became a surgeon and prided himself on running the operating room as a "well-oiled machine." He was not averse to being regarded by nurses as "intimidating" and "arrogant," despite being told by colleagues that he needed to "tone it down."

Doug discovered to his surprise that he had a "soft spot" for his daughter. He was affectionate toward her and extremely protective. He recalled his "terror" when she was hospitalized for pneumonia and nearly died. After becoming a mother, Penny discovered to her surprise that she needed more than a strong and successful man; she needed a supportive partner. She resented Doug's single-minded focus on work, and she resented his affection for their daughter and seeming emotional indifference to her, particularly in light of the limited time they had together. Doug dismissed Penny's protests and resigned himself to the emotional distance in their relationship, coupled with the waning of her admiration. Like his father, he wanted his home to run like a factory wherein the needed work would get done to his satisfaction. Penny objected to his demands that everything be orderly and that all tasks be done with "surgical precision," especially when it came to raising their daughter.

Doug was "shocked" when Penny filed for divorce, having been oblivious to the emotional significance of her protests, even when underscored by her occasional requests that they seek marriage counseling. He said he "crashed" after she moved out and took their daughter with her; he couldn't believe it when he collapsed into sobbing when they drove away. He tried to carry on with his practice but, over a period of weeks, he became increasingly depressed and took leave. He said he just sat on the couch and stared for hours. He'd been a "binge drinker" in college and he started drinking again. He'd also "flirted" with cocaine in medical school and, in desperation, binged on cocaine to pull him out of his despondency. He knew he needed help and called a colleague; three of his colleagues showed up at his home, and they brought him to the hospital.

When he began recovering from his acute depression and binge on alcohol and cocaine, Doug regained his footing and adopted a critical stance toward the hospital, pointing out all the deficiencies and the "lackadaisical" attitudes of some of the staff members. He was equally critical of some of his peers for "whining" and behaving like "victims." Over time, he came to appreciate that his peers—equally capable and successful—tolerated and "saw through" him. He could acknowledge his "tender" side, although doing so put him in an exquisitely vulnerable position. His tenderness was evident in his love for the family dog and the pain of her loss; in his love for his daughter and terror during her acute illness; and in his feeling bereft when his wife drove away. He also acknowledged that his respect and admiration for his father was infused with fear, and he remembered a long-forgotten childhood event when his father had reduced his mother to tears and Doug helplessly tried to comfort her when she was inconsolable. He could see the defensiveness in his obliviousness to Penny's confronting him with her unmet needs for affection. Although he was not able to stop the divorce proceedings, Doug's emotional openness enabled him to begin developing a more amicable relationship with Penny that bolstered his hope in maintaining his loving relationship with their daughter.

Relationships

The story on avoidant attachment is short: given a low level of intimacy, closeness, affection, commitment, and emotional dependence, there is little to say. The prototype of avoidant attachment is the self-sufficient loner. If you are avoidant, you are more invested in activities than in relationships. As is true in childhood, this attachment pattern does not preclude relationships—including attachment relationships—but it *does* preclude closeness in such relationships. Being avoidant, you nevertheless may be highly social and extroverted, perhaps downright charming and witty. But such sociability is superficial in the sense that your relationships lack intimacy and, especially, you will find it difficult to depend on others emotionally. This contrast illustrates the difference between sociability on the one hand and attachment on the other hand. Sociability is consistent with a focus on exploration—in this context, to the exclusion of attachment.

Secure attachment is consistent with constructive attempts to resolve conflicts, and ambivalent attachment involves distressed efforts to reinstate closeness. In contrast, relationship problems are liable to reinforce distance in avoidant attachment. Being avoidant, you might respond to your partner's expressions of emotional dependence or efforts to address problems by stonewalling or even expressing contempt. Thus, as it is in childhood, avoidant attachment in adulthood often is evident in hostility.

Consistent with the low level of emotional intimacy, and in contrast with secure attachment, sex is relatively divorced from love. That is, being avoidant, you are more likely to have positive attitudes toward casual sex and interest in relatively emotionless sex—sex with strangers and one-night stands, for example. You might use sex as a means to enhance your self-image or social prestige as evident, for example, in bragging about sexual conquests. You are liable to be coercive in sexual relationships, focusing more on your needs and desire than those of your partner. You might also use sex to achieve a sense of power and control in a relationship. In contrast with ambivalent attachment, you would find sex more appealing than cuddling and kissing. Similarly, your jealousy is more likely to focus on your partner's sexual intimacy than emotional intimacy with others. Too, your romantic relationships may be characterized by sexual avoidance evident, for example, in a relatively low frequency of sexual activity.

Avoidant attachment is relatively incompatible with caregiving; your emotional distance is consistent with limited responsiveness to your partner's distress and, at worst, you might be emotionally neglectful. Moreover, your partner's distress and needs for comfort might evoke anger and hostility, such that you might withdraw your support when your partner most needs it. Recall that, in infancy, avoidant attachment is a strategy for maintaining a relationship in the face of consistent emotional unavailability; in adulthood, this childhood experience is mirrored in the pattern of caregiving—namely, being rejecting of others' needs. You are inclined to repeat what you have observed and learned, and you might have learned this pattern as far back as the first year of life.

Internal working models

Plainly, avoidant attachment is associated with negative expectations for others' emotional responsiveness, but the negativity extends to a more general inclination to view others with suspicion—assuming the worst. For example, being avoidant, you are liable to see others as hostile or as lacking in remorse for their hurtful behavior. Such attributions, of course, can be based on sheer projection of your own negativity onto others. Sometimes, such projection can be associated with disowning negative traits—you externalize blame onto others instead of taking a self-critical stance. Whereas ambivalent attachment is associated with over-estimating the similarity between yourself and others (exaggerating closeness), avoidant attachment is associated with overestimating differences and with a sense of your own uniqueness (exaggerating distance).

Avoidant attachment is obviously defensive in being self-protective—that is, you do not depend on others whom you expect to be rejecting.

Avoidant attachment also can be defensive in being associated with a distorted working model of yourself, that is, with defensive self-inflation. In sum, secure attachment is associated with a balanced self-image, which allows for negative as well as positive traits; ambivalent attachment is imbalanced in the direction of self-criticism (you feel one-down); whereas avoidant attachment is imbalanced in the direction of self-enhancement, reinforced by criticism of others (you feel one-up).

Emotion regulation

To reiterate, being avoidant, you try to deactivate your attachment needs and downplay your emotional distress. You downplay threats and vulnerabilities, suppress your worries and needs, and disavow any desire for support and comfort. You view experiencing and acknowledging distress as a weakness that threatens your self-image of self-reliance. Thus, facing a stressful visit to a doctor in the company of your partner, you are more likely to rely on distraction (e.g., reading a magazine) than to seek comforting conversation. You are inclined to block your awareness of the full range of distressing emotions: anxiety, fear, anger, shame, guilt, loneliness, and sadness. This does not mean, of course, that you are impervious to emotions; on the contrary, your suppressed emotions may be transparent to others in your facial expressions as well as being evident to psychologists if you were to let them measure your level of physiological arousal.

Avoidance is a workable strategy for managing your distress—up to a point. And you might have developed an avoidant pattern in part on the basis of your strengths and resourcefulness; that is, you might have been very successful at managing on your own. Yet, when you encounter severe stress, your avoidant defenses are liable to collapse. Then your history of success in going it alone can become your Achilles heel. At that point, like those who are ambivalently attached, you are faced with a severe conflict: seeking needed emotional help puts you at risk for rejection. Thus, in the face of escalating stress, you may rely on impersonal strategies to regulate your unmanageable emotions— quite commonly, alcohol and drugs or other addictive behavior. But these strategies further erode your emotion regulation and necessitate that you ultimately reach out for help in desperation. Yet, when you are compelled to seek help, your avoidant pattern renders you hard to help, as much-needed comfort is hard to take in, even as you seek it.

Of course, allowing yourself to seek help is the only pathway to security. You cannot help feeling this pathway to be risky as your avoidance is founded on past experience of feeling your emotional needs to have been rejected. Seeking security therefore takes courage.

Partner matching

I have been discussing secure and insecure attachment as characteristics that individuals bring to relationships, and the research reviewed in this chapter attests to the significance of these individual characteristics. But attachment is a twosome; it is only natural to wonder how one partner's attachment pattern interacts with that of the other partner. Attachment researchers have investigated matches and mismatches between partners (Feeney, 2008; Mikulincer & Shaver, 2007a); the findings are complex for two reasons: first, there are six possible combinations of these patterns; second, gender may interact with mismatches (e.g., an ambivalent woman with an avoidant man might differ from an ambivalent man with an avoidant woman). I will merely highlight some common and straightforward findings to emphasize the twosome.

Not surprisingly, secure individuals tend to partner with each other, and relationships in which both partners are secure are associated with greater satisfaction and better adjustment. Some studies also suggest that, in mismatched couples, one secure partner might buffer the negative effects of the other's insecurity. Indeed, one pathway to change from insecure to secure attachment is forming an attachment with an individual with a disposition toward attachment security. Ideally, two partners can use whatever level of security each possesses to ratchet up the level of security in the relationship over time. Each will be testing the others' emotional responsiveness. We should not be ashamed about testing each other: we started learning to do so in the first year of life, by the end of which our attachment patterns displayed the results of innumerable daily quizzes.

While it is true that secure and insecure individuals alike are more attracted to others who are secure, there is also some evidence that ambivalent persons are relatively attracted to others who are ambivalent, whereas avoidant persons are relatively attracted to others who are avoidant. Not surprisingly, ambivalently attached persons are relatively dissatisfied with their relationships. As is easy to imagine, an ambivalent-avoidant pair is a recipe for trouble, and ambivalent wives are particularly dissatisfied with avoidant husbands.

These mismatched relationships often are enduring but unhappy. The husband's avoidance confirms the wife's view that attachment relationships are unsupportive; the wife's demands confirm the husband's view that it is unwise to get too close. Thus the relationships are characterized by power struggles and escalating pursuing-distancing cycles. At worst, such conflict can lead to violence in the relationship. As my account implies, insecure attachment tends to be associated with behavior that exemplifies sex-role stereotypes. But similar conflicts are likely to ensue in relationships of ambivalent men and avoidant women as well as in same-sex relationships characterized by this mismatch. At worst, two insecure partners' insecurity can feed off each other in vicious circles.

> Earl and Earline were mirror images of each other, both vying for security and each undermining the other's security. Earl was afraid Earline would leave him for another man, and he was extremely possessive. Resenting his possessive and controlling behavior, Earline retaliated by staying out late and sometimes flirting with other men in Earl's presence. Earl retaliated in turn by drinking, which enabled him to let loose with jealous rages. He also drove recklessly while drunk and let Earline know about it. Alarmed, she told him she was afraid he'd kill himself. He responded, "So what? You'd be better off." Distraught, Earline started bingeing and purging, trying to calm her anger while only fueling her self-loathing. She became more isolated and withdrawn, in part because of her shame. She was sliding into depression, feeling more and more alone.
>
> Unwittingly, Earl and Earline tried to manage their insecurity in ways that increased it, adding fuel to each other's insecurity and, in turn, their own. Each felt fearful, angry, helpless, and out of control. Earl wanted Earline close but drove her away. His reckless behavior was an expression of his desperate need for help, but his actions rendered Earline too terrified and angry to be able to provide any support and comfort. Likewise, Earl was in no position emotionally to reach out to Earline as she became increasingly mired in her bingeing, purging, and depression.

Stability and change in attachment security

Bowlby (1973) made a strong claim about the stability of attachment in adulthood: "confidence in the availability of attachment figures, or a lack of it, is built up slowly during the years of immaturity—infancy, childhood, and adolescence—and … whatever expectations are developed during those years tend to persist relatively unchanged throughout the rest of life" (p. 202).

Bowlby's claim has been validated to some extent by subsequent research on adult attachment: individual differences in attachment security are more stable in adulthood than in childhood, and studies of stability in attachment patterns over periods ranging from one week to twenty-five years show that, on average, about 70% of persons show a consistent pattern (Mikulincer & Shaver, 2007a). Internal working models tend to foster stability (Feeney, 2008): individuals select partners consistent with their beliefs; they pay attention to relationship events that are consistent with these beliefs; and they behave in ways that confirm their working models. In short, attachment patterns tend to be self-perpetuating. In secure attachment, trust begets trust, and conflicts are addressed and resolved. Ambivalent attachment is associated with a high sensitivity to insensitivity and a push-pull pattern that leads to partner withdrawal, exacerbating insecurity. Avoidance is self-perpetuating in being a relatively rigid pattern of emotional distancing that precludes learning that others can be depended upon and responsive.

We should be glad for relative stability when it comes to secure attachment and concerned about stability in relation to insecure attachment. Yet stability in adulthood is a matter of degree, and change is possible. As in childhood, security is modifiable by life experience; to reiterate, internal models are *working* models, to some degree open to revision. Mikulincer and Shaver (2007a) summarize:

> A handful of studies have explored whether changes in adult attachment style can be explained by attachment-relevant experiences that challenge existing working models. For people who enter the adult world with a secure attachment style, these destabilizing experiences include experiences of rejection, disapproval, or criticism, the breaking of an attachment bond, and separation or loss of an attachment figure. For insecure people, the formation of a stable, secure attachment bond with a romantic partner; positive interpersonal interactions; a good marriage; successful psychotherapy; becoming a loving and caring parent; and encounters with available, sensitive, and supportive relationship partners can contradict their negative models of self and others. As in childhood

and adolescence, these changing life circumstances can encourage people to reflect upon and reevaluate their attachment behavior and working models. (p. 143)

As is typical in psychology, not all research is consistent on these points, and the authors note that some of the fluctuations in security seemingly unrelated to major relationship events might be a reflection of instability associated with a core sense of insecurity. As the tenor of the findings attests, security and stability tend to beget security and stability, and treatment relationships are one pathway toward this end— but by no means the only pathway.

In their painstaking developmental research on the relation between childhood maltreatment, attachment security, and adulthood psychiatric disorder, Antonia Bifulco and Geraldine Thomas (in press) did *not* find a direct link between maltreatment and adulthood disorder. Rather, disorder was associated with ongoing insecurity in attachment. A substantial proportion of persons with a history of maltreatment subsequently developed relatively secure attachment relationships outside the home. Notably, adolescence often served as a route to change, not only through peer relationships but also through esteem-building success in school. This research backs up common sense that orients our therapeutic efforts: good relationships heal.

Intergenerational transmission of attachment security

In reviewing childhood attachment, I proclaimed an astounding research finding: observing an infant's attachment behavior in relation to a caregiver in a twenty-minute laboratory situation (i.e., Ainsworth's Strange Situation) predicts (albeit far less than perfectly) attachment and adjustment in adulthood. Here is an equally amazing finding: an interview with an expectant mother about her childhood attachment relationships predicts the security of her infant's attachment to her in that twenty-minute laboratory situation a year after the birth (Fonagy, Steele & Steele, 1991).

Based on her extensive experience observing and classifying attachment and caregiving in the Strange Situation, Mary Main and her colleagues developed the AAI and a way of coding participants' responses with an eye toward matching parents' attachment patterns with those of their infants (Main & Goldwyn, 1994; Main, Hesse & Kaplan, 2005;

Main, Kaplan & Cassidy, 1985). In this section, I will describe the AAI and then summarize the patterns of parental attachment that correspond to secure, ambivalent-resistant, and avoidant attachment in infancy. The fact that Main and colleagues succeeded in finding a match between parents' and infants' attachment security allows us to speak of intergenerational transmission: attachment security tends to be passed on from one generation to the next, for better or for worse. Thus attachment patterns can be inherited across generations—not by genetic mechanisms but rather through experience, that is, on the basis of internal working models developed from countless attachment-caregiving interactions.

My focus in this section takes a different slant on adult attachment: earlier in this chapter, I concentrated on attachment in adult romantic relationships as well as caregiving in those relationships. Now I focus on adults' attachment in relation to *their* parents as it relates to their infants' attachment to them. Thus I am considering the same basic patterns of secure and insecure attachment but in the context of different relationships (i.e., parents and children versus romantic partners). Moreover, the methods of assessing these relationships—self-report questionnaires about adult romantic relationships versus interviews about childhood experiences—are very different. Accordingly, to the frustration of psychologists like me who like everything to be neat and tidy, there is limited agreement in attachment classification between these different assessments (Crowell, Fraley & Shaver, 2008; Mikulincer & Shaver, 2007a). But this area of attachment research commands our attention by virtue of the sheer fact that parents' childhood attachments—as they are represented in their adult mind—strongly influence their children's attachment to them.

Adult Attachment Interview (AAI)

Main and colleagues' AAI is a counterpart to Ainsworth's Strange Situation in two senses. First, these two assessments have become joint foundations of attachment research and, used together, have yielded some remarkable findings. Second, like the Strange Situation, the AAI is designed to evaluate attachment security in the context of emotional stress—where attachment counts. That is, the interview questions have the potential to evoke painful memories and strong emotions. I've been interviewed by a highly sensitive expert (Mary Target) and can attest to this—blindsided by sadness as I was during the interview. Thus the participant is challenged to provide a meaningful account of complex experience in the midst of emotional arousal; the capacity to do so is a mark of secure attachment.

The interview asks you about your life history with respect to attachment. It consists of twenty questions and takes about an hour on average (Hesse, 2008; Main, Hesse & Goldwyn, 2008). The following is a synopsis of the interview questions. After orienting the interviewer to your family constellation while you were growing up, you are asked to describe your relationships with your parents, as far back as you can remember. Specifically, you provide five adjectives characterizing your mother and then your father (e.g., "loving," "distracted," "harsh," "affectionate," "confusing," and so forth). Then, for each adjective and each parent, you are asked for specific memories that illustrate; for example, you describe a specific childhood incident in which your father was "confusing." To investigate attachment experiences in particular, you are asked about your feelings of closeness to your parents; how your parents responded when you were upset or hurt or ill; your experiences of being separated from your parents; and whether you ever felt rejected or threatened by your parents. You also are asked about your attachment relationships with other adults as well as about losses of close attachment figures throughout your life. All these experiences are explored in concrete detail, drawing on your memories of specific events.

The interview also invites you to *reflect on the meaning of your early experiences* and your understanding of the long-term influence of these early attachment relationships. For example, you are asked how the experiences affected the development of your personality, your understanding of the reasons your parents behaved as they did, and how your relationships with your parents changed from childhood to adulthood as well as the nature of your current relationships with your parents if they are still living. In addition, you are asked about your relationships with your children (or how you imagine these would be if you do not have children). You are asked about experiences of being separated from your children and how your relationships with your parents have influenced your relationships with your children. You also are asked about your wishes for your children's future.

In many ways, the hour-long AAI parallels a psychotherapy session in its exploration of potentially painful childhood attachment relationships. The interview encourages emotional expression and reflection on the meaning of emotional experiences. Thus the AAI can be incorporated relatively seamlessly into the psychotherapy process as an assessment. The questions "serve as an alert to the patient that current troubles may possibly be based on childhood experiences, and ways of thinking, feeling, and behaving as a consequence of childhood experiences" (Steele & Steele, 2008, p. 12). Accordingly, the AAI can be employed to gauge the patient's suitability for an exploratory therapeutic process, to build a therapeutic alliance, to elucidate core relationship problems, and to assess benefit from treatment (Jacobvitz, 2008; Jones, 2008).

Plainly, its clinical relevance is a main reason for the AAI's substantial contribution to attachment research. Following Bowlby's view that internal working models are tolerably accurate representations of actual experiences with caregivers, interviewers make judgments about the quality of your early relationships. In addition to recording significant losses, they assess negative experiences such as your parents' rejecting your attachment needs, being abusive or neglectful, pressuring you to achieve, or reversing roles (i.e., putting you in the role of confidant or caregiver). Interviewers then make an overall judgment about the extent to which each of your parents was loving or unloving. Although your memories of actual experiences are important, they are *not* the main basis of determining your attachment security. In and of themselves, positive childhood experiences do not necessarily translate into secure attachment, nor do negative experiences translate into insecure attachment.

More important than the actual experiences that you describe in childhood is your *current state of mind with respect to attachment* as shown by your attitudes toward attachment and the manner in which you discuss their experiences. The form of the interview is more important than the content. As Main and colleagues (Main, Hesse & Goldwyn, 2008) put it, the interview requires that you juggle two tasks: "(1) produce and reflect upon relationships and experiences related to attachment history, *while simultaneously* (2) maintaining coherent conversation with the interviewer" (p. 35, emphasis in original). Thus you are challenged to remember, reflect, and communicate effectively about emotion-laden experiences. Accordingly, the interview "is designed and structured to bring into relief individual differences in deeply internalized strategies for regulating emotion and attention in response to the discussion of attachment" (p. 37). Making use of her background in linguistics, Main evaluated the quality of communication in the interview on the basis of four maxims (pp. 39–40) that constitute "requirements for an ideally rational and cooperative conversation," namely,

Quality:	"Be truthful, and have evidence for what you say."
Quantity:	"Be succinct, yet complete."
Relation:	"Be relevant to the topic as presented."
Manner:	"Be clear and orderly."

The ability to follow these communicative maxims in the AAI is a hallmark of secure attachment and—remarkably—the parent's ability to talk about attachment in this way with an interviewer predicts the infant's attachment security with the parent. Following these maxims consistently might be challenging in any conversation; doing so when talking about painful or frightening attachment experiences is especially so.

The terminology for the parent-infant matches in attachment prototypes is slightly different from that used in other areas of adult attachment literature; these differences facilitate keeping in mind whether we are referring to parents or infants:

- infant "secure" attachment goes with parent "secure-autonomous" attachment;
- infant "ambivalent-resistant" attachment goes with parent "preoccupied" attachment; and
- infant "avoidant" attachment goes with parent "dismissing" attachment.

Secure-autonomous attachment

As just described, in the Adult Attachment Interview, the hallmark of the secure-autonomous attachment pattern is *narrative coherence*, that is, being able to tell an understandable, emotionally engaged, and credible story about your early attachment relationships, complete with illustrative memories and experiences. Such narrative coherence is precisely what we strive to achieve in psychotherapy. Of all the characteristics of Adult Attachment Interviews, parents' narrative coherence is most predictive of their infants' attachment security. Narrative coherence implies *coherence of mind* with respect to attachment, which would include the internal secure base discussed earlier. As "security" implies, participants are at ease with their attachment history and relationships.

Main and colleagues (Main, Hesse & Goldwyn, 2008) characterized narrative coherence as follows:

> the speaker exhibits a steady and developing flow of ideas regarding attachment. The person may be reflective and slow to speak, with some pauses and hesitation, or speak quickly with a rapid flow of ideas. Overall, however, the person seems at ease with the topic, and discussions often have a quality of freshness. (p. 53)

A crucial aspect of narrative coherence is the match between general descriptions of parents (i.e., the adjectives) and specific memories that are emotionally authentic and convincing. Main and colleagues give an example for the description of mother as being "loving" as follows:

RESPONSE: Ah … sure, well I, when I was really little and had nightmares she would come into my room and sit with me until I felt better, just talk to me until she pretty much took away my fears. And if I was sick, she was always right there, guess she coddled me a bit then if I played it up right.

INTERVIEWER: OK, well, I wonder if you remember a specific time or incident where you found her loving.

RESPONSE: That's hard …. Oh, I remember once I had been mean, no question, to another kid I was mad at in my class, and had spoiled his chemistry experiment, and the teacher punished me. She was right, too. Well when I got home, my mom asked me what was wrong, and we talked about it. She said I should apologize to the other kid, and she called his parents for me, and somehow it wasn't too hard to apologize *with her sitting there*. (Main, Hesse & Goldwyn, 2008, pp. 42–43, emphasis added to underscore the secure base)

The quality of *freshness* in such secure-autonomous interviews indicates that participants are thinking on their feet, often coming up with new perspectives and insights; the antithesis of freshness is a stale, rote, or clichéd account—one that hardly requires thought, much less active emotional engagement. Consistent with freshness is a capacity for *reflection.* Participants recognize and comment on contradictions and are aware of the fallibility of their memory. They also recognize their biases and different points of view, such as a sibling viewing a relationship differently. In effect, without having been educated about attachment theory, they recognize that they are talking about their *working* models of attachment and that these *models* are mental representations that can be more or less accurate and always open to revision. Indeed, even in the course of the AAI, participants might reevaluate their thinking (e.g., "As I think about these memories now, maybe my father was a lot more important to me than I have realized"). This reflective quality of secure-autonomous interviews exemplifies the secure-base side of attachment, that is, the psychological freedom to *explore* relationships.

Last, secure-autonomous interviews are characterized by a positive attitude toward attachment, that is, valuing attachment relationships. This attitude includes acceptance of dependency, evident in accounts of missing others as well as needing and relying on them. This positive attitude also includes tolerance, forgiveness, acceptance, and compassion—not only for parents but also for yourself. Hence secure-autonomous persons convey ease with imperfections in themselves and parents, taking a balanced and realistic view.

Participants for whom both parents are judged by the interviewer to have been loving are likely to be classified secure-autonomous (Main, Hesse & Goldwyn, 2008). Yet, as stated earlier, it is not your actual experience but rather the way you currently relate to that experience that determines your security (i.e., your current state of mind with respect to attachment). You might give a history of adversity—including a history of traumatic attachments—and yet show the interviewer that you have come to terms with these experiences. That is, despite adversity, you can provide a coherent narrative of your relationships with your parents as well as placing a high value on attachment relationships in the present. If you provide a coherent narrative and your interviewer concludes that your parents were not loving in childhood, you are considered to show "earned" security. In this case, the (relatively untested) assumption is that you were likely to have been insecure in childhood but nonetheless have managed to achieve attachment security later in life (Hesse, 2008). Psychotherapy is one way that you can "earn" such security (Levy et al., 2006), that is, by working toward it. As described earlier, other secure relationships also enable you to attain security (Bifulco & Thomas, in press).

Attaining security is one way of interrupting the intergenerational transmission of attachment security. With a history of traumatic relationships with parents, security must be achieved through other relationships. As Jacobvitz (2008) reported,

> Among women who recalled having unloving relationships with *both* parents during childhood, those who received higher levels of emotional support from a subsidiary attachment figure were more often classified as secure-autonomous on the AAI, and their infants were classified as secure, as assessed by the Strange Situation. (p. 480, emphasis in original)

These subsidiary relationships included teachers, neighbors, and therapists. Hence, as Sroufe and colleagues point out, resilience in the face of adversity is consistent with attachment theory. Regarding individuals who describe negative experiences with parents yet are coded as secure-autonomous on the AAI,

> when one looks at prospectively gathered information, these people were not more likely to have been anxiously attached as infants, and the observed parental support available to them was comparable to that of others achieving autonomous status .... *Those who overcome adversity do so because of a positive platform or balancing supports available later*. (Sroufe, Egeland, Carlson & Collins, 2005, p. 227, emphasis in original)

Preoccupied attachment

The adult counterpart of infant ambivalent-resistant attachment is *preoccupied* attachment, that is, being "preoccupied with or by early attachments or attachment-related experiences" (Hesse, 2008, p. 552). Preoccupation thus reflects an obvious *lack of ease* in discussing attachment.

Preoccupied interviews are rambling, vague, and overly detailed, with participants wandering into irrelevant topics. Lacking in coherence, the interviews are characterized by grammatically entangled sentences and thus are hard to follow, as in this example:

INTERVIEWER: Could you tell me a little bit more about why you used the word *close* to describe the relationship?

RESPONSE: Well, my mom, you know like she kind of shaded
me in her. And I remember mornings I runned to be
with her uh walking the ... well the dog was pulling
on her, leash was like this big long leather thing I
don't know whether you can still get those I haven't
seen one long like that since I was little but a lot's
changed since then, you know even when you think
about like just going downtown and you look at the
storefronts and things and the way the signs are and
the lights and this and that and the other it's like a
different world now ... (Main, Hesse & Goldwyn,
2008, p. 53, emphasis in original)

In addition to being rambling and off the topic, preoccupied interviews
also can be contradictory, with no efforts to reconcile the contradictions, for example, "Great mother—well, not really. Mothering wasn't
her area. No, I mean actually really grateful to her ... " (Main, Hesse &
Goldwyn, 2008, p. 58).

Preoccupied interviews also are liable to be infused with ongoing
anger, complaints about parents, lengthy discussions of small offenses,
and filled with blame—blaming of parents as well as self-blame. If you
are preoccupied, you will find it hard to reflect on the past, because you
will become absorbed in memories that bring the past emotionally into
the present. Your absorption may include addressing your absent parent as if he or she were present. Asked to provide an example to support
a description of a mother as "troublesome," an interviewee responded
as follows:

That was an understatement. It was yell, yell, yell—'Why didn't
you do this, why didn't you do that?' Well, Mom, it was because
you were just at me all the time, like last week you start yelling
at the only grandkid you've got when we had you over to dinner.
And angry? She's angry at me, she's angry at her latest husband—
that's the latest in the series—now she's angry at her neighbor
about a tree that's supposed to be blocking her view, and so on and
so on. She's more than troublesome; she stirs up little things, like
I was saying last week at dinner, and ... (Hesse, 2008, p. 560)

This response exemplifies the kick-and-cling quality of ambivalent
attachment described earlier in this chapter. The interviewee cannot

let go of the relationship yet feels resentful and angry. This is the hyperactivating pattern, keeping the emotional dial turned up in relation to attachment. Such emotional preoccupation with your own attachment history may interfere—at least intermittently—with your sensitivity to the attachment needs of others. You might understand the correspondence between parents' preoccupation and their infants' ambivalent-resistant attachment in this way: the preoccupied caregiver is liable to be unresponsive or inconsistently responsive to the infant's attachment needs, leading the infant to adopt a similarly hyperactivating strategy in an effort to draw the caregiver's attention to these needs. It takes work—perhaps in the form of angry protest—to keep the preoccupied caregiver emotionally engaged.

Dismissing attachment

The adult counterpart of infant avoidance is *dismissing* attachment, that is, being "dismissing, devaluing, or cut off from attachment relationships or experiences" (Hesse, 2008, p. 552). In stark contrast to preoccupied interviews, dismissing interviews are brief—too succinct. If you are dismissing, you might settle for abstract descriptions, being unable to back up your adjectives with evidence. Then your responses will be lacking in detail, or you might simply insist that you cannot remember anything that far back in your childhood. Your interview responses emphasize facts over the emotional qualities of relationships. You might justify your father's being loving, for example, by his giving you a lot of presents for your birthday. Here is a dismissing account of a mother as having been loving: "I guess like, well, you know, she was really pretty, and she took a lot of care with her appearance. Whenever she drove me to school, I was always really proud of that when we pulled up at the playground" (Hesse, 2008, p. 558).

Being dismissing, you might idealize or devalue your parents. For example, despite giving a history that suggests to the interviewer that your mother was unloving, you might characterize her as "wonderful" or as being "the best Mom." For example, an adolescent reported that his mother repeatedly threatened to place him in care outside the home, and she ultimately did so. Yet he maintained that his parents never pushed him away and characterized his mother as "outstanding," which he explained as follows:

INTERVIEWER: What about *outstanding*? You used that word to describe your relationship with your mother.

RESPONSE: Um, my mother is an outstanding person. She knows what is going on inside my head and she can understand me better than anyone else in the world and she just, oh, how can I describe it? She has always been there for me and I do find that outstanding. (Main, Hesse & Goldwyn, 2008, p. 50)

Alternatively, you might speak about your attachment relationships in a derogating manner—that is, with cool and contemptuous dismissal, as if the relationships are unworthy of your thought or concern, in effect, a waste of your time. As one interviewee responded, "My mother? A nobody. No relationship. Next question?" (Hesse, 2008, p. 565). Another interviewee, asked what is most satisfying in her relationship with her mother responded, "When she is out of my way" (Main, Hesse & Goldwyn, 2008, p. 51). Or the contempt may be even more blatant: [in relation to mother] "Well, from 6 onwards I just thought she was a total cow and I hated her" (Main, Hesse & Goldwyn, 2008, p. 51).

Conveying that you have no need for attachment and care, you are likely to present yourself as strong and independent. You downplay painful emotions or negative experiences, even to the point of interpreting negative experiences in a positive light. An example:

My parents raised me strictly. They used the belt on me when I needed it, didn't with my little brother. I'm, a lot stronger than he is because of it. I handle stress at work a lot better than he does, and I'm more independent, I've noticed. (Main, Hesse & Goldwyn, 2008, p. 57)

As described earlier, dismissing attachment in adulthood is a *deactivating* pattern: turning down the dial on attachment needs and painful experiences. Thus it is not surprising that the infants of dismissing parents are likely to be avoidant in relation to them: they are liable to be as rejecting of the infant's needs and emotional pain as they are of their own. Hence, as evident in the Strange Situation, the infant does not turn to them for comfort when distressed.

Attachment prototypes: qualifications and limitations

Having championed the value of attachment classifications thus far, I now introduce several qualifications. First, useful as categories may be, degrees matter. Following Hazan and Shaver's (1987) pioneering study, a large number of more refined questionnaires have been developed to measure adult attachment (Crowell, Fraley & Shaver, 2008). In contrast to the do-it-yourself approach (i.e., picking a paragraph description that best fits your attachment proclivities), questionnaires assess attachment security from a dimensional perspective such that security and different forms of insecurity are assessed as a matter of degree. In these multi-item assessments, two broad dimensions stand out: closeness versus distance and comfort versus anxiety (Brennan, Clark & Shaver, 1998). In varying degrees, security entails comfort with closeness; ambivalence entails anxiety in conjunction with closeness; and avoidance entails (relative) comfort with distance.

Second, notwithstanding the robust research findings related to assigning individuals to a single attachment classification, attachment patterns also are relationship-specific (Bretherton & Munholland, 2008). In childhood and adulthood, you can be relatively secure with one parent and relatively insecure (ambivalent or avoidant) with the other. Similarly, you can be relatively secure in one romantic relationship and insecure in another. Similar variation might occur among friendships to the extent that they entail attachment.

A third and related qualification: within a given relationship, different forms of insecurity can be intermingled. Commonly, for example, avoidance masks ambivalence, that is, longing for comforting coupled with fear of rejection. This intermingling is not surprising: as reviewed in the last chapter, with varying admixtures, both forms of infant insecurity can be associated with intrusiveness as well as unresponsiveness in caregiving. Concomitantly, to some degree, attachment is fluid within a given relationship, be it with a parent or romantic partner. Plainly, for example, a betrayal will create insecurity, and reconciliation will move the relationship back in the direction of security. Moreover, aspiring to move from a more avoidant to a more secure stance in a relationship might well entail a transition through ambivalence inasmuch as avoidance stems from prior rejection and moving toward closeness inevitably will evoke anxiety.

Fourth, thus far I have concentrated on the three typical and organized attachment strategies; belatedly, in the context of trauma, attachment researchers discovered a fourth pattern in infancy: disorganized attachment. Subsequently, infant disorganized attachment was associated not only with maltreatment but also with unresolved trauma and loss in parents. Such traumatic attachment patterns in infancy and adulthood do not trump the three organized categories; rather, signs of traumatic attachment are superimposed on these organized patterns (potentially, including secure attachment). This fourth pattern is the subject of the chapter on attachment trauma.

Fifth, I am partial to an idea that Mario Mikulincer (Shaver & Mikulincer, 2011) introduced in a lecture, namely, *islands of security*. This idea is profoundly hopeful and rings true: even persons who struggle with substantial insecurity borne of traumatic relationships have had some positive attachment experience that affords islands of security. We necessarily build on these islands to strengthen the foundations of security. Without islands of security, small as they might be, patients would never arrive at therapists' doors—or, even if they were coerced through the doors, they would not begin to engage in a therapeutic process. In educating patients about traumatic attachments, I routinely emphasize islands of security as a basis for some trust. Mikulincer and colleagues' work on security priming entails setting foot on these islands. Notably, when I brought up this idea in an educational group, a patient presciently raised the possibility of *islands of insecurity* in generally secure relationships. This idea also rings true, highlighting areas of conflict or shame that impinge on ideal security. The existence of islands of security and insecurity reinforces the principle that security is a matter of degree and that different patterns of attachment can be intermingled in relationships. In sum, useful as they are, the classifications represent ideal types; reality is messy by comparison.

Sixth, as the organization of this chapter attests, the field of adult attachment research is somewhat divided into two camps: a social psychological tradition focusing on questionnaire assessment of romantic relationships and a clinical psychological tradition employing structured interviews focusing on adults' states of mind regarding their childhood attachments. As I hope this chapter attests, both lines of research contain much to inform clinical practice. Yet, in my view, *thorough assessment of patients' emotional support in current attachment networks should be a high clinical priority*. Bifulco and colleagues' Attachment Style Interview is an exemplar (Bifulco, Jacobs, Bunn, Thomas & Irving, 2008; Bifulco, Moran, Ball & Bernazzani, 2002; Bifulco & Thomas, in press). The interview assesses the quality of attachment not only with a partner but also with one or two additional "very close others" as well the history of attachments with parents. Thus the interview assesses the generality of attachment styles across relationships as well as the network of relationships that constitute the broader context of social support. Although the interview is designed to arrive at an overall attachment classification, the assessment allows for the possibility of double classifications when (a) different styles are evident across relationships or (b) different styles are evident in different relationships.

Bifulco's classification scheme overlaps the others I have discussed to a considerable degree: she distinguishes among secure, enmeshed (ambivalent-preoccupied) and fearful attachment styles, the last being associated most prominently with attachment trauma. Yet, within avoidance, she usefully distinguishes between angry-dismissive and withdrawn attachment styles, both of which entail a high level of self-reliance. The *angry-dismissive* style reflects angry avoidance, with relationships marked by hostility, distrust, and denigration of others. In contrast, the *withdrawn* style reflects a preference for emotional distance and personal privacy concomitant with a relatively unemotional, rational, and practical way of relating. This distinction merits attention, because the angry-dismissive style is associated with clinical disorder, whereas the withdrawn style is not. This finding is unsurprising inasmuch as the angry-dismissive style is associated with a high level of stress and relationship conflict; by contrast, although falling short of the secure ideal, the withdrawn style can be self-protective. Notably, Bifulco's findings also underscore the crucial point that degrees matter: mild levels of insecurity, even when associated with childhood maltreatment, were not associated with clinical disorder.

Clinical implications

As much ground as I have covered thus far, the caveats just introduced highlight the fact that I have oversimplified in identifying prototypical secure and insecure attachment patterns. In psychotherapy, we do not treat patterns; we treat individuals. We should heed Alan Sroufe and colleagues' (Sroufe, Egeland, Carlson & Collins, 2005) conclusion from their landmark Minnesota longitudinal study: "We knew, of course, that development was complicated, but it has proven to be complex beyond our imaginations" (p. 301). We therapists do our patients a disservice when we impose over-simplifying theories on them. Yet we need theories to structure our inquiry and the conduct of psychotherapy.

We therapists develop implicit and explicit internal working models of our patients and our relationships with them; they do likewise with us. Attachment theory informs these models and implies that, as working models, they are open to continual revision. We therapists must maintain openness to complexity, because our evolving working models of our patients will influence their internal working models. Above all, we should promote open-mindedness.

In these first two chapters, I have been laying the groundwork for understanding trauma. Attachment is pertinent to all types of trauma—from hurricanes to assaults to combat—simply because traumatic stress is associated with being endangered and contending with a range of painful emotions. As I will continue to elaborate, from infancy through adulthood, you learn emotion regulation through attachment, and attachment remains your main way of alleviating emotional distress. Moreover, you learn best in secure attachment relationships, and your learning is compromised to varying degrees in the context of insecure attachments. Traumatic attachment relationships pose the greatest difficulty, because you learn to fear the very thing you need to assuage your fear: attachment.

I am fond of Aristotle's (Bartlett & Collins, 2011) point that you are more likely to achieve your aim if you have a target. Attachment theory and research provides that target, namely, secure attachment relationships. Banking on your endurance, I have gone to considerable lengths to paint a big, bold target by describing secure attachment as it is evident from infancy to adulthood. This target helps orient us to what we need to achieve in treatment ranging from parent-infant therapy to adult psychotherapy. Nowhere is attaining this goal of increasing secure attachment more crucial—or more challenging—than in the context of attachment trauma. I have proposed that there are three key facets to psychological security: (1) security in attachment, that is, relying on the safe haven for comfort and a feeling of security when you are distressed; (2) security in exploration, that is, relying on the secure base of attachment in becoming self-reliant in exploring the world, including the world of relationships; and (3) developing an internal secure base, that is, a way of relating to yourself with compassion, care, and encouragement—in effect, developing a secure attachment relationship with yourself, in your own mind. Of course, as attachment research makes plain, you cannot achieve psychological security by yourself; doing so requires secure attachment relationships.

I find it helpful not only to have a clear target in secure attachment but also to appreciate the ways of falling short of the target. The basic patterns of insecurity are elegant in their simplicity, and each is a stark contrast to the other. In anxious-ambivalent (preoccupied) attachment, you adopt the strategy of trying harder when your attachment needs are not being met reliably. You make your distress and frustration well known, hoping to evoke more emotional responsiveness from those you are depending on for comfort and security. In avoidant (dismissing) attachment, you feel you are on your own in managing your distress, so you divert your attention away from your emotional pain and do not express it to others. Ambivalence and avoidance are reasonable ways of adapting to less than optimal care, and these strategies are learned well in the first year of life. Obviously, early in life these strategies are not based on conscious decisions; they are relatively automatic procedures for managing your attachment needs in light of the way those upon whom you depend have responded to them.

Over the course of your lifetime, beginning in infancy, you have developed internal working models of attachment relationships on the basis of your experience and how you have interpreted it. These models include expectations you have built up for others' responsiveness as well as your view of yourself, for example, as worthy of love or not, capable or not. And these models include ways of interacting with others on whom you are dependent—that is, in ways that are secure, ambivalent, or avoidant. Your models can be more or less accurate or useful guides to your relationships. Being working models, they are always works in progress, potentially open to revision on the basis of new experience—provided that you are open to new experience. Thus the concept of working models is ideally suited to appreciating the balance of stability and change in attachment security—for better or for worse, depending on the fate of your key relationships. You rely on your working models to provide some predictability in your relationships, based on your past learning. And you are able to change these models for the better by cultivating relationships with reliably responsive and trustworthy partners.

I hope you have come to appreciate that attachment theory and the results of research are utterly commonsensical. You learn what to expect in the way of comfort and security from the responsiveness of those upon whom you rely. You are inclined to repeat what you have learned and to generalize what you have learned from previous experience to your current relationships. To the extent that stability prevails, attachment research has established an intergenerational pattern of learning for secure, ambivalent, and avoidant strategies. Potentially, for each pattern, you can envision the links in the chain as follows: (1) parents' currents states of mind with respect to their attachment history relate to (2) the way parents interact with their infants which, in turn, relate to (3) the patterns of security their infants display toward them and then to (4) adjustment in childhood, adolescence, and adulthood, which includes adult attachment patterns and caregiving behavior. Imaginably, if all were to remain stable indefinitely, these patterns could be transmitted generation after generation.

Thus far, I have been setting the stage for trauma in attachment relationships, which can lead to the most profound form of insecurity. Stability of insecure attachment is a major problem, such that I am concerned mainly with promoting change. Thus I am looking for leverage to enhance security and, concomitantly, to strengthen the capacity for emotion regulation. I have embraced Ainsworth's concept of sensitive responsiveness as the basis for developing attachment security. As Peter Fonagy's groundbreaking contribution to attachment theory and research has brought into bold relief, sensitive responsiveness requires a meeting of minds. In my view, we cannot understand attachment trauma fully without taking account of failures at the level of meeting of minds, the subject of the next chapter, which will finish laying the foundation for understanding attachment trauma.

CHAPTER THREE

Holding mind in mind

Now that you have a good grasp of attachment theory, I hope that the concept of *sensitive responsiveness* has taken hold in your mind. The caregiver's sensitive responsiveness is essential for the development of secure attachment. And your sensitive responsiveness to your own emotional distress is essential for you to maintain an internal secure base in your relationship with yourself. In identifying maternal sensitive responsiveness as the linchpin for secure attachment, Mary Ainsworth dramatically propelled developmental research forward. But sensitive responsiveness remains a broad and somewhat vague concept, and its modest link to secure attachment in studies of the intergenerational transmission of attachment security leaves room for further clarification; we are left with a "transmission gap" (van IJzendoorn, 1995) that needs filling: how do we get from parental security to infant security? There is no single or simple answer to this question, but this chapter addresses an important piece of the puzzle. The next chapter on attachment trauma addresses what is missing in the transmission of attachment security.

Sensitive responsiveness—to an infant, a partner, or yourself—requires psychological attunement: holding mind in mind, to use Fonagy's memorable phrase. In this chapter, I will ask you to hold two more concepts in mind: mindfulness and mentalizing. I think we need to engage in mental juggling of mindfulness and mentalizing to understand what goes into psychological attunement and sensitive responsiveness. Mentalizing is particularly noteworthy in being proposed as one way to begin filling the intergenerational transmission gap (Fonagy & Target, 2005).

To assist you with this mental juggling act, here is an overview: You can think of mindfulness as attentive awareness of present experience. Thus you can be mindful of a flower, your breathing, or washing the dishes. Because present experience includes what is going on in your mind—what you are thinking and feeling—you also can be mindful of your mind. While mindfulness practices generally cultivate awareness of your own mental states, mindfulness also extends to attentiveness to other persons' experience—you can be mindful of another person's mental states as well as your own.

Mentalizing not only requires mindful attentiveness to mental states in yourself and others but also includes more complex understanding of behavior in relation to mental states. If you suddenly start feeling anxious as you are reading this book, you would naturally try to figure out why; then you would be mentalizing. If you were sitting in a coffee shop with a friend who suddenly started laughing out loud for no apparent reason, you'd wonder why and ask your friend, "What's so funny?" You'd be mentalizing, and your friend would be mentalizing in explaining himself.

To make the long story of this chapter short, mindful attentiveness to mental states is the foundation for mentalizing, that is, more complex understanding of the reasons for these states—their context and history. I give great weight to mentalizing in this book because of its role in attachment, trauma, and psychotherapy. But I am also giving mindfulness its due in this book for three reasons. First, the rich literature on mindfulness illuminates the foundation of mentalizing: attentive awareness. Second, mindfulness—attentive awareness of the present moment—is an extremely valuable skill. Rooted in Buddhist thought and practice, mindfulness has a venerable history. And mindfulness practice has become popular among psychologists; it is garnering extensive research and is being incorporated into a wide range of psychotherapies, including trauma therapies. The connection with trauma is straightforward: mindfulness promotes stress reduction and emotion regulation; accordingly, mindfulness practice has been shown to diminish stress, anxiety and depression—pervasive trauma-related problems.

Third, if you already are familiar with mindfulness, you might wonder when I refer to mentalizing, "Isn't that the same as mindfulness?" As I already have implied, the two concepts are similar but not identical, and I think we need both concepts to understand attachment and trauma. I will start with mindfulness, the simpler and more basic of the two. Then, after discussing mentalizing, I will spell out how the two concepts fit together.

Mindfulness

One of my supervisors known for his inquisitive open-mindedness, Peter Novotny, introduced me to mindfulness a couple of decades ago. He spearheaded a meditation group that I joined and suggested that I read a book by Vietnam Buddhist, Tich Nhat Hanh, entitled *Peace is Every Step*. This book is a masterpiece, a work of art in its elegant simplicity, and an exemplar of mindful writing. He begins his book by drawing attention to the precious gift of being alive and urges us to keep this gift in mind:

> We can smile, breathe, walk, and eat our meals in a way that allows us to be in touch with the abundance of happiness that is available. We are very good at preparing to live, but not very good at living. We know how to sacrifice ten years for a diploma, and we are willing to work very hard to get a job, a car, a house, and so on. But we have difficulty remembering that we are alive in the present moment, the only moment there is for us to be alive. Every breath we take, every step we make, can be filled with peace, joy, and serenity. We need only to be awake, alive in the present moment. (Hahn, 1991, p. 5)

Sound appealing? Of course, when psychologists embrace a seemingly simple concept like mindfulness, they complicate it, research it, and disagree about it (K. W. Brown, Ryan & Creswell, 2007; Davis & Hayes, 2011; Mikulas, 2011). Interest in mindfulness has exploded in the two decades since I first became acquainted with it, fueled in no small part by the demonstrable benefit of mindfulness practice for a wide range of health problems, including mental health problems. The burgeoning research literature led a group of experts on mindfulness to convene a series of meetings to achieve some consensus. They did so in a way I find compelling and elegant (Bishop et al., 2004; S. L. Shapiro,

Carlson, Astin & Freedman, 2006). Their consensus follows the lead of Jon Kabat-Zinn (1990), who lit a fire under mindfulness research by developing an intervention to provide emotional help to persons struggling with chronic medical conditions, that is, Mindfulness-Based Stress Reduction. Kabat-Zinn (2003) proposed the following working definition of mindfulness, which guides the organization of my review: "the awareness that emerges through paying attention on purpose, in the present moment, and nonjudgmentally to the unfolding of experience moment by moment" (p. 145).

Consistent with Kabat-Zinn's definition, as Bishop and colleagues (Bishop et al., 2004) elaborated, two fundamental components of mindfulness are paying *attention* to your present experience and cultivating a nonjudgmental and *accepting attitude* toward your experience, even when it is emotionally painful. As all these authors agreed, a third facet of mindfulness practice is its intention or purpose, which we might also think of as the desired outcome of mindfulness practice. I view this third facet of the mindfulness literature through the lens of ethics. That is, since its inception, mindfulness evolved in the context of a solid ethical foundation, which, in many practices, also includes a spiritual dimension (Aronson, 2004; Wallace, 2009). After reviewing these three facets of mindfulness, I will illustrate some ways in which mindfulness is being cultivated in meditation and psychotherapies, and I will conclude with a sketch of research on the therapeutic effects of mindfulness.

Attentiveness to present experience

A patient once told me of his experience in a lecture at Hazelden, a prominent treatment center in the United States for persons struggling with alcohol and substance abuse. He said that one day the instructor came in and wrote on the board, in big bold letters, "Attention. Attention. Attention." I cannot overstate the importance of attention, which is not only a prerequisite for consciousness (Dehaene & Naccache, 2001) but also the *"primary structuring feature of consciousness"* (Shallice & Cooper, 2011, p. 447, emphasis in original) and thus the basis of all our intentional action. Impressed as I am with the fundamental role of attention in our mental life, I often have mentioned this patient's experience to others since. So I was pleased to discover what could have been the instructor's source, the following words of a Zen master, cited in a paper by William McIntosh (1997):

> Even though it was the Master's day of silence, a traveler begged
> for a word of wisdom that would guide him through life's journey.
> The Master nodded affably, took a sheet of paper, and wrote a sin-
> gle word on it: 'Attention.' The visitor was perplexed. 'That is too
> brief. Would you please expand on it a bit?' The master took the
> paper back and wrote 'Attention, attention, attention.' 'But what
> do these words MEAN?' said the stranger helplessly. The Master
> reached for the paper and wrote: 'Attention, attention, attention
> means ATTENTION.' (p. 47)

The core of mindfulness is *bare attention* (Mace, 2008), that is, attention
to what you perceive or feel without thinking or making judgments
about it. Accordingly, Bishop and colleagues (Bishop et al., 2004) construe mindfulness as skill in regulating the focus of attention, that is,
staying alert to what is happening here and now. Mindfulness requires
not only skill in sustained attention (e.g., focusing on your breath, if you
are striving to do that) but also in switching attention flexibly when you
notice that you have lost mindfulness. Typically, you lose mindfulness
by becoming caught up in thinking about the past or the future and
thus drifting away from the present moment. For example, while trying
to remain mindful of the present, you might find yourself ruminating
about an argument you regret and the mess you made of a relationship.
Or you might start worrying about a conflict you need to deal with the
next day and all the ways in which things might go wrong. In so doing,
you immerse yourself in misery. As William James wrote a century ago,
"To wrestle with a bad feeling only pins our attention on it, and keeps it
still fastened in the mind" (Richardson, 2010, p. 132).

Tich Nhat Hanh (1991) believes that "Most of the time, we think too
much" and that "quite a lot of our thinking is useless." He goes on,

> It is as if, in our head, each of us has a cassette tape that is always
> running, day and night. We think of this and we think of that, and it
> is difficult to stop. With a cassette, we can just press the stop button.
> But with our thinking, we do not have any button. (p. 11)

Technically put, to remain mindful, you must develop "the ability to
inhibit secondary elaborative processing of thoughts, feelings and sensations" (S. L. Shapiro, Carlson, Astin & Freedman, 2006, p. 376). Thus,
while aspiring to be mindful of walking, you might think "This is boring"

and then go on to think, "I'm no good at this," and further, "I'll never get my mind under control," and so on. The paradox: to catch yourself drifting into elaborative thinking, you need to be mindful! To reiterate, you must be *mindful of mind*, just as you can be mindful of your breath or a flower: "With the mind … observe the mind" (Kornfield, 2009, p. 37). As you will quickly discover when you try to put your mind to it, being mindful is *simple but difficult*. In short, "Mindfulness is about losing your focus 100 times and returning to it 101 times" (Roemer & Orsillo, 2009, p. 137).

Accepting attitude toward experience

Now I go from simple but difficult to even *more* difficult, that is, cultivating an accepting attitude toward your experience. Mindfulness entails being open-minded in maintaining an *attitude of curiosity* as well as a *stance of nonjudgmental acceptance* toward *all* experience. Owing to the fundamental role of acceptance in mindfulness, the treatment approaches to be considered here can be lumped together as mindfulness- and acceptance-based behavioral therapies (Roemer & Orsillo, 2009). I prefer to view this acceptance facet of mindfulness through the lens of attachment theory. That is, adopting an accepting attitude toward your emotional distress is a way of relating to yourself consistent with secure attachment. Hence acceptance of distressing emotion is a pillar of your internal secure base.

Like mindfulness, acceptance is a venerable and complex concept embedded in many spiritual and religious traditions (Williams & Lynn, 2010). For more than a half-century, psychologists and psychotherapists have paid keen attention to self-acceptance and acceptance of others, as well as their substantial correlation. Viewed as a key facet of mindfulness, acceptance pertains to states of mind; in this context, avoidance is the antithesis of acceptance. Maintaining a curious, accepting attitude toward your experience might seem easy, until you realize that this attitude also must incorporate emotionally painful experience (Bishop et al., 2004). Now consider that this accepting attitude also would apply to frightening and painful feelings associated with traumatic experiences. Imagine being *curious* about your feelings of fear, outrage, disgust, shame, and guilt as well as about posttraumatic images from your past that haunt you. Simple in principle but extremely difficult in practice.

I must make a strong case for acceptance when it comes to facing traumatic emotions. To do so, I will begin by drawing a contrast between acceptance and avoidance. Then I will discuss two strategies that make acceptance easier: first, being mindful of the difference between the internal world of the mind and the external world of reality and, second, being willing to engage in valued actions while experiencing distressing emotions.

As you can tell from its title, Acceptance and Commitment Therapy, developed by Steven Hayes and colleagues (Hayes & Strosahl, 2004; Hayes, Strosahl & Wilson, 1999) gives primacy to acceptance. Hayes points to avoidance as the polar opposite of acceptance. Notoriously, persons who have been traumatized are inclined to avoid reminders of trauma so as to block the painful feelings, images, and sensations associated with traumatic memories. Avoidance is central to the diagnosis of posttraumatic stress disorder, in part because avoiding—rather than coping—keeps you stuck.

Hayes and colleagues usefully distinguish between situational avoidance and experiential avoidance. *Situational avoidance* is straightforward: if you were assaulted in a hotel room, you might avoid sleeping in hotels. *Experiential avoidance* is far more complicated:

> Experiential avoidance … occurs when a person is unwilling to remain in contact with particular private experiences (e.g., bodily sensations, emotions, thoughts, memories, behavioral predispositions) and takes steps to alter the form or frequency of these events and the contexts that occasion them. (Hayes, Strosahl & Wilson, 1999, p. 58)

Thus, caught up in experiential avoidance, you might strive to avoid remembering, imagining, thinking about, or talking about traumatic experiences, so as to avoid the painful feelings associated with them. It is one thing to avoid specific situations; it is another thing to try to avoid your own mind. Experiential avoidance tends to backfire, as research on ironic mental processes attests (Roemer & Orsillo, 2009; Wegner, 1994): you must remain alert to whatever you do not want to think about in order to avoid having it come to mind. But your alertness ironically tends to keep the avoided thoughts, feelings, and memories on your mind. Imagine being told that you will receive a painful electric shock if you think of a tiger in the next five minutes. How could you help doing so?

Situational and experiential avoidance are utterly natural; there is no more powerful reward than escaping from pain. Of course you should avoid pain, but only to a point. Using narcotics to block the pain of a broken arm is no substitute for seeing an orthopedist. Avoiding emotional pain can prevent you from facing problems and coming to terms with them; at worst, as in posttraumatic stress disorder, you live in fear of your own mind. And avoidance can restrict your freedom to live your life. It is one thing to avoid hotels and another to avoid going out anywhere by yourself.

Accordingly, a major goal of mindfulness practice is to counter experiential avoidance with *experiential acceptance,* that is, an openhearted receptiveness toward your thoughts, feelings, and sensations—however distressing they may be. Acceptance is easier if you can refrain from getting caught up in elaborative thought such as ruminating, obsessing, worrying, or feeling guilty about what is going on in your mind. Such mindful attention makes acceptance easier by rendering disturbing and painful thoughts and feelings *transient.* If you refrain from wrestling with them, you will discover that they will pass through your mind. Accordingly, mindfulness exercises have been designed to enhance the process of allowing thoughts to come and go in your mind (Hayes, Strosahl & Wilson, 1999). For example, you can imagine being on a river bank looking at leaves floating by in the stream, and letting the words of your thoughts be written on the leaves passing through.

Now I come to a fundamental principle of mindfulness and mentalizing: *what goes on in your mind is separate from reality.* Your capacity to maintain an accepting stance toward painful experience hinges on this distinction. My colleague, cognitive therapist Tom Ellis, has a sign in bold letters in his office: "Don't Believe Everything You Think!" One meditation teacher estimated that "the average person has seventeen thousand thoughts a day" (Kornfield, 2009, p. 139). I have no idea how accurate this estimate is, but it makes the point: how many of these thoughts are worth taking seriously? How many things that you have worried about actually happened? Mark Twain reportedly quipped, "My life has been filled with terrible misfortunes—most of which never happened!" (Kornfield, 2009, p. 294). The mind is imaginative—the creative mind, the worrying mind, the frightened mind, and the angry mind alike. You can work yourself up to a frenzy by imagining all that can go wrong. You can terrorize yourself in your mind—catastrophizing, in the lingo of cognitive therapists. When you catastrophize and have an anxiety attack, you have lost the separation between the inner world and the outer world. You can feel afraid without being in danger. You can crave alcohol without drinking. You can remember traumatic events without actually going through them. And you can think about suicide without killing yourself. Mindfulness gives you space, as if you are standing back from your mind (the thought of suicide) and the world (the act of suicide) and recognizing that they are not the same (J. Holmes, 2011).

Thus maintaining a feeling of separateness between your internal world and the external world is central to mindfulness. It requires a degree of mindful detachment from what is going on in your mind— standing back from it, observing it, accepting it as your experience without giving it undue weight or credibility. Cognitive therapists have used two terms to refer to maintaining the separation between mind and reality: decentering and defusion. At the risk of overkill, I will present both to drive home the point. Segal and colleagues (Segal, Ma, Teasdale & Williams, 2007) employ *decentering* to refer to "the ability to observe one's thoughts and feelings as temporary, objective events in the mind, as opposed to reflections of the self that are necessarily true" (p. 234). Decentering captures the difference between *feeling* worthless and *being* worthless. Hayes and colleagues (Hayes, Strosahl & Wilson, 1999) use the term, cognitive defusion, best understood in contrast to *cognitive fusion*, which refers to the failure to distinguish mental events from reality (believing everything you think). Technically put, cognitive fusion stems from a failure to be aware of the mental process (worrying) that generates the mental content (the imagined danger) and thereby accepting unquestioningly the content at face value; in short, there is a "fusion of the symbol and the event" (Hayes, Strosahl & Wilson., 1999, p. 73). Such fusion leads to experiential avoidance insofar as mental events are experienced as too real, often overwhelmingly so. You do not want to think or remember if your thoughts or memories terrify you. Hence Acceptance and Commitment Therapy interventions aim to promote cognitive *defusion*, shifting attention from mental content to mental process:

> Clinically, we want to teach clients to see thoughts as thoughts, feelings as feelings, memories as memories, and physical sensations as physical sensations. None of these private events are inherently toxic to human welfare when experienced for what they are.

Their toxicity derives from seeing them as harmful, unhealthy, bad experiences that are what they claim to be, and thus need to be controlled and eliminated. (Hayes, Strosahl, Bunting, Twohig & Wilson, 2004, p. 8)

Being mindful and employing decentering or defusion, you do not take your thoughts literally. Thinking you are a failure is not the same as being a failure. Feeling an urge to gamble does not mean that you must go to the casino. You give yourself some space from your mind. Of course, there are many thoughts you need to believe. If you drive your car into a wall, you will get hurt. If you are afraid of someone who is actually threatening you, you must take action. Indeed, you need to "fuse" with such thoughts. But much of your mental life, especially your thoughts and feelings about yourself and others, are far more loosely tied to reality, and you are better off not getting too caught up in them. Sometimes, a mere nudge in the direction of mindful acceptance can be helpful.

> I worked with a patient hospitalized with depression who, in the first session of psychotherapy, confessed that he had been plagued by blasphemous religious thoughts of a sexual nature that he had never talked about with anyone. We were not able to figure out what set off this chain of intrusive thinking. No matter. Without using the word, I counseled him to take a mindful attitude toward these thoughts, encouraging him to let them be in his mind and pass through his mind without making too much of them. In the subsequent sessions, he reported that he was far less troubled by these thoughts.
>
> I suspect that my own attitude of curiosity and acceptance had rubbed off a bit. I also told him my belief that all of us have private thoughts about which we are ashamed; I assured him that I do. That surprised him—he thought he was unusual in this regard. Then I suggested that he survey a group of his fellow patients as to whether they had private thoughts they are so ashamed of that they would not want to tell anyone about them. He came back in the next session having conducted his survey, which revealed that the vast majority of his peers also acknowledged such thoughts. After adopting a more accepting attitude toward the thoughts, he experienced them far less frequently, and he was no longer so troubled by them.

As already stated, experiential avoidance is natural, whereas experiential acceptance goes against the grain. Making this mental shift requires a 180-degree turn for many persons. In addition to working on detachment (decentering or defusion), you can promote mindful acceptance through *action*. I see many patients who, understandably, want therapy to help them get rid of their anxiety. No wonder, if they have been traumatized and experience crippling anxiety. Fear of anxiety—at worst, panicking when you notice a hint of anxiety such as a rapid heartbeat—escalates anxiety (Craske & Barlow, 2008). Anxiety becomes the childhood monster under the bed; avoiding looking under the bed makes the monster all the more real. Paradoxically, avoiding anxiety can escalate anxiety. The university student who procrastinates in writing her intimidating term paper becomes increasingly panicky as the window of time to do so closes. On the other hand, doing things that make you anxious will increase your anxiety in the short run but decrease your anxiety in the long run, the fundamental basis of exposure therapy.

Here I am referring to a core principle of Acceptance and Commitment Therapy (Hayes, Strosahl & Wilson, 1999), which promotes willingness and commitment to taking action. The aim is to reverse your priorities: it is more important to engage in valued activities than to avoid distressing feelings. Experience and accept the feelings while doing what you want or need to do. You want a raise but the prospect of asking your boss increases your anxiety. You want to go out on a date but you are anxious about being turned down if you make the phone call. Your best strategy is to ask for the raise and make the call—while feeling the anxiety. I think of this strategy as *functioning while anxious*. Sleep in a hotel room like one where you were assaulted (when it is safe) while anxious. Give a speech while anxious. Confront someone who is annoying you while anxious. Talk about shameful feelings in psychotherapy while anxious. Accept that others will observe your anxiety. Quite likely, they will be accepting and will not condemn you for it. And accept that they may not be accepting. You can make a list of all the things you might need to do while anxious. Ditto for functioning while angry, while depressed, while feeling guilty, and so forth.

This principle of changing your feelings by taking action, a cornerstone of behavior therapy, is not new. In 1899 William James wrote:

There is ... no better known or more generally useful precept ... in one's personal self-discipline, than that which bids us to pay

> primary attention to what we do and express, and not to care too
> much for what we feel …. Action seems to follow feeling, but really
> action and feeling go together; and by regulating the action, which
> is under the more direct control of the will, we can indirectly regu-
> late the feeling, which is not. (Richardson, 2010, p. 131)

To sum up, mindfulness entails attentiveness to present experience, which includes mindful awareness of the inner world as well as the outer world. And mindfulness entails awareness with an attitude—an accepting attitude that buttresses your internal secure base. Such accept- ance is fostered by not taking your mind too seriously—not conflating inner and outer reality, and not letting your feelings stand in the way of things you want and need to do. I hope it is obvious that mindfulness plays an important role in coping with trauma. But mindfulness is more than a technique or coping strategy; ideally, it is a way of life embedded in an ethical value system.

Ethical purpose of mindfulness

Many psychotherapists, not wanting to proselytize or to step on toes, have taken pains to emphasize the secular nature of mindfulness instruction (Roemer & Orsillo, 2009). Stripped of its origins in spiritual- ity, mindfulness practice can be employed in a thoroughly pragmatic way for example, to enhance coping with a general medical condition or to decrease anxiety. Thus acceptance has a pragmatic aim in its "rather interesting compound paradox: that we are to accept internal events in order to be rid of them, and we control them by letting go" (Williams & Lynn, 2010, p. 11).

Yet we should not overlook the ethical and spiritual dimensions of mindfulness. I agree with Shauna Shapiro and colleagues:

> When Western psychology attempted to extract the essence of
> mindfulness practice from its original religious/cultural roots, we
> lost, to some extent, the aspect of intention, which for Buddhism
> was enlightenment and compassion for all beings. It seems valuable
> to explicitly bring this aspect back into our model. (S. L. Shapiro,
> Carlson, Astin & Freedman,, 2006, p. 375)

Enlightenment is a high aspiration; compassion is more accessi- ble. Cultivating *compassion* is a pervasive theme in the mindfulness literature, Buddhist and secular, and compassion is nowhere more needed than in the realm of trauma, which entails extreme suffering. We must not confuse compassion with pity. Martha Nussbaum (2001) defines compassion simply as "a painful emotion occasioned by the awareness of another person's undeserved misfortune" (p. 301), and she distinguishes compassion from pity, which entails condescension, that is, looking down on the sufferer. Developing an accepting and nonjudgmental attitude toward your own painful experience provides a basis for self-compassion, which is essential in healing from trauma (Allen, 2005). A foundation of major religions (Armstrong, 2010), promoting compassion for self and others is gaining popularity in the mental health literature (P. Gilbert, 2010; Neff, 2011).

Concomitant with promoting compassion, some mindfulness practices include loving-kindness meditation, and loving-kindness applies equally to self and others. Kabat-Zinn (1990) begins this meditation by inviting participants to consciously invoke feelings of love and kindness toward the self: "May I be free from anger, may I be free from hatred; may I be filled with compassion, may I feel kindness toward myself" (p. 183). Then you extend the meditation toward someone you care about: "May he or she be happy, may he (she) be free from pain and suffering, may he (she) experience love and joy" (p. 183). Then you extend the meditation to a person with whom you have a difficult relationship, someone with whom you are not sympathetic. Then you extend the feeling to all people who are suffering or in need of kindness or caring—indeed extended to all living creatures on the planet.

I think it is fitting that, with secure attachment as our backdrop, we have wound our way from acceptance to compassion to *love*. We should call a spade a spade and not be timid about referring to love in our work. But we must not simply slide from self-compassion to compassion for others and from self-love to love for others without taking notice of the shift. No doubt, just as you can be mindful of your own emotional states, you can be mindful of others' emotional states— and should be. But research on mindfulness is noteworthy for generally sidelining attunement to others in favor of self-focused attention (Mace, 2008). The predominant emphasis on self-awareness in mindfulness therapies and research is ironic, given the Buddhist emphasis on self-transcendence (Wallace, 2009), that is, the aim of letting go of our ferocious attachment to "ego."

I have found Iris Murdoch's writing to be inspiring, and I used her work previously to illustrate ethical dimensions of mentalizing

(J. G. Allen, 2008b; Allen, Fonagy & Bateman, 2008). I now realize that I was unwittingly smuggling into mentalizing the ethics from mindfulness. But Murdoch's thinking bridges mindfulness and mentalizing in drawing attention to others' mental states, the basis of sensitive responsiveness. Murdoch gave great weight to *attention*, and note how she characterized it: "I have used the word 'attention' … to express the idea of a just and loving gaze directed upon an individual reality" (Murdoch, 1971, p. 33). Simply put, "Love is knowledge of the individual" (p. 27). Murdoch also gave great weight to *imagination* as crucial in being mindful of others; imagination is "an ability to picture what is quite other; especially of course to picture and realise, make real to oneself, the existence of other people" (Murdoch, 1992, p. 322). Furthermore, Murdoch construed "unselfing" as the core challenge in perceiving others as they really are. She decried the "usual egoistic fuzz of self-protective anxiety" (p. 174) and asserted, "egoistic anxiety veils the world" (p. 244). She treasured unfettered imagination as "freely and creatively exploring the world, moving toward the expression and elucidation (and in art celebration) of what is true and deep" (p. 321). As she recognized, employing attention and imagination to overcome egoism is no mean feat: "our ordinary consciousness is full of illusions. Our 'grasp' is superficial. Anxiety, malice, envy, greed, all sorts of selfish preoccupations and instinctive attachments may deform or hide what confronts us …. At every moment we are 'attending' or failing to attend" (Murdoch, 1992, pp. 295–296). This quotation easily could have come from the Buddhist mindfulness literature.

Murdoch (1971) construed "reality" as "that which is revealed to the patient eye of love" (p. 39) and thus brought ethics and morality to the forefront of mindfulness: "consciousness is a form of moral activity: what we attend to, how we attend, whether we attend" (Murdoch, 1992, p. 167). More elaborately,

> it is perfectly obvious that goodness is connected with knowledge: not with impersonal quasi-scientific knowledge of the ordinary world, whatever that may be, but with a refined and honest perception of what is really the case, a patient and just discernment and exploration of what confronts one, which is the result not simply of opening one's eyes but of a certainly perfectly familiar kind of moral discipline. (Murdoch, 1971, p. 37)

Accordingly, Murdoch (1992) argued that we practitioners of psychotherapy "cannot avoid being involved in moral judgment, in moral reflection and insight in the widest sense" inasmuch as "It is the soul that is being treated" (p. 307). Nowhere is her formulation more apt than in confronting trauma. No doubt, embracing this ethical dimension of mindfulness puts us on an unavoidable slippery slope: we must find a way to engage in this inescapably moral activity without moralizing in a narrowly judgmental fashion (J. G. Allen, 2008b). But I am not bashful in acknowledging the values that I am advocating; not infrequently, in an educational group I acknowledge, "Now I'm going from teaching to preaching." I believe that all of us therapists preach, but we do not always face up to the fact that we are doing so. The values espoused in the mindfulness literature are hardly parochial (Armstrong, 2010).

We psychotherapists could not do better than following Murdoch's lead in aspiring to be mindful of the reality of self and others. As Murdoch (1971) articulated it, mindful attention is a high aspiration:

> The love which brings the right answer is an exercise of justice and realism and really looking. The difficulty is to keep the attention fixed upon the real situation and to prevent it from returning surreptitiously to the self with consolations of self-pity, resentment, fantasy and despair .... It is a *task* to come to see the world as it is .... We act rightly 'when the time comes' not out of strength of will but out of the quality of our usual attachments and with the kind of energy and discernment which we have available. And to this the whole activity of our consciousness is relevant. (p. 89; emphasis in original)

Now I hope you will see that my path from mindfulness of self to mindfulness of others and my plunge into the territory of love leads straight to the realm of attachment. Think of Ainsworth's sensitive responsiveness as emanating from mindful attention in Murdoch's words: a just and loving gaze directed upon an individual reality. Plainly, childrearing is a moral endeavor. Here I am in agreement with Jeremy Holmes (2001), who referred to the "implicit moral overtones" in attachment theory and who proposed that patterns of secure and insecure attachment are not only developmental models but also "moral maps" (p. xiii). I will return to these themes later in this chapter when considering the relation between attachment and the conceptual sibling of mindfulness, mentalizing.

Cultivating mindfulness

We must be careful to distinguish the activity of mindful attentiveness from the practices designed to promote it, meditation most prominent among them (Davis & Hayes, 2011). The mindfulness literature makes an important distinction between concentration meditation and insight meditation. *Concentration meditation* entails directing your attention to a single focus, such as your breathing. Concentrating, you find that you lose your focus (100 times) and then gently bring it back (101 times). In contrast, *insight meditation* is especially pertinent to cultivating mindfulness *of mind*. Insight meditation promotes attentiveness to mental states and exemplifies the principles of acceptance and decentering discussed earlier, as Goldstein and Kornfield's (1987) instructions indicate. They draw the meditator's attention to the continual flux of mental states while aspiring to "loosen the sense of identification with them" (p. 35):

> maintain a quality of openness and alertness so that whatever presents itself becomes the object of awareness, and let all objects of body and mind arise and pass away by themselves. Our practice is simply to settle back and note in each moment what is arising, without judgment, without evaluation, without interpretation. It is simple, bare attention to what is happening. (p. 36)

Innumerable strategies for cultivating mindfulness are covered in a huge and burgeoning literature. Kabat-Zinn (1990) developed a stand-alone intervention for stress reduction, which is distinct from applications of mindfulness in various psychotherapies, where mindfulness is incorporated alongside established practices. I offer a quick tour, starting with Kabat-Zinn's pioneering stress-reduction program and then noting how mindfulness has been incorporated into cognitive therapy for depression, Dialectical Behavior Therapy for borderline personality disorder, and Acceptance and Commitment Therapy, as well as Metacognitive Therapy for anxiety disorders, which directly overlaps mindfulness and mentalizing. Given the panoply of stress-related problems and psychiatric disorders associated with attachment trauma, all these interventions are pertinent to the main concerns of this book. I look for help wherever I can get it.

Kabat-Zinn (1990, 2003) began developing Mindfulness-Based Stress Reduction in 1979 as an eight-week, outpatient group intervention for patients with a range of general medical conditions (e.g., heart disease, lung disease, cancer, and chronic pain) who were not responding fully to standard medical care. The mindfulness intervention was not designed to replace but rather to complement standard care. The program includes education about stress and stress-management strategies, but it centers on various mindfulness exercises that place considerable emphasis on the body (e.g., including focus on the breath, attentively scanning all of the body, and attentiveness to movement in yoga and walking meditation). In addition, mindfulness exercises are directed toward thoughts and emotions with the attitude of acceptance described earlier in this section. To supplement formal training, Kabat-Zinn wrote *Full Catastrophe Living* (Kabat-Zinn, 2003) to guide readers through the program and *Wherever You Go, There You Are* (Kabat-Zinn, 1994) to instruct readers in more informal practice. The Center for Mindfulness at the University of Massachusetts Medical School offers a variety of audiovisual materials to support mindfulness practice.

Zindel Segal and colleagues developed Mindfulness-Based Cognitive Therapy for Depression (Segal, Teasdale & Williams, 2004; Segal, Williams & Teasdale, 2002) with an eye toward preventing further relapses in patients with chronic, recurrent depression. This approach employs eight weekly two-hour group sessions. The intervention adapts core facets of Mindfulness-Based Stress Reduction to depressive thinking. As in Kabat-Zinn's program, patients are educated about depressive relapses as well as mindfulness, but the heart of the intervention is developing mindfulness skills through exercises and daily practice. In its standard form (Beck, Rush, Shaw & Emery, 1979), cognitive therapy for depression helps patients to modify the content of automatic, unrealistic and depressing thoughts (e.g., "I can't do anything right—I'll never amount to anything!") by learning to identify them, challenge their validity, and thus cultivate more reasonable thoughts (e.g., "I've succeeded at many things when I've worked hard at them").

As already described, mindfulness differs from cognitive therapy: it does not focus on the *content* of your thoughts but rather the way you *relate* to your thoughts. It is not a problem to have the thought, "I can't do anything right," as long as you do not take it seriously: you observe the thought, accept it, and let it go. Recall the mantra, Don't believe everything you think. Notoriously, depressed persons are inclined to ruminate about their problems; in so doing, they labor under the illusion that they are engaging in problem solving whereas their ruminating actually leads to poorer coping and exacerbates depressed mood (Nolen-Hoeksema, 2000). Thus depressive mood and depressive thinking are self-perpetuating. I like the admonition, "When you're in a hole, the first thing to do is stop digging." Through mindfulness, patients learn to disengage from depressing patterns of thinking such that they can feel sad or entertain depressing thoughts without ruminating themselves back into a full-blown depressive episode when things go wrong. Thus, along with other relapse-prevention strategies, mindfulness skills enable patients to nip the potential recurrence of depression in the bud, as the authors put it (Segal, Teasdale & Williams, 2004).

Marsha Linehan (1993) developed Dialectical Behavior Therapy, the most extensively researched treatment for persons with recurrent nonsuicidal self-injury and suicidality who are diagnosed with borderline personality disorder, a disorder to which attachment trauma commonly makes a major contribution. Such self-injurious behaviors as self-cutting can be seen, in part, as relatively desperate and ineffective strategies for managing and expressing painful emotions (Nock, 2009). The dialectic in Dialectical Behavior Therapy refers to the need to balance *acceptance* of things as they are with the need to *change*. Linehan's treatment, which involves a combination of individual therapy and group skills training, is complex and multifaceted. Yet, as other clinicians have done, Linehan identified mindfulness as a core skill in recovery, although formal meditation practice is not part of the treatment. Linehan brings mindfulness to bear on what she calls "what" skills and "how" skills. Three "what" skills are learning to mindfully *observe* events and emotions, even if they are distressing; learning to *describe* events and personal responses in words for the sake of communication and personal control; and learning to *participate* attentively and spontaneously in activities without self-consciousness. The three "how" skills are taking a *nonjudgmental* stance toward experiences; focusing attention on the *current moment* and on one thing at a time; and being *effective in actions* in the service of meeting goals. Consistent with adopting a mindful attitude toward experience, Linehan teaches distress tolerance skills and advocates *radical acceptance*:

Radical acceptance is the fully open experience of what is, entering
into reality just as it is, at this moment. Fully open acceptance is
without constrictions, and without distortion, without judgment,
without evaluation, and without attempts to keep an experience or
to get rid of it .... Another way of thinking about it is that radical
acceptance is radical truth. In other words, acceptance is experiencing something without the haze of what one wants and does not
want it to be. It is the unrivaled entering into reality as it exists.
(Robins, Schmidt & Linehan, 2004, p. 39)

Acceptance and Commitment Therapy (ACT) (Hayes, 2004; Hayes,
Strosahl & Wilson, 1999) is an eclectic approach to treatment that builds
on cognitive-behavior therapy but cannot be reduced to a set of techniques; indeed, going far beyond method, "it provides an underlying
theory and philosophy of the human condition" (p. 16). As Hayes and
colleagues summarize, "Said simply, *ACT is a therapy approach that uses
acceptance and mindfulness processes, and commitment and behavior change
processes, to produce greater psychological flexibility*" (Hayes, Strosahl,
Bunting, Twohig & Wilson, 2004, p. 13, emphasis in original). ACT shares
mindful acceptance with other approaches, more specifically, striving to
move from experiential avoidance to experiential acceptance, as noted
earlier in this section. But, as Hayes (2008) argues, the emphasis on commitment along with acceptance is a substantial additional contribution
to traditional cognitive therapy that I want to highlight here. To expand
on a point made earlier, constricting your life is a high price to pay for
avoiding emotional distress. ACT places a premium on identifying core
values and engaging in valued action—even if doing so is emotionally
distressing. Thus ACT emphasizes the cardinal importance of commitment in the sense of willingness to take action. Put simply and force-
fully, "*You can choose to try to control what you feel and lose control over your
life, or let go of control over discomfort and get control over your life*" (p. 135,
emphasis added). As Hayes and colleagues summarize:

ACT is at its core a behavioral treatment. Its ultimate goal is to help
the client develop and maintain a behavioral trajectory in life that
is vital and valued. All ACT techniques are eventually subordi-
nated to helping the client live in accord with his or her chosen
values .... although ACT is emotionally evocative, it differs from
some emotion-focused approaches in that there is no interest in

confronting painful or avoided private experiences for their own sake. Instead, acceptance of negative thoughts, memories, or emotions, and other private events is legitimate and honorable only to the extent that it serves ends that are valued by the client. Helping the client identify valued life goals ... and implement them in the fact of emotional obstacles ... both directs and dignifies ACT. (Hayes, Strosahl & Wilson, 1999, p. 205)

A cognitive treatment approach with particular theoretical kinship to mindfulness and mentalizing is Metacognitive Therapy, developed by Adrian Wells (2009). Metacognition refers narrowly to thinking about thinking and, more broadly, to "any knowledge or cognitive process that is involved in the interpretation, monitoring, or control of cognition" (p. 5). As in mentalizing, the key goal in treatment is maintaining the distinction between mental states and real events (e.g., distinguishing memories from current reality). Metacognitive therapy promotes an attitude of *detached mindfulness:*

a state of awareness of internal events, without responding to them with sustained evaluation, attempts to control or suppress them, or respond to them behaviorally. It is exemplified by strategies such as deciding not to worry in response to an intrusive thought, but instead allowing the thought to occupy its own mental space without further action or interpretation in the knowledge that it is merely an event in the mind. (p. 71)

To promote such detached mindfulness, the treatment includes attention training in addition to facilitating mindfulness in relation to negative thoughts and intrusive symptoms.

Benefits of mindfulness

Mindfulness has been practiced for millennia, but only recently have the benefits of this practice garnered the attention of mental health professionals who have subjected them to systematic research. Mindfulness practice, such as meditation, is intended initially to promote *states* of mindfulness and, ultimately, to enhance *traits* of mindfulness, that is, enduring dispositions to be mindful (Garland, Gaylord & Fredrickson, 2011). In its pragmatic applications, mindfulness has been employed in the treatment of a wide range of psychiatric disturbances, including not only anxiety and depression but also borderline personality disorder, substance abuse, eating disorders, and psychotic symptoms (Roemer & Orsillo, 2009). Evaluating comprehensively the effectiveness of mindfulness interventions is complicated by the fact that treatment approaches vary (K. W. Brown, Ryan & Creswell, 2007); while all are multifaceted, some focus more exclusively on meditative practices (e.g., Mindfulness-Based Stress Reduction and Mindfulness-Based Cognitive Therapy), whereas others incorporate mindfulness in more eclectic interventions (e.g., Dialectical Behavior Therapy and Acceptance and Commitment Therapy).

Reviews of recent research on the impact of mindfulness interventions reveal wide-ranging benefits (K. W. Brown, Ryan & Creswell, 2007; Davis & Hayes, 2011). Mindfulness is associated with basic psychological competencies, including improved attention, greater cognitive flexibility, increased emotion regulation, diminished stress reactivity, faster recovery from negative emotions, decreased propensity to ruminate, along with increased awareness, understanding, and acceptance of emotion. Accordingly, mindfulness is associated with increased well-being and positive emotionality; improved physical health and pain management; and diminished anxiety, depression, and impulsivity. A meta-analysis of results from thirty-nine studies that included a combined sample of 1,140 patients (Hoffmann, Sawyer, Witt & Oh, 2010) showed significant decreases in levels of anxiety and depression from the beginning to the end of mindfulness treatment. Moreover, nineteen of these studies included follow-up assessments (averaging twenty-seven weeks) that showed enduring benefit. Although the aggregated studies assessed changes in anxiety and depression associated with a wide range of other problems, including general medical conditions, the beneficial effects were strongest for patients with psychiatric disorders, that is, decreases in anxiety for patients with anxiety disorders and decreases in depression for patients with depressive disorders.

The application of mindfulness to the treatment of chronic depression warrants particular attention owing to the impressive findings and the sheer ubiquity of depression-related disability in patients with a history of attachment trauma. As it was designed to do, Segal and colleagues' (Segal, Williams & Teasdale, 2002) Mindfulness-Based Cognitive Therapy for depression has been shown to prevent recurrence of depressive episodes for patients who are at especially high risk, that is, patients with a history of multiple prior episodes. Notably, this psychological treatment intervention is administered *after* recovery from the acute depressive episode, at which point patients have the capacity to engage in mindfulness practice. Impressively, the mindfulness intervention has been shown to prevent relapse as effectively as continuation of antidepressant medication (Segal et al., 2010).

To repeat William James's century-old observation, wrestling with a bad feeling keeps it fastened in the mind. In my way of thinking, it is utterly natural—indeed, like a reflex—to feel depressed when things go badly. But mindfulness can block the process of spiraling from *feeling* depressed to becoming *ill* with depression, a crucial distinction (Allen, 2006a). As discussed earlier, decentering from negative thoughts—observing them without believing them—plays a significant role in the treatment. Segal and colleagues (Segal, Ma, Teasdale & Williams, 2007) showed decentering to be associated with lower levels of anxiety and depression as well as less proclivity to ruminate. In addition, decentering was associated with less experiential avoidance. These authors note emerging findings suggesting that depressed patients treated to remission with cognitive-behavioral therapy showed increases in decentering, in contrast to those treated to remission with antidepressant medication. This finding is of particular significance because a high level of decentering following treatment is associated with a more enduring treatment response.

Further research explored the psychological mechanisms by which the mindfulness intervention exerted its effects (Kuyken et al., 2010). Participants were patients with a history of three or more prior depressive episodes who had been successfully treated with antidepressant medication. Half of the patients were randomly assigned to continued medication; the other half discontinued their medication and began Mindfulness-Based Cognitive Therapy. All patients were followed up at three-month intervals for fifteen months. With a history of multiple recurrences, these patients were selected because of their high risk of relapse, and the relapse rates were substantial: 47% of those in the mindfulness group relapsed, compared to 60% in the continued medication group (a difference that was not statistically significant). But the researchers were primarily interested in the determinants of depression severity at follow-up. Not surprisingly, they found that, compared to medication treatment, the mindfulness group showed higher levels of mindfulness and self-compassion at the end of treatment. And the increases in mindfulness and self-compassion led to less severe depression at fifteen months.

The researchers went beyond relating mindfulness to depression by subjecting participants to a challenge—examining their reaction to feeling transiently depressed. That is, the researchers experimentally induced a low mood by having participants listen to sad music while rehearsing a sad memory, and then they examined the impact of this sad mood induction on participants' depressive thinking. For the group maintained on medication, the increase in depressive thinking after they became sad forecasted a high level of depression at fifteen months and a greater likelihood of relapse into another depressive episode. In contrast, for the mindfulness group, the increase in depressive thinking evidently was more transient, because it was *not* associated with subsequent depression. I do not mean to imply that the experimental induction of sadness triggered depression for some participants. Presumably, their reaction in the laboratory was a sign of their typical coping with depressed mood in daily life. Now, the most interesting finding: although the mindfulness group responded to sadness with depressive thinking, they also showed increases in self-compassion; moreover, it appears that their increased self-compassion prevented them from being stuck in depressive thinking and thus from sliding back into depressive illness.

Mentalizing in attachment relationships

I have been gradually desensitizing you to the technical term, mentalizing, and the time has come for full exposure. I will start by defining the word more fully and spelling out some of its complexity, as I have done with mindfulness. Then I will present an overview of the way mentalizing develops in attachment relationships, which is tantamount to addressing the profoundly intriguing question of how you come to have a mind. I can hardly begin to do justice to that profound question, but I hope at least to pique your interest in it. All the prior material in this book has been leading up to the last concern of this section, the intergenerational transmission of mentalizing in attachment relationships. That process sets the stage for understanding fully the nature of attachment trauma in the next chapter.

Defining mentalizing

Our colleague, Jeremy Holmes, rightly calls mentalizing an *ungainly* word. A patient I worked with was less charitable; she called it an abomination of the English language. I have said it, read it, and written it so many times that mentalizing seems like a perfectly ordinary word to me. And, in our family, it has become a household word. Staff members throughout The Menninger Clinic know the word, and our patients cannot go through treatment without being exposed to it. But many patients in our educational groups say it takes some weeks to "get it."

If you browse the dictionaries in a bookstore looking for "mentalizing," as I have done, you will find it only rarely. I did not find it in my trusted volumes of the *Shorter Oxford English Dictionary* until I ordered the CD-ROM version. I typed in "mentalize" and, to my surprise, it came up in the fine print under the main entry, mental. The definition: to develop or *cultivate mentally* (as we hope to do in therapy) or to *give a mental quality* to something (e.g., seeing anger in your spouse's face). This CD-ROM discovery prompted me to contact the staff at the Oxford English Dictionary to find out about the history of the word. Katherine Connor Martin was graciously helpful. Although it is not a commonly used word, "mentalizing" has been in the lexicon for two centuries, and the word has been included in the Oxford English Dictionary for a century. French psychoanalysts have used the word, mentalisation, for several decades (Lecours & Bouchard, 1997), and two publications brought mentalizing into the English professional literature in 1989. John Morton (1989) pointed to enduring impairments of mentalizing capacity as the central and pervasive problem in autism, and Peter Fonagy (1989) identified more limited and transient impairments of mentalizing associated with traumatic attachment relationships in persons with borderline personality disorder.

Like mindfulness, mentalizing is a multifaceted concept (Allen, Fonagy & Bateman 2008; Fonagy, Bateman & Luyten, 2012), which can make for some confusion (Choi-Kain & Gunderson, 2008). We think of mentalizing as an umbrella term because it covers a wide range of mental activity. At the most basic level, overlapping mindfulness, mentalizing refers to *awareness of mental states*. Of course, the variety of mental states is enormous. Broadly, we distinguish between mentalizing cognition (e.g., thoughts and beliefs) and mentalizing emotion (e.g., feelings and emotional expressions). Yet mental states are extremely diverse, encompassing sensations, perceptions, thoughts, feelings, desires, impulses, hallucinations, dreams, posttraumatic flashbacks, dissociative experiences, and the like. And mentalizing encompasses awareness of mental states in others as well as oneself. As it pertains to awareness of mental states in others, mentalizing includes external and internal facets. On the exterior, you can be aware of a scowling facial expression or a looming posture; from this external appearance, you can infer internal states of mind, such as anger and critical or hostile thoughts.

We also make a more subtle but utterly crucial distinction between mentalizing explicitly and mentalizing implicitly (Allen, 2003); including implicit along with explicit mentalizing accounts for much of the breadth of the term—the sheer size of the umbrella. *Mentalizing explicitly* is easiest to understand, because it is a more fully conscious process. Mostly, we mentalize explicitly using language. When you name a feeling or anything else going on in your mind, you are mentalizing explicitly (e.g., "I'm feeling angry," "I'm craving a drink," "I'm imagining a beach on the French Riviera"). When you consciously interpret behavior, you're mentalizing explicitly (e.g., "I think I snapped at you because I was annoyed about your being late," "When you didn't return my call, I thought you'd lost interest in me"). Much of our explicit mentalizing takes the form of narrative—stories. Indeed, each of us has a life story, which is a mentalizing creation, always open to revision. Thus, along with advocating, Don't believe everything you think, we commend, Don't believe every story you create. We all have attachment stories, as called for in the Adult Attachment Interview; I will discuss attachment stories further in this section and again in conjunction with attachment trauma.

Mentalizing explicitly is a conscious process, something you do deliberately and oftentimes with effort. Imagine the thought you would need to put into a narrative account of a serious transgression that was impulsive and was hurtful to someone you love (e.g., an alcoholic relapse after a commitment to sobriety). In contrast, *mentalizing implicitly* is a relatively automatic, effortless, nonconscious process. Mentalizing implicitly is like driving a car. Having learned to do it, you do it automatically, without having to think about it. You do not need to think about turning the steering wheel in a certain direction to avoid a pothole; you just do it. Examples of mentalizing implicitly are taking turns in a conversation or taking account of your partner's background knowledge when explaining something (e.g., not referring to "Anne" without explaining who Anne is when your conversation partner does not know her). Much of the implicit mentalizing that concerns us, however, relates to emotion. We naturally resonate emotionally to each other without having to think about it (Iacoboni, 2008); we can think of this process as emotional contagion (Hatfield, Cacioppo & Rapson, 1994). When your friend comes in looking crestfallen, you naturally alter your posture (lean forward showing interest) and adjust your voice (to be soft and soothing). You are mentalizing in the sense of being aware of your friend's mental state, but your behavioral response is automatic, based on an intuitive, gut-level response. If you tried to adapt your behavior deliberately, you would mess it up—appearing stilted and wooden. Of course, if your friend comes to you looking crestfallen, you also would mentalize explicitly, wondering about the reason and asking him about it.

As we do with mindfulness, we can think of mentalizing as a skill. Short of profound autism, all of us learn to mentalize. Some of us are better at mentalizing than others, and all of us mentalize well sometimes and poorly at others. We do not mentalize well, for example, when we are frightened, angry, or ashamed; then we get defensive. Our variable mentalizing capacity will be a main concern of this book. But you also should be aware that mentalizing is like intelligence in the sense that you can be better at some facets of it than others. Some of us are adept at mechanics and not at academics, others the reverse. Similarly, you can be better or worse at mentalizing in relation to yourself in comparison with others. Commonly, it is easier to spot faults in others than in yourself. Or you might be in touch with some of your feelings (e.g., sadness) and not with others (e.g., anger). We all mentalize implicitly in having gut-level emotional reactions to someone, but we are not necessarily able to mentalize explicitly in the sense of understanding the reason for our reaction.

Like mindfulness, mentalizing is not an all-or-none phenomenon: you can be more or less mindful, and you can mentalize more or less skillfully. Following the French psychoanalysts (Lecours & Bouchard, 1997), we can think of degrees of mentalizing in terms of *mental elaboration*, for example, in mentalizing emotion. If you were to notice your heart racing without any awareness that your racing heart is a reflection of your anxiety, you would not be mentalizing. Merely identifying that you are anxious would be a first step in mentalizing. Understanding the reasons for your anxiety would be an even higher level of mentalizing, and this understanding might even include some historical context (e.g., awareness of your sensitivity to being dominated or controlled based on earlier traumatic relationships).

One last matter of definition: there are many concepts that overlap the territory of mentalizing—mindfulness being one that occupies us in this chapter. Empathy is a prime example. You might think of empathy as requiring mentalizing of others' emotional states, implicitly and explicitly. That is, when you empathize, you not only resonate at a gut level but also strive to understand the other person's experience. Moreover, while resonating you also maintain a sense of separateness between the other person's experience and your own. Thus empathy requires complex mentalizing. Empathy is narrower than mentalizing in pertaining to understanding others' mental states. Sometimes for shorthand in explaining mentalizing, I say that mentalizing is empathy if you also include empathy for yourself. Yet, along with mindfulness, empathy is only one of many terms that overlap mentalizing (Allen, Fonagy & Bateman, 2008); others include psychological mindedness, observing ego, insight, metacognition, mindreading, theory of mind, social cognition, and emotional intelligence.

As just detailed, we have many words available besides mentalizing. Why use this uncommon and ungainly word? I confess, there are a number of things I do not like about the word. The main thing I do not like: many other people—colleagues and patients—dislike it! I often find myself feeling apologetic for it. Another thing I do not like is its technical sound, which, as Holmes contends, is "off-putting" (J. Holmes, 2010, p. 9). I find this technical connotation dismaying, because I am convinced that the capacity to mentalize is the essence of our humanity; it is what most distinguishes us from other animals, including the great apes, domesticated dogs, and dolphins: they have plenty of social intelligence but nowhere near our mentalizing capacity. Mentalizing sounds too much like psychological jargon to capture the essence of our humanity. More substantively, I do not like the intellectual or cognitive connotations of mentalizing; mentalizing would seem to relate more to thinking than to feeling. "Mental" might even seem opposed to "emotional," and yet I am primarily concerned with mentalizing emotion in attachment relationships. Mentalizing is an emotional process that requires gut-level emotional experience as well as involving reflective thinking. Finally, I find that colleagues who initially are put off by the term mentalizing conclude that, once they grasp the meaning of the word, they already knew all about it and there is nothing more they have to learn. On the contrary, there is much to learn, as the increasingly extensive literature on mentalizing attests. And, as we say repeatedly in our educational groups, while we all mentalize, we all could do it better—*all* including us clinicians as well as our patients.

What do I like about mentalizing? There is an advantage in using an uncommon word: it captures attention. As with any other skill, we can improve our mentalizing in part by paying more attention to doing it—or failing to do it. Thus it is helpful to have an attention-getting word: Mentalize! Although there is a downside to it (Choi-Kain & Gunderson, 2008), I like the breadth of mentalizing. As an umbrella term, mentalizing puts us in the right ballpark when it comes to aspiring to be self-aware, to be attuned to others, and to communicate well—all these are interconnected through mentalizing. I also am convinced that, while there are many related concepts, there is no synonym for mentalizing. For example, when we can use mindfulness, empathy, or psychological mindedness instead, we should do so. But none is equivalent.

Finally, a seemingly nit-picky point: I believe strongly that we need a verb, my reason for preferring mentalizing to the more widely used word in this literature, mentalization. Mentalizing is something we *do* (or should do more often or better). Empathy is a good word in this respect, because we can empathize. Mindfulness and many other perfectly fine terms, such as psychological mindedness, observing ego, and social cognition do not have a verb form. We can be mindful, and we can attend mindfully, but we can't mindfulize. But we can mentalize, mindfully.

Development of mentalizing

As I emphasized in discussing mindfulness, adopting an accepting attitude toward painful experience is bolstered by not taking your thoughts and feelings too seriously, not believing everything you think, detaching yourself somewhat by observing what is going on in your mind, and decentering and defusing yourself from your states of mind. All of us have this capacity, which is not to say that we always make use of it. How did you develop this capacity? The answer is tantamount to understanding how you developed at least an intuitive sense of what a mind is, that you have a mind, and that others have a mind. This development might seem like a philosophical problem of peripheral interest to us in this book. On the contrary, it is central, because the answer lies in attachment security, which is pivotal in our capacity to mentalize in the mindful way I have been praising.

In discussing detached mindfulness, I have been skirting around the linchpin of appreciating the separation between mental states and reality, that is, our intuitive sense of the *representational nature of mental states* (Perner, 1991). A simple analogy: we must distinguish between the map (a representation) and the territory (the actual terrain). Similarly, we distinguish between the portrait and the subject. Mentalizing, we are at least intuitively aware that the mental portraits of self and others that we continually create are just that—portraits, representations that can be more or less sketchy, more or less accurate. In sum, mentalizing entails keeping this representational nature of mental states in mind—in the back of your mind when all goes well and in the forefront when you become aware that you might be off base in your interpretations.

You are not born with full-fledged attachment relationships, and you are not born with anything like an intuitive sense of what a mind is, having a mind, or relating to others with minds. Like the road to attachment, the road to full-fledged mentalizing is long, complex, and subject to continuing research and understanding (Gergely & Unoka, 2008). There is a milestone in this developmental road, a false-belief test employed with children (Wimmer & Perner, 1983), administered as follows:

> Maxi is helping his mother to unpack the shopping bag. He puts the chocolate into the GREEN cupboard. Maxi remembers exactly where he put the chocolate so that he can come back later and get some. Then he leaves for the playground. In his absence his mother needs some chocolate. She takes the chocolate out of the GREEN cupboard and uses some of it for her cake. Then she puts it back not into the GREEN but into the BLUE cupboard. She leaves to get some eggs and Maxi returns from the playground, hungry.

> *Test Question:* "Where will Maxi look for the chocolate?"

> (Perner, 1991, p. 179)

Prior to developing an understanding of the representational nature of mental states, the child answers that Maxi will look in the blue cupboard, because he knows that is where the chocolate is. Capable of mentalizing (recognizing that mental states can *mis*represent reality), the child answers that Maxi will look in the green cupboard, falsely believing that the chocolate remains where he put it.

Most children fail the false belief test before age three and pass by age four (Wellman & Lagattuta, 2000). Notably, passing this test requires full-fledged explicit mentalizing (making a declarative statement about beliefs), and there is some evidence that children implicitly or intuitively appreciate false beliefs as early as fifteen months (Onishi & Baillargeon, 2005). I am going to take you on a rapid transit along the developmental road to mentalizing with signposts identified by Fonagy and colleagues (Fonagy, Gergely, Jurist & Target, 2002). In their earliest months, infants learn that they and others are agents, initiators of action and exerting an influence over the world. As *physical* agents, they influence objects (e.g., moving a mobile, shaking a rattle and hearing the sound). As *social* agents, the influence others (e.g., evoking a smile from mother). Around nine months, they develop an intuitive sense of others as being *teleological* agents, that is, expecting actions to be rational and goal directed as evidenced, for example, by a clever experiment (Csibra & Gergely, 1998). The nine-month old infant anticipates that one computer-animated agent will take a straight path as if to make contact with another, or will jump over an obstacle to do so if need be; yet the infant registers surprise when one agent jumps needlessly to reach the other when no obstacle lies in its path.

Beginning in the second year of life, infants begin *mentalizing* their teleological understanding, that is, they begin to appreciate intuitively that goal-directed actions are associated with mental states, such as desires and feelings (Gergely, Nadasdy, Csibra & Biro, 1995). Yet, as their failure to pass false-belief tests attests, the distinction between internal states and external reality remains blurry (Fonagy, 2006): they conflate another child's understanding of reality with their own. Between the third and fourth year of life, with the aid of language development, children mentalize goal-directed actions more fully in the sense of appreciating that actions can be based on mental states that are out of sync with reality, a main theme of mindfulness that I am continuing to replay. For a coda, here is an expert rendition:

representation is not just one aspect among others of the mind, but provides the basis for explaining what the mind is. In other words, by conceptualizing the mind as a system of representations, the child switches from a *mentalistic theory of behavior*, in which mental states serve as concepts for explaining action, to a *representational theory of mind*, in which mental states are understood as serving a representational function. One can think of the concept of 'representation' as playing a catalytic role in children's reconceptualization of what the mind is. (Perner, 1991, p. 11; emphasis in original)

But you continue to refine your mentalizing capacity beyond childhood, particularly as you create and continually revise your autobiographical narrative; through this narrative, you explicate your understanding of yourself, other persons, and your relationships. Take note: it is through your mentalizing capacity that you develop and revise implicit and explicit working models of yourself and others in your attachment relationships—a primary endeavor of psychotherapy and nowhere more crucial than in treating attachment trauma. As Fonagy summarizes, mentalizing

> enables children to conceive of others' beliefs, feelings, attitudes, desires, hopes, knowledge, imagination, pretense, plans, and so on. At the same time as making others' behavior meaningful and predictable, they are also able flexibly to activate from multiple sets of self-other representations the one most appropriate in a particular interpersonal context. Exploring the meaning of actions of others is crucially linked to the child's ability to label and find meaningful his or her own experience. This ability may make a critical contribution to affect regulation, impulse control, self-monitoring, and the experience of self-agency. (Fonagy, 2001, p. 165)

As reviewed in detail elsewhere (Allen, Fonagy & Bateman, 2008) we develop our understanding of mind in a way that is profoundly counter-intuitive and thus challenging to understand. As an advanced mentalizer, you know your own mind, and you empathize in part by simulating others' experience, for example, intuiting what a friend feels by imagining how you would feel in the same circumstances (Goldman, 2006). So it is natural to assume that a child first recognizes that he or she has a mind (desires, feelings, and thoughts) and then infers that others are similar: they also have a mind. This natural assumption has it backward: our understanding of mind develops not from the inside out but rather from the outside in, based on our social experience (Gergely & Unoka, 2008; Vygotsky, 1978). In his wonderfully titled book, *The Cradle of Thought*, Peter Hobson (2002) put it right: "if an infant were not involved with other people, then she would not come to think" (p. xiv). Moreover, this early development is mainly emotional: "The links that can join one person's mind with the mind of someone else—especially, to begin with, emotional links—are the very links that draw us into thought" (p. 2). In short, as Hobson and Daniel Stern (1985) before him explicated, we develop our sense of self and our understanding of mind through *social engagement*, fundamentally, in attachment relationships.

Donald Winnicott (1971) proposed that the infant's sense of self develops from the "mirroring" responses of caregivers. Through social referencing, where the infant is the object of joint attention, the infant learns what he feels—from the outside in. That is, the mother mirrors the infant's emotional state, such as sadness or frustration, in her own emotional expression—in her face and her voice. Our colleague, George Gergely (Gergely & Watson, 1996) instructively dubbed this process social biofeedback. In physiological biofeedback (Green & Green, 1986), you can tell how anxious or relaxed you are by hooking yourself up to monitors that gauge your skin temperature or muscle tension. With social biofeedback, you become aware of your emotional state through others' emotional responses to your emotions—to the extent that they are emotionally in sync.

A crucial point: the mother's emotional mirroring is not direct; rather, she *represents* the infant's emotional state back to the infant through her own expression of that state (Fonagy, Gergely, Jurist & Target, 2002; Gergely, 2007; Gergely & Unoka, 2008). That is, she does not merely respond to fear with fear, sadness with sadness, excitement with excitement, and frustration with frustration. Such direct responses are liable to escalate the infant's emotions rather than regulating them. Rather, she intermingles her resonance with the infant's emotion with cues that she is expressing *his* emotions, not *hers*. Thus she might soothe while mirroring sadness or show concern while mimicking the infant's frustration; or she might raise her eyebrows to convey that her emotional expression is intended for the infant's attention. She might well use emotion language as well: "Oh! That's scary!" Ultimately, such responsiveness will enable the child to put feelings into words, by matching his internal experience with his mother's external representation of it—in expression and in language. Of course, ideally, she also will talk about her own emotional experience. Such discourse about mental states, inside and outside the family, enables us to develop a language for the mind, ultimately articulated in biographical and autobiographical narrative, the pinnacle of mental elaboration.

Intergenerational transmission of mentalizing

I hope I have made it adequately clear that mentalizing—indeed our sense of ourselves as minded beings—develops in the context of attachment relationships. Now I am in a position to address a mystery that might have gone unnoticed earlier when I reviewed remarkable research showing that the parents' security of attachment in relation to their parents—as revealed in the AAI, even when administered prior to the birth of the infant—predicts the infant's security of attachment to the parent at twelve months. This finding holds for fathers (Steele, Steele & Fonagy, 1996) as well as mothers (Fonagy, Steele & Steele, 1991). The mystery: how do we get from parental security to infant security? Here we are in the transmission gap (Fonagy & Target, 2005). One answer lies in the most fundamental principle of this book: *mentalizing begets mentalizing*.

As described in the previous chapter, narrative coherence in the AAI is the hallmark of attachment security. Mary Main (1991) identified metacognitive-monitoring as a contributor to narrative coherence. *Metacognition* is one of many terms that overlap with mentalizing; in short, it refers to cognition about cognition or thinking about thinking (Smith, Shields & Washburn, 2003). Along these lines, Main distinguished representation from meta-representation as the difference between "*thinking vs. thinking about thought*, or, at a deeper level, possessing a mental representation of an experience vs. being able to reflect on its validity, nature, and source" (p. 128, emphasis in original). If you recall that narrative coherence is evident in the capacity to *reflect* on the meaning of early attachment experiences and their impact on development, the role of metacognitive monitoring in the interview should be evident. For example, you would be engaged in metacognitive monitoring if you were to reevaluate your thinking as follows: I used to feel resentful of my father for what I experienced as his critical pressuring of me to do things that made me anxious, but I now see that that he might have been expressing more confidence in me than I had in myself (to take an example from my own experience).

Fonagy and colleagues (Fonagy, Target, Steele & Steele, 1998) further refined Main's appreciation for metacognitive monitoring in their measure of *reflective functioning* as applied to the AAI, that is, a way of assessing mentalizing capacity as it pertains to attachment relationships. As this measure attests, mentalizing capacity is not an all-or-none phenomenon but rather a matter of degree. Some key components of reflective functioning that may be evident in the AAI are as follows:

- *Awareness of the nature of mental states in self and others*, which includes acknowledging that you cannot be certain of your judgments or inferences about others' feelings, thoughts, or intentions—or even your own; that you are capable of deception and disguising your mental states; and that you can block or distort your awareness of mental states by means of psychological defenses.
- *Efforts to tease out mental states underlying behavior*, which includes giving plausible explanations for your own and others' behavior; recognizing that different individuals have different perspectives on the same situation; being aware of the impact of your mental states (e.g., feelings or biases) on your perceptions and judgments; appreciating the impact of your behavior on others; being aware of how you are seen by others; and being able to revise your thinking about mental states on the fly and to see things in new ways (e.g., in the course of the AAI).
- *Recognizing the developmental aspects of mental states*, including appreciating the impact of early attachment relationships on your current states of mind as well as awareness of how your parents' mental states were affected by their developmental history; appreciating the impact of your influence as a child on your parents' behavior; being aware of family dynamics, that is, relationships among family members; revising thoughts and feelings about your childhood based on more recent understanding; appreciating that your perspective changes over time, not only that you think and feel differently in the present compared to the past but also that your perspective will be different in the future.

- *Awareness of mental states in interaction with the interviewer*, including taking the interviewer's perspective into account and helping the interviewer understand (e.g., seeming contradictions); providing adequate context; sticking to the point in responding to the interviewer's questions; and being aware of the impact of your narrative on the interviewer (e.g., how painful the interviewer might find it to hear about your traumatic experiences).

Fonagy's research demonstrated that reflective functioning and coherence of transcript are highly correlated; yet, in the context of a maternal trauma history, reflective functioning bore a stronger relation to infant attachment security than narrative coherence. Accordingly, narrative coherence can be subsumed under mentalizing:

> of the 18 or so rating scales standardly used with the AAI, internal coherence of the transcript was the best single indicator of AAI classification and child's attachment status. The coherence of the parents' perception of their past derives from their unhindered capacity to observe their own mental functioning, to have a plausible view of themselves and their objects as human beings, thinking, feeling, wishing, believing, wanting, and desiring. We assume, then, that *coherence may be a measure of reflectiveness*, and it is the latter attribute of the caregivers that has direct implications for their relationship to the infant. (Fonagy, Steele, Steele, Moran & Higgitt, 1991, p. 215, emphasis added)

Thus the crux of attachment security in the child's mind is the expectation that "his or her mental state will be appropriately reflected on and responded to accurately" and, to this extent, "she or he will feel secure in relation to her or his mental world" (p. 215).

Now a whole line of research relates parental attachment security and mentalizing capacity to parental mentalizing of infants and hence to infant attachment security (Allen, Fonagy & Bateman, 2008; Fonagy, Gergely & Target, 2008). In the context of secure attachment, mentalizing begets mentalizing. This finding is commonsensical: why would the infant seek comfort from a parent who is not mentalizing, that is, who is not psychologically and emotionally attuned, not mindful of the infant's emotional state? Incipient mentalizers, infants intuitively interact with their parents according to their parents' mentalizing capacity.

Arietta Slade and colleagues (Slade, 2005; Slade, Grienenberger, Bernbach, Levy & Locker, 2005) adapted Fonagy's assessment of reflective functioning to parents' capacities to mentalize their child, as contrasted with their capacity to mentalize in relation to their own attachment history in the AAI. These researchers assess parental reflective functioning from a ninety-minute Parental Development Interview designed to capture parents' internal working models of their relationship with their child. Parallel to the AAI, parents provide adjectives to describe their relationship with their child, evidenced by specific examples from ongoing daily life. Thus the interview provides information about the mother's understanding of the child's behavior, thoughts, and feelings. The interview specifically addresses emotionally charged interactions, for example, "'Describe a time in the last week when you and your child really clicked', and then 'a time when you and your child really didn't click'" (Slade, 2005, p. 276). Low parental mentalizing is evident, for example, when parents are oblivious to their child's feelings: "'She clings to me, but she's fine', 'She wakes up in the night screaming, screaming, but nothing really bothers her'" (p. 278). Poor mentalizing also is evident in parents' attributions of malevolence to the child (e.g., as being a devil) and their lack of awareness of their own emotions in parenting (e.g., denial of anger, guilt feelings, or joy). Higher levels of mentalizing are evident in parents' recognition of their child's emotional states and, especially, by their ability to link their own mental states with those of their child: "'I was just so *sad* and *frightened* (mental state) by the fight I had with my husband. I wasn't *myself* at all (behavior) and this was so *disorienting to my baby* (implies effect on baby's mental state)'" (p. 279, emphasis in original).

Slade (2008b) contrasted high and low levels of maternal mentalizing in a hypothetical scenario that we easily recognize: A mother comes from work, picks up her two-year-old child from daycare, has nothing for dinner, and stops at the grocery on her way home. As she pulls into the parking lot, her child starts to fuss. The mentalizing mother recognizes that her child is fussy because he has missed her during the day; moreover, he is tired, hungry, eager to get home, and senses her distress about needing to shop. She acknowledges his feelings, gives him something to eat when he asks, and makes the trip short. If he has a tantrum despite her mentalizing, she provides physical comforting, comments on his feelings, and strives to balance his needs with hers. In the midst of this distressing situation, the child is learning to mentalize. In contrast, the nonmentalizing mother feels angry and agitated at her child's distress, denies his requests (e.g., for food), and moves methodically through the aisles. When her child throws a tantrum, she yells, "You're doing this on purpose! You're trying to drive me crazy! You never let me do what I need to do!" (p. 319). Upon leaving the store, the mother and the child are both dysregulated. Moreover, the child is learning coercive (nonmentalizing) strategies for interacting in times of duress.

Slade and colleagues (Slade, Grienenberger, Bernbach, Levy & Locker, 2005) studied mentalizing and attachment in 40 mothers and their babies. They assessed the mothers' attachment in relation to their parents in the AAI in last trimester of the mother's pregnancy; then they measured the mother's mentalizing (maternal reflective functioning) in relation to her ten-month-old infant; last, they assessed the infant's attachment security with the mother in the Strange Situation when the infant was fourteen months old. As predicted, maternal attachment security measured prior to the birth predicted higher levels of mentalizing in relation to the ten-month-old infant; in turn, higher levels of mentalizing were associated with greater infant security. Moreover, the authors presented evidence that maternal attachment security linked to infant attachment security by virtue of mothers' better capacity to mentalize in relation to their infant.

Whereas Slade and colleagues assessed maternal mentalizing from an interview about parent-child relationships, Elizabeth Meins and colleagues (Meins, 1997; Meins, Fernyhough, Fradley & Tuckey, 2001) assessed mentalizing from observations of mother-infant interactions. These researchers studied what they called mothers' *mind-minded* commentary during interactions with their six-month-old infant, indicative of their psychological attunement. Mind-minded comments might refer to the infant's knowledge ("You know what that is, it's a ball"), interests ("What toy do you prefer?"), or thought processes ("Are you thinking?"); they might refer to the infant's state of mind, voicing feelings of being bored, worried, or excited; and they might refer to efforts to manipulate beliefs ("You're joking"; "You're just teasing me") (Meins, Fernyhough, Fradley & Tuckey, 2001, p. 641). Mothers' mind-minded commentary predicted their infant's attachment security at twelve months. Arnott and Meins (2007) investigated the entire transmission model for mothers and fathers and found that the parents' security of attachment related positively to mentalizing regarding those attachments; security of attachment and mentalizing related to mind-minded comments in interaction with their six-month-old infant; and their mind-minded commentary predicted infant security at twelve months. They identified two developmental pathways: parental secure attachment was linked to infant security through a high level of parental mind-mindedness, whereas parental insecurity linked to infant insecurity through a low level of mind-mindedness.

In doing research for this book, I was astounded to find that Ainsworth (1963) had discovered in Uganda the importance of what we now call parental mentalizing of the child. One of the predictors of infant security was the mother's excellence as an informant, that is, she "sticks to the topic, volunteers information, gives much spontaneous detail about the child, and never seems impatient in the interview" (p. 97). In discussing their securely attached infants, the mothers were exemplifying narrative coherence, which they also might well have done in a Parental Development Interview or regarding their own attachment history if they had been administered the AAI. Consider this summary with the concept of mentalizing in mind:

> The mothers of the secure-attached infants tend to be above the median in excellence as informants, and this is believed to reflect their keen interest in the development of the babies, which led them to want to talk about them and to offer spontaneous and detailed descriptions of their behaviour. The mothers of the non-attached [insecure] infants tend to be below the median in excellence as informants, which seems to reflect a relative lack of involvement with their infants, so that they preferred to talk of other things, and some had not even observed their infants closely enough to be able to give details about their behaviour. In this sample, at any rate, this variable seems to reflect more real involvement with the infant than does any superficial impression of the warmth of the mother's behaviour to the infant. (Ainsworth, 1963, p. 98)

This last statement bears repeating: mentalizing—*not* maternal warmth and affection—related to attachment differences in Ainsworth's initial research. As noted earlier, also in line with Ainsworth's discovery, in their Minnesota longitudinal study, Alan Sroufe and colleagues found secure attachment to be related to parental *psychological complexity*, defined as "the caregiver's psychological understanding of the infant"

(Sroufe, Egeland, Carlson & Collins, 2005, p. 91), which included parents' understanding of the complexity of the infant and an appreciation for the fact that the infant is a separate person from them. A related powerful predictor in this study was the variable, "the mother's interest in the baby" (p. 57) as assessed by hospital nurses' ratings of mothers of newborns. Ainsworth revisited.

The research just reviewed shows that mentalizing begets mentalizing insofar as parents' mentalizing in relation to their attachment history begets mentalizing in relation to their infants. But there is one more piece to this puzzle: securely attached infants, who have experienced being mentalized by their parents, become better mentalizers as children. Meins and colleagues (Meins, Fernyhough, Russell & Clark-Carter, 1998), for example, found that secure attachment at twelve months predicted subsequent performance on theory-of-mind tasks. For example, whereas 83% of children with previous secure attachment passed a false-belief test at age four, only 33% of those with insecure attachment did so. Subsequent research showed that maternal mind-mindedness at six months of age was the critical predictor of the child's mentalizing performance at four years of age. Again, these findings are commonsensical: the intergenerational transmission of mentalizing entails a process of teaching and learning, through words and actions (i.e., modeling mentalizing for the child); Gergely and colleagues rightly call this a "pedagogical" process (Gergely, Egyed & Kiraly, 2007; Gergely & Unoka, 2008). Given this history of being taught and learning mentalizing, it is not surprising securely attached children are more empathic, caring, and socially competent.

Slade (2005) summarized eloquently the principle that mentalizing begets mentalizing:

> A mother's capacity to hold in her own mind a representation of her child as having feelings, desires, and intentions allows the child to discover his own internal experience via his mother's representation of it; this re-presentation takes place in different ways at different stages of the child's development and of the mother-child interaction. It is the mother's observations of the moment to moment changes in the child's mental state, and her representation of these first in gesture and action, and later in words and play, that is at the heart of sensitive caregiving, and is crucial to the child's ultimately developing mentalizing capacities of his own. (p. 271)

To sum up, mentalizing puts another link into the chain of intergenerational transmission: securely attached parents, by means of their mentalizing capacity, are able to provide a coherent and emotionally authentic account of their attachment history; using their mentalizing capacity, they are able to engage in psychologically attuned interactions with their infants, most notably when their infants are emotionally distressed; consequently, their infants are able to rely on them for sensitively responsive emotional support; in turn, these securely attached children become relatively capable mentalizers, for example, able to talk about their emotions and to empathize with others.

Plainly, the synergy between mentalizing and attachment security would have limited implications for psychotherapy if the process were confined to childhood. Hence research reviewed by Mikulincer and Shaver (2007b) warrants mention in this developmental context. One hundred young couples who had begun dating were assessed and followed up several months later. Initial assessments of relationship partners' accuracy in decoding emotional expressions and supportive behaviors in response to disclosure of a personal problem were examined in relation to subsequent changes in attachment security. The findings were clear-cut: "Partners who were more accurate in decoding their partner's facial expressions and nonverbal expressions of negative emotions and were coded by judges as more supportive during the dyadic interaction task induced a decline in within-relationship attachment anxiety and avoidance across the 8-month period" (p. 202). In the language of this chapter, mindful attentiveness to emotion and mentalizing enhanced attachment security over time. Consistent with research on childhood attachment, this finding hardly defies common sense.

Forms of impaired mentalizing

What are you doing when you're not mentalizing? Much of the time, you do not need to mentalize, for example, when you're planting flowers, painting a landscape, or cleaning up the dishes. How about writing a book? Writing seems an impersonal task, but you need to mentalize by keeping the imagined reader's mind in mind. The readability of a book is a test of the author's mentalizing. How about an architect designing a building? This, too, requires mentalizing as does designing anything for human use. But we are concerned in clinical practice with mentalizing in specific relationships, and particularly attachment relationships. Not mentalizing—not taking your partner's feelings into account—is a basic problem in relationships. In addition, we are concerned with mentalizing in relation to the self in the sense of being self-aware and reflective. Not mentalizing with respect to yourself can lead to mindless repetition of maladaptive behavior in relationships or otherwise.

Following Murdoch, I view mentalizing as an imaginative activity. Empathizing is a prime example: hearing your friend's story about a painful experience, you need to imagine the situation as she describes it and imagine how she might have felt—in part by imagining how you might have felt. From the standpoint of imagination, there are two basic ways of going wrong: too little and too much imagination (Allen, 2006b). On the side of too little imagination, you can be oblivious, obtuse, or indifferent to mentalizing—not making the effort to do it. Or you can be too simplistic or concrete in your thinking: I was curt because I didn't get enough sleep. She's lethargic because she hasn't been eating right. Both explanations might have some truth, but they don't rate high on mental elaboration.

On the other hand, you can be too imaginative, engaging in distorted mentalizing. Thanks to my daughter, Yvonne, a speech and language therapist, we have a slang term for distorted mentalizing: *excrementalizing*, that is, mentalizing but doing a crappy job of it (Allen, Fonagy & Bateman, 2008). A related problem is hypermentalizing (Fonagy, Bateman & Luyten, 2012), that is, being preoccupied and obsessed with what's going on in your mind or someone else's mind. Social anxiety, for example, can be associated with hypermentalizing and excrementalizing. For example, I worked with a patient who was afraid to go into a mall by himself or to eat in a restaurant by himself; he was fine if he was accompanied. In a mall by himself, hypermentalizing, he believed that everyone was looking at him; he was extremely self-conscious. And, excrementalizing, he believed that others viewed him as a loser, because he was alone without friends. So he was not only paying too much attention to others' thinking and feelings but also distorting his perceptions of what they were thinking. Moreover, he had no understanding of the reasons for these distortions until we thought about his loneliness and fears of being alone—indeed, dying alone, notwithstanding that he was a young man.

I have already accumulated some major jargon, not only mentalizing, but also hypermentalizing and excrementalizing as two forms of impaired mentalizing. But we have more. Fonagy and colleagues (Fonagy, Gergely, Jurist & Target, 2002) have identified three *premental-izing* modes of experience, that is, ways of experience in infancy and early childhood that precede the development of full mentalizing. All of us adults regress into prementalizing modes of functioning, especially when we are emotionally aroused. I will be referring to these non-mentalizing modes at various points in the book.

1. *Psychic equivalence.* I have discussed how, when you are mentalizing, you are able to recognize that your thoughts and feelings represent reality in a certain way—more or less accurately. In psychic-equivalence mode, you equate your mental state with reality (i.e., as in cognitive fusion). You have lost sight of the maxim, Don't believe everything you think. Dreaming is the starkest example of psychic equivalence: your dream seems utterly real. You mentalize on awakening: it was only a dream. Paranoia is another example: you are convinced they are out to get you, whether they are or not. Posttraumatic flashbacks also exemplify psychic equivalence: you lose the distinction between experiencing the traumatic event and remembering it. You are mentalizing when you orient yourself: It's not happening now; I'm remembering the past.
2. *Pretend.* The pretend mode is the opposite of psychic equivalence: instead of mental states being too real, they are too disconnected from reality. The pretend mode is a significant danger in psychotherapy, for example, in the use of psychobabble, for which I am giving you much fodder. To put it in plain language, bullshitting is an example of the pretend mode, and a significant potential danger in psychotherapy—having the illusion of doing significant work and in fact getting nowhere (Allen, Fonagy & Bateman, 2008).
3. *Teleological.* In the teleological mode, goal-directed behavior substitutes for mentalizing. Actions speak louder than words. For example, a suicide attempt may express in behavior a feeling of sheer desperation along with outrage about being neglected. While actions may speak louder than words, they can be so loud (e.g., frightening) as to preclude hearing.

Were it not for the various forms of nonmentalizing just discussed, there would be no need for this book—indeed, much less need for a lot of psychotherapy. We would all be getting along much better, with each other and in our own minds. And we would be less likely to traumatize each other in attachment relationships or otherwise.

Integrating mindfulness and mentalizing

I began this chapter by inviting you to engage in some mental juggling, holding in your mind two concepts—mindfulness and mentalizing— that pertain to the way in which you hold minds in mind, your own mind and the minds of others. I will ask you to continue juggling them periodically throughout this book henceforth because of their pertinence to attachment trauma and treatment. I bring this chapter to a close by presenting my understanding of the way the two concepts fit together: summarizing what they have in common, how they are distinct from one another, and how they complement each other.

In talking with Peter Fonagy about this intersection, we came to agree on an overall point: the overlap reflects a remarkable convergence, namely, that two radically different traditions came to focus on mindfulness of mind. The mindfulness literature evolved from Buddhism, philosophy, and ethics; whereas the focus on mentalizing evolved from psychoanalysis, developmental psychopathology, and attachment theory (Fonagy, 2001; Fonagy, Gergely & Target, 2008). Both traditions were inspired by a common concern: suffering and its amelioration, the crux of trauma treatment.

Commonality

I find it problematic that mindfulness and mentalizing are similar in their breadth and complexity—each concept is multifaceted. Some facets overlap; some do not. Moreover, the extent of overlap will vary to the extent that different authors view the two concepts differently.

I envision four main areas of overlap between mindfulness and mentalizing. First and most basic, both concepts include *awareness* of mental states. Second, both emphasize awareness of the separateness of internal mental states and external reality. In the cognitive-behavioral literature on mindfulness, decentering and cognitive defusion are employed to refer to this separateness; the mentalizing literature emphasizes the representational nature of mind and distinguishes the mentalizing mode from the psychic-equivalence mode of thought. Third, with this sense of separateness in mind, mindfulness and mentalizing commend an accepting and non-judgmental attitude toward mental states, most notably, in explicitly advocating an open-minded and inquisitive curiosity about what is going on in the mind. Paralleling the mindfulness literature, we advocate the *mentalizing stance* (Allen, Fonagy & Bateman, 2008; Bateman & Fonagy, 2006). That is, we commend a tentative, not-knowing attitude in the mentalizing stance: we do not know with certainty what is going on in another persons' mind—or even in our own. Thus inquisitive curiosity is a fitting approach to mentalizing. Similarly, as recounted by Kornfield (2009) in the mindfulness literature, a Zen master commends students who answer, "I don't know" when queried about the mind: "Keep this 'don't-know mind.' It is an open mind, a clear mind" (p. 375). Apropos the not-knowing attitude, Kornfield provides a charming anecdote:

> I love this story told by the mother of a five-year-old girl. The child had taken a stethoscope out of her mother's doctor bag and was playing with it. As she put he stethoscope to her ears, her mother thought proudly, *She seems interested in medicine. Maybe she will grow up and become a doctor like me.* After a time the little girl put the listening end of the stethoscope up to her mouth and exclaimed, 'Welcome to McDonald's. May I take your order, please?' At this, the mother had to laugh with her daughter, and smiled to herself about how easily we can project our ideas on one another. (Kornfield, 2009, p. 375, emphasis in original)

There is a fourth domain of overlap that I will elaborate in discussing treatment later in this book. In the face of unending proliferation of different brands of psychotherapy, the literature contains a long-standing debate about the extent to which the demonstrable effectiveness of psychotherapy rests on factors that all the different brands have in common (Frank, 1961). We have proposed that mentalizing is a fundamental common factor in psychotherapy (Allen & Fonagy, 2006; Allen, Fonagy & Bateman, 2008); indeed, I find the prospect of conducting psychotherapy with no attempt to understand mental states to be unimaginable. Similarly, mindfulness also has been proposed as being a common factor among psychotherapies (Martin, 1997; Siegal, 2007). I agree: I cannot imagine effective therapy that does not entail mindful attention to mental states. Likewise, experiential acceptance can be regarded as a factor common to psychotherapy since its inception in psychoanalysis

(Block-Lerner, Wulfert & Moses, 2009). It follows that, if mindfulness, mentalizing, and acceptance are common factors, it is essential that, in conducting psychotherapy, the therapist be skilled at mentalizing (D. Diamond, Stovall-McClough, Clarkin & Levy, 2003) and mindfulness (Siegal, 2010) as well as accepting of a wide range of experience.

I am inclined to extend our fundamental developmental principle for mentalizing to mindfulness and acceptance: just as research shows that mentalizing begets mentalizing, I would expect research to show that mindfulness begets mindfulness and acceptance begets acceptance. Accordingly, by mentalizing and being mindful and accepting in doing so, the therapist cultivates the patient's skill in mentalizing and mindfulness, both of which are central to coping with traumatic attachment relationships.

Distinctness

If *bare attention* is the core of mindfulness (Mace, 2008), mentalizing is broader: mentalizing includes interpreting behavior in relation to mental states, reflecting on the meaning of mental states, and constructing narratives in the process. As Holmes (J. Holmes, 1999) put it in the context of psychotherapy, mentalizing entails story making and story breaking. In contrast, mindfulness is nonconceptual: "it does not compare, categorize, or evaluate, nor does it contemplate, introspect, reflect, or ruminate upon events or experiences based on memory" (K. W. Brown, Ryan & Creswell, 2007, p. 213). Note, however, that ruminating is not an effective form of mentalizing insofar as rumination is inflexible and closed to alternative perspectives.

In addition to being broader than mindfulness in encompassing reflection, mentalizing is broader in being more social. Mindfulness practices focus primarily on enhanced awareness and acceptance of mental states in oneself, whereas mentalizing is inherently social in two senses. First, mentalizing balances awareness of mental states in self and others. Second, and more fundamentally, the developmental research on attachment and mentalizing underscores the profoundly social nature of mind: mind comes into being in the context of attachment relationships. To the extent that mindfulness and mentalizing overlap, the mentalizing literature sheds light on how mindfulness of mind develops in attachment relationships. No doubt, as research demonstrates, improvement in *self-regulation* of emotion is a huge contribution of mindfulness interventions. Yet I have emphasized in the first two chapters of this book that *interpersonal regulation* through attachment security is our primary means of emotion regulation and, indeed, the wellspring of self-regulation. As attachment research attests, a full understanding of emotion regulation requires a developmental approach.

Yet here matters of definition come into play such that distinctions are a matter of degree. Extending mindfulness to attentive awareness of mental states in others as well as oneself, as I am inclined to do, brings mindfulness into the social realm with mentalizing. Taking this extension to the limit, the developmental story I have presented can be retold, substituting mindfulness for mentalizing in the context of attachment relationships (Siegal, 2007, 2010). Although it is the exception rather than the rule (Mace, 2008), newer research assesses the benefits of mindfulness for interpersonal relationships (K. W. Brown, Ryan & Creswell, 2007; Davis & Hayes, 2011). Mindfulness enhances empathy, buffers stress associated with interpersonal conflicts, enhances communication, and increases the sense of social connectedness.

James Carson and colleagues (Carson, Carson, Gil & Baucom, 2004) adapted mindfulness to an intervention for couples, Mindfulness-Based Relationship Enhancement. After the intervention, the already well-adjusted couples showed increased relationship satisfaction, enhanced closeness, greater acceptance, and diminished distress, among other salutary benefits. This effectiveness is consistent with Brown and colleagues' summary of the interpersonal benefits of mindfulness:

> the receptive attentiveness that characterizes mindfulness may promote a greater ability or willingness to take interest in the partner's thoughts, emotions, and welfare; it may also enhance an ability to attend to the content of a partner's communication while also being aware of the partner's (sometimes subtle) affective tone and non-verbal behavior .... At the same time, such a person may be more aware to their own cognitive, emotional, and verbal responses to the communication. (K. W. Brown, Ryan & Creswell, 2007, p. 225)

Yet this research on interpersonal applications of mindfulness blurs the fundamental difference: mindfulness entails bare attention, whereas mentalizing includes reflection. Brown and colleagues' summary includes both, and Carson and colleagues' intervention included not only mindfulness practice (with a couples' focus) but also communication exercises, consideration of emotion-focused and problem-focused approaches to relationship stress, discussion of the impact of broader areas of life (e.g., work) on the relationship, and recording new understandings arising from interactions. Plainly this is the territory of mentalizing, as is Dan Siegal's (2007) reference to "the reflective aspects of mindfulness" in the context of research with AAI (p. 205).

There is a sense which mindfulness and mentalizing are not only distinct but also might seem downright contradictory: in discussing mentalizing, I have championed attachment, whereas the Buddhist literature advocates nonattachment. In his masterful effort to reconcile the Buddhist perspective on mindfulness with Western psychotherapy practice, Harvey Aronson (2004) frames this problem regarding "attachment" as follows: "It is worth considering how this word can represent something so negative in one context—that is, the detrimental attitude blamed for leading us into repeated suffering—and so valuable in another—the critical nurturant bond central to human development" (p. 156). As Aronson explains, in the Buddhist literature, attachment connotes craving, fixated clinging, and greed; it has the sticky quality you might associate with *insecure* (ambivalent) attachment, which includes possessiveness, jealousy, and aversion to separation. This kind of problematic attachment pertains to more than relationships; examples include obsessive preoccupation with wealth, fame, and popularity. In contrast, nonattachment is the "value of being not struck or fixated on things or ideas" (p. 159). Note that, as in the mentalizing literature, nonattachment includes decentering or defusion in the sense of not being overly identified with your thoughts, feelings, and desires. Aronson clarifies that nonattachment in this sense of clinging does not preclude active *engagement*, including engagement in loving and compassionate relationships. Balance is the key: "we can be involved and engaged in the world without being ensnared by it" (p. 172). Thus health involves "our capacity to be psychologically attached in a flexible way" (p. 184). This flexibility is characteristic of *secure* attachment which, as I have described, entails balance in many senses: balance between the safe haven and secure base, closeness and distance, as well as relatedness and autonomy.

Research by Phil Shaver and colleagues (Shaver, Lavy, Saron & Mikulincer, 2007) clearly supports Aronson's (2004) line of thinking. Shaver summarizes research indicating that mindfulness and secure attachment have similar benefits in relating to numerous aspects of mental and physical health as well as relationship strengths. Hence it is not surprising that measures of mindfulness and attachment security are highly correlated; that is, persons who are more mindful show less attachment anxiety and avoidance. As these authors summarize, "the more attachment-anxious participants were less capable of maintaining a nonreactive, nonjudgmental stance toward their experience, and the more avoidant participants were less mindful in general, including being less able to notice their experiences and label them in words" (pp. 269–270). But this line of research went farther in the seemingly paradoxical endeavor to relate secure attachment to the Buddhist stance of *non*attachment (Sahdra, Shaver & Brown, 2010). As already noted, in the Buddhist literature, attachment has the negative connotations of clinging, grasping, and possessiveness as well as defensive avoidance; whereas nonattachment has the positive connotations of being able to let go and to recognize the constructed and impermanent nature of mental states. As the researchers anticipated, their nonattachment measure related positively to secure attachment (that is, to lower levels of attachment anxiety and avoidance) as well as to mindfulness. Hence, ironically, secure attachment is conducive to nonattachment and vice versa. Both are associated with a balance of relatedness and autonomy.

Complementarity

I have taken the position that mindfulness and mentalizing are complementary concepts worth juggling in our approach to understanding emotion regulation, attachment trauma, and psychotherapy. Here I am following in the footsteps of David Wallin (2007), whose marvelous book, *Attachment in Psychotherapy*, heralded burgeoning interest in making greater clinical use of attachment theory and research on the foundation that Bowlby (Bowlby, 1988) created some decades ago. Also juggling these two concepts, Wallin proposed an apt analogy to DNA, the genetic basis of intergenerational transmission:

> The relationship between a mentalizing and a mindful stance in psychotherapy can be likened to a double helix: a pair of partially overlapping spirals that converge and diverge, again and again. Mentalizing and mindfulness are distinct, but complementary and interweaving, ways of knowing and responding to experience— and each potentiates the other. (p. 312)

With the fundamental distinction between attention and reflection in mind, I view mindfulness as a *necessary condition* for effective mentalizing. *Effective mentalizing must be built on a foundation of mindful attentiveness to mental states, supported by an accepting attitude and inquisitive curiosity* as advocated in the mindfulness and mentalizing literatures. We might consider mindfulness distinct from mentalizing (i.e., its foundation) or as part and parcel of mentalizing (i.e., as one of its many facets). Analogously, reflection can be incorporated into mindfulness. As my review attests, in the hands of some writers, each concept tends to encroach on the territory of the other.

We psychologists are prone to turf wars; it is easy for me to see how mentalizing could claim territory from mindfulness (as I have done previously in importing the ethical framework) and how mindfulness could claim territory from mentalizing (e.g., as it pertains to attachment relationships). I like Wallin's approach: these concepts as synergistic rather than competing. I like the user-friendliness of mindfulness, and I like especially the *spirit* of mindfulness, particularly the richness with which the mindfulness literature has addressed the ideal attitude we might adopt toward our mental states—painful feelings in particular. If mindful attention toward mental sates is a necessary condition for effective mentalizing, those of us who are partial to mentalizing have much to learn from the mindfulness literature—the main reason for my review. Finally, given their overlap, I wonder if mindfulness practice might be a way to enhance mentalizing in psychotherapy. But mindfulness practice does not address mentalizing where it counts most as regards the subject matter of this book: mentalizing in the midst of painful emotional states associated with a history of trauma in attachment relationships, the subject of the next chapter.

Clinical implications

As I hope to have made plain, the clinical benefits of mindfulness are legion, and I cannot imagine anyone disputing the proposition that therapists should perform their work mindfully. Yet I am in full agreement with Aronson (2004), who makes a compelling case that mindfulness practice is no substitute for psychotherapy. At worst, mindfulness practice can abet dissociative detachment, an extreme form of avoidance. Consistent with the greater intrapersonal than interpersonal focus of mindfulness, Aronson notes, "The skills related to one's capacity to sustain a relationship differ significantly from the capacity to concentrate on the breath or understand the subtle nature of reality" (p. 196). Accordingly, "Buddhist meditation was not devised to deal explicitly with pervasive interpersonal and emotional issues related to attachment difficulties" (p. 193). Specifically, he points out that persons with a history of attachment trauma may have difficulty with meditation (e.g., becoming caught up in traumatic memories or dissociative states) and that trauma-related problems "are best addressed and resolved outside of traditional meditation practice" (p. 192). That said, "Buddhist meditation, when applied appropriately, can work with therapy synergistically" (p. 192).

My bias is transparent: mentalizing develops or falters in attachment relationships, and problems in attachment relationships must be addressed in a mentalizing process—at both implicit and explicit levels. Explicitly, we foster mentalizing to examine and revise internal working models of attachment as they apply not only to interpersonal relationships but also to ways of relating to oneself. Explicit mentalizing is manifested in psychotherapeutic narrative—story making and story breaking, as Holmes characterizes it. With the AAI as a model, we strive for narrative coherence in relation to painful attachment experience, evident in clearly communicated, emotionally rich, and concretely detailed accounts that include fresh perspectives. Mentalizing is the psychological and intersubjective process by which narrative coherence is achieved. From early in life, we understand ourselves through interactive synchrony and dialogue. Accordingly, in psychotherapy as in childrearing, implicit processes occur in parallel with explicit processes. Working models are revised at the implicit level insofar as patients feel increasingly safe in expressing and exploring their internal experience, intuitively feeling understood at an emotional level through the therapist's complex mirroring process, as Gergely (Gergely & Unoka, 2008; Gergely & Watson, 1996) has characterized it. Siegel (1999) neatly articulates the blend of explicit and implicit processes applicable to psychotherapy and other attachment relationships:

> The capacity of an individual to reflect upon the mental state of another person may be an essential ingredient in many forms of close, emotionally engaging relationships. This reflection on mental states is more than a conceptual ability; it permits the two

individuals minds to enter a form of resonance in which each is able to *'feel felt'* by the other. (p. 89, emphasis added)

In sum, by means of such mindfully attentive, mentalizing interactions, at implicit and explicit levels, security evolves in attachment relationships.

Building on the chapters on attachment in childhood and adulthood, I have written this chapter to set the stage for understanding attachment trauma, which poses the greatest challenges to our psychotherapeutic efforts. Attachment trauma—abuse and neglect at the extreme—exemplifies the antithesis of mindful attention to mental states and reflective discourse. In short, attachment trauma stems from obliviousness to mental states, often coupled with silencing of the child. Thus I have set the stage for what I consider to be the crux of traumatizing attachment experience: being left alone and feeling invisible in extreme psychological pain, as elaborated in the next chapter.

CHAPTER FOUR

Attachment trauma

I have taken pains in the previous three chapters to establish a foundation in attachment and mentalizing that I consider necessary for understanding the core of trauma, namely, feeling alone in the midst of unbearably painful emotion. In this chapter, I will drive home this basic point by immersing you further in the findings of attachment research.

I use the term, *attachment trauma*, in two senses: first, to refer to trauma that takes place in attachment relationships; second, to refer to the adverse long-term impact of such trauma on your capacity to develop and maintain secure attachment relationships. Put simply, profound distrust is a central manifestation of attachment trauma. Plainly, such distrust undermines your relationship in which the trauma occurs. But you also can be traumatized more broadly in being unable to find comfort and security in *other* attachment relationships later on—including psychotherapy relationships.

Peter Fonagy and Mary Target (1997) refer to the *dual liability* associated with attachment trauma in early life: first, such trauma evokes intense emotional distress; second, it undermines the *development* of the capacity to regulate the emotional distress it evokes. As I have described, secure attachment provides the foundation of emotion regulation; by undermining attachment security, trauma in attachment relationships impedes the development of ways to cope with emotional distress. Moreover, as we also have seen, within attachment relationships you develop emotion-regulation capacity through mentalizing; as this chapter will explain, attachment trauma also compromises the development of mentalizing.

All this preparation leads to my main thesis about attachment trauma, which I will explicate in this chapter and beyond: mentalizing failure renders painful emotional states unbearable; treatment restores mentalizing and thereby fosters attachment security such that painful experiences can be expressed, understood, and reflected upon; this process renders previously unbearable traumatic experience more meaningful and bearable.

Given what I have stated thus far, you will rightly associate attachment trauma with childhood maltreatment, namely, abuse and neglect. The thesis I just proposed emphasizes how abuse and neglect are somewhat inextricable: to abuse a child—physically, sexually, or emotionally—is also to neglect the child in the sense of leaving the child psychologically alone in the midst of emotional distress. Conversely, to neglect a child also is abusive in the sense of evoking painful emotional distress such as fear or despair. To make this point with extreme simplicity, the essence of traumatic experience is being *afraid and alone* (Allen, 2001). Here I am using "alone" in the sense of no one holding your mind in mind. I cannot overstate the "alone" part of this combination, and traumatized persons will resonate with it. It is the "alone" part that forms the basis of my thoroughgoing attention to mindful mentalizing.

I still remember vividly an educational group on trauma I conducted a decade ago for patients who were hospitalized during acute crises. I had been talking about the stress pileup that typically precedes hospitalization, and I wrote on the board, AFRAID + *ALONE*, underlining "alone" a few times for emphasis. At that moment, I saw tears start to run down the cheeks of a woman who, up to that point, had been sitting quietly and attentively in the group. Invited to talk about what she was feeling, she recounted her painful childhood experience with her mother's psychotic episodes. She had not previously appreciated or acknowledged the profound impact of her early experience of aloneness on her subsequent vulnerability to depression.

Sadly, as this chapter explains, you can see the seeds of attachment trauma in infancy—indeed, in the early months of infancy, even before full-fledged attachment develops. You are now familiar with secure attachment and two relatively common forms of insecurity: ambivalent and avoidant attachment. Trauma brings us to a fourth pattern: disorganized attachment. Thus I will start with disorganized attachment in infancy as it came to be recognized in the Strange Situation. As I have done with the three organized patterns, I will describe infants' disorganized behavior along with kind of caregiver behavior that is disorganizing to the infant. Next, with an eye toward intergenerational transmission of attachment trauma, I will discuss the adult counterpart to infant disorganization as assessed in the AAI, namely, unresolved-disorganized attachment. With the background established in earlier chapters, this research will enable you to appreciate a central theme of this book: the role of mentalizing failures in the intergenerational transmission of attachment trauma. My review of intergenerational transmission sets the stage for subsequent consideration of the developmental impact of attachment disorganization, that is, the ways in which disorganization persists beyond infancy as well as its contribution to problem behavior and later psychiatric disorder. As this discussion also will make plain, attachment disorganization contributes to vulnerability to being traumatized by later abuse and neglect, which is one reason for my giving so much attention to disorganization. Having set this stage, I will consider various forms of abuse and neglect as traditionally conceived. Sadly, as I will describe later in this chapter, attachment trauma pertains to adulthood as well as childhood.

Before proceeding with this detailed account of all that can go wrong in development, I need to introduce two caveats akin to the warning label on cigarette packs. First, occasional disruption in caregiving does not lead to attachment disorganization; recurrent patterns of disruption in relationships that entail a consistent failure to hold the child's mind in mind will have the greatest impact. Second, disorganized infant attachment is not irreparably traumatizing. As I reviewed in relation to the organized attachment patterns, development is characterized by interplay of stability and change. Disorganization, coupled with other persistent developmental adversities, can initiate a problematic trajectory. But change to greater attachment security—sooner or later—always remains a possibility. Professional intervention—sooner or later—is one route to such favorable change. Keep in mind the balance between stability and change. There would be no point in writing this book, on the one hand, if early development were carved in stone or, on the other hand, if early development had no lasting impact. As I say frequently (with some hyperbole) in our educational groups on mentalizing at the Menninger Clinic, if change in attachment security were not possible, we might as well close the doors to the place.

Disorganized attachment in childhood

As I described in Chapter 1, Ainsworth began developing ways of classifying infant attachment on the basis of home observations in Uganda and Baltimore and then refined this assessment in the laboratory, employing the Strange Situation. The basic distinctions between secure, ambivalent-resistant, and avoidant attachment have been powerful predictors of childhood functioning as well as having adult counterparts that play a fundamental role in intergenerational transmission of attachment. Although most infants are readily classified into one of the three attachment categories, some are not. Repeated observations of such unclassifiable infants led Mary Main and her colleagues to create a new category, disorganized-disoriented, and then to the discovery of the complex role of trauma in attachment disorganization.

At first, these unclassifiable infant behaviors appeared anomalous—odd and inexplicable. In Main and Solomon's words, "What these infants shared in common was ... bouts or sequences of behavior which seemed to lack a readily observable goal, intention, or explanation" (Main & Solomon, 1990, p. 122). Typically, these anomalous behaviors are relatively transient in the Strange Situation. Indeed, a bout of disorganized behavior may be as short as ten to thirty seconds (Main, Hesse & Kaplan, 2005). Amazingly, such a brief episode of anomalous behavior can be indicative of serious trouble in the attachment relationship as well as forecasting significant developmental problems—even into adulthood. Presumably, such transient behaviors in a carefully structured and monitored laboratory situation are indicative of more pervasive instances in the natural environment. We can view these bouts of contradictory and confusing behaviors as extreme forms of conflict and ambivalence, with dramatic alternations between proximity seeking, resistance, and avoidance. Because disorganized behavior is so intermittent, it is intermingled with the more common patterns of attachment behavior, and thus the infants are assigned to the disorganized category alongside the best-fitting traditional category (i.e., disorganized-secure, disorganized-ambivalent, or disorganized-avoidant). In this section, I will give examples of disorganized infant behavior and then describe the caregiver behavior that promotes disorganization.

Disorganization in infancy

A sequence like the following in the Strange Situation is downright painful to watch: The mother gets up to leave the room and the toddler runs after her, screaming and then pounding on the door after his mother's exit. Yet, when his mother returns, the toddler becomes fearful and immediately runs away from her to the other side of the room. This extremely stressful separation is endured with no emotional reunion and no solace. Main and Solomon (1990) categorized several kinds of disorganized/disoriented behavior in the Strange Situation with rich descriptive examples, a sample of which follows:

- *Sequential display of contradictory behavior*: after a bright greeting with raised arms, the infant freezes with a dazed expression; or the infant appears calm and content during the separations and then, on reunion, becomes intensely focused on the parent, showing distress or anger.
- *Simultaneous displays of contradictory behavior patterns*: the infant clings to the parent while sharply averting his head and gaze; approaches by backing toward the parent; reaches up toward the parent with arms extended but with head turned down or averted; smiles at the parent with an expression that also conveys fear; or strikes or pushes against the parent while in an apparently good mood.
- *Undirected, misdirected, or interrupted movements*: upon becoming distressed, the infant moves away from the parent; seemingly approaching the parent, the infant attempts to follow the stranger out of the door; moves his hand toward the parent and then quickly withdraws it; makes extremely slow or limp movements toward the parent; or suddenly and inexplicably cries or shows anger in the midst of otherwise contented play.
- *Stereotypical or anomalous movements*: the infant engages in extended rocking or hair twisting; shows tics; or displays jerky, automaton-like movements.
- *Freezing and stilling*: the infant sits or stands with arms held out for prolonged periods, or maintains a slack or dazed expression.

- *Apprehension* regarding the parent: the infant jerks back from the parent with a frightened expression; moves behind a chair to avoid the parent; or shows vigilance or tension in interacting with the parent.
- *Direct indices of disorganization or disorientation*: the infant engages in disorganized wandering; shows a disoriented expression or blind look in his eyes; or greets and approaches the stranger with raised arms as the parent enters the room.

The concept of *dissociation* has been used to describe many aspects of disorganized infant behavior in the Strange Situation, and dissociation is a common trauma-related problem. You can view dissociation as a self-protective, defensive way of coping with anxiety and fear. Whereas *a*ssociation refers to joining things together, *dis*sociation refers to keeping things separate. I find it helpful to distinguish two broad forms of dissociation: detachment and compartmentalization (Allen, 2001; E. A. Holmes, Brown et al., 2005). Dissociative *detachment* is evident in being disconnected from present reality—"spaced out" in one form or another. Thus dissociative detachment is the opposite of mindful attention to the present moment, and it also stands in contrast to detached mindfulness, which involves an engaged but observing stance toward present experience. Dissociative detachment is evident in the Strange Situation examples of freezing and stilling as well a showing a dazed, trance-like expression. Dissociative *compartmentalization*—keeping things in separate compartments—includes maintaining emotions or memories out of awareness, until they erupt suddenly. The extreme alternation of approach and avoidance behavior in the Strange Situation can be viewed as dissociative in this sense (e.g., clinging with gaze averted, backing toward the parent, or showing sudden outbursts of crying or anger in the midst of apparently good mood). As the examples also show, such dissociative defenses can alternate with direct expressions of fear.

The central theme in disorganized attachment is *fear of the parent*, which is expressed either directly or in dissociative defenses. Thus, like the three organized attachment patterns, disorganization is not a trait of the infant but rather embedded in a specific relationship: infants rarely show disorganized attachment with more than one parent (Lyons-Ruth & Jacobvitz, 2008). Being afraid of a parent puts the infant in an intolerable dilemma, which Main (Main, Hesse & Kaplan, 2005) characterized as *fright without solution*. That is, being with the parent evokes fear, and fear activates the need for attachment, which ordinarily would evoke proximity seeking to provide a feeling of security. Yet proximity only escalates the fear, which then evokes simultaneous needs for closeness and distance: "an infant who is frightened by the attachment figure is presented with a paradoxical problem—namely, *an attachment figure who is at once the source of and the solution to its alarm*" (Main & Hesse, 1990, p. 163, emphasis in original). No wonder the infant might become fearfully detached from the situation emotionally (e.g., in a daze or spaced out) or attempt to compartmentalize the contradictory emotions and behavior tendencies (e.g., pounding on the door and then running away when the parent returns). There is simply no organized way to obtain comfort from someone who is frightening.

Disorganization in early childhood

As Main and colleagues (Main, Hesse & Kaplan, 2005, p. 283) discovered, in contrast to the three organized attachment patterns, which show continuity over the course of development, a radical shift is evident in the behavior of six-year-old children who showed disorganization in infancy: "an unanticipated behavioral transformation had occurred, in that these children were organized in structuring the reunion with their mothers" (p. 283). Specifically, many such children, during the three-to-five-year-old period, have developed controlling strategies of interacting with their mother; these role reversals can be viewed as "desperate attempts by the child to reestablish the protective caregiving-attachment relationship" (George & Solomon, 2011, p. 139). These controlling strategies take two different forms, punitive and caregiving. Although the majority of disorganized infants develop one of these controlling patterns, about a third remain behaviorally disorganized (Moss, Bureau, St-Laurent & Tarabulsy, 2011).

Controlling-*punitive* children employ harsh commands, verbal threats, and physical aggression, attacking and humiliating the parent to manage the relationship. Ellen Moss and colleagues paint a vivid picture:

> A mother and her 5-year-old son arrive at our laboratory playroom for their scheduled visit. We ask them to sit down. Two chairs are provided; one is a regular adult-sized chair and the other is a small chair …. The mother sits down in the large chair. Suddenly, the

child becomes angry and says in a commanding voice, 'Get up from that chair! It's for me. Go sit in the other one.' The mother says nothing, looks sheepish, and quietly gets up and goes to sit in the small chair. (Moss, Bureau, St-Laurent & Tarabulsy, 2011, p. 52)

In stark contrast, controlling-*caregiving* children are animated, cheerful, polite, helpful, and attentive to their mother. Moss and colleagues give an example of an interaction between mother and child upon entering a playroom:

The mother sits down and the child immediately becomes involved in showing her mother a toy. The mother quickly loses interest and the child finds a second object which she brings to the mother's attention. The child appears to be quite animated and adopts a lively, happy voice when addressing her mother. By contrast, the mother appears deflated, unfocused, and expresses little emotion in voice or mannerisms. The play interaction continues with the child initiating most of the interactive exchanges and the mother sitting quite passively, sometimes in what appears to be a dissociated state. (pp. 52–53)

Akin to their infant counterparts, some children remain disorganized, showing erratic behavior and confusion, unable to adopt any effective strategy for maintaining proximity to their mother. Moss and colleagues describe an interaction between a behaviorally disorganized child and his mother in the playroom:

a 5-year-old boy is playing independently while his mother tries to draw his attention toward her. At one point, she asks the child to sing a song for her. He refuses, insisting that he wants to play on his own. The mother persists, saying that it will make her happy and that he is a good singer. The child continues to refuse to sing a song. As the tension escalates between them, the child breaks down, saying, 'I will get beat up if I sing.' The mother, surprised by his answer, asks him to explain himself. The child answers, 'I'm ugly, like my father." The mother seems quite shocked and says, 'You're not ugly and neither is Dad!' The child then seems very surprised as if he did not remember his previous statement, and asks, 'What are you talking about?' Strikingly, during this whole interaction, the child's nonverbal behavior and posture remain neutral, and he keeps playing with his toys. (p. 53)

Caregiver behavior

The recognition of the anomalous pattern of disorganized attachment behavior in the Strange Situation has led to meticulous research on associated patterns of caregiving that has dramatically shaped our understanding of attachment trauma. More than two decades of research has uncovered increasingly subtle and yet potentially traumatic patterns of disruption in parent-child interaction, all of which are best understood as failures of mindful attentiveness and mentalizing. I will chronicle the development of this research from the initial focus on blatant maltreatment to the ensuing examination of disrupted emotional communication. I will give particular attention to recent research on patterns of interaction between four-month-old infants and their mothers that captures what I consider to be the crux of attachment trauma.

Main and colleagues (Main & Solomon, 1990) quickly linked their recognition of disorganized infant attachment to maltreatment, and ongoing research has continued to confirm this connection (Sroufe, Egeland, Carlson & Collins, 2005). Extensive research (van IJzendoorn, Schuengel & Bakermans-Kranenburg, 1999) shows a relatively low prevalence of infant disorganization (15%) in typical middle-class families as compared with a substantially higher prevalence in high-risk groups (e.g., 43% in infants of mothers addicted to alcohol or drugs) and in children exposed to maltreatment (with estimates ranging from 48% to 77% depending on how disorganization is coded). In the Minnesota longitudinal study (Sroufe, Egeland, Carlson & Collins, 2005), different forms of maltreatment were identified in several contexts: a series of home observations from the first weeks after birth to twelve months of age; home interviews with mothers; observations and interviews during visits to the public health clinic; and from a series of laboratory observations. Three forms of early maltreatment were linked to infant disorganization in the Strange Situation (E. A. Carlson, 1998): physical abuse (e.g., frequent and intense spanking, angry parental outbursts resulting in serious injuries such as cigarette burns), psychological unavailability (e.g., parental unresponsiveness, passive rejection, withdrawal, or detachment), and neglect (failure to provide health or physical care, or failure to protect the child from dangers in the home).

Plainly, maltreatment will be frightening to the infant and will present the infant with an irresolvable dilemma: needing yet fearing emotional closeness. Yet Main and colleagues (Main & Hesse, 1990; Main, Hesse & Kaplan, 2005) launched an extensive line of research relating infant disorganization to a wide range of parental behavior beyond maltreatment that is liable to evoke fear in the infant. As I will describe in considering the intergenerational transmission of trauma, a more subtle process also leads to disorganization: the parent's unresolved attachment trauma can lead to frightening interactions with the infant. Thus the parent not only might be directly frightening to the infant (e.g., abusive) but also might be indirectly frightening by virtue of being *frightened*. For example, the frightened parent might be anxious, timid, disorganized, or in a dissociatively detached state—any of which will be distressing or alarming to the distressed infant who is in need of comfort and security. In short, both frightening and frightened parental behavior can be frightening to the infant: parental fear not only is contagious but also renders the parent psychologically unavailable when the infant is distressed.

Other researchers have extended Main and colleagues' findings in showing an even wider range of disturbed parent-infant interactions to be associated with infant disorganization. Karlen Lyons-Ruth and colleagues (Lyons-Ruth, Bronfman & Atwood, 1999) proposed that *misattuned caregiver responses* to the infant's attachment needs are frightening to the infant because of the infant's inability to influence the behavior of the caregiver when the infant is distressed; cries for comfort go unheard. Paralleling Main's frightening-frightened distinction, these authors identified two patterns of misattunement: *hostile intrusiveness* and *helpless withdrawal*. In contrast to helpless-withdrawn maternal behavior, where non-hostile and superficially responsive behavior is intermingled with subtle fearfulness, hostile-intrusive behavior is directly frightening to the infant. Both patterns are associated with disorganized infant attachment, but there is a difference between them regarding infants' secondary attachment classifications: hostile-intrusiveness is more pernicious in being associated with disorganized-insecure (avoidant or ambivalent) attachment; whereas helpless withdrawal is associated with somewhat more adaptive disorganized-secure attachment.

Additional aspects of Lyons-Ruth and colleagues' research show that frightening caregiver behavior is not the only pathway to disorganized infant attachment (Lyons-Ruth & Jacobvitz, 2008). More generally, infant disorganization is associated with *disrupted emotional communication*. This disrupted communication renders the caregiver emotionally unavailable to comfort the infant in times of distress and thus "should lead to unmodulated infant fear and contradictory approach-avoidance behavior, *whether or not the mother herself is the source of the fear*" (Lyons-Ruth & Jacobvitz, 2008, p. 677, emphasis added). These authors distinguished several types of disrupted communication: negative-intrusive behavior (e.g., mocking the infant); role confusion (e.g., seeking reassurance from the infant); withdrawal (e.g., silence); communication errors (e.g., contradictory cues such as verbally encouraging the infant to come close and then physically distancing from the infant); and disorientation (e.g., unusual changes in voice during an interaction). Notably, disrupted communication is predictive of infant disorganization *even when directly frightening behavior is excluded,* leading the authors to conclude that frightening behavior "is occurring within a broader matrix of disturbed communication between mother and child" (p. 678). Keep in mind that such disturbed communication will include a lack of psychological availability, that is, mentalizing.

Beatrice Beebe and colleagues' (Beebe et al., 2010) landmark study of four-month-old infants interacting with their mother provides an exceptionally fine-grained understanding of attachment trauma. Beebe sought early predictors of disorganized attachment evident in the Strange Situation at twelve months of age. At the four-month point, infants were placed in an infant seat on a table and mothers were instructed to play with their infant without the use of toys. Beebe analyzed second-by-second analyses of two and a half minutes of mother-infant interactions to predict subsequent disorganization. In my view, this research provides the clearest prototype of attachment trauma, a model that remains pertinent throughout the lifetime.

Compared to their secure counterparts, future disorganized infants showed more vocal and facial distress as well as discordant emotions, for example, "one future D [disorganized] infant joined sweet maternal smiles with smiles of his own, but meanwhile he whimpered as his mother pushed his head back and roughly smacked his hands together" (p. 93). Moreover, these infants were more erratic and unstable from moment to moment, which would make them more difficult for their mothers to read emotionally. In addition, these infants engaged in less self-touch, which is a crucial means of emotional self-soothing.

The future disorganized infants' distressed is unmitigated by their mother's behavior, several features of which are striking: their mothers (1) gazed away from their infant's face more often and unpredictably; (2) loomed into the infant's face more often and unpredictably; (3) did not respond to their infant's self-touch with complementary affectionate touch; (4) showed less variable emotional responsiveness, that is, relatively rigid, closed-up facial expressions; (5) were less likely to follow the infant's shifts between positive and negative emotions, for example, less able to "emotionally 'enter' and 'go with' infant facial and vocal distress" (p. 90); and (6) showed discordant emotional responses, specifically, responding to their infant's distress with surprise or positive emotion. Beebe interpreted these discordant responses as being defensive, indicative of denial of the infant's emotional distress, attempting to "ride negative into positive," evident in such comments as "Don't be that way" or "No fussing, no fussing, you should be very happy" (p. 94).

Beebe makes the crucial point that mothers of future disorganized infants do not show a global failure of empathy or engagement but rather a far more specific *failure of attunement during moments of infant distress*. In these moments, their mother fails to provide the foundation of mentalizing, namely, mindful attentiveness to their emotional states. Thus the infants are left alone in distress; moreover, their agency is undermined inasmuch as they are unable to engage their mother in alleviating their distress and they are unable to regulate their distress on their own (e.g., through self-touch). In these distressed states, they are deprived of the fundamental experience of mentalizing, that is, a mind influencing a mind as well as the experience of being experienced, as Beebe puts it. At the procedural or implicit level, they are developing profoundly insecure working models of attachment. Beebe speaks for the infant destined for disorganization:

> I'm so upset and you're not helping me. I'm smiling at you and whimpering; don't you see I want you to love me? When I'm upset, you smile or close up or look away. You make me feel worse. I feel confused about what I feel and about what you feel. I can't predict you. I don't know what is going on. What am I supposed to do?

I feel helpless to affect you. I feel helpless to help myself. I feel frantic. (p. 101)

As I have stated repeatedly, this experience of being psychologically alone in emotional pain typifies attachment trauma; the experience Beebe articulates at four months can be reexperienced throughout life. The combination of intrusiveness (e.g., looming into the infant's space and striving to override distress) and withdrawal (e.g., gazing away, even while looming) typifies a failure to promote relatedness and autonomy, that is, a failure to engage coupled with a failure to give the infant space and to allow the infant to exert influence in the relationship. The upshot is a gross failure on the ground floor of the development of mentalizing. As Beebe summarizes, the infant's emerging working model of relationships includes "confusion about their own basic emotional organization, their mothers' emotional organization, and their mothers' response to their distress, setting a trajectory in development which may disturb the fundamental integration of the person" (p. 119).

As just reviewed, disorganized attachment develops in a wide range of caregiving contexts, varying from frank maltreatment to recurrent failures of attunement to distress. Similarly problematic and ongoing patterns of disrupted caregiving are evident in conjunction with disorganized-controlling attachment in early childhood (George & Solomon, 2011; Moss, Bureau, St-Laurent & Tarabulsy, 2011). Carol George and Judith Solomon (2008) have characterized parenting related to infant disorganization as reflecting a *disabled caregiving system*, marked by the caregiver's helplessness (George & Solomon, 2011). Helpless caregivers are unable to help the child with emotion regulation, and they are equally unable to regulate their own emotions—alternating between emotional flooding and emotional constriction.

Here it is important to keep in mind that the problems in caregiving just reviewed do not occur in a vacuum. As described in the chapter on attachment in childhood, secure attachment relationships require a stable and supportive family context. For example, problematic maternal care stems from both parents' attachment insecurity in conjunction with severe and chronic marital discord (Bifulco, Moran, Jacobs & Bunn, 2009; Bifulco & Thomas, in press). George and Solomon (2008) describe how a potentially wide range of "assaults to the caregiving system" (p. 848) can result in what they call an *abdication of care*, which in turn can lead to disorganized attachment. These assaults include perinatal loss of a previous child; child prematurity or disability; parental psychiatric disorders including depression, anxiety, and substance abuse; parental divorce; and living in a violent environment, such as in the midst of terrorism or a war zone (George & Solomon, 2008; Lyons-Ruth & Jacobvitz, 2008). As I describe next, one common assault to the caregiving system that leads to disorganized infant attachment is the parent's history of attachment trauma.

Intergenerational transmission of attachment trauma

I have delineated parallels between parents and infants in the three organized attachment patterns: although the correspondence is far from perfect, securely attached infants are likely to have secure-autonomous parents; ambivalent-resistant infants to have preoccupied parents; and avoidant infants to have dismissing parents. I begin this section reviewing research with the AAI showing that disorganized infants are likely to have parents who are classified as unresolved with respect to their own history of loss and trauma. Then I will discuss the ways in which the intergenerational transmission of trauma is associated with mentalizing failures. There is hope in this finding because, as I will then review, mentalizing promotes resilience; accordingly, clinicians are developing parent-child therapies that promote mentalizing and, thereby, greater attachment security.

Adult attachment and infant disorganization

Secure-autonomous adults, who have securely attached infants, provide coherent narratives in the AAI. That is, they discuss their attachment experiences in an emotionally authentic and richly detailed way, which the interviewer can follow easily. In contrast, parents of disorganized infants show striking lapses in coherence in the AAI. The relative incoherence of these interviews takes one of two forms (Hesse, 2008; Main, Hesse & Goldwyn, 2008). First, infant disorganization is associated with unresolved-disorganized interviews, in which the lack of resolution of loss or trauma is evident in lapses in coherence when these unresolved experiences are brought to mind in the interview by questions pertaining to loss and abuse. Just as infant disorganization is identified in short bursts of anomalous behavior, unresolved interviews are associated with transient lapses rather than pervasive incoherence.

For example, a parent may slip into dissociatively detached states when discussing a traumatic experience—seeming momentarily spaced out or lost in the past. Amazingly, just a few sentences in the AAI showing such lapses can reveal significant attachment problems that have profound consequences. Presumably, such lapses in the interview are indicative of more pervasive disruptions in daily life. Because of the transience of the disturbance, disorganized interviews are assigned a best-fitting secondary classification (as is done with disorganized infant attachment). Thus an adult might be classified as unresolved-secure, unresolved-preoccupied, or unresolved-dismissing. Infant disorganization also is associated with a second type of difficulty in the AAI. Paralleling infant disorganization, the parental interview might be coded "Cannot Classify," owing to lack of any clear pattern, an extreme intermingling of contradictory patterns (e.g., preoccupied and dismissing), or, in rare cases, a pervasive incoherence that makes the whole interview difficult to understand.

Main and colleagues (Main, Hesse & Goldwyn, 2008) construe the unresolved-disorganized classification as follows:

> what the parents of disorganized infants exhibited could be termed *lapses in the monitoring of reasoning or discourse* during discussions of loss or other potentially traumatic experiences. These discourse-reasoning lapses suggested temporary alterations in consciousness, and are now believed to represent either interference from normally dissociated memory or belief systems, or unusual absorptions involving memories triggered by the discussion of traumatic events. (p. 61, emphasis in original)

Such lapses include references to deceased persons as if they are still living, such as the following: "It was almost better when she died, because then she could get on with being dead and I could get on with raising my family" (p. 61). Here is an example of frank incoherence: "I'm still afraid he died that night because I forgot to think about him. I promised to think about him and I did, but that night I went out, and so he died" (p. 61). Such incoherence exemplifies severely impaired mentalizing in the context of trauma and loss.

Many studies have revealed a relationship between parental unresolved loss and trauma in the AAI and infant disorganization in the Strange Situation (van IJzendoorn, Schuengel & Bakermans-Kranenburg,

1999). Yet, because they reflect temporary lapses in coherence, unresolved interviews can be coded as secure or insecure based on the quality of the interview as a whole, and this classification makes a difference. A group of researchers conducted two, two-hour home visits during which they used a camcorder to videotape mother-infant interactions (Schuengel, Bakermans-Kranenburg & van IJzendoorn, 1999). They coded these interactions for frightening behavior (i.e., threatening, frightened, or dissociative states) and, as previous research would suggest, such behavior was associated with infant disorganization in the Strange Situation. Yet, despite the fact that they shared an experience of unresolved loss, the otherwise secure and insecure mothers differed substantially from each other: the insecure mothers had the highest frightening-behavior scores, whereas the secure mothers had the lowest. Thus, when coupled with generally insecure attachment, it is noteworthy that unresolved mourning can be associated with transient subtly frightening—not abusive—behavior in parents who relate sensitively to their infants most of the time. Yet, even such subtly frightening behavior can contribute to the infant's disorganized attachment.

To reiterate, Main's unresolved-disorganized coding reflects lapses in coherence at specific points that are related to memories of loss or trauma evoked by interview questions addressed to these topics. In contrast, Lyons-Ruth and colleagues (Melnick, Finger, Hans, Patrick & Lyons-Ruth, 2008) formulated a way of coding AAI transcripts as a whole for *hostile-helpless* states of mind based on "identifications with hostile or helpless childhood attachment figures that appear unintegrated in the mind of the speaker" (p. 399). Such lack of integration can be construed as dissociative compartmentalization and, as these authors noted, such severe dissociation commonly occurs in the context of "repeated, early, and prolonged interpersonal trauma" (p. 403). Persons in the *hostile* subtype describe attachment figures as malevolent and tend to identify with them: "My mother was horrible/I'm just like my mother" (p. 403). Those in the *helpless* subtype are pervasively fearful and passive, identifying with a parent who abdicated the caregiving role. As anticipated, Lyons-Ruth and colleagues found that the hostile-helpless coding of AAIs relates significantly to infant disorganization; moreover, parental hostile-helpless states of mind promote infant disorganization in part because they are conducive to disrupted parent-infant communication.

Solomon and George (2011) studied the origins of caregiver helplessness in conjunction with disorganized-controlling attachment in children ranging from four to seven years old. Mothers of these children described their childhood attachment figures—often both parents—as being out of control and unpredictable in their rages and other frightening behaviors. A history of unresolved loss of an attachment figure characterized the mothers of controlling-caregiving children in particular; the mother's loss in the child's early years was conducive to the role reversal in caregiving. Yet Solomon and George observed that not only a frightening maternal history but also the lack of protective factors—most notably, other sources of security—played a significant role in caregivers' helplessness. This finding attests to the value of islands of security: "mothers who experienced comparable frightening parental behavior and fear but who also described a family figure or friend who served as a source of reassurance had children who were judged to be organized in attachment" (p. 42).

The simplest way to understand the intergenerational transmission of trauma implied by these attachment findings is to view the parent's frightening-frightened or hostile-helpless behavior as a posttraumatic stress response marked by reexperiencing trauma and hyperarousal, coupled with avoidance strategies. The parent's trauma shows through in the AAI when interview questions evoke painful memories. Similarly, in the Strange Situation, the infant's distress and attachment needs are liable to evoke the parent's traumatic memories and emotions as the parent resonates with the infant's distress. At least momentarily, the traumatized parent, caught up in emotion from the past, loses mindful connection with the present, and becomes psychologically unavailable to the infant:

> If a parent has not experienced comfort in relation to his or her own fear or shame-evoking experiences, we would expect that parent to lack an inner dialogue through which to integrate and contain the activation of intense reexperiencing of his or her own early vulnerability in the presence of the infant's pain, distress, fear, anger, or perceived rejection. This may place parents in jeopardy of becoming flooded by intense affects that they cannot regulate or act on adaptively, leading to the display of hostile (e.g., suppressing children's emotions, yelling) or helpless (dissociating, withdrawing)

responses to their children. (Melnick, Finger, Hans, Patrick & Lyons-Ruth, 2008, pp. 413–414)

When the infant's distress evokes the parent's traumatic memories, the parent is responding to the past rather than the present. As Main and Hesse (1990) propose, the traumatized parent's continuing fear and frightened-frightening behavior "could be particularly puzzling or frightening to the infant because its immediate cause would often lie in the parent's response to memories aroused by ongoing events rather than resulting from those events directly" (p. 163). As Beebe (Beebe et al., 2010) described eloquently, the parent's behavior will not make sense to the infant; it won't fit. We can understand this out-of-sync response as a failure of mentalizing: in the moment, the parent as well as the infant is psychologically alone in distressed states.

Mentalizing failures in intergenerational transmission

I have outlined a straightforward and commonsensical process of inter-generational transmission as follows: parents with secure attachment are able to provide coherent narrative in the AAI by virtue of their capacity to mentalize regarding their attachment history; such parents engage in mentalizing interactions with their infants; counting on par-ents holding their mind in mind, the infants become securely attached; and, with their experience of mentalizing interactions, the infants develop into children with solid mentalizing capacities. Mentalizing begets mentalizing.

Now consider the opposite and equally commonsensical scenario: in the AAI, parents with unresolved-disorganized attachment show lapses in coherence associated with impaired mentalizing capacity; by virtue of reexperiencing trauma in the face of infants' distress, their capacity to mentalize their infant is impaired; anticipating frightening interac-tions in which their mind will not be held in mind while they are in distress, the infants show disorganized attachment; as a consequence of parental mentalizing failures, the infants do not learn to mentalize when emotionally distressed; and, consequently, they develop into chil-dren whose mentalizing capacities are compromised. Nonmentalizing begets nonmentalizing.

Gergely (Gergely & Unoka, 2008) argued that secure attachment does not promote mentalizing; rather, adverse caregiving undermines what is otherwise a natural developmental process: "an implicit and automatic capacity for mentalizing about others is … an innate social-cognitive evolutionary adaptation implemented by a specialized and pre-wired mindreading mechanism that seems active and functional at least as early as 12 months of age in humans" (pp. 58–59). Yet the patterns of interaction conducive to disorganized attachment impair the development of mentalizing:

> There are, in fact, good empirical reasons to believe that certain dysfunctional types of early attachment relations involving severe neglect, abuse, dissociative, highly intrusive, or grossly unpredictable patterns of parental reactivity have significant and long-term detrimental and disruptive effects on one's later capacity to functionally use the innate competence for online mentalizaiton as an adaptive interpersonal coping strategy to deal with the vicissitudes of affectively charged intimate and affiliative relationships of later life. (p. 59)

As Gergely proposed, research supports the proposition that adverse attachment relationships undermine the development of mentalizing. As described in the previous chapter, Slade and colleagues (Slade, 2005; Slade, Grienenberger, Bernbach, Levy & Locker, 2005) developed the Parent Development Interview to assess parents' capacities to mentalize in their relationship with their infant. Slade's research revealed the flip side of attachment security: maternal unresolved-disorganized attachment was associated with poor mentalizing in relation to the infant; in turn, poor maternal mentalizing was associated with disorganized (as well as ambivalent-resistant) infant attachment. Further research by this group (Grienenberger, Kelly & Slade, 2005) showed that poor maternal mentalizing was associated with disrupted parent-infant emotional communication, as assessed by Lyons-Ruth and colleagues' measure (Lyons-Ruth & Jacobvitz, 2008) discussed earlier in this chapter. As Lyons-Ruth also had found, disrupted communication predicted disorganized infant attachment.

From the research just reviewed, you can discern the intergenerational transmission of attachment trauma: the parent who has not resolved her own history of attachment trauma is liable self-protectively to turn attention away from the infant's distress to avoid reexperiencing her own trauma (Lyons-Ruth, Bronfman & Atwood, 1999).

This failure of mindful attentiveness is precisely what Beebe (Beebe et al., 2010) discovered in her observations of four-month-old infants who subsequently showed disorganized attachment: when the infant was distressed, the mother might direct her gaze away or smile as if blinding herself to distress. Thus parent-infant communication is liable to be disrupted; mentalizing collapses, and the infant does not have the experience of the parent holding his mind in mind. Accordingly, the infant does not become securely attached to the parent but rather, at worst, attachment is disorganized; such disorganization, coupled with impaired mentalizing, potentially has long-lasting traumatic conse- quences, as Gergely (Gergely & Unoka, 2008) delineated.

To take extreme cases, as Slade (2005) put it, "Disturbed and abu- sive parents obliterate their children's experience with their own rage, hatred, fear, and malevolence. The child (and his mental states) is not seen for who he is, but in light of the parents' projections and distor- tions" (p. 273). In Slade and colleagues' view, mentalizing is the crucial factor in attachment: "attachment categories may, in essence, be prox- ies for a more basic and organizing psychological capacity, namely the reflective function" (Slade, Grienenberger, Bernbach, Levy & Locker, 2005, p. 294). They summarize the connection between attachment and mentalizing as follows:

> AAI categories offer a way of describing the dimensions of high and low reflectiveness, with security linked to high reflective- ness, with dismissing, preoccupied, and unresolved sates of mind indicative of varying types of failure to mentalize. But, what is intrinsic to all insecure categories is the inability to envision men- tal states. The dismissing individual rejects mental state reasoning, the preoccupied individual cannot think about mental states but rather is buffeted by them, and the unresolved individual is pro- foundly dysregulated by mental states. Nevertheless, the classifica- tion of an adult as 'secure' or 'insecure' in relation to attachment serves as a kind of shorthand for the presence or absence of a more basic capacity to make sense of and thus regulate powerful inter- subjective and interpersonal experiences. (Slade, Grienenberger, Bernbach, Levy & Locker, 2005, p. 294)

The last link in the chain of transmission is this: maltreatment and disorganized attachment are associated with impaired child mentalizing.

To reiterate, as mentalizing begets mentalizing, nonmentalizing begets nonmentalizing. Hence, as Fonagy and colleagues have reviewed (Fonagy, Gergely & Target, 2007; Fonagy, Gergely & Target, 2008), attachment-related mentalizing impairment is evident in difficulty appreciating what others are thinking and feeling, limited capacity to talk about mental states, difficulty understanding emotions, failure to empathize with other children's distress, and difficulty managing emotional distress. All these difficulties are liable to contribute to problems in relationships with parents, peers, teachers, and others. These impairments make relationships more stressful for a child who has special difficulty coping with stress, which can create a vicious circle: relationship conflicts escalate stress, and poor coping escalates relationship conflicts.

Mentalizing in resilience

All is not lost. A primary justification for focusing on mentalizing is the potential for mentalizing capacity to promote resilience, in effect, by serving to buffer potentially traumatic experiences. As discussed in the previous chapter, Fonagy and colleagues (Fonagy, Steele, Steele, Moran & Higgitt, 1991) showed that a high level of parental mentalizing measured prior to the infant's birth predicted infant security at twelve months. Subsequent findings showed that mentalizing capacity can serve as a protective factor in coping with stress (Fonagy et al., 1995). Mothers were divided into high and low stress and deprivation groups, based on interviews regarding childhood adversity (e.g., prolonged separations) as well as adulthood stress (e.g., parental unemployment or illness). All ten of the highly stressed and deprived mothers whose mentalizing was preserved had securely attached infants; whereas only one of the seventeen highly stressed mothers with poor mentalizing capacity had a securely attached infant.

This research also showed a relation between mentalizing capacity and the development of borderline personality disorder. That is, among a group of patients with different types of personality disorder, those with borderline disorder were distinctive in having a trauma history (e.g., sexual abuse) in combination with a low level of mentalizing capacity in the AAI, which would interfere with the resolution of trauma. That is, neither trauma nor impaired mentalizing alone suffices, from which we can infer that preserved mentalizing in the context of trauma affords some protection against the development of borderline disorder.

In this context, it is important to keep in mind that disorganized attachment is commonly observed in relation to one and not both parents. Fonagy and colleagues (Fonagy, Steele, Steele, Moran & Higgitt, 1991) propose that, by virtue of this relationship-specific nature of early attachment, the resilient maltreated child may have had the opportunity to develop a secure internal working model alongside an insecure model; such islands of security might permit the child to develop mentalizing capacities that ultimately enable the child to come to some resolution with regard to the abuse and thus be less likely to develop severe personality disorder. Similarly, Bifulco and Thomas (in press) found that, in the context of a history of abuse and neglect, closeness to a parent and positive peer relationships contributed to later attachment security; in turn, security provided a buffer against the development of psychiatric disorder.

Mentalizing interventions interrupt intergenerational transmission

Perhaps the most powerful evidence for the influence of parental behavior and mentalizing on the development of attachment comes from research on therapeutic interventions, that is, parent-infant and parent-child psychotherapy. Think of this research as if it were an experiment: does changing mentalizing and parenting behavior lead to changes in attachment security? Yes. I will review briefly some of these therapeutic efforts here and will focus more on psychotherapy for adults in the last chapter.

Arietta Slade and colleagues developed a program designed to promote maternal mentalizing in parent-infant interactions, aptly titled *Minding the Baby* (Sadler, Slade & Mayes, 2006; Slade, 2006; Slade et al., 2004). This program is designed for high-risk, inner city, first-time parents and their infants. The intervention helps the mother to mentalize with respect to herself, her infant, and their relationship. As Sadler and colleagues (Sadler, Slade & Mayes, 2006) state, "Understanding that the baby *has* feelings and desires is an achievement for most of our mothers" (p. 280, emphasis in original). The home visitors assist mothers to mentalize by speaking for the baby. When a mother teased her baby for crying after he hurt his finger in the door, calling him a "faker," the clinician gently spoke, "Ooh, that hurt. You're kinda' scared and want Mommy to make it feel better" (p. 282). Modeling such mind-minded interactions for the mother enables the mother to become more responsive to the infant. Home visitors also videotape mother-infant interactions and review the videotapes with the mothers to enhance their awareness of the baby's mental states and the impact of their interactions on the baby's feelings and behavior. As a consequence, mothers improve in mentalizing capacity, and their infants are more likely to become securely attached (as contrasted with the high rates of disorganized attachment typically observed in high-risk groups).

Over the past two decades, clinicians and researchers have devised a number of parent-infant and parent-child intervention programs to assist parents in regulating their own emotional responses to their children's distress and thus to help them to become more sensitively responsive to their infants attachment needs—all with the aim of promoting greater attachment security (Berlin, Zeanah & Lieberman, 2008; Zanetti, Powell, Cooper & Hoffman, 2011). As Slade (2008b), summarizes, current child therapists may "touch upon the parent's own history," but the therapy is "focused on the *child* … helping the parent to better understand the child," and they "view such deepening empathy and engagement as crucial to creating changes in the parent-child relationship and in the internal life of the child" (p. 311). Whether or not the clinicians consciously use the concept, such programs enhance mentalizing (or mindfulness, or empathy, if you prefer). The proliferation of programs has led to diverse interventions and goals; the charge for the future, as it is with psychotherapy more generally, is to discover which aspects of the interventions are most effective.

As a footnote to the point that mentalizing has the potential to interrupt the intergenerational transmission of trauma, I note a study regarding the cycle of violence. You have likely heard some version of the apparent truism that "Abused children become abusers and victims of violence become violent offenders" (Widom, 1989, p. 244). Fortunately, repeating the cycle is by no means inevitable. A comprehensive and critical review of the research literature came to a more refined conclusion: "one-third of the children will continue the pattern, one-third will not, and the last one-third will continue to be vulnerable, their eventual parental behavior depending on extrafamilial pressures" (Oliver, 1993, p. 1321). I emphasized the crucial contribution of the environmental context of care in discussing the development of attachment security in childhood. As reviewed elsewhere (Allen, 2001), a host of factors besides trauma history contribute to parental abusiveness: social stressors, stressful life events, extent of social support in childhood and adulthood, attitudes toward punishment, and the health and behavior of the child. But research also has identified a critical psychological factor related to repeating the past: "The single most important modifying factor in intergenerational transmission of child abuse is the capacity of the child victim to grow up with the ability to face the reality of past and present personal relationships" (Oliver, 1993, p. 1322). This finding highlights the importance of mentalizing: I can easily imagine that these parents who interrupt the cycle of violence would provide coherent narrative in the AAI, indicating that they are keenly aware of their past trauma and have come to terms with it. Such is the aim of parent-infant therapy, as Selma Fraiberg and her colleagues (Fraiberg, Adelson & Shapiro, 1975) pioneered it, where the ghosts of the past can be laid to rest—or at least identified as such when they show up.

Developmental impact of disorganized attachment

Disorganized attachment would not merit as much of psychotherapists' attention if it were confined to infancy. As I already stated, however, disorganized attachment also is evident in adulthood in the AAI, that is, in the form of brief lapses in coherence that occur during discussions of loss or trauma as well as in more pervasive loss of coherence that renders interviews unclassifiable. Moreover, when a parent is disorganized in the AAI, the infant is likely to be disorganized in relating to that parent in the Strange Situation. But I have yet another matter to consider, that is, the developmental trajectory of infants who show disorganization in the Strange Situation. As with other attachment patterns, a combination of continuity and discontinuity of disorganized attachment is evident from infancy and childhood into adulthood. When disorganization and its effects persist, the child is at risk for subsequent development of problem behavior and psychopathology. Given its prominence in trauma and disorganized attachment, I will single out dissociation for discussion. Then I will consider a wider range of disturbance as it relates to disorganization in childhood and adulthood. All this is a lot to digest, and I will conclude this section by summarizing the role of disorganization in vulnerability to trauma and psychopathology.

Continuity and discontinuity of disorganized attachment

As with the three organized patterns, disorganized attachment shows a balance of continuity and change over the course of development. Indeed, in this instance, we count on the capacity for change and, as research on parent-child interventions demonstrates most directly, improvement in the quality of relationships in which disorganization occurs will promote greater security. A broad finding emerges from a review of fourteen studies, most of which first assessed attachment at twelve months (van IJzendoorn, Schuengel & Bakermans-Kranenburg, 1999). The time lags from the first to the subsequent assessment ranged from one month to five years. The research showed substantial long-term stability, although the stability varied considerably from sample to sample and left ample room for change.

Although the form of behavior from infancy to early childhood changes from disorganized to organized (i.e., controlling), the findings show stability in disorganization in the sense that profound insecurity remains. Main and colleagues (Main, Hesse & Kaplan, 2005) administered a Separation Anxiety Test to disorganized-controlling six-year-old children. The test depicts various kinds of parent-child separations, and the child is asked to about what the separated child might feel or do. The children responded fearfully, describing catastrophic fantasies about injuries to the parents or the child and characterizing the child as afraid and at a loss as to what to do. Showing significant developmental continuity, disorganization and fearful responses to the Separation Anxiety Test predicted one form or another of insecure attachment when these participants were administered the AAI at age nineteen. There was a consistent tendency for early disorganization to predict unresolved or cannot-classify AAI coding in particular. Similarly, the Minnesota study (Sroufe, Egeland, Carlson & Collins, 2005) also revealed some continuity from infancy to adulthood: disorganized attachment predicted insecure attachment in the AAI administered at ages nineteen and twenty-six and, more specifically, predicted lack of resolution of trauma at both ages.

One study of the stability of disorganized attachment in adulthood bears mention. Judith Crowell and Stuart Hauser (2008) obtained

AAIs at three points in adulthood (ages 26, 34, and 39) for a group of individuals—many with a trauma history—who had been psychiatrically hospitalized in adolescence. They also assessed quality of social adjustment over this period. As with all other research, they found a combination of stability and change. Specifically, 37.5% of the individuals showed unresolved-disorganized attachment at all three points, and 44% varied, showing unresolved-disorganized attachment at one point and not another, with some moving into disorganized attachment and others moving out of it. Not surprisingly, a high prevalence of different forms of insecure attachment was evident in this high-risk group. Yet, despite their early history, some participants showed secure attachment, and their security served a protective function: "the ability to coordinate thoughts, feelings, and reported behaviors that is required to be classified as coherent-secure regarding attachment may also be a requirement of successful social adjustment/functioning in daily life" (p. 365). In short, such coherence, indicative of mentalizing capacity, "would seem especially important as a buffering system for individuals who have experienced many adversities and stresses, including mental illness" (p. 366).

Dissociative disturbance

Because dissociation is so intertwined with fear, trauma, and posttraumatic stress disorder (Allen, 2001, 2013), I find it striking that attachment research has revealed the intergenerational transmission of dissociative disturbance in particular. As already stated, lack of resolution of trauma in the AAI sometimes is marked by dissociative lapses, that is, alterations of consciousness in which the parent loses touch with the present. Parents with such disorganized attachment also are liable to dissociate in the Strange Situation, for example, by tuning out and withdrawing into a frightened state. Similarly, their infants, responding to parental fear, show dissociative disturbance in the Strange Situation (e.g., appearing as if in a daze or trance, engaging in aimless behavior). Thus disorganized attachment is a route to later dissociative disorders, namely, "the first step in a developmental pathway leading, perhaps through a long sequence of dramatic or violent family interactions from infancy onward, to pathological dissociation in adult life" (Liotti, 1999, p. 296).

A dramatic demonstration of developmental continuity in the Minnesota study (Sroufe, Egeland, Carlson & Collins, 2005) revealed that infants who showed disorganization in the Strange Situation continued to show dissociative behavior in childhood and up to nineteen years of age. Elizabeth Carlson and colleagues (1998) obtained teacher ratings in grades 1, 2, 3, 6, and high school and the dissociative scales included the items such as "Confused or seems to be in a fog," and "Strange behavior" as well as items pertaining to self-injury, which often occurs in conjunction with trauma and dissociation (i.e., in middle childhood, "Gets hurt a lot, accident prone" and in high school, "Deliberately harms self or attempts suicide"). Infant disorganization was significantly correlated with these dissociative items in middle childhood and high school. In addition, earlier disorganization related significantly to dissociative disturbance shown in a clinical interview at age seventeen and a half and to a widely used self-report measure of dissociation, the Dissociative Experiences Scale (E. B. Carlson & Putnam, 1993) at age nineteen. Keep in mind that, although these correlations are statistically significant, the strengths of relationships are modest—far from a perfect correspondence. Yet I find it truly remarkable that a brief bout of disorganized behavior in a laboratory situation at twelve months of age would have *any* relation to a specific psychiatric symptom nearly two decades later.

Research has continued to show a relatively robust relation between infant disorganization and subsequent dissociative pathology (Dozier, Stovall-McClough & Albus, 2008). Although Lyons-Ruth and colleagues did not find a direct link between disorganization and later dissociation, they did find that maternal disrupted communication in the laboratory (a contributor to disorganization) predicted dissociation in young adulthood. Notably, low levels of maternal positive emotion, as well as lack of emotional responsiveness, were associated with later dissociation (Lyons-Ruth & Jacobvitz, 2008). Hence Lyons-Ruth and colleagues concluded, "chronic impairment in caregiver responsiveness may be more central to the etiology of dissociative symptoms than abusive events per se" (Melnick, Finger, Hans, Patrick & Lyons-Ruth, 2008, p. 415). Either abuse or lack of attunement undermines the infant's ability to influence the parent's attention and behavior, resulting in a state of helplessness; thus the infant is liable to dissociatively detach or to become self-absorbed (Koos & Gergely, 2001).

What is the link between disorganization and dissociation? Main and colleagues attributed disorganization to placing infants in a situation for which they are not biologically prepared:

The mother (or any other primary attachment figure) is the haven of
safety that must be approached in times of danger. However, when
the infant's biologically channeled haven of safety has simultaneously become a source of fright, the infant is placed in an irresolvable and disorganizing approach-flight paradox. We have proposed
that when this occurs, anomalies in behavior, attention, and reasoning may arise and … may ultimately increase vulnerability to
disorders involving dissociative processes. (Main, Hesse & Kaplan,
2005, p. 281)

Sroufe and colleagues (Sroufe, Egeland, Carlson & Collins, 2005) made
the telling point that, in the face of such inescapable conflict, "infants
can only *leave the situation psychologically,* that is, with breakdowns in
organized behavior and gaps in awareness" (p. 248, emphasis added).
This point echoes what I have found to be one of the most apt charac-
terizations of dissociative defenses, proposed by Richard Kluft (1992):
dissociation is a form of mental flight when physical flight is not possible. Dissociation can be construed as a conflict-based mental paralysis;
as Carlson and colleagues (1998) put it, "Proximity-seeking mixed with
avoidance may result as infants attempt to balance conflicting tendencies. Freezing, dazing, and stilling may be the result of their mutual
inhibition" (E. A. Carlson, 1998, p. 1108).

Considering Kluft's point that dissociation is a form of mental flight
when physical flight is impossible, the self-protective nature of this
defense is plain. Yet a proclivity to dissociate in the face of fear and anxiety also can undermine more adaptive coping; you cannot cope with a
situation effectively if you are not psychologically present (i.e., mindful and mentalizing). Thus disorganized attachment and dissociative
defenses constitute a vulnerability to additional forms of disturbance;
indeed, disorganized attachment renders the individual more vulnerable to subsequent trauma.

Childhood disorganization and subsequent psychopathology

Although disorganized attachment is not a disorder, it can initiate developmental pathways that increase the risk of later disorder
(Sroufe, Egeland, Carlson & Collins, 2005), especially when disorganization is combined with other risk factors (Deklyen & Greenberg,
2008). Specifically, either disorganization or maltreatment is potentially

problematic, but their combination presents the greatest risk for psychopathology (Melnick, Finger, Hans, Patrick & Lyons-Ruth, 2008). Research summarized next shows that attachment disorganization is associated with diverse problems from infancy into school age, and it is predictive of psychopathology into adulthood (Lyons-Ruth & Jacobvitz, 2008).

As described earlier, many children who show disorganized attachment in infancy develop a pattern of controlling behavior in early childhood while also remaining fearful. When disorganized children are invited to imagine attachment relationships or scenarios, they envision fear, confusion, and destruction—at worst, with a nightmarish quality. The inner world of imagination can be as frightening as the outer world. Yet the form that disorganization takes in childhood relates to the pattern of disturbance. Whereas the controlling-caregiving pattern is associated with internalizing problems (i.e., anxiety and depression), the controlling-punitive and (continuing) disorganized behavior patterns are associated with externalizing problems: anger and aggression along with problems in relationships with peers and teachers, combined with poorer academic performance (Moss, Bureau, St-Laurent & Tarabulsy, 2011).

Of particular concern in this book is the vulnerability that attachment disorganization confers to later trauma. Thus a study of the relation between infant disorganization and the development of posttraumatic stress disorder (PTSD) in childhood is particularly noteworthy (MacDonald et al., 2008). The sample consisted of seventy-eight eight-year-old children from low-income urban backgrounds, many of whom were affected by intrauterine cocaine exposure. Attachment was assessed at twelve months in the Strange Situation, and diagnostic interviews were administered at age eight to assess trauma history and related symptoms. PTSD was assessed in relation to the "scariest" things the children had experienced. Children with a history of disorganized attachment showed higher levels of the two central symptoms of PTSD, namely, reexperiencing the traumatic events and avoidance. Notably, disorganization was not associated with other anxiety disorders, leading the researchers to conclude, "children with a history of disorganized attachment in infancy may *evidence greater difficulty than other children coping with stressful experiences* later in childhood" (p. 503, emphasis added). Making a point that is central to this book, the authors infer that these children "may evidence particular difficulty coping with frightening situations or regulating negative affect, in part because caregivers may not have responded to their children effectively or consistently in the past" (p. 503). Noting that avoidance symptoms of PTSD overlap with dissociative defenses that are also associated with disorganized attachment, the authors point out that such defensive coping will interfere with learning more adaptive ways of coping with stress—a primary justification for addressing trauma actively in psychotherapy.

But the effects of infant disorganization extend beyond childhood. In the Minnesota study, Sroufe and colleagues (Sroufe, Egeland, Carlson & Collins, 2005) found disorganized attachment in infancy to be the strongest predictor of global psychopathology at age seventeen and a half years (i.e., number and severity of diagnoses). As described earlier in this chapter, infant disorganization also was associated with disorganized attachment at ages nineteen and twenty-six, which is noteworthy for lack of resolution of loss and trauma. To reiterate, this study provides further evidence that disorganization has the potential to undermine coping capacities.

One additional study is noteworthy in showing how disorganized infant attachment interacts with other developmental factors to initiate a trajectory toward disturbance in adulthood. Carlson and colleagues (E. A. Carlson, Egeland & Sroufe, 2009) reported on results from the Minnesota study that correlated extensive assessments from infancy onward with symptoms of borderline personality disorder diagnosed from structured interviews at age twenty-eight. Borderline personality disorder is noteworthy for combining attachment problems with difficulty in regulating emotional distress, often evident in impulsive and self-destructive behavior. The following early developmental observations related to borderline personality symptoms: attachment disorganization (twelve to eighteen months), maltreatment (twelve to eighteen months), maternal hostility (forty-two months), family disruption related to father presence (twelve to sixty-four months), and family life stress (three to forty-two months). Several harbingers of borderline disorder were evident at twelve years: attentional disturbance, emotional instability, behavioral instability, and relationship disturbance. The findings suggested that identity disturbances evident at twelve years of age may be the link between earlier attachment disorganization and later personality disorder. Imaginative story-telling tasks, for example, revealed violence related to the self, unresolved feelings of guilt or fear, and bizarre images. As in earlier childhood, such findings are suggestive of a nightmarish inner world of relationships. Secure attachments are hard to envision (mentalize), and there is no internal secure base—no compassionate and caring relationship with oneself. Thus, as these authors noted in relation to identity disturbance, "representations and related mentalizing processes are viewed as the carriers of experience" (p. 1328) that link early attachment to later personality disorder.

Adult unresolved-disorganized attachment and psychopathology

Paralleling longitudinal studies relating early attachment to later psychopathology, researchers have investigated the relation between assessments of adult attachment with the AAI and concurrent measures of psychopathology. A review of combined results of AAI studies that incorporated more than 4,200 participants (van Ijzendoorn & Bakermans-Kranenburg, 2008) revealed a strong relationship between the unresolved classification and likelihood of diagnosis with a psychiatric disorder. That is, the prevalence of unresolved-disorganized AAI status was relatively low in non-clinical adolescent and adult samples (16.5% and 15%, respectively); whereas the prevalence was much higher—41%—in the adult the clinical sample. Notably, these combined studies showed an especially strong association between unresolved-disorganized adult attachment and borderline personality disorder, suicidality, and PTSD in relation to a history of abuse.

Stovall-McClough and colleagues (Stovall-McClough, Cloitre & McClough, 2008) reported AAI findings for a sample of 150 women with a history of severe physical, sexual and emotional abuse by a caregiver before age eighteen, coupled with trauma-related symptoms for which they sought psychotherapy. Remarkably, about 50% of the patients were rated as secure; 38% were preoccupied and 12% were dismissing. Yet 43% were unresolved regarding abuse, and being unresolved was associated with a 7.5-fold increase in the likelihood of a PTSD diagnosis (and especially with avoidance symptoms). Moreover, resolution of trauma through treatment was associated with improvement in symptoms of PTSD. Notably, treatment that involved working with traumatic memories was more effective than skills training in promoting resolution.

Such treatment can help in moving from experiential avoidance to experiential acceptance and thereby promote mentalizing.

Summary: disorganization and vulnerability to trauma

Disorganized attachment is associated with early trauma and, sadly, abuse and neglect can be evident in conjunction with disorganized attachment in the first year of life. Yet disorganization also can be associated with non-maltreating patterns of caregiving that are nonetheless frightening to the infant: these include frightened parental states (e.g., dissociative withdrawal) as well as disrupted emotional communication. As Beebe's (Beebe et al., 2010) research documented most starkly, the crux of these precursors of attachment disorganization—whether or not frank maltreatment is involved—is a lack of psychological attunement when the infant is emotional distressed. This lack of attunement can be characterized as an absence of mindful attentiveness and parental mentalizing when the infant most needs these. Consequently, the infant is unable to obtain soothing from others or to self-soothe.

I have reviewed this infant attachment research for two main reasons. First, clinicians must be mindful of this early trauma so as to identify and ameliorate it. The effectiveness of parent-infant and parent-child interventions is encouraging in this regard. Second, disorganized attachment can undermine the developing child's ability to cope with subsequent trauma. That is, throughout development, attachment disorganization is associated with compromise to emotion regulation, mindful attention, and mentalizing capacities. Obviously, abuse and neglect will tax the coping capacities of the most resilient individuals; any of us can be traumatized. But disorganized attachment renders the individual even *more reactive* to stress and *more vulnerable* to being overwhelmed by distress by virtue of impaired emotion regulation coupled with compromised mentalizing capacities. In my view, the most profound limitation to coping is the child's fear of reaching out for comfort at times of distress. This fear robs the child of the most basic and potentially effective means of coping with emotional pain: contact with someone to whom the child is securely attached. To put it simply, disorganized children cannot manage emotions well on their own, and they cannot rely on others for help. In the midst of emotional distress, they evidence impairment in both developmental lines: autonomy and relatedness.

To bring home the significance of this attachment research for later development, I quote Karlen Lyons-Ruth once again: "deviant early caregiving is likely to potentiate the occurrence of later loss or trauma, as well as to increase the likelihood that the trauma will not be resolved" (Lyons-Ruth, Bronfman & Atwood, 1999, p. 44). Furthermore, "attachment disorganization is likely to index a broad relational contribution to maladaptation and psychopathology that cuts across conventional diagnostic categories and interacts with individual biological vulnerability to contribute to a range of psychiatric disorders" (Lyons-Ruth & Jacobvitz, 2008, p. 689).

I present these profoundly troubling findings to set the stage for considering abuse and neglect as traditionally understood next in this chapter. I will reexamine these traditional categories of childhood trauma from the perspective of mentalizing. But I must emphasize now a fundamental fact: attachment disorganization, like any other attachment pattern, is not carved in stone. I am writing about *vulnerability, not destiny*. Attachment research shows that loss and trauma can remain unresolved or be resolved. Improved coping and greater security can develop in infancy, childhood, adolescence, and adulthood. Such change, at any developmental juncture, will stem from greater security in relationships. Professional help is one route to improving relationships. Therapists and patients must remain mindful of the possibility of change as we also face the harsh reality of abuse and neglect and their potential for harm.

Varieties of childhood attachment trauma

Karl Menninger's (1983) litany of child maltreatment is a place to start, and I find it noteworthy that his last sentence implicates the intergenerational transmission of abuse:

> A great deal remains unknown about ideal parenting, although there have been millions of experiments and prescriptions. Some parents learn their task, some never do, and often by the time some find wisdom, their children are no longer children. We know that there are some terrifyingly wrong parental behaviors. Children are beaten, burned, slapped, whipped, thrown about, kicked, and raped daily. Children have been objects of discipline and punishment and senseless cruelty for centuries, since civilization

began. Is there any form of physical abuse that they have not been subjected to?

Worse yet, children are abandoned and neglected and mistaught, lied to, and misinformed. The more we investigate the details of family life in recent centuries of 'civilization'—and even in previous centuries and other cultures—the more we find that child abuse, which is thought of as a modern evil, has been prevalent for eons and eons in older European cultures. Child abuse is a long-standing stain on the record of the human race. Children are weak and small, parents are strong and big; parents can get their way by sheer force, proving (to the child) that 'might makes right.'

No one actually knows or can even imagine how much children are made to suffer by parents who—at least at times—are heartless, sadistic, brutal, or filled with vengeance nursed since their own childhood days! (p. 329)

As it was to Karl Menninger, the basic territory of childhood trauma will be all too familiar to any reader of this book. After barraging you with trauma in childhood, I do not want to belabor the painfully obvious. To say the least, contemplating abuse and neglect is unpleasant—and far worse when it brings back painful memories. I will summarize what I find to be the most useful distinctions so as to highlight mentalizing challenges and failures associated with traumatic experiences.

The first systematic study of childhood abuse was reported in 1860 (Dorahy, van der Hart & Middleton, 2010), but it is only in the past half century that a full range of adversities have been systematically distinguished and documented. Here, I rely heavily on the careful thinking and meticulous research of Bifulco and her colleagues. Bifulco explored the origins of adult episodes of depression in childhood trauma, summarized in an accessible book, *Wednesday's Child* (Bifulco & Moran, 1998). In her research, Bifulco was expanding her mentors' pioneering study of the relation between social stress and depression (G. W. Brown & Harris, 1978).

Here is the list—all too long—of experiences that I will review: physical abuse, sexual abuse, antipathy (rejection), psychological abuse, witnessing domestic violence, physical neglect, and psychological (emotional) neglect. Typically, different forms of abuse and neglect are combined—and repeated—in complex trauma. I will conclude this section with a brief review of recent research on the long-term consequences of childhood trauma.

As you read about these various forms of maltreatment, I invite you to imagine two aspects of the child's experience: first, the feeling of being psychologically alone with no one holding his or her mind in mind; second the challenge of mentalizing, understanding the mind of the abusive person and making sense of what is happening in the relationship. You might contrast such maltreatment with what you would wish for a child who is undergoing a frightening experience, for example, a painful medical procedure. Most of all, you might wish for the comforting presence of a compassionate parent who is emotionally attuned and reassuring. You would want the child to know as much as possible about what will happen and to understand that the procedures are being done with good will, that is, to help and protect the child or to relieve pain. Keep in mind how all this emotional support is absent in frightening and painful abusive experience. I used a painful medical procedure as an example because it is unimaginable—indeed horrifying—to contemplate a parent mindfully mentalizing a child in the midst of abuse. As Fonagy describes, maltreatment is incompatible with promoting mentalizing but rather undermines it:

> In normal circumstances, a parent will be able to protect the child from some of the frightening force of reality, not so much by concealing some events and feelings but by conveying to the child that there is more than one way of seeing things. Perhaps the child has seen the parent being angry, even frightening; if the parent is able to recognize the child's experience, but also to communicate that the fear is unjustified, the child is safe. However, in cases of maltreatment, the child is not safe. Any reassuring communication of containment will be false, further undermining the child's capacity to trust inner reality. (Fonagy, 2001, p. 174)

Physical abuse

Modern awareness of childhood physical abuse began with the identification of the *battered child syndrome* in the early 1960s (Kempe, Silverman, Steele, Droegemueller & Silver, 1962). At some level, the distinction between physical punishment and physical abuse is a matter of degree, and the threshold for distinguishing these varies among subcultures. Obvious distinctions of degree relate to the potential for injury, for example, the differences among being spanked with an open hand, being hit with a belt or a whip, being punched with a closed fist, or being struck with a board—or being hit on the buttocks, the legs, the torso, the head, or the face. The sheer frequency of such events also is a matter of degree.

Yet, with attachment security and mentalizing in mind, we must pay attention to the psychological and relationship context of such abuse. Bifulco and colleagues (Bifulco, Brown & Harris, 1994; Bifulco & Moran, 1998) emphasize the importance of the *threatfulness* of abuse, which not only includes its objective severity (e.g., frequency and extent of injury) but also the nature of the relationship (e.g., a key attachment relationship) and the state of mind of the abuser. Most threatening is the perception that the abuser is out of control in a rage:

> You could really gauge my father because his expression would change—his eyes would become quite manic. He definitely lost control without a doubt. You could see it happen. He would be sitting there and he would be annoyed. Then there would be an explosion and he was completely different. It would be very frightening. (Bifulco & Moran, 1998, p. 69)

To say that the parent in such a violent state has lost mindful attention and mentalizing seems absurdly understated. In thinking about traumatizing behavior (Allen, 2007), I borrow Simon Baron-Cohen's (1995) term for mentalizing impairments in autism: *mindblindness*. The mindblindness of the abuser is central to the potentially terrifying nature of physical abuse. Unpredictability and uncontrollability are hallmarks of traumatic experience (Foa, Zinbarg & Rothbaum, 1992). When the parent fails to mentalize the child, the child loses all influence over the parent's behavior, resulting in a feeling of utter helplessness. And it is not only the parent's behavior but also the parent's state of mind that is terrifying to the child. Not only is the child *unable* to mentalize the parent's state of mind—to make any sense of it—but also the child is *fearful* of mentalizing: the parent's rage, hatred, cruelty, and indifference are too painful to recognize (Fonagy & Target, 1997). Thus, while we generally champion mentalizing, we also must appreciate reasons for defending against mentalizing. Indeed, to recognize the parent's hatred is potentially to experience oneself as hateful. This instance is one of innumerable examples of needing most to mentalize when it is most difficult to do. It is virtually impossible for a young child—or a person of any age—to mentalize in the midst of such terrifying rage or hatred. Yet, ultimately, it is crucial to mentalize—if only years later in psychotherapy—to make the distinction between the parent's hatred and being hateful, or the distinction between *feeling* hateful and *being* hateful.

Sexual abuse

Lagging behind physical abuse, the scope of sexual abuse of females (Herman, 1981) and males (Finkelhor, 1984) first became clear in the 1980s. Even more than physical abuse, sexual abuse covers an extremely wide range of behavior. Without minimizing any of its forms, like physical abuse, sexual abuse varies widely in severity, depending on age inappropriateness, the stressful and threatening nature of the activities, extent of physical contact, frequency and duration of the abusive events, extent of coercion, and—not least—the nature of the relationship with the perpetrator, which includes the abuse of power and trust (Bifulco, Brown, Neubauer, Moran & Harris, 1994). Sexual abuse within an attachment relationship can be particularly traumatic (Trickett, Reiffman, Horowitz & Putnam, 1997).

Sexual abuse, and the mindblindness of the sexually abusive parent, is extraordinary difficult to mentalize and abets defenses against mentalizing. Jennifer Freyd (DePrince & Freyd, 2007; Freyd, 1996) has highlighted this challenge in her theory of *betrayal trauma*. Such betrayal puts the child in an impossible bind: "the person doing the betraying is someone the child cannot afford *not* to trust" (Freyd, 1996, p. 11, emphasis in original). Plainly, protective parenting and a sexual relationship cannot be reconciled in the mind of the abuser or the abused; they are psychologically and biologically incompatible (M. T. Erickson, 1993). Hence, as Freyd's research has demonstrated, a common way of coping with a relationship that defies mentalizing is dissociation—specifically, compartmentalizing the relationship by blocking awareness of the sexual relationship so as to maintain the attachment relationship. The motivation is clear: awareness of the betrayal would endanger the child by threatening the attachment relationship. Dissociation keeps the sexual aspect of the relationship out of mind. Moreover, in the midst of the sexual interaction, dissociative detachment is common, as evident in trance-like states, out-of-body experiences, or deep absorption in imagination, such as imagining oneself elsewhere, such as a flower garden outside the window. With such detachment goes a feeling of unreality. Thus, if the abuse is remembered, it may be recalled with a sense of unreality that bolsters the dissociative compartmentalization, which keeps the abuse separate from ordinary life or identity. And other factors besides dissociation foster compartmentalization: a sense of alternate realities (nightly abuse versus the appearance of daily normality), denial of abuse by the perpetrator, and demands for secrecy, which may be reinforced by dire threats.

Antipathy and psychological abuse

While physical and sexual abuses rightly command our attention, we should not underestimate the impact of what is loosely called "emotional abuse." I still remember with painful embarrassment a moment in a patient education group in which we were discussing where to draw the line in terminating an abusive (adult) relationship. I suggested drawing the line at being hit. A group member was outraged: "The hateful words were far more damaging than being hit!" Here I am contrasting a direct assault on the self with an assault on the body—although an assault to the body surely is an indirect assault on the self.

Bifulco and colleagues usefully distinguish between antipathy and psychological abuse (Bifulco, Brown, Neubauer, Moran & Harris, 1994; Bifulco & Moran, 1998). Antipathy is a deep-seated feeling of dislike, felt by the child as rejection—for example, in relentless criticism and disapproval. Antipathy can be *hot*, as in screaming at the child in a verbally abusive way; and it can be *cold*, as in the silent treatment, ignoring the child, or cold indifference. Antipathy also is evident in favoritism toward one child over another and in scapegoating a particular child. At the extreme, antipathy is the expression of hatred toward the child. To mentalize such antipathy, the child would need to understand the reasons for it. Does it stem from the parent's chronic depression, irritability, and marital dissatisfaction? Is the father's antipathy toward his son rooted in his jealousy of his wife's affection and protectiveness toward the son—something the father lacked in *his* childhood? How can the young child understand such motivation? More likely, the child will mentalize inaccurately—make sense of it—by self-blame.

When such rejection is internalized—taken to heart—it can develop into a deep-seated feeling of dislike toward oneself and, at worst, self-contempt or frank self-hatred, and an internal insecure base.

Although there is no bright line between the two, psychological abuse goes beyond antipathy in entailing outright cruelty, often with malevolent intent (Bifulco, Moran, Baines, Bunn & Stanford, 2002; Moran, Bifulco, Ball, Jacobs & Benaim, 2002). Sadly, psychological abuse takes many forms (Moran, Bifulco, Ball, Jacobs & Benaim, 2002) and gruesome examples abound: deprivation of basic needs (e.g., for food and sleep), deprivation of valued objects (e.g., a stepparent tearing up a treasured photo of a beloved, deceased biological parent; killing a pet); inflicting marked distress (e.g., forcing a child to eat something that makes him vomit; punishing a child by forcing her to kneel on cheese graters); humiliation (e.g., public shaming; rubbing the bedwetting child's face in soiled sheets); extreme rejection (e.g., telling the child of a wish for him to die and describing a horrific death); terrorizing (e.g., playing on the child's fears, such as taking the light bulbs out of the bedroom of a child who is terrified of the dark); emotional blackmail (e.g., a sexually abusive father telling his daughter that he will kill her mother if she doesn't hold the secret); and corruption (e.g., forcing the child into illegal activities, such as pornography).

As these examples attest, at the extreme, psychological abuse can be regarded as *sadistic* abuse (Goodwin, 1993), and we have a rich language to characterize such abusive persons: controlling, demeaning, nasty, vindictive, mean, cruel, malicious, menacing, malevolent, brutal, callous. How does the child mentalize this attitude? As a therapist, I often find myself dumbfounded by patients' experience of cruel treatment. Frequently enough, patients will simply conclude that the sadistically abusive person was "evil," although this attribution calls for explanation more than being an explanation (Allen, 2007, 2013). To repeat Karl Menninger, we are likely to look to the parents' past; perhaps, to repeat his words, sadistic parents are "filled with vengeance nursed since their own childhood days." But this explanation only pushes the mystery back a generation. And this mentalizing option hardly is available to the bewildered child. Moreover, in any case, no such explanation is a justification. Fortunately, to most of us, there is something simply unfathomable about sadistic cruelty, especially directed toward children. As Fonagy and Target (1997) proposed, perhaps the most natural thing the child can do is to shut down mentalizing—to try to avoid awareness of the mind of the parent. Dissociation is one way to do this.

To their detriment, as they do with antipathy, many children find a way of mentalizing such cruelty; they infer that they deserve it. Their badness, stupidity, forgetfulness, weakness, hatefulness brings it on. And all too often the child need not make an inference: the child is blamed explicitly for whatever imagined failings bring about the sadism. Taking on this responsibility provides the child with hope: rather than being completely helpless, if the child only could reform in some way, he or she could prevent the abuse. The potentially lifelong feelings of guilt and shame associated with taking on this responsibility are a high price to pay for an illusory sense of control. But you are inclined to do whatever you can to avoid utter helplessness.

Being terrorized or treated with sadistic cruelty not only is frightening but also is enraging. When you are threatened, there is a fine line between flight and fight. The child's rage only adds another layer to the conflict. The natural impulse to strike back or even to protest in anger puts the child in even greater danger: to fight back risks being hurt worse. Not just expressing the anger but even *feeling* the anger becomes dangerous, because it may lead to protest. Dissociation is one option. Turning the anger inward, from hating the parent to hating oneself, in another option. Little wonder that psychological abuse is associated with a high risk of chronic and recurrent depression in adulthood. Moreover, a history of psychological abuse also is associated with suicidal behavior: self-hate can motivate self-destruction (Bifulco, Moran, Baines, Bunn & Stanford, 2002; Firestone, 2006).

Witnessing domestic violence

Trauma in attachment relationships does not require that the child be the direct target of abuse. Witnessing parental violence not only can be terrifying in its own right but also threatens the child with the loss of the attachment relationships (Lieberman & Zeanah, 1999): mother may be injured or killed, and father may be hauled off to jail.

Even if violence occurs behind closed doors, children hear it. But rarely does the violence remain behind closed doors (Christian, Scribano, Seidl & Pinto-Martin, 1997; Jaffe, Sudermann & Reitzel, 1992). Children not only may witness violence but also are liable to become embroiled in it: infants may be hit while being held; adolescents may be injured while trying to intervene, for example, to protect their mother from their father. And children may feel responsible for the violence if it erupts in relation to them: the child breaks something; the father screams at the child for doing so; the mother screams at the father for screaming at the child; and the father assaults the mother. Moreover, if one parent is hitting another, it is highly likely that the parent also is hitting the child (Ross, 1996).

As with other forms of trauma, witnessing violence is associated with a wide range of behavioral and emotional problems (Osofsky, 1995), one of the most pernicious being the likelihood of repeating what one has observed in childhood in later romantic relationships (Maker, Kemmelmeier & Peterson, 1998). This is one of many instances in which mentalizing is required to break the intergenerational pattern. But, like other forms of abuse, the parental violence itself bespeaks a failure of parental mentalizing, that is, mindblindness to the impact of the violence on the child.

The child's sense of invisibility in the face of parental violence is striking, as work with two patients illustrates. Jane told me of her terror in childhood as her alcoholic mother repeatedly went at her temperamentally volatile father until he erupted in a rage and assaulted her. Such episodes occurred unpredictably, and she lived in fear of them. To make matters worse, her parents forbad her to close her bedroom door at night. Her fear was palpable, even as she recalled these episodes in therapy. But even more painful was her feeling of invisibility to her mindblind parents—the fact that they did not seem to care about what she went through. They never talked about it; and there was never any consolation, no effort at repair. Being psychologically alone with her fear was the most damaging facet of this experience. Similarly, James was repeatedly terrorized by his father's brutal beatings of his mother. After the assaults, he climbed in his mother's bed, shaking in fear. Although his equally frightened mother comforted him as best she could, she forbad him to talk about the violence. In adulthood, he could not feel anger, much less express it—except indirectly in dangerous substance abuse, self-cutting, and suicide attempts.

Physical and psychological neglect

Here is a sad irony: with all the needed attention to abuse, a glaring problem in child protective services is the neglect of neglect

(Wolock & Horowitz, 1984). I think of abuse as involving acts of commission whereas neglect usually entails acts of omission. And I distinguish between physical and psychological neglect.

Two forms of physical neglect have been distinguished (Barnett, Manly & Cicchetti, 1993). Failure to provide for physical needs includes the areas of food, clothing, shelter, healthcare and hygiene. Lack of supervision compromises the child's safety; this includes time left unsupervised ("latchkey children"), dangers unattended in the physical environment (e.g., accessibility of loaded guns), and inadequacy of substitute caregivers (e.g., leaving the child with abusive or neglectful caregivers). As some of these examples attest, at worst, physical neglect can be fatal. In the Minnesota longitudinal study (Sroufe, Egeland, Carlson & Collins, 2005), physical neglect in the four- to six-year-old age group had particularly serious effects, which included anxiety, aggression, unpopularity with peers, and academic failure (Egeland, 1997; M. F. Erickson & Egeland, 1996). To state the obvious, physical neglect exemplifies a lack of mindful attention, not to mention failure to mentalize.

Psychological neglect is the main subject of this book, focusing as I am on caregivers' mentalizing failures—potentially, mindblindness that leaves the child alone in unbearable emotional pain. Here I am in the arena of Bowlby's (1973) initial concern: separation in the sense of psychological disconnection. In the Minnesota study, psychological neglect was aptly termed *psychological unavailability* (M. F. Erickson & Egeland, 1996). Notably, psychological unavailability in infancy had a greater adverse impact on development than physical neglect or other forms of maltreatment. Thus the subtlest form of maltreatment had the most severe consequences. Virtually all psychologically neglected infants were insecurely attached, and their developmental difficulties observed in elementary school included anger, non-compliance, lack of persistence, negativism, impulsivity, dependency, nervousness, and self-destructive behavior.

Physically neglected children are likely to be emotionally neglected as well, but the converse is not true: children can live amongst material plenty while remaining emotionally neglected. As we all know, money is no substitute for love, although it is not uncommonly used as such. Stern (1985) gave an example of the potentially stark contrast between a mother's attentiveness to her infant's physical needs and her obliviousness to the infant's psychological being.

When we first observed the baby arriving for one of her visits, the child was asleep. The mother gently took her sleeping baby and began to lay her on the bed so she would stay asleep. The mother did this with enormous concentration that left us closed out. After she had ever-so-slowly eased the baby's head onto the bed, she took one of the baby's arms, which was awkwardly positioned, and with her two hands carefully guided it to a feather-like landing on the bed, as though the arm were made of eggshells and the bed made of marble. She poured herself into this activity with complete and total participation of her body and preoccupation of her mind. (p. 205)

In light of her mindful attentiveness to the infant's physical wellbeing, it was striking that this mother was evaluated to be the *least emotionally attuned* of all the mothers observed. All her attention was absorbed in ensuring that no physical harm came to the infant; she failed to engage her infant as a person, that is, in a mentalizing or mind-minded way.

Complex trauma and long-term consequences

The distinct forms of abuse and neglect I just delineated rarely occur in isolation from one another. I already noted that marital violence typically is intertwined with physical abuse of children. As you might surmise, psychological abuse is commonly intertwined with other forms of maltreatment (Bifulco, Moran, Baines, Bunn & Stanford, 2002). Other forms of abuse and neglect also commonly accompany sexual abuse, as is true for psychological abuse. Indeed, familial sexual abuse can be viewed as an indicator of severe family dysfunction (Zanarini et al., 1997). In fact, because various forms of maltreatment are so often intermingled, researchers are challenged to distinguish the effects of any one form of abuse from any another.

Research on PTSD reveals a well-established dose-response relationship: the greater the stress, the more severe the resulting disturbance (March, 1993). Thus it is no surprise that exposing a child to multiple forms of maltreatment magnifies the risk of subsequent disturbance (Bifulco & Moran, 1998). Here I am echoing a point made in the chapter on attachment in childhood: long-term adverse consequences typically result from an *accumulation* of risk factors in childhood rather than any single form of adversity.

The research literature on the relation between childhood trauma and adulthood illness is vast (Lanius, Vermetten & Pain, 2010), and I will merely summarize the results of one landmark study for illustrative purposes (Felitti & Anda, 2010). The Adverse Childhood Experiences (ACE) study, carried out in Kaiser Permanente's Department of Preventive Medicine in San Diego, included over 17,000 middle-class participants, 80% of whom were white, and equally divided between males and females. Ten categories of childhood adversity reported to have occurred before eighteen years of age were tallied, and the prevalence of many (in parentheses) was high: emotional abuse (11%); physical abuse (28%); contact sexual abuse (28% of women and 16% of men); mother treated violently (13%); alcoholic- or drug-abusing household member (27%); imprisoned household member (6%); chronically depressed, suicidal, mentally ill, or psychiatrically hospitalized household member (17%); not raised by both biological parents (23%); physical neglect (19%); and emotional neglect (15%). Each participant was assigned a total ACE score based on the number of categories of abuse reported.

The findings of the ACE study are dramatic. Adversities go together: if any one category is reported, there is an 87% likelihood of exposure to at least one other. Concomitantly, the number of individuals with high ACE scores is far greater than it would be if each adversity occurred independently of the others. The likelihood of long-term adverse consequences increases dramatically as the childhood adversities pile up. Reporting four or more adversities, for example, typically was associated with highly elevated rates of later problems in a wide range of domains. Some examples: lifetime history of depression and suicide attempts; rates of antidepressant medication prescriptions; rates of smoking, alcohol dependence, and intravenous drug use; serious financial and job performance problems; teen pregnancy, teen paternity, and likelihood of more than fifty sexual partners; and risk of liver disease or chronic obstructive pulmonary disease. Perhaps most striking: those with an ACE score of six or more had a lifespan almost two decades shorter than those with an ACE score of zero. Plainly, childhood trauma, including attachment trauma, is a social problem of monumental proportions.

Attachment trauma in adulthood

Recall that attachment trauma refers to traumatic experience within an attachment relationship as well as the traumatizing effects of that experience. Attachment trauma in childhood is especially troubling, owing to its potential influence on the entire course of subsequent development. Nevertheless, the various forms of childhood abuse and neglect just reviewed have their adult counterparts, and such adulthood experience also can undermine the capacity to form secure attachments. Obviously, the traumatic adulthood attachment relationship will be insecure; yet subsequent attachment relationships also are liable to become infused with fear and distrust. Naturally, you learn to fear what has hurt you: if you have been hurt in emotionally close relationships in adulthood, even if your childhood relationships were secure, you might learn to fear emotional closeness thereafter.

> Marjorie sought psychotherapy after months of social withdrawal, during which time she became progressively more depressed and dependent on alcohol, which only worsened her depression. Her depression had become especially severe in the aftermath of her divorce from her husband, Mark, whose behavior had escalated from criticism to verbal abuse and then to violent arguments in which he became physically threatening.
>
> This abusive and violent behavior was unlike anything Marjorie had experienced previously in her lifetime. Her father had been somewhat domineering and demanding, but he was highly protective and never downright frightening. Marjorie recognized that she identified with her mother, who was relatively compliant with her father's controlling behavior and who had learned to avoid making waves. In hindsight, she was able to see that Mark's domineering style had appealed to her in its familiarity, giving her some sense of security. Yet she was blindsided by the abusive turn in his behavior and faulted herself for being naïve. After the divorce, she was afraid that she could not trust her own judgment about men, and she feared being alone indefinitely. She was able to use the therapy to reflect on the development of problems in the relationship and to rekindle her hope of exploring future intimate relationships, albeit with more caution.

As indicated in reviewing attachment in adulthood, romantic relationships are the prototype of adult attachments, and these relationships have been the focus of theory and research on attachment trauma in adulthood. Lenore Walker's (1979) classic book, *The Battered Woman*, based on interviews of more than 100 women, staked out the full territory—encompassing physical, sexual, and psychological abuse as well as neglect. In the decades since Walker's pioneering work, the alarming worldwide prevalence of battering has been documented (Walker, 1999), and women have been found to be as physically aggressive as men in intimate relationships, albeit with less intensity and damaging consequences (Schafer, Caetano & Clark, 1998).

Walker (1979) identified a now well-known three-phase cycle: escalating tension and minor incidents of aggression lead to an acute battering incident, followed by reconciliation as exemplified by the batterer's contrition and loving behavior. As Walker observed, "The women interviewed consistently admitted, although somewhat shamefacedly, that they loved their men dearly during this phase. The effect of their men's generosity, dependability, helpfulness, and genuine interest cannot be minimized" (p. 69). Hence, paradoxically, battered women become more intensely attached to their batterer in a pattern of *traumatic bonding* (Dutton & Painter, 1981) that makes sense in attachment terms: abuse escalates fear; fear heightens attachment needs; and attachment is reinforced by the illusory safe haven during the third phase of reconciliation.

Coercion is a prototypical form of exerting interpersonal influence by nonmentalizing means. Coercion lies at the heart of battering relationships, and coercive power is at the core of sadistic psychological abuse. Terrorizing is evident in threats not only to the partner but also to her children, other family members, and friends. Moreover, as Walker documented, battering relationships are characterized not only by abusive coercion but also by neglect. The adult counterpart to childhood physical neglect is economic deprivation, and the counterpart to psychological neglect is the blatant lack of emotional attunement to the pain inflicted except during the intermittent periods of ostensibly loving respite.

As it is in childhood, the combination of abuse and psychological neglect, alternating with care and respite from fear, are profoundly challenging to mentalize in adult attachment relationships. It is natural to turn your mind away from hate and sadism, especially in an attachment relationship. Dissociative detachment and compartmentalizing—putting blinkers on—are understandable alternatives to mentalizing. Yet denial and emotional numbing can put the battered person at risk for further abuse. Moreover, in adulthood as in childhood, you are vulnerable to distorted mentalizing: criticism, derogation, and blame can be internalized as self-blame and self-hate, with attendant anxiety, guilt feelings, and shame.

It is common for persons who have been abused in childhood to enter unwittingly into abusive relationships in adulthood. This process strikes me as involving a profound mentalizing challenge. It is understandable for someone who has lived in fear to seek a protective mate, for example, for a woman to select a man who appears strong, self-confident, and dominant—willing to take over in a protective way. Yet such ostensible strength can be an illusion, a cover for insecure attachment. Recall the apparent independence associated with avoidant attachment and the later controlling caregiving behavior associated with infant disorganization. It is sadly common for marriage to be a turning point.

> Nichole married Patrick in her early twenties; they had been high school sweethearts and he had become like a member of their family. Patrick's father had died when Patrick was a child, and he developed a close relationship with Nichole's father. Nichole had long been concerned about Patrick's irritability, and she described him as being "pushy" in a literal sense: he occasionally pushed her when she was in his way or not moving fast enough to suit him. But, like the rest of Nichole's family, Patrick came under the orbit of Nichole's father's protectiveness: he was an imposing full-bearded man who indeed resembled a big teddy bear. Apart from his occasional irritability and pushy behavior, Patrick adopted the mantle of Nichole's father, treating her affectionately and kindly.
>
> Tragically, Nichole's father was killed in an accident two years after her marriage. Soon thereafter, she and Patrick moved to another state where he had taken a new job. Stressed by the loss of his "adopted father" and by the move and new job, Patrick became more consistently sullen and irritable. Worse yet, with Nichole outside the protective orbit of her family, Patrick became downright derisive and aggressive, particularly after he'd been out drinking. Although Nichole was able to see the seeds of his aggression, she felt as if Patrick had made a 180-degree turn once he felt she was under his total control.

Perhaps it is never more important to mentalize accurately than when selecting a mate. But how good are any of us in judging character? I tend to be trusting—believing what I am told—and I have been blindsided by patients' behavior often enough, even when I felt I knew them well. And making such judgments is even harder if defenses have been erected against seeing malevolence. The best way forward for persons who have been blindsided by betrayal and battering is to learn from experience, identify red flags, move cautiously, and talk through the relationship as it is evolving, with trusted confidants and, potentially, in psychotherapy.

Clinical implications

The inclusion of PTSD in the diagnostic lexicon in the 1980s has contributed to a narrow conception of trauma, which I have endeavored to dispel in this chapter. To a large extent, potentially traumatic events are defined in relation to physical danger, namely, "actual or threatened death or serious injury, or a threat to the physical integrity of self or others" (APA, 2000, p. 467). I have taken a far wider view in emphasizing the potentially traumatic consequences associated with repeated experiences of psychological disconnection in attachment relationships in the context of extreme distress. Feeling endangered is especially likely to be traumatic in an attachment context lacking in mindful mentalizing. To reiterate Fonagy and Target's understanding, attachment trauma poses a dual liability not only in evoking extreme distress but also in undermining the development of the capacity to regulate distress.

I will discuss treatment in the final chapter of this book, but I provide a glimpse of this material here while the review of attachment theory and research is fresh. Attachment trauma is the bane of psychotherapy, because traumatized patients most need what they most fear: attachment. Hence our patients share the plight of the disorganized infant: they are in the throes of fright without solution. Moreover, psychotherapy is founded in a mindful, mentalizing process; attachment trauma undermines the capacity to engage in that process *while in a state of distress*—the very reason patients seek psychotherapy. Accordingly, seeking psychotherapy in desperation, patients are liable to avoid experiencing and expressing distress and, when they do so, they are unlikely to be able to make use of the elusive security of the psychotherapy relationship to assuage their distress.

As countless clinicians who have conducted psychotherapy with traumatized patients are likely to attest, treatment is difficult but not impossible. Perforce, patients who seek psychotherapy have not given up on attachment. I am convinced that they come to us psychotherapists with islands of security as well as substantially intact albeit precarious mentalizing capacity. I have employed the first four chapters of this book to set the stage for the seamless transition to the application of a fundamental developmental principle to psychotherapy: mentalizing begets mentalizing in a way that is conducive to increasing security in attachment relationships. Paralleling the pattern of caregiving that is conducive to secure attachment, we psychotherapists must endeavor to be mindfully attentive and psychologically available while taking care not to be too intrusive so as to give our patients needed space. In so doing, we support a balance of relatedness and autonomy.

I have an interim step to take before discussing treatment at more length, namely, linking attachment and mentalizing to neurobiological research. We have arrived at an era in which seeing is believing: we are more convinced of the validity of our theories when they are demonstrated in physiological markers and patterns of brain activity made manifest by neuroimaging. While the behavioral findings I have reviewed in the chapters thus far stand on their own, I find the neurobiological research illuminating as well as important in underscoring the reality—and seriousness—of attachment trauma.

CHAPTER FIVE

Neurobiological connections

It is a truism that all the processes I have discussed in this book have a biological basis; this chapter provides some substance for that truism. I am not keen on what I have dubbed *biomania*, that is, excessive enthusiasm for exclusive focus on neurobiological findings as the be-all and end-all of understanding psychological processes and psychiatric disorders. Yet neuroscience is yielding findings that are not only intrinsically fascinating but also promise to enhance our self-understanding. Put simply, we are now in a position to begin using our expanding knowledge about the brain to understand the organization of the mind (Shallice & Cooper, 2011).

This chapter links current neurobiological research to the main topics of previous chapters: attachment and attachment trauma, mindfulness, and mentalizing. I also use the neurobiological framework to highlight the role of consciousness in the development of the self and in emotion regulation, giving prominence to the role of the prefrontal cortex in these processes. I make no pretense of providing a comprehensive review but rather aim to illustrate the potential contributions of neuroscience to our understanding of attachment and mentalizing and to illuminate some of their key facets along the way.

Attachment

Bowlby construed attachment as a biological phenomenon, and we now have the benefit of decades of neurobiological research that promises to refine our understanding of attachment. We can hardly link attachment to a localized brain area; as Jim Coan (2008) stated, "because so many neural structures are involved one way or another in attachment behavior, it is possible to think of the entire human brain as a neural attachment system" (p. 244). Acknowledging the huge scope of this domain of knowledge, I will hit a few highlights. I start where Bowlby did, with evolution. Then I will focus on an obvious point: we develop attachment relationships because they are rewarding. To underscore this point, I will summarize research on maternal preoccupation and then review research on two brain systems associated with attachment and reward, that is, systems activated by dopamine and endogenous opioids. This review will set the stage for discussion of a neuropeptide that has taken center stage in attachment research, oxytocin, which activates these reward processes. After a note on the relation of addictive substances to attachment circuitry, I conclude this section with consideration of the neurobiological impact of attachment trauma.

Evolution

Bowlby (1958) was on solid ground when he anchored attachment theory in evolutionary biology. As Coan (2008) put it, "One of the most striking things about humans (and many other mammals) is how well *designed* we are for affiliation" (p. 247, emphasis in original). Jaak Panksepp (1998) pointed out, "Momentous evolutionary changes must have occurred when animals with an urge to take care of their offspring emerged on the face of the earth" (p. 246).

Attachment plays a central role in Paul MacLean's (1985, 1990) influential conception of the triune brain, which evolved in three broad stages: reptilian, paleo-mammalian, and neo-mammalian. Of interest here is the paleo-mammalian brain, loosely called the limbic brain (and even more loosely the emotional brain), in contrast to the late-evolving neocortex. In MacLean's (1985) view, the development of the paleo-mammalian brain set the stage for a family way of life:

> If one were to choose three outward behavioral manifestations that most clearly distinguish the evolutionary transition from reptiles

to mammals, the triad would be (1) nursing, in conjunction with maternal care, (2) the separation call, and (3) play. I single out the separation call because it is probably the most primitive and basic mammalian vocalization, serving originally to maintain maternal-offspring contact. (p. 405)

MacLean's interests were not far from Freud's and Bowlby's when he wrote, "When mammals opted for a family way of life, they set the stage for one of the most distressful forms of suffering. A condition that, for us, makes being a mammal so painful is having to endure separation or isolation from loved ones" (p. 415). He gave this problem of separation ancient roots: "Some 180 million years ago there must have been a first time when the first mammalian ancestor let out a separation call" (p. 415). Two of MacLean's core functions of the paleo-mammalian brain—maternal care and the separation cry—obviously lie at the heart of attachment, but we should not lose sight of the related function of the third: "one of the main functions of PLAY circuitry is to help construct social brains" (Panksepp, 2009). I think of play in the context of the secure base for exploration in the realm of social learning.

Inasmuch as the capacity for intensive caregiving evolved in tandem with humans' prolonged dependence, Fonagy (2006) proposed, "Evolution has charged attachment relationships with ensuring the full development of the social brain" (p. 60). The brain remains plastic throughout life, but its plasticity is greatest in the earliest years of life, as brain volume quadruples between birth and age six; this early plasticity makes for monumental learning capacity but also renders the developing brain vulnerable to trauma (Giedd, 2003). Thus attachment not only played a major role in brain evolution but also plays an equally significant role in individual brain development (Fonagy, Gergely & Target, 2007; Schore, 2001; Siegel, 1999).

Attachment and reward

As every parent knows, raising a child is enormously costly in time, energy, effort, and material resources. Moreover, as just noted, we humans require an exceptionally prolonged period of childrearing (now extending into early adulthood!). Plainly, the rewards outweigh the costs—unless something goes drastically awry in attachment, as it does in conjunction with child neglect. Given the costs, the rewards of parenting must be powerful, and evolution has ensured this incentive through parental love which, early in development, takes the form of *preoccupation.*

James Swain and colleagues (Swain, Thomas, Leckman & Mayes, 2008a) characterize the period that begins toward the end of pregnancy and extends through the first months of the infant's life as one that "would resemble a mental illness of acute onset" were it not for the context. More specifically,

> In this period, mothers are deeply focused on the infant to the apparent conscious exclusion of all else; this preoccupation heightens their ability to anticipate the infant's needs, learn his or her unique signals, and over time to develop a sense of the infant as an individual. (p. 266)

Prior to delivery, this preoccupation can be focused on preparing the environment for the infant (e.g., the nursery). Preoccupation peaks around the time of delivery and, at two weeks postpartum, mothers spend an average of fourteen hours a day focused exclusively on the infant. Fathers share this preoccupation but to a lesser degree, spending about half this time focused on the infant. This gender difference also is evident in responsiveness to infants' cries in the early weeks postpartum: patterns of brain activation in response to their baby's cries show more arousal in mothers than fathers.

Maternal preoccupation includes feelings of unity and reciprocity with the infant as well as thoughts about the infant's perfection. The preoccupation also includes worries and concerns about parental adequacy and the wellbeing of the infant. Either too much or too little preoccupation can be problematic: too much preoccupation can be evidenced in anxious obsessiveness; at worst, too little preoccupation could be associated with neglect or abuse. Notably, by undermining the capacity for interest and pleasure that makes caregiving rewarding, maternal depression also can interfere with the normal level of preoccupation and thus hamper the development of attachment.

Our survival as a species and as individuals depends not only on taking care of offspring but also a host of other activities, including eating, drinking, and having sex. Evolution has ensured that all these activities are tied to brain reward circuitry. One such circuit is activated by the neurotransmitter, dopamine, which is produced in the ventral tegmental area and activates a cascade of brain areas including the amygdala, bed nucleus of the stria terminalis, ventral striatum (including the nucleus accumbens), and the frontal cortex. As Panksepp (1998) argued, it is misleading to construe this dopaminergic circuit simply as a brain reward system, although its activation is associated with pleasurable feelings. Instead, Panksepp labels it the SEEKING system, attuned to stimuli that predict rewards. This system thus energizes exploration and goal-directed behavior, and you experience its activation as engaged curiosity, eager anticipation, intense interest, and excitement. Psychostimulants, such as cocaine and amphetamines, activate this circuitry, and animals offered the opportunity to stimulate the circuits through implanted electrodes will do so until they collapse in exhaustion or die—sadly suggestive of addicts who take cocaine to the point that their heart stops.

As you might have surmised from my bringing it up, the dopaminergic circuit is active in attachment relationships, contributing to their rewarding nature. Dopamine activity is associated with sexual interest and arousal, thus motivating relationships that can evolve into enduring attachments (or pair bonds, in the animal world). Dopamine activity also is associated with maternal interest in infants. Exposing rat mothers to their pups induces dopamine activity, and blocking this circuitry disrupts maternal behavior (Insel, 2003). Notably, rat mothers prefer access to their pups to access to cocaine at eight days postpartum, but they prefer cocaine to their pups at sixteen days postpartum, perhaps indicative of waning maternal preoccupation!

A number of researchers have studied differences in mothers' patterns of brain activation in response to seeing pictures of their own infants compared to other infants (Swain, 2011; Swain, Thomas, Leckman & Mayes, 2008b); these studies also reveal activation of dopamine-related reward processes. Research by Andreas Bartles and Semir Zeki (Bartles & Zeki, 2000, 2004; Zeki, 2009) illustrates. For an initial study of romantic love, male and female participants who were deeply and madly in love were recruited for brain scans while viewing pictures of their romantic partner as contrasted with pictures of friends. A subsequent study recruited mothers for brain scans while they viewed pictures of their own child as contrasted with a child with whom they were acquainted, their best friend, and another person with whom they were acquainted. Although these researchers found differences between romantic and maternal love in patterns of brain activity evoked by pictures of loved ones, both were associated with activation of the dopaminergic system. A subsequent study (Strathearn, Li, Fonagy & Montague, 2008) in which first-time mothers were exposed to pictures of their own infant and matched pictures of unknown infants controlled for the emotional expression of the infants, that is, showing happy, sad, or emotionally neutral expressions. In this study, the happy faces, not the sad faces, activated dopaminergic pathways.

Whereas the dopaminergic system is active in appetitive behavior, or wanting, the endogenous opioid system is active in consummatory behavior, or liking (Panksepp, 1998). In Panksepp's view, the opioid system is active in conjunction with "the emotional gratification of social connectedness" (Panksepp, Nelson & Bekkedal, 1999, p. 225). Thus brain opioid activity is associated with childbirth, nursing, caregiving, soothing touch, grooming, sex, and play (Coan, 2008). External opiates, such as morphine and heroin, artificially induce gratification akin to that achieved by release of endogenous opioids (Panksepp, 1998).

Given the relation between social interaction and opioid activity, it is not surprising that opioids are associated with the alleviation of separation distress through comforting contact, which Panksepp (1998) construes as a "secure neurochemical base" (p. 266). Opioid release suppresses separation cries, and MacLean long ago noted that morphine eliminated the separation call in squirrel monkeys, whereas administration of an opiate antagonist reinstated the calls. Thus the opioid system is provides powerful reinforcement for social contact in two senses: first, such contact is inherently pleasurable (positive reinforcement); second such contact can reduce emotional distress (negative reinforcement). Indeed, nothing is more reinforcing than escaping pain. It is little wonder that Bowlby centered attachment theory around proximity seeking; these bonds are cemented through potent reward systems and relief from distress in particular.

Earlier in this chapter I commented on the interplay of romantic love and attachment, and here it is worth noting their neurochemical interplay. Panksepp (1998) associates erotic love primarily with dopaminergic activation and maternal love with opioid activation. Yet dopamine activation is common to both; moreover these two systems interact in a number of ways, for example, through arousal of dopamine by opiate receptors in the ventral tegmental area and through opiate inhibition of dopamine activity in the striatum. Accordingly, Panksepp muses that, with the experimental disentangling of these brain systems, "it will be remarkable to behold how erotic love and nurturant love are dynamically intertwined within subcortical neural circuits," and he proposes that "we may begin to understand why they are often tangled in the higher cognitive reaches of our minds" (p. 265).

When he noted that morphine reduces the separation call, Paul MacLean (1985) mused, "Is it possible that one of the attractions of opiate drugs is that they provide some people a surcease from persisting feelings of 'separation' or alienation?" (p. 414). Thomas Insel (2003) addressed this question as to whether substance abuse and drug addiction are attempts to replace the neurobiological effects of attachment relationships in his article, "Is social attachment an addictive disorder?" Given the research reviewed in this section, it seems a short leap to an affirmative answer to MacLean's question. As we will see, oxytocin enhances activity in two prominent brain systems linked to reward: dopaminergic and opioid. Think of cocaine (dopamine) and heroin (opioid).

As Insel states, research on drugs of abuse has yielded a great deal of knowledge about brain reward systems. As he notes, these reward pathways "evolved not for drug abuse but for mediating the motivational aspects of social interaction, including pair bonding, maternal attachment to infants, and presumably infant attachment to mother" (p. 356). Accordingly, Insel proposed that drugs such as cocaine and heroin "hijack" the neural systems that evolved in conjunction with attachment (p. 352). In educating patients, we make the point that addictions serve as an alternate means of alleviating stress in the context of insecure (e.g., avoidant) attachment. This phenomenon evidently has long evolutionary roots: compared to their satisfied cohorts, rejected-isolated fruit flies (having experienced repeated rejection of their sexual advances) showed an elevated preference for alcohol (Shohat-Ophir, Kaun, Azanchi & Heberlein, 2012). For us humans, it is little wonder that restoring social bonds, as support groups do, is a mainstay of addictions treatment.

Oxytocin and maternal love

Nearly forty years ago when we lived in northern Illinois, my wife and I travelled to the University of Illinois in the southern part of the state to visit her former biology professor, Lowell Getz. Ignorant as I was, I was somewhat bemused by his keen interest in voles—small rodents resembling mice, of which there is a multitude of species. I remember watching them scurrying along the fencerows. Thus I was amused decades later to find that he and his colleagues were pioneering research that has since captured the attention of attachment researchers (Carter et al., 1999).

Handily, nature has provided attachment researchers with experimental and control groups in different species of voles (Insel & Young, 2001; Young & Wang, 2004). Prairie voles are monogamous; they form enduring pair bonds and provide biparental care to their young. Moreover, if they lose a mate, they do not take another partner. Their monogamy is based on the formation of partner preferences during mating, and even cohabitation without mating can lead to partner preferences in this species. In contrast, nonmonogamous montane and meadow voles are promiscuous; they do not form partner preferences. These species differences are neatly tied to the neuropeptide, oxytocin, and a closely related neuropeptide, vasopressin; both neuropeptides facilitate pair bonding, although oxytocin plays a more important role in females and vasopressin in males (Neumann, 2008).

All aspects of monogamy are enhanced in prairie voles by central injections of oxytocin or vasopressin (Insel & Young, 2001) and inhibited by injections of their antagonists. Blocking of the neuropeptides does not inhibit mating, but it does inhibit formation of partner preferences during mating. In contrast, neither of these neuropeptides affects behavior in nonmonogamous voles. The species differences are clear: receptors for both neuropeptides are expressed in the dopaminergic pathways of monogamous voles (oxytocin in the nucleus accumbens, vasopressin in the ventral pallidum) but not in those of nonmonogamous voles. Hence the release of these neuropeptides, which occurs during mating, activates the dopaminergic reward circuits in monogamous (but not nonmonogamous) voles, resulting in bonding to unique individuals.

Sue Carter (1998) referred to oxytocin as the "hormone of maternal love" (p. 792), and decades of research on our mammalian kin has documented the extensive role of oxytocin in attachment (Neumann, 2008; Strathearn, 2011; Striepens, Kendrick, Maier & Hurlemann, 2011). Oxytocin plays a role in delivery by facilitating intrauterine contractions and after birth by triggering milk letdown. Oxytocin also promotes partner preferences and bonding in a bidirectional fashion, promoting maternal bonding to infants and infant attachment to mothers.

Moreover, oxytocin is a candidate for a neurobiological mediator of intergenerational transmission of attachment (Strathearn, 2011): maternal oxytocin is associated with maternal nurturing; maternal nurturing might influence the development of the oxytocin system in female offspring; ultimately, such influence could affect the offspring's maternal behavior. Conversely, deficiencies on oxytocin could portend a trajectory of intergenerational maternal neglect.

Animal research also attests to the ongoing role of oxytocin in adult attachment (Neumann, 2008; Striepens, Kendrick, Maier & Hurlemann, 2011). Oxytocin promotes social recognition and memory, hence facilitates pair bonding. In addition, oxytocin levels are enhanced by positive social interactions, including mating, and oxytocin activates brain reward systems. Moreover, oxytocin attenuates anxiety and stress by inhibiting activation of the amygdala and the hypothalamic-pituitary-adrenal axis. Accordingly, oxytocin plays a key role in the calming effect of social contact in the face of stress. The combination of enhanced pleasure and diminished distress is hard to beat, underscoring the parallel between attachment and addiction discussed earlier.

Oxytocin and human social bonds

Experimental study of the influence of oxytocin on human social behavior has been facilitated by the fact that intranasal inhalation can be employed to increase brain levels of oxytocin—a few puffs in each nostril will do. Rapidly proliferating studies are demonstrating the influence of oxytocin on cooperation, trust, judgments of trustworthiness, emotional empathy, and generosity (Striepens, Kendrick, Maier & Hurlemann, 2011). A sample of studies illustrates.

A study by Adam Guastella and colleagues (Guastella, Mitchell & Dadds, 2008) illustrates the fundamental level at which oxytocin exerts its effects. After sniffing oxytocin, males were exposed to a set of twenty-four human faces with neutral emotional expressions. Compared to the control (placebo) group, those who were administered oxytocin gazed longer at the eye region of the faces, notable because the eye region is the primary source of facial information pertinent to detection of emotional states. In a subsequent study, Guastella and colleagues (Guastella & Mitchell, 2008) demonstrated that oxytocin enhanced memory for happy faces, from which they inferred that oxytocin facilitates encoding of positive social information conducive to social approach, intimacy, and bonding. In a similar vein, Gregor Domes and colleagues (Domes, Heinrichs & Michel, 2007) explored the impact of oxytocin on perception of facial expressions of emotion. Participants were administered the Reading the Mind in the Eyes Test, which has been employed to study mentalizing ability. Participants state what emotions are displayed in photographs of faces that are cropped around the eye region (Baron-Cohen, Wheelwright, Hill, Raste & Plumb, 2001). Intranasal administration of oxytocin improved participants' scores on this test, consistent with the positive role of oxytocin in social relationships. In a subsequent study, Domes and colleagues (Domes, Heinrichs, Glascher et al., 2007) found that oxytocin administration diminished amygdala responses to perceptions of faces displaying a range of emotions (fearful, angry, and happy) and, consistent with Guastella and colleagues, they concluded that oxytocin facilitates social approach behavior. Notably, however, with respect to the role of oxytocin in reading emotions, a subsequent study (Pincus et al., 2010) failed to show that oxytocin improved accuracy on Reading the Mind in the Eyes Test, although the researchers found differences in brain activity among depressed and healthy participants in response to oxytocin as they were performing this task.

Given its well-known role in fear responses, Peter Kirsch and colleagues (Kirsch et al., 2005) employed amygdala activity as a marker of threat response to fear-inducing pictures (i.e., threatening faces or scenes). Prior to the brain scan, the male participants were administered either oxytocin or placebo. Oxytocin attenuated amygdala activation in response to both forms of threatening stimuli, especially for the faces. Moreover, oxytocin decreased the functional connectivity of the amygdala to the brainstem, reducing the amygdala's characteristic orchestration of the fear response. In a related study with direct clinical significance, another group of researchers found that oxytocin administration normalized amygdala hyperactivity in persons with social phobia (Labuschagne et al., 2010). Notably, however, the effects of oxytocin on amygdala activity extend beyond attenuating distressing emotions. As noted earlier, oxytocin reduced males' amygdala activation not only in response to fearful and angry facial expressions but also to happy expressions (Domes, Heinrichs, Glascher et al., 2007). The authors concluded that amygdala responses to social cues reflect uncertainty, and oxytocin reduces uncertainty, thereby facilitating social approach.

One study illustrates the potential social impact of administering oxytocin (Kosfeld, Heinrichs, Zak, Fischbacher & Fehr, 2005). Participants were males who played a trust game with monetary stakes. Investors (exposed to oxytocin or placebo) were invited to transfer varying amounts of money to trustees, who had the option of returning various amounts of money to investors. Investors could maximize their gains by transferring more money to trustees—but only if the trustees shared their earnings. The results were clear: under the influence of oxytocin, investors transferred more money, indicating greater trust and greater willingness to accept risk in social interactions. As discussed next, and especially pertinent to attachment, oxytocin also plays a significant role in social regulation of emotional stress.

Markus Heinrichs and colleagues (Heinrichs, Baumgartner, Kirschbaum & Ehlert, 2003) exposed a group of men to a significant social stressor: in front of a panel, the men participated in a mock job interview and also performed mental arithmetic. Their level of stress was measured by secretion of cortisol, a stress hormone. One group of participants had the social support of their best friend prior to the stress; another group had no social support. In addition, some participants were given intranasal oxytocin at the beginning of the experiment, whereas others were administered a placebo. The results were straightforward: both social support and oxytocin decreased stress, but their combination was most powerful, suggesting that oxytocin enhanced the stress-buffering effect of social support.

Owing to its role in attachment, we might view oxytocin as an anti-stress hormone, but some research findings caution about going overboard with this idea. Shelly Taylor and colleagues (Taylor, Saphire-Bernstein & Seeman, 2010) found that oxytocin levels in women and vasopressin levels in men were elevated in conjunction with *distress* in their primary attachment relationship, and they proposed that oxytocin might be a biological signal to seek other sources of social support. Moreover, the extent to which oxytocin facilitates or hinders social relationships appears to depend on security of attachment. In one study, Jennifer Bartz and colleagues (Bartz, Zaki et al., 2010) found that administering oxytocin positively biased securely attached males' recollections of their childhood relationship with their mother (i.e., as having been more caring and close), whereas it had the opposite effect for males who were insecurely attached: oxytocin led them to remember their relationships as *less* caring and close. Moreover, these researchers also contrasted participants with and without borderline personality disorder in their behavior in a trust game that involved exchange of money (Bartz, Simeon et al., 2010). For participants with borderline personality disorder, oxytocin *decreased* trust and cooperation, an effect that was particularly pronounced for participants who showed a high level of anxiety in attachments combined with an aversion to closeness. Thus the effects of increasing oxytocin levels may be positive or negative, depending on the quality of attachment.

This cursory review of ongoing research merely hints at the complexity of findings. Yet the experimental research generally supports the broad hypothesis that oxytocin promotes bonding to individuals by virtue of rendering social cues more memorable and rewarding. Moreover, oxytocin plays a significant role in social stress regulation. Accordingly, the potential therapeutic uses of oxytocin in treating patients with psychiatric disorders (including PTSD) are being explored actively (Striepens, Kendrick, Maier & Hurlemann, 2011). Stay tuned.

Oxytocin and human parental bonds

I have not concealed my enthusiasm for many facets of attachment research, and I consider the sample of studies to be reviewed next to be particularly remarkable. Again, I am merely hitting some highlights from a burgeoning research literature evaluating the complex network of brain regions associated with parental responsiveness, complicated by the fact that "The parental brain is also a moving target, subject to adaptive plastic changes associated with postpartum, so richly affected by the baby" (Swain, 2011, p. 1251).

Ruth Feldman and colleagues' research program has yielded powerful and informative findings. These authors (Feldman, Weller, Zagoory-Sharon & Levine, 2007) sampled plasma levels of oxytocin in married, pregnant women at three points: the first trimester, the third trimester, and in the first postpartum month. At this third point, they videotaped fifteen minutes of mother-infant interaction, computing a composite score for maternal bonding based on the extent of gaze at the infant's face, positive emotion, affectionate touch, and "motherese" speech (i.e., high-pitched, sing-song, infant-directed vocalizations). They also assessed mothers' thoughts and feelings about their infant. They found that oxytocin levels were stable across time (suggesting stable traits) and that higher levels of oxytocin were associated with higher scores on bonding behaviors; more attachment-related thoughts about the infant (e.g., imagining the infant when apart from the infant); and more frequent checking on the infant.

In a subsequent study, Feldman and colleagues (Feldman, Gordon, Schneiderman, Weisman & Zagoory-Sharon, 2010) related plasma oxytocin levels to mothers' and fathers' manner of touching their four-to-six-month-old infants in a fifteen-minute play situation. Baseline oxytocin levels were assessed prior to play, and levels were reassessed after the play session. Prior research had indicated that mothers are more prone to engage in affectionate touch whereas fathers are more inclined to engage in rough-and-tumble, stimulatory touch that promotes exploratory play (i.e., in effect, mothers are more inclined to provide a safe haven and fathers a secure base for exploration). These typical parental gender differences were evident in the findings: greater increases in oxytocin levels were associated with more affectionate touch in mothers and with more stimulatory touch in fathers, suggesting differences between fathers and mothers in patterns of touch that they found most rewarding. In related experimental study, Fabienne Naber and colleagues (Naber, van Ijzendoorn, Deschamps, van Engeland & Bakermans-Kranenburg, 2010) found that intranasal administration of oxytocin increased fathers' stimulation of their toddlers' exploratory play while decreasing signs of hostility—again, attesting to the role of oxytocin in fathers' promotion of a secure base.

In a more recent and comprehensive study, Feldman and colleagues (Feldman, Gordon & Zagoory-Sharon, 2011) assessed mothers' and fathers' bonding to their parents and the quality of their romantic attachment as well as their attachment representations of their infants. They also assessed parental and infant engagement and affective synchrony during play, and the related all these assessments to oxytocin samples in plasma, saliva, and urine. They found high oxytocin levels to be associated with more positive parental bonding and more secure romantic attachment as well as with parent-infant attachment representations. In addition, high oxytocin levels related to higher levels of parent and infant positive engagement as well as affective synchrony in interactive play. These findings held for fathers and mothers. Moreover, as the researchers had hypothesized, maternal oxytocin levels were elevated in conjunction with interactive stress, which they interpreted as indicative of mothers' inclination to rely on social engagement as a means of restoring well-being. They summarized these impressive findings as follows:

> The present findings indicate that [oxytocin] is related to the entire constellation of attachment in humans, including the parent's experience of being card for as a child, attachment to romantic partner, and the ability to provide optimal parenting to the next generation, as expressed in developmentally adequate preoccupations and worries regarding infant well-being, clear and coherent representations of the parent infant attachment, and the ability to engage in positive, well-timed synchronous interactions with the child. (p. 759)

As MacLean's (1990) early observations would imply, parental responses to infants' crying are especially influential in attachment security. Psychological attunement and soothing behaviors promote attachment security; yet infant crying also can trigger abuse and neglect. Madelon Riem and colleagues (Riem et al., 2011) administered oxytocin intranasally and examined patterns of brain activity in women (without children) while they were exposed to sounds of two-day-old healthy infants' crying. Compared to placebo, oxytocin was associated with diminished amygdala activation and enhanced insula and inferior frontal gyrus activation, which the researchers interpreted to reflect a combination of diminished anxiety and enhanced empathy.

Lane Strathearn and his colleagues (Strathearn, Fonagy, Amico & Montague, 2009) conducted a landmark study that is unique in examining the impact of mothers' attachment security on the role of oxytocin in mother-infant interactions. In my view, this research has direct bearing on the crux of attachment trauma. These researchers assessed first-time mothers' attachment security with the AAI administered during pregnancy; they measured mothers' serum oxytocin response to a period of interaction with their infant; and, a few months later, they also measured patterns of brain activation as mothers viewed pictures of their infant's crying and smiling faces. Mothers who showed secure attachment on the AAI were contrasted with a group who showed avoidant-dismissing attachment (which has been associated with avoidant infant attachment). In the first phase of the study, securely attached mothers showed greater increases in oxytocin levels than did insecure mothers after interacting with their infant, implying that the secure mothers found the interactions to be more rewarding. Consistent with this hypothesis, oxytocin response to interacting with the infant was correlated with activation of brain reward circuits in the subsequent viewing of the infant's face.

Here is the finding in Strathearn's research most pertinent to my thesis about attachment trauma: securely attached mothers showed activation in dopaminergic reward pathways when viewing their infant's *sad* faces as well as happy faces. By contrast, in response to their infant's sad faces, dismissing mothers showed patterns of brain activation consistent with negative emotions and efforts to control these emotions. The three-month delay between the mother-infant interaction phase and the neuroimaging phase is noteworthy in suggesting that the oxytocinergic effects are indicative of enduring characteristics of the secure mothers. This trait-like quality of oxytocin responsiveness was confirmed in a subsequent study (Strathearn, Iyengar, Fonagy & Kim, 2012) relating mothers' oxytocin response to interacting with their infant to mothers' temperament. Oxytocin responsiveness was positively associated with temperamental Orienting Sensitivity, which includes responsiveness to sensory cues, moods, and emotions; in contrast, oxytocin response was inversely related to a temperamental proclivity to rely on Effortful Control, consistent with a more compulsively task-oriented approach to childrearing.

Strathearn and colleagues (Strathearn, Fonagy, Amico & Montague, 2009) conclude that, for securely attached mothers, oxytocin might contribute to the rewarding quality of their relationship with their infant and thus (in my terms) to their mindful attentiveness; in turn, their attentiveness potentially contributes to their nurturing care—most notably, not only when their infant is happy but also when their infant is distressed. In contrast to the approach response of secure mothers to infant distress, dismissing mothers are more likely to respond with avoidance of distress—their infant's and their own. Such avoidance is the crux of attachment trauma, as exemplified by Beebe's (Beebe et al., 2010) research showing that maternal aversion to infant distress at four months of age portends disorganized infant attachment at twelve months of age.

Expanding on findings just reviewed, Pilyoung Kim and colleagues (Kim et al., 2010) studied brain structure as well as brain activation in relation to mothers' responsiveness to (others') infants' cries. Mothers who reported higher levels of maternal care in their upbringing showed larger brain volumes and greater activation of areas hypothesized to play a role in sensitivity to infants' emotional signals (e.g., superior and middle frontal and superior temporal regions), which the authors associated with greater mentalizing capacity. Notably, mothers who reported a history of poor maternal care showed activation in brain regions associated with stress responding (i.e., hippocampus), which implies aversion to infants' cries.

Attachment trauma

Research on attachment trauma yields a simple and worrisome finding: early-life trauma can have long-term adverse effects on the neurobiological substrates of emotion regulation, my main concern in this book. Such trauma—abuse and neglect—intensifies stress reactivity and impairs stress regulation, underscoring the dual liability of attachment trauma explicated by Fonagy and Target (1997). Research on other mammals who share much of our biological equipment for attachment and emotion has been highly informative in this regard.

Animal research dramatically demonstrates that disruption and trauma in early attachment relationships compounds the challenges of stress regulation. Focusing on research with rats, Jonathan Polan and Myron Hofer (2008) note that the adaptive function of attachment goes far beyond providing protection from predators, as Bowlby (1982) initially had proposed: attachment processes influence neurobiological development in ways that shape basic emotion regulation and adaptive strategies. Specifically, high levels of maternal stimulation immediately after birth, including licking and grooming, lead to toned-down stress reactivity into adulthood, coupled with a proclivity toward exploration and learning. Conversely, low levels of stimulation and interaction (e.g., as associated with prolonged separations) portend high levels of fear, defensiveness, and avoidance, along with lower levels of exploratory activity. This research demonstrates the animal parallels of secure and insecure attachment. The molecular biological mechanisms are being elucidated, down to the level of the influence of rearing patterns on gene activity that affects the development of stress-response systems (Weaver et al., 2004).

I have described how the organized patterns of insecure attachment are optimal secondary strategies for managing emotion in the face of less than optimal caregiving (Mikulincer & Shaver, 2007a). But what would be the evolutionary (survival) value of insecure attachment? Jeffry Simpson and Jay Belsky (2008) speculate that the fearful-defensive (insecure) pattern prepares the animal for a harsh environment with few resources; whereas the converse (secure) pattern prepares the animal for exploratory learning in a stable, resource-rich environment. In effect, these early rearing experiences are predictive of future environmental conditions to which the animal's stress response systems and behavior will be adapted. Hence, these adaptive patterns, mediated by epigenetic mechanisms (i.e., environmental influences on gene activity), constitute a form of "soft inheritance" (Polan & Hofer, 2008, p. 167) as they are passed on through the generations from mothers through their daughters.

Stephen Suomi (2008) summarized research with monkeys, wherein the parallels to human attachment are relatively transparent, for example, in the use of attachment as a safe haven and secure base as well as in individual differences in security of attachment. Experimentally induced disruption in early mother-infant attachment relationships leads not only to insecure attachment and social withdrawal but also to adverse effects on physiological stress regulation that persist into adulthood. Notably, peer reared monkeys (separated from their mother at birth) show inhibited exploration and social play, coupled with long-term heightened stress reactivity and impulsivity. Suomi also reported results of downright traumatic attachments in matrilines of physically abusive and neglecting monkeys: their infants were observed to show extreme distress (e.g., screaming and tantrums) for months after the active abuse stopped; they were inhibited in exploration and play; and they showed long-term physiological changes in stress reactivity. The intergenerational transmission of maternal abuse was striking in these monkeys, and cross fostering showed dramatic environmental effects:

> whereas half of the female offspring of nonabusive mothers who were reared by abusive foster mothers grew up to be abusive toward their own offspring, *none* of the female offspring of abusive mothers who had nonabusive foster mothers subsequently abused their own infants! (p. 186, emphasis in original)

Research on the long-range impact of early trauma on emotion regulation capacities in animals underscores our concerns about the neurobiological effects of childhood maltreatment. More specifically, stress sensitization and associated impairment of emotion-regulation capacities can contribute to trauma-related psychiatric disorders in adults—most notably, depression and PTSD (Nemeroff et al., 2006). Consistent with animal models, Julian Ford (2009) reviews literature suggesting that brain development can be skewed toward a focus on either survival or learning; of particular concern is the possibility of adverse impact on brain development during sensitive periods (Alter & Hen, 2009).

Summarizing adverse effects of trauma on brain development, and consistent with Patrick Luyten and colleagues' (Luyten, Mayes, Fonagy & Van Houdenhove, submitted) review, Michael De Bellis and colleagues (De Bellis, Hooper & Sapia, 2005) stated, "PTSD in maltreated children may be regarded as a complex environmentally induced developmental disorder" (p. 168). They cite evidence for a dose-response relationship insofar as earlier onset and longer duration of abuse, as well as severity of PTSD symptoms, have the greatest impact on development. They point to dysregulation in sympathetic nervous system and hypothalamic-pituitary-adrenal axis stress-response systems as well as evidence for smaller brain volumes in multiple areas, including the prefrontal cortex. They also note indications of compromised neuronal integrity in the anterior cingulate region of the medial prefrontal cortex, which is particularly pertinent to our concerns, given the prominent role of this region in mentalizing, as I will discuss in the next section of this chapter.

In educational groups, we routinely inform patients of the inverse relationship between emotional arousal and mentalizing, noting the neurochemical switch process that shuts down reflective thinking in favor of more reflexive action—fighting, fleeing, or freezing. As you likely know from personal experience, your capacity to inhibit impulsively defensive action varies from time to time, depending on how overwhelmed you are at any given moment (Arnsten, 1998). Yet the neurobiological research also suggests that early stress and trauma may have enduring effects on emotional reactivity that generally lower the threshold for switching from the mentalizing to the fight-flight-freeze mode (Mayes, 2000). Then, in effect, a lower level of emotional arousal can take mentalizing offline. In the last chapter, I argued that attachment trauma is the bane of psychotherapy in undermining the capacity for mentalizing, the bedrock of therapy. Neurobiological research underscores this point by documenting the adverse impact of early attachment trauma on the development of brain-based regulatory processes that support mindful mentalizing.

Plainly, neurobiological research on the adverse impact of trauma in early attachment relationships underscores the daunting challenges therapists and their patients face in fostering greater capacity to regulate unbearable emotional states. Moreover, this research supports my continual emphasis of the point that attachment security is the antidote to attachment trauma. Coan (2008) elegantly conceptualized the role of attachment in emotion regulation from a neurobiological perspective. He started from the premise that the attachment system is "primarily concerned with the social regulation of emotion responding" (p. 251). He and his colleagues provided direct evidence for this premise in a clever experiment with married couples (Coan, Schaefer & Davidson, 2006). With electrodes fastened to their ankles, women in the couples were exposed to electric shocks on selected trials; anticipating shock presumably activated their attachment needs. At different points, as patterns of brain activity were assessed, the women were permitted to hold their husband's hand, an anonymous experimenter's hand, or no one's hand. Holding hands decreased activation in brain areas associated with threat responding and emotion regulation (including the hypothalamus, insula, cingulate, and dorsolateral prefrontal cortex); moreover, holding the spouse's hand was especially powerful in this regard, as measured not only by brain activity but also subjective emotional distress. Furthermore, based on prior questionnaire assessments of marital satisfaction, high-quality marriages were associated with lowered activation of threat-responsive brain areas. The authors interpret their findings as showing that holding one's spouse's hand decreases the need for vigilance and self-regulation of emotion, although this beneficial effect may not be true of insecure relationships. Given what is known about neurochemistry, they speculate that hand holding might enhance oxytocin activity and, in turn, activate dopaminergic and opioid reward activity. As reviewed earlier, other research has demonstrated a role for oxytocin in stress regulation.

Attachment and stress regulation revisited

Based on his review of neurobiological studies in attachment research, Coan (2008) makes the case for the sheer *efficiency* of secure attachment in emotion regulation; attachment is economical in minimizing utilization of brain resources for stress management. At least in the context of secure relationships, social emotion regulation is a relatively effortless, bottom-up process that ameliorates the initial perception of threat and thus decreases the need for effortful distress regulation. In contrast, self-regulating by a top-down process involves more effortful control over attention and cognition, relying to a greater degree on the prefrontal cortex. As described earlier, maternal effortful control is inversely related to oxytocin responsiveness (Strathearn, Iyengar, Fonagy & Kim, 2012). As handholding attests, Coan contends that simpler is better:

> the brain's first and most powerful approach to affect regulation is via social proximity and interaction. This is most obvious in infancy .... Because the PFC [prefrontal cortex] is underdeveloped in infancy, the caregiver effectively serves as a kind of 'surrogate PFC'—a function that attachment figures probably continue to serve for each other to varying degrees throughout life. (p. 255)

Given his premise that attachment figures can serve the role of surrogate prefrontal cortex throughout life, as Coan (2008) proposes, "Simply put, affect regulation is possible, but more difficult, in isolation" (p. 256). Hence he notes the irony that stress-reduction training relies so heavily on self-regulation, and he advocates the alternative of "training in how to allow oneself to be soothed by another person" (p. 259). I concur: allowing oneself to be soothed by another person cuts to the chase of attachment security; yet "training" implies a simple therapeutic process. In my view, the social regulation of stress through attachment hinges significantly on emotional attunement during times of stress, and this is by no means a simple process. Importantly, attachment trauma undermines attunement, such that social contact may exacerbate rather than ameliorate stress (Luyten et al., submitted). In this context, we psychotherapists find ourselves rowing upstream, aspiring to cultivate mindfulness and mentalizing in patients whose capacities are compromised by their attachment insecurity.

Mindfulness

Clinicians' burgeoning interest in mindfulness has been equaled by neuroscientists' enthusiasm for relating these capacities to brain function and structure. The wide availability of neuroimaging has contributed to an explosion of research with enormously complex results. A comprehensive review of this research is far beyond the scope of this book as well as beyond my expertise. At this early stage of research, results are more intriguing than definitive, but the general directions of research merit our attention as they reinforce some of the major psychological themes in this book. Before delving into the neuroimaging research, however, studies of the physiological health benefits of mindfulness are worth noting insofar as they complement the mental health benefits noted earlier in this book.

Impact on physical health and stress activation

Kabat-Zinn's (Kabat-Zinn et al., 1992) Mindfulness-Based Stress Reduction program for general medical patients has been found not only to alleviate their emotional distress (e.g., anxiety and depression) but also to contribute to physiological benefits. Kabat-Zinn (2003) reported, for example, that mindfulness practice accelerated the process of skin clearing in patients with psoriasis, a skin disease that is strongly influenced by psychological stress. A study by Richard Davidson and colleagues (Davidson et al., 2003) was the first to show that Mindfulness-Based Stress Reduction had a positive impact on an *in vivo* measure of immune function: in comparison with a control group, those who had engaged in mindfulness meditation showed an increase in antibody titers following administration of influenza vaccine. Moreover, the meditation group also showed an increase in left-anterior brain activation (as measured by EEG), consistent with prior findings that relative left-anterior activation is associated with positive emotionality (whereas relative right-anterior activation is associated with negative emotion). Most striking in this study was the finding that the magnitude of increase in left-anterior brain activation predicted the extent of antibody titer rise following vaccination.

Before reviewing neuroimaging research with persons who have been trained in mindfulness, a study of the impact of a simple instruction promoting detached mindfulness is worth noting. Schardt and colleagues (Schardt et al., 2010) studied amygdala reactivity to threat-related stimuli in a high-risk group. Previous research had shown that genetic vulnerability to heightened amygdala activation in response to threat is associated with the short allele of the serotonin transporter gene;

this vulnerability, in turn, is associated with increased risk for anxiety and mood disorders (Munafo, Brown & Hariri, 2008). Consistent with previous research, participants with the short allele showed increased amygdala response to fear-inducing pictures. Yet merely instructing these participants to look at the pictures while adopting the stance of a detached observer ameliorated amygdala hyperactivity, and this amygdala regulation was mediated by activity of prefrontal cortex.

Impact on brain activity and structure

Two neuroimaging studies by Norman Farb and his colleagues not only tie formal meditation practice to the neurobiology of emotion regulation but also point to neurobiological differences between mindful attention to present experiences and more reflective mentalizing. In reading about these findings, it will be helpful to know in advance that the medial prefrontal cortex has been dubbed the "mentalizing region" of the brain, as will be discussed further in the next section on the neurobiology of mentalizing.

In the first study (Farb et al., 2007), participants who had completed eight-week mindfulness training were compared with a control group as they engaged in two different kinds of mental activity in response to hearing adjectives pertaining to personality traits (e.g., "greedy," "charming"). One activity, narrative focus, was consistent with reflective mentalizing: participants were instructed to think about what the word means to them and whether it is characteristic of them. The other activity, experiential focus, was consistent with present-centered mindfulness: participants were instructed to sense and notice their thoughts, feelings, and bodily state without any elaborative thinking. Results showed that narrative focus was associated with medial prefrontal cortical activation as well as activation in left hemisphere language areas. The primary focus of the study, however, was on the impact of mindfulness training on experiential focus. The mindfulness group showed distinctive deactivation of the medial prefrontal areas coupled with increased activation of a right-lateralized cortical network including the dorsal prefrontal cortex, insular cortex, and somatosensory cortex. Notably, right insula activation is associated with awareness of bodily aspects of emotional states (gut feelings), and the lateral prefrontal activation might reflect a more detached awareness of these bodily feelings. Moreover, when they were focusing mindfully on their experiences, the meditators' right-lateralized activity was decoupled from the medial prefrontal activation, which was not true of the untrained participants. The authors concluded that "meditation practice is associated with developing moment-to-moment awareness of all available stimuli" (p. 319) with an experience of detachment, as contrasted with the more ordinary experience of engaging in self-focused thinking.

In a second study (Farb et al., 2010), these researchers studied the brain activity of meditation-trained and untrained participants in response to sad moods evoked by films. Sadness was associated with increased activation in the medial prefrontal cortex and areas of the left hemisphere, along with deactivations in the right insula and other areas representing visceral responses. Yet the meditation-trained group showed reduced activation in areas associated with self-referential thinking (e.g., medial prefrontal and language areas) without the reductions in areas associated with visceral awareness (e.g., insula). The authors concluded that mindfulness training promoted "detached viewing of emotions, rather than the elaboration of emotional content through cognitive reappraisal" and that mindfulness fosters the "objectification of emotion as innocuous sensory information rather than as affect-laden threat to self requiring a regulatory response" (p. 31). In short, participants were able to be mindful without needing to mentalize.

Alongside active research employing *functional* neuroimaging to study the impact of mindfulness on brain activity, *structural* neuroimaging is being employed to investigate enduring changes in volume of brain tissue associated with mindfulness practice. In a seminal study, Sara Lazar and colleagues (Lazar et al., 2005) examined the thickness of the cerebral cortex in two groups of participants, experienced Buddhist insight meditation practitioners and persons with no meditation experience. Meditators showed greater cortical thickness in multiple brain areas, including prefrontal cortex and right anterior insula; these areas are associated with attention and awareness of bodily experience, both of which are promoted by mindfulness practice. Put simply, given neural plasticity in the brain (in effect, potential for rewiring), one might infer that greater use of these areas promotes growth (e.g., greater neural arborization or increased vasculature).

Lazar and colleagues' findings are dramatic, yet a subsequent group of researchers including Lazar (Holzel et al., 2011) pointed out that later studies have not shown consistent differences between meditators and non-meditators and, moreover, such cross-sectional studies cannot rule out the possibility that brain differences are a cause of engaging in meditation practice rather than a result of it. Accordingly, employing a control group without meditation training, this research group examined gray matter concentration before and after the eight-week course of Mindfulness-Based Stress Reduction. In the meditation group, they found increased density of gray matter in several regions: left hippocampus, posterior cingulate, temporo-parietal junction, and cerebellum—areas related to emotion regulation, self-reflection, and perspective taking.

Reflections

Given the inconsistencies among prior contrasts between meditators and non-meditators, coupled with the small numbers of participants in these expensive neuroimaging studies, it is premature to draw firm conclusions about brain areas that are involved in meditation and enduringly affected by meditation practice. Moreover, there are wide variations among participants and types of meditation practice, and it is impossible to know what aspects of complex programs such as Mindfulness-Based Stress Reduction might account for the effects. Mindfulness training can promote mentalizing as well as mindful attention, recruiting a wide range of brain regions. Accordingly, I present these studies merely to attest to the excitement in the field and the prospects for better understanding how we might better use our minds to change our brain activity and even our brain structure. It is, of course, a truism that learning changes brain structure; this truism is increasingly being elucidated at the level of molecular biology (Kandel, 2005, 2006) and, given that psychotherapy can be effective only by means of learning, we increasingly appreciate that psychotherapy as well as medication is associated with enduring brain changes (Cozolino, 2010).

Mentalizing

I have presented mentalizing as an umbrella concept that includes many facets. We are now in a position to begin clarifying these facets in relation to neurobiological research, linking mentalizing to patterns of activity in different brain regions. I begin this section noting research on mirror neurons that bears on implicit mentalizing. Then I review the contributions of various brain areas to mentalizing, paying particular attention to the medial prefrontal cortex. I conclude by mentioning neurobiological research pertaining to a catch-22 of mentalizing: the more you need to do it, the less capable you are of doing it.

Implicit mentalizing and mirror neurons

Your implicit, unreflective awareness of others' emotional states is partly founded in mirror neuron activity. The discovery of mirror neurons has garnered a great deal of interest as it sheds light on the foundations of empathy at the implicit level (Iacoboni, 2008). The initial discovery was somewhat fortuitous, when an Italian research team discovered that the same neurons in the premotor cortex that fire when a monkey grasps something also fire when the monkey observes another individual grasp something. When you observe intentional behavior, you also partially enact it (or not so partially as when you flinch in a movie theater when you see a boxer hit his opponent in the face). Linking observation to action, mirror neurons also contribute to imitative behavior. Moreover, mirror neurons are involved not only in perception of action but also perception of sensation: these neurons in the somatosensory cortex fire not only when you are being touched but also when you observe someone else being touched (Keysers et al., 2004).

Of particular concern here, mirror neurons also link observing emotion to feeling emotion (Gallese, 2001). For example, one study showed that the anterior insula and anterior cingulate cortexes are activated not only while smelling something disgusting but also when watching someone else smell something while showing facial expressions of disgust (Wicker et al., 2003). Another study compared participants' responses to directly experiencing pain with their responses to observing their romantic partner experiencing pain (Singer et al., 2004). Both conditions activated the anterior insula and anterior cingulate; moreover, those participants who scored higher on a questionnaire measure of empathy showed the highest activation of these structures. Vittorio Gallese summarized the implications of such findings:

> With this mechanism we do not just 'see' or 'hear' an action or an emotion. Side by side with the sensory description of the observed social stimuli, internal representations of the state associated with these actions are evoked in the observer, 'as if' they were performing

a similar action or experiencing a similar emotion .... crucial for
both first- and third-person comprehension of social behavior is
the activation of the cortical motor or viscero-motor centers, the
outcome of which, when activating downstream centers, determines a specific 'behavior', be it an action or an emotional state.
When only the cortical centers, decoupled from the peripheral
effects, are active, the observed actions or emotions are 'simulated'
and thereby understood. (Gallese et al., 2004, p. 400)

You might think of mirror neuron activity as providing a substrate for
empathy, but full-fledged empathy also requires more explicit mentalizing, not only resonating with the other person's emotion but also
regulating your emotion (to avoid contagion), maintaining a sense of
distinctness from the other person, and being able to identify imaginatively with the other person's perspective, including being able to
put this resonance and imaginative activity into words. Thus empathy is a prime example of the need to integrate implicit and explicit
mentalizing.

An intriguing study bearing on maternal responsiveness links mentalizing capacity to mirror neuron activity (Lenzi et al., 2009). Mothers'
brain activity was measured while they observed and imitated various
types of emotional expression in their own and other mothers' infants.
Their mentalizing capacity (reflective functioning) was assessed in the
Adult Attachment Interview. Responding to emotional expressions activated the mirror neuron system as well as the amygdala and anterior
insula, and this responsiveness was especially prominent in relation to
their own infants. Notably, mentalizing capacity was correlated with
activation in the anterior insula, which plays a role in processing mirror
neuron activity and thus, in the authors' view, "a greater ability to bodily feel the emotions of others" (p. 1130).

Cortical regions contributing to mentalizing

Given the multifaceted nature of social cognition and its sheer complexity, it is unsurprising that the activity of multiple brain regions
must be coordinated in mentalizing. Moreover, this coordinated
activity shows considerable commonality with respect to mentalizing the self and others (Lombardo et al., 2010; Vanderwal, Hunyadi,
Grupe, Connors & Schulz, 2008). I provide a capsule summary of

the contribution to mentalizing of several cortical areas: amygdala, temporal lobes, temporo-parietal junction, and the anterior insula.

The amygdala plays a central role in immediate and nonconscious fear responses to threatening stimuli as well as in orchestrating the fear response. The amygdala also contributes to mentalizing in assigning emotional significance to social stimuli (Adolphs, 2003; Aggleton & Young, 2000; Brothers, 1997). The amygdala is responsive to gaze, facial expressions, and bodily movements. It biases attention to the eye region of the face and is especially sensitive to threat and, hence, judgments of others' trustworthiness. Yet the amygdala also responds to a wider range of emotional expression, including positive emotions (Rolls, 1999). The amygdala has been shown to be responsive to threatening faces in a small fraction of a second (33 milliseconds), far below the threshold of conscious detection (Whalen et al., 1998).

In the temporal lobe, two areas contribute to preferential orientation toward social stimuli: the *fusiform gyrus* contributes to the perception of appearances and, in particular, the identification of individual faces; in contrast, the *superior temporal sulcus* is active in the perception of biological motion and thus the perception of animacy, agency, and intentionality (Adolphs, 2003; U. Frith & Frith, 2003). The *temporal poles* (superior anterior temporal lobes) play a role in applying abstract conceptual knowledge of social behavior to interpreting individuals' actions at a particular time and in a particular context, including the application of autobiographical memory to such interpretation (C. D. Frith & Frith, 2006; Zahn et al., 2007). In short, the temporal poles contribute to the application of knowledge of social scripts to interpreting behavior in particular contexts.

The temporo-parietal junction (TPJ; adjacent to the superior temporal sulcus) responds selectively to attributing thoughts to other persons (Saxe & Powell, 2006). Whereas the left TPJ plays a role in the attribution of enduring socially relevant traits, the right TPJ plays a role in attributing transient mental states to others and is especially responsive in reconciling incongruities when interpreting others' mental states (Saxe & Wexler, 2005). A study obtaining functional brain images during a live interaction (via video) was notable in showing right TPJ activity during the actual interaction, as contrasted with activity during viewing a recording of the same interaction (Redclay et al., 2010).

The insula is noteworthy for rendering bodily activity accessible to subjective awareness, as reviewed comprehensively by Bud Craig

(2009). Yet the anterior portion of the insula is especially pertinent to mentalizing inasmuch as it engenders self-awareness, including awareness of the full range of emotions. Perhaps making a central contribution to mindfulness, the anterior insula is associated with mental representations of the self at a given moment in time, that is, providing for the experience of a sentient self, feelings about engaging with objects (including other persons), and a feeling of knowing (e.g., familiarity) when interacting with objects. Thus insula activation is associated not with the role of a passive observer but rather with the experience of an active agent. The insula also contributes to anticipated feelings and thus to the guidance of behavior. Given its broad role in subjective awareness, in Craig's view, the insula yields a "unified final meta-representation of the 'global emotional moment'" (p. 67) and, more broadly, "the feeling that 'I am'" (p. 65). Hence Craig concluded that the insula facilitates emotional awareness and communication among conspecifics and thus provided a major evolutionary advantage to hominoid primates.

The "mentalizing region" in the prefrontal cortex

Based on a series of experimental studies, Chris and Uta Frith (U. Frith & Frith, 2003) dubbed a broad area of the medial prefrontal cortex overlapping the anterior cingulate cortex the *mentalizing region.* Frith and colleagues (Amodio & Frith, 2006; C. D. Frith & Frith, 1999, 2006) documented extensive research attesting to the role of this prefrontal region in mentalizing. One of the most instructive experiments showed the selective activation of the mentalizing region when participants in a game believe that they are interacting with a person versus interacting with a computer, notwithstanding that the (programmed) moves of the opponent were identical in both conditions (Gallagher, Jack, Roepstorff & Frith, 2002). By no means is mentalizing a unique function of this broad mentalizing region; rather, the region "supports a general mechanism for the integration of complex representation of possible actions and anticipated outcomes, and … such integration is particularly relevant to the domain of social cognition" (Amodio & Frith, 2006, p. 269). In short, this multipurpose region plays a key role in mentalizing along with many other complex mental activities.

The medial frontal cortex consists of a large territory, and three broad regions can be distinguished (Amodio & Frith, 2006;

C. D. Frith & Frith, 2006). (1) The *posterior* region of the *rostral* medial frontal cortex (the uppermost region) represents the expected values of actions and contributes to selecting among competing actions as well as continual monitoring of actions in relation to outcomes. The region is activated when responses must be inhibited, when the action is not fully determined by the context, and when errors are committed. (2) The *orbital* medial prefrontal cortex (lowermost region) is sensitive to rewards and punishments associated with actions, and it guides behavior in relation to the value of possible outcomes. The lateral portion of the orbital region suppresses behavior associated with previously rewarded actions when they are no longer rewarded. (3) In between the posterior-rostral and orbital regions, the more anterior region of the rostral medial frontal cortex contributes to self-knowledge, person perception, and mentalizing. This region contributes to complex social cognition and to reflection about mental states (thoughts, feelings, intentions); this activity includes not only reflection on your own mental states as well as others' mental states but also reflection on how others see you. Within this region, the inferior portion (bordering the orbital region) is associated with mentalizing more similar others (e.g., on the basis of similar feelings), whereas the superior portion (bordering the posterior-rostral region) is associated with interpreting actions of unfamiliar or unknown others. A further distinction: thinking about private (unobservable) intentions activates the anterior-rostral area, whereas interpreting communicative (observable) intentions activates the posterior-rostral area. I highlight such distinctions to emphasize the multifaceted nature of mentalizing and the ways in which neuroscience might gradually contribute to elucidating the various facets and their relationships.

The mentalizing catch-22

You most need to mentalize when you are least capable of doing it. You need to bring in the big guns—mentalizing and elaborate cortical networks—when emotions are intense; yet, as I described in the context of attachment trauma, intense emotions impair your mentalizing capacity by deactivating prefrontal areas. Amy Arnsten (1998) addressed this catch-22 in her memorably titled paper, "The Biology of Being Frazzled." Escalating levels of emotional stress lead up to a neurochemical switch, a shift in the balance or activity in various cortical and subcortical areas. That is, with increasing arousal, you shift from relatively slow executive functions mediated by the prefrontal cortex to faster habitual and instinctual behaviors mediated by posterior cortical (e.g., parietal) and subcortical structures (e.g., amygdala, hippocampus, and striatum). Accordingly, mentalizing goes offline, and defensive responses (fight, flight, freeze) come into play. This capacity for rapid switching has obvious survival value: when dire threat is immanent (an approaching predator), you must act, not reflect. Yet such mindlessly automatic responses are maladaptive in less dire situations of interpersonal conflict that call for mentalizing and flexible responding. Unfortunately, traumatized persons are sensitized to stress such that defensive responses are triggered more readily; then more robust mentalizing capacities must be developed through hard, effortful work. This work requires cultivating conscious regulation through explicit mentalizing, as we strive to do in psychotherapy.

Conscious regulation and the prefrontal cortex

Contra the traditional argument that the human capacity for tool making drove the evolution of the neocortex, the more compelling view is that the sheer complexity of social cognition—the need to cooperate and compete—was the main evolutionary arms race that propelled brain development (Bogdan, 1997; Hrdy, 2009; Humphrey, 1988). The human brain was not designed for social cognition per se but rather for the kind of problem solving that social cognition exemplifies. Thus we use this problem-solving brain machinery to manage ourselves and to relate to each other. In this section, I will step back from the trees to see the forest so as to place mentalizing in the broader context of complex problem solving. I start with the role of consciousness in mentalizing and then describe how mentalizing fits into the functional role of the prefrontal cortex, an especially refined area of the brain in us humans. Understanding this research is conducive to mentalizing in the most abstract sense, that is, understanding how our minds work.

The self in consciousness

Antonio Damasio (2010) makes a convincing case that consciousness requires a sense of self at implicit and explicit levels: "consciousness is a state of mind that occurs when we are awake and in which there is a private and personal knowledge of our own existence, situated relative to whatever its surround may be at a given moment" (p. 158). In short, consciousness requires a mind coupled with a sense of self:

> to get a passing standard consciousness score, it is indispensable (1) to be awake; (2) to have an operational mind; *and* (3) to have, within that mind, an automatic, unprompted, undeduced sense of self as a protagonist of the experience, no matter how subtle the self sense may be. (p. 161, emphasis in original)

The distinction I have drawn between mindfulness and mentalizing relates to the extent of conscious elaboration of experience: mindfulness entails attention, and mentalizing entails reflection. Moreover, in the broad domain of mentalizing, we can distinguish levels of elaboration (Lecours & Bouchard, 1997), ranging from labeling a feeling to ever-expanding narratives regarding the reasons for the feelings. Damasio's (2010) explication of increasing self-awareness parallels this view of mindfulness and mentalizing as entailing different levels of mental elaboration. Specifically, he distinguishes three levels, each developing over the course of evolution, and each built on top of the other: proto-self, core self, and autobiographical self.

The *protoself*, grounded in relatively stable, homeostatic physiological processes, provides a continuous foundation of subjectivity, anchored in primordial feelings reflecting the state of the internal milieu. These primordial feelings include a sense of vitality along with feelings of hunger and thirst as well as pleasure and pain. The protoself is supported by brainstem structures (nucleus tractus solitarius, parabrachial nucleus, and periaqueductal gray) and the hypothalamus as well as the insula and anterior cingulate cortex, where the sense of bodily well-being is integrated with and elaborated into emotional feelings.

The *core self* emerges from interactions with objects, and thereby introduces a protagonist and sense of agency into consciousness. The core self is an intermediary between the protoself and the auto-biographical self, the latter providing our full-fledged sense of identity. Interactions with objects modify the protoself (i.e., bodily processes), creating a feeling of engagement and a feeling of knowing, anchored in saliency and attention: the core self is "created by linking the modified protoself to the object that caused the modification, an object that has now been hallmarked by feeling and enhanced by attention" (p. 203). Keep in mind that the "objects" of greatest concern to us in this book are other persons. Thus the core self puts us in the territory of mindful attention to others. The constituents of this core self process are a set of intertwined images: an image of the momentarily salient causative object (or person); an image of the organism as modified by the interaction with the object; and an image of the object-related emotional response. In Damasio's view, "the core self mechanism ... anchored in the protoself and its primordial feelings, is the central mechanism for the production of conscious minds" (p. 204).

The *autobiographical self*, the basis of human personhood and the explicit subject of psychotherapy, is constructed from personal (episodic) memories and from personal knowledge. In Damasio's view, "Autobiographical selves are autobiographies made conscious" (p. 210). The neural architecture for the autobiographical self is highly integrative in requiring coordination of activity in multiple brain sites, just as would be expected from neuroimaging research related to mentalizing. The integrative regions that Damasio postulates as being involved in the creation of the autobiographical self include the lateral and medial temporal cortices, the lateral parietal cortices, the lateral and medial frontal cortices, and the posteromedial cortices.

Our activity—physical, mental, and interpersonal—is overwhelmingly based on nonconscious processes. In Damasio's view, a mind without a self is not conscious; consciousness evolved after nonconscious minds were established and is founded on an increasingly elaborate sense of self. What is the value of this conscious complexity? The benefits boil down to the capacity for planning and deliberation, based on reflecting on previous experience and knowledge, which enables us to "survey the possible future and to either delay or inhibit automatic responses" (p. 268). When all goes smoothly and problem solving is relatively routine—in your interpersonal interactions, in your mind, or in any other activity—you need not reflect, deliberate, and plan. Yet much of life is hardly so routine, and novelty is especially characteristic of interpersonal interactions. We need conscious regulation to come up with strategies to cope with novelty and to monitor our successes and failures (Shallice & Cooper, 2011). In short, as Damasio put it, "We use conscious deliberation to govern our loves and friendships, our education, our professional activities, [and] or relations to others" and, furthermore, conscious deliberation is guided by a "robust sense of self built on an organized autobiography and a defined identity" (p. 271). Its value: "We cannot run our kind of life, in the physical and social environments that have become the human habitat, without reflective, conscious deliberation" (p. 272). Thus, in broad terms, consciousness serves an integrative and supervisory function (Shallice & Cooper, 2011), and this mental function is mirrored in the finding that consciousness is associated with coordinated and temporally sustained activation in widespread cortical networks, with the prefrontal and anterior cingulate cortices playing a central role in this coordination (Dehaene, Changeux, Naccache, Sackur & Sergent, 2006; Dehaene & Naccache, 2001).

Plainly, explicit mentalizing requires consciousness. As already stated, nothing is more fraught with novelty and the unexpected than your social relationships. But you also meet up with the unexpected in your own mind—puzzling or disturbing images, desires, feelings, thoughts and actions. Then you need higher-order consciousness to sort yourself out—often with the help of dialog with others. Hence, as Damasio recognized and Roy Baumeister and colleagues (Baumeister & Masicampo, 2010; Baumeister, Masicampo & Vohs, 2011) elaborated, whereas basic awareness enables you to interact with the physical environment, conscious thought enables you to deal with the more complex social and cultural environment. You need conscious thought to understand yourself and others, to resolve conflicts within yourself and with others, as well as to explain yourself to others. You come to understand yourself better in the process of explaining yourself to others. You do all this through narrative, constructing stories to give an account of yourself—often in the privacy of your own mind.

I want to underscore the importance of narrative here. Much of your mental life as well as your interpersonal relationships revolve around constructing narrative, elaborating stories. Conscious mentalizing is the basis of the stories you tell yourself and others as well as the stories you create about others and your capacity to interpret stories others tell. Hence conscious mentalizing is mainly what patients and therapists are doing in psychotherapy—when it is going well.

The value of conscious deliberation and narrative construction is nowhere more evident than in the realm of mentalizing emotion. Plainly, intense, painful, and nonmentalized emotion can be diffused in self-destructive action as exemplified in addictions and self-injury. Yet Baumeister (Baumeister, Vohs, DeWall & Zhang, 2007) contends that our emotional feelings are adaptive primarily in informing future behavior rather than in driving current behavior. Conscious feelings do not necessarily cause emotional behavior directly; we often experience them after the fact. We mistakenly believe that we run from the assailant because we are afraid; by the time we realize we are afraid, we are already running. Nonetheless, our conscious fear might add fuel to our running. Yet Baumeister argues that the main adaptive function of emotion is its *indirect* effect on behavior by influencing how we think: "the proper function of emotion is to influence cognition" (p. 197). Emotion captures our attention and potentially enhances the adaptive functions of conscious thought: emotion promotes learning from the past, especially owing to the negative emotional effects of past actions. Your emotional responses can ensure that you learn your lessons from your past missteps. For example, if you have ignored your spouse's grief, you are liable to grapple with painful guilt feelings when you fully appreciate the hurtful consequences of your emotional neglect. If you make room for your guilt feelings and reflect on them, you will feel a twinge of guilt if you start to repeat the same pattern of neglect in the future. The twinge of guilt can prompt you to stay engaged and psychologically attuned when the opportunity arises.

The adaptive scenario that Baumeister envisions requires mindful mentalizing of emotion. Ideally, you feel the emotion, accept it, understand it, learn from it, and use it as a signal to guide your future behavior. With a history of attachment trauma, however, mentalizing emotion does not come easily. Your capacity for higher-order consciousness evolved in the context of social relationships, and it needs to be maintained and enhanced in relationships throughout life. Psychotherapy is one avenue to expand your consciousness of emotion.

Prefrontal cortex

Now to the piece de résistance: numerous brain regions contribute to mentalizing, but the rostral (anterior) prefrontal cortex (PFC) plays the central role. Yet, to reiterate my earlier point, you should not think of the PFC as having evolved specifically for social cognition but rather as evolved for complex problem solving, with mentalizing being a prime example. Hence, to appreciate the complexity of mentalizing, it is helpful to step back and consider the broader function of the rostral PFC within which mentalizing is encompassed.

Paul Burgess and colleagues (Burgess, Gonen-Yaacovi & Volle, 2012; Burgess, Simons, Dumontheil & Gilbert, 2005) identified several tasks that depend on intact rostral PFC functioning. I start with *prospective memory*, defined as "the ability to remember to carry out an intended action (or thought) after a delay period where one has been occupied with another task" (Burgess, Gonen-Yaacovi & Volle, 2012, p. 83). Remembering to stop at the market on the way home from work is a common example; your prospective memory fails when you forget to remember to make the detour. Prospective memory plays a key role in conducting psychotherapy; for example, you might need to keep in mind your intention to find an opening in a session for exploring an aspect of the patient's trauma history that he seems to brush off as unimportant. The rostral PFC also plays a role in *multitasking*, that is, prioritizing, juggling, dovetailing, and completing multiple tasks in a given time period. A common example: getting your children out of bed, dressed, fed, and out the door while also preparing yourself to go to work. Yet multitasking also applies to an individual psychotherapy session (interweaving multiple agendas of the patient and therapist) and even more obviously to group interactions where competing agendas and multiple perspectives must be addressed in some sort of order (e.g., group therapy, family therapy, or a work group).

Beyond prospective memory and multitasking, additional features of problem-solving challenges supported by the rostral PFC bear noting. The rostral PFC is essential to performance of *ill-structured* and *open-ended* tasks. That is, you need your rostral PFC operating when it is up to you to decide which task among several to work on at a given time, how long to work on each task, what constitutes adequate progress on a given task before switching to the next, and how to prioritize tasks in a sequence as you work your way through them. Frequently enough, you must do this multitasking in the face of interruptions and shifts in priorities. You should be able to recognize this kind of complex problem solving as characteristic of many lines of work as well as raising children and running a household. Yet this same complexity also applies to social interactions, as the following general characterization attests: "Rostral PFC would seem to be most involved in situations for which there is not a well-rehearsed or well-specified way of behaving, and therefore where behavioral organization needs to be self-determined" (Burgess, Simons, Dumontheil & Gilbert, 2005, p. 229). Hence Burgess and colleagues (Burgess, Gonen-Yaacovi & Volle, 2012) include mentalizing among the functions of the rostral PFC, consistent with well-known social deficits related to damage in this brain region. Note how this characterization of PFC function applies to the work of psychotherapists and their patients alike, as it does pervasively to myriad social interactions. A psychotherapy process certainly consists of multiple ill-defined and open-ended tasks that must be dovetailed on the basis of ever-changing priorities.

Burgess and colleagues (Burgess, Simons, Dumontheil & Gilbert, 2005) also link the rostral PFC to a pervasive multitasking challenge of alternating attention between two fundamental forms of thought that have garnered much interest in current neuroscience: *stimulus-oriented thought* (SOT) is "either *provoked by* something being experienced through the senses, or *oriented toward* something to be experienced through the senses" (p. 233, emphasis in original). In contrast, *stimulus-independent thought* (SIT) includes "any cognition that has not been provoked by, or directed toward, an external stimulus" (p. 234). Examples of SIT include daydreaming, zoning out, ruminating, and creative thinking. Plainly, rostral prefrontal functioning relates to mentalizing in this respect; mentalizing in interpersonal interactions requires mindful attentiveness to your interaction partners (SOT) as well as reflection on their mental states and your own (SIT). A simple example in the Adult Attachment Interview: you listen (SOT) to the interviewer's request to give an example of an instance in which your mother was "unfeeling," and search your memory (SIT) to do so, while attending to the interviewer's response (SOT) and perhaps thinking about her comprehension of your response or gauging your credibility in her mind (SIT). Ubiquitously, mentalizing requires applying past experience to current interactions, thus exemplifying the need to alternate between SIT and SOT.

Gilbert and colleagues (S. J. Gilbert et al., 2007) conducted an elegant experiment employing neuroimaging to tease out the relation between mentalizing and switching between SOT and SIT inasmuch as both activities have been associated with medial PFC functioning. Participants were cued to switch between making decisions about visual images while viewing the images (SOT) versus picturing the images in their mind (SIT). Moreover, they were led to believe that the timing of the cues to switch was being decided by the experimenter versus a computer. In the mentalizing condition, participants believed they were interacting with an experimenter who was controlling the timing of the switches between SOT and SIT, and they subsequently judged the experimenter to have been helpful or unhelpful. In the nonmentalizing condition, participants believed the switches to be controlled by the computer, and they judged the timing of transitions to have been faster or slower than usual. In fact, all attentional switches were cued randomly. The results showed that both SOT (externally focused attention) and mentalizing (believing they were interacting with the experimenter) activated participants' medial PFC functioning. Yet the areas of activation were distinct within this broad region: the area active in attentional selection (switching between SOT and SIT) was rostral and inferior to the area active in mentalizing (i.e., caudal and superior). Thus there is no contradiction between these dual roles of the medial PFC; they work together in attention selection and mentalizing.

The distinction between SOT and SIT has come into play in a fascinating line of inquiry in neuroimaging research regarding broad patterns of brain functioning pertinent to mindful attention and mentalizing. Prototypically, researchers administer tasks while patients are scanned, and they look for areas of the brain that are "activated" or, more colloquially, areas that "light up." For example, many social-cognition tasks light up the mentalizing region, that is, the rostral medial PFC. This language obscures the fact that, when participants are lying in the scanner and not performing any task (i.e., doing nothing in particular, the control or baseline condition), the brain is continuously lit up. Task participation typically yields activations at a level less than 5% above baseline; as Debra Gusnard (2005) put it, "These [activations] are modest modulations in ongoing or baseline activity and do not appreciably effect the overall metabolic rate of the brain" (p. 685). Expanding on this point, Marcus Raichle and Abraham Snyder (2007) observed,

> it is estimated that 60% to 80% of the brain's enormous energy budget is used to support communication among neurons, functional activity by definition. The additional energy burden associated with momentary demands of the environment may be as little as 0.5% to 1.0% of the total energy budget. This cost-based analysis alone implies that intrinsic activity may be at least as important as evoked activity in the understanding of overall brain functioning. (p. 1087)

Engaging in specific tasks not only leads to selective (albeit modest) activation in specific brain areas but also results in a consistent pattern of decreased activity in other regions, regardless of the nature of the task: "The consistency with which certain areas of the brain participated in these decreases indicated that there might be an organized mode of brain function, which is attenuated during various goal-directed behaviours" (Gusnard & Raichle, 2001, p. 687). To summarize,

> There is a consistent set of brain areas that are active at rest with eyes closed, as well as during visual fixation and the passive viewing of simple visual stimuli. The activity in these areas is attenuated during the performance of various goal-directed actions. Because these areas arise from the baseline activity of the brain in these passive conditions, we suggest that they are functionally active, although they are not 'activated.' In contrast to the transient nature of typical activations ... the presence of this functional activity in the baseline implies the presence of sustained information processing. (p. 689)

The network supporting this baseline activity includes widespread brain regions, encompassing various regions of the parietal, temporal, cingulate, and prefrontal cortexes. Neuroimaging has demonstrated not only functional connectivity among these areas but also structural connectivity (Greicius, Supekar, Menon & Dougherty, 2009). The activity of this network has been dubbed the *default mode* (Gusnard, Akbudak, Shulman & Raichle, 2001), and the significance of this discovery bears underscoring: "The frequently expressed concern that, left unconstrained, brain activity would vary unpredictably, does not apply to the passive resting state of the human brain. Rather, it is intrinsically constrained by the default functionality of the baseline or resting state" (Gusnard & Raichle, 2001, p. 689). Pertinent to my concerns in this chapter, Gusnard and Raichle conclude that the unifying concept for this default mode of brain functioning is "the continuity of a stable, unified perspective of the organism relative to its environment (a 'self')" (p. 692). In effect, your brain is operating in the default mode when you are not engaged in any particular task but rather are merely being you. Accordingly, inasmuch as the default mode is conductive to self-awareness (including self-reflection), active engagement in complex tasks, by deactivating this mode, will diminish self-awareness (Gusnard, 2005).

Research suggests that the default mode is associated with a particular attentive stance, which has been construed as "surveillance of the internal and external environment and some assessment of salience of stimuli for the individual" (Gusnard, Akbudak, Shulman & Raichle, 2001, p. 4263). This "attentional mode during rest" is conducive to "toggling between introspective and extrospective modes of attention" (Sonuga-Barke & Castellanos, 2007, p. 980). As Raichle and Snyder (2007) put it, "Among the possible functions of this intrinsic (default) activity is facilitation of responses to stimuli," namely, by "the maintenance of information for interpreting, responding to and even *predicting* environmental demands" (p. 1087, emphasis added).

When I first learned about the default mode, I viewed it as consistent with mentalizing (e.g., idly thinking about yourself). Yet the concepts just reviewed suggest that the default mode is better associated with broad awareness and preparedness to respond to a wide range of stimuli. Accordingly, Michael Lombardo and colleagues (Lombardo et al., 2010) present neuroimaging findings suggesting that we should resist the temptation to associate mentalizing with default mode functioning: "we suggest that the intrinsic mode of functional brain organization is exactly the opposite of what occurs during task-specific shared mentalizing processes for both self and other. Thus, if there are any interpretations to be made about the current findings in relation to the DMN [Default Mode Network] literature, it would be that during mentalizing about the self and other, there is possibly an adaptive reconfiguration of dynamic functional organization from how the brain is naturally functionally organized" (p. 1633). I wonder if we might better think of default mode functioning is consistent with mindful attention (as in insight meditation), that is, flexible and open awareness of the full potential range of internal and external stimuli without sustained focus on any particular content. Potentially balancing SOT and SIT, such mindful attention would be conducive to rapid engagement in a wide range of tasks, should such engagement become adaptive. Such engagement would include mentalizing. In sum, we might view the default mode of open-minded attention as a platform for mentalizing (and much else).

Clinical implications

Neurobiological research attests to the fundamental role of attachment in modulating distress and providing a pleasurable feeling of security. The continuity across mammalian species in neuroendocrine mechanisms is impressive, leaving no doubt about Bowlby's wisdom in adopting an evolutionary view of the functions of attachment. In educating patients about attachment, I seize every opportunity to refer to Jim Coan's (Coan, Schaefer & Davidson, 2006) study on hand-holding, emphasizing his insistence that secure attachment is our most efficient and potent means of regulating distress (Coan, 2008); as I put it, attach and give your brain a break. I also press his point that popular therapies tend to emphasize skills in self-regulation; essential as these skills might be, I give primacy to bolstering security in attachment relationships, employing the therapeutic relationship as a model.

Sadly, neurobiological research also demonstrates interspecies continuity in attachment trauma; early abuse and neglect potentially exert a lifelong adverse effect on emotion regulation by increasing stress sensitization and decreasing the capacity to down-regulate distress—the crux of the developmental dual liability associated with attachment trauma identified by Fonagy and Target (1997).

I reviewed research on attachment, mindfulness, and mentalizing in the previous chapters to establish the foundation for a treatment model for attachment trauma, and the neurobiological research in this chapter also supports that model. The basic principle has been self-evident throughout, although bringing it to fruition is anything but easy: we must help traumatized patients achieve greater security in a network of attachment relationships by means of cultivating mindful attention to mental states as a platform for mentalizing more effectively in relation to self and others. Unfortunately, the neurobiological research underscores the sheer difficulty of this task, a level of difficulty that is all too evident in routine clinical practice: prefrontal regulation is undermined by high reactivity to stress, often exacerbated by addiction to alcohol and drugs, which have served as a substitute for attachment in regulating distress. Hence endeavors to promote mindful mentalizing confront a catch-22: you most need to mentalize (i.e., in emotionally stressful interpersonal or intrapsychic contexts) when you are least able to do so (i.e., owing to heightened emotional arousal). Psychotherapy addresses this catch-22 by promoting mindfulness and mentalizing in the context of an increasingly secure attachment relationship. In this endeavor, we must count on neuronal plasticity (rewiring) insofar as the effectiveness of psychotherapy is based on restoring the integration and balance among the prefrontal and subcortical brain circuits that regulate emotion (Cozolino, 2010).

CHAPTER SIX

Treatment

In the Introduction to this book, I proposed that understanding *is* the treatment, and the preceding five chapters have laid out a way of understanding attachment trauma, based on extensive research. In effect, I have established—in the abstract—ways of mentalizing attachment truama for the purpose of orienting treatment and guiding the process of mentalizing individal patients' experience. I respect the value of specialized, evidence-based treatments for particular psychiatric disorders. Yet these specialized approaches are of limited value in treating attachment trauma, owing to the fact that our patients present us with a panoply of disorders and problems. As in general medicine, we need specialists. But we also need generalists, and I count myself as one. Accordingly, as this book attests, I am far more invested in working collaboratively with patients to achieve understanding—a meeting of minds—than in applying any particular therapeutic techniques.

My generalist practice and broad orientation to trauma treatment is compatible with the long-held observation that horse races among psychotherapies rarely yield winners (Luborsky, Singer & Luborsky, 1975). A half century ago, Jerome Frank (1961) saw the forest for the trees: "much, if not all, of the effectiveness of different forms of psychotherapy may be due to those features that all have in common rather than to those that distinguish them from each other" (p. 104). Subsequent research has borne out Frank's supposition, while also providing extensive evidence for the substantial contribution of the patient-therapist relationship to treatment outcomes (Castonguay & Beutler, 2006; Norcross, 2011). I have taken pains in the preceding chapters to establish the foundation for what I consider to be the core process in the patient-therapist relationship: mentalizing in the service of bolstering attachment security in the therapeutic relationship and beyond. Accordingly, while I am keen to refer patients to specialists when necessary, I have declared myself (somewhat tendentiously) to be a practioner of plain old therapy (Allen, 2013), albeit now anchored in contemporary attachment research.

This chapter begins by elaborating my point that patients with a history of attachment trauma present us generalists with a multiplicity of problems and disorders, thus defying narrowly focused treatment approaches. Nevertheless, we generalists have much to learn from specialists, and the following section reviews some evidence-based trauma treatments. With this overview of disorder-specific treatments as a backdrop, I summarize briefly key research on attachment in psychotherapy and then proceed to my main agenda, mentalizing. First, I discuss mentalizing as a general style of psychotherapy, and then I focus on the threapeutic process of mentalizing traumatic experience.

What are we treating?

Therapists who prefer prescriptive treatments for focal problems will be flummoxed by patients struggling with a host of disorders and problems related to attachment trauma. I will catalog the most prominent trauma-related disorders in this section, commenting on PTSD, dissociation, depression, substance abuse, eating disorders, nonsuicidal self-injury, suicidal states, and borderline personality disorder. I have reviewed these disorders in conjunction with attachment trauma more extensively elsewhere (Allen, 2001, 2013), and each of these disorders has a huge associated literature. From this perspective, understanding trauma fully is a staggering undertaking, and we must approach our therapeutic work with an attitude of humility. I intend this admittedly cursory review merely to emphasize the sheer complexity of trauma-related problems and the role of attachment and mentalizing in these problems.

Posttraumatic Stress Disorder (PTSD)

No doubt, many patients who have suffered trauma in early attachment relationships develop PTSD at different points in their lifetime, and a history of attachment trauma increases the risk of developing PTSD after subsequent traumas. A number of patients with a history of attachment trauma are bewildered by the eruption of PTSD in later life, which invariably raises the question, Why now? Notoriously, core PTSD symptoms of intrusive memories and associated avoidance strategies are evoked by reminders of past trauma; not uncommonly, these reminders take the form of painful experiences in current attachment relationships. A prototypical example is a woman with a childhood history of psychological, physical, and sexual abuse who becomes embroiled in a battering relationship in adulthood, which is not only traumatic in itself but also liable to evoke memories of past trauma. Yet the broad view of trauma I have proposed—the experience of being psychologically alone in unbearable emotional states—suggests that a wide range of current stressors in attachment relationships might evoke intrusive memories related to earlier trauma. Feeling betrayed, let down, abandoned, dismissed, and psychologically invisible in the midst of extreme distress and feeling helplessly out of control are liable to bring the past back into the present, consciously or not.

In stating that our therapeutic task would be relatively simple if we merely faced the disorder of PTSD, I do not intend to imply that PTSD is a simple problem. On the contrary, the diagnosis of PTSD is fraught with controversy (Brewin, 2003; Rosen & Lilienfeld, 2008; Spitzer, First & Wakefield, 2007). The foundation of the diagnosis is exposure to a traumatic stressor, but it is difficult to agree on an objective threshold for a "traumatic" level of stress. Moreover, *physical* threat and danger takes center stage in the psychiatric definition of trauma (APA, 2000), whereas threat to *psychological* integrity is more prominent in the experience of traumatized persons (Grey & Holmes, 2008; E. A. Holmes, Grey & Young, 2005) and more relevant to a mentalizing treatment focus. Plainly, I have set the threshold for what constitutes traumatic stress relatively low in my broad definition, and I have focused on the psychological and interpersonal context of trauma. Yet this broad approach is consistent with the finding that a sizeable proportion of persons develop the full PTSD syndrome after experiencing stressors that are not prototypically traumatic, such as the breakup of a relationship (Long et al., 2008). Furthermore, painful intrusive memories and emotions, the hallmark of PTSD, are just as common in depression (Brewin, Reynolds & Tata, 1999), the problem for which many traumatized patients seek treatment.

Perhaps more pertinent to my agenda in this book is the fact that the etiology of PTSD is remarkably complex, going far beyond exposure to traumatic stress. This fact attests to the importance of the broader context in which the stress is experienced. Consistent with the developmental perspective I have been advocating throughout this book, an *accumulation of developmental risk factors* and adversities creates vulnerability to PTSD after exposure (Koenen, Moffitt, Poulton, Martin & Caspi, 2007). Moreover, this developmental perspective pertains not only to processes that preceded stress exposure but also to subsequent experience. Chris Brewin (2003) concluded, "What happens *after* a trauma has been shown consistently to have the biggest impact on whether a person develops PTSD" (p. 56, emphasis added). Most notably, Brewin found the most potent post-trauma predictor of PTSD to be lack of social support, for example, as exemplified by coldness, lack of sympathy, and criticism—all of which leave the individual alone in distress.

Brewin's finding regarding social support is consistent with my understanding of trauma: vulnerability to PTSD is associated with a failure of mentalizing in attachment relationships in the aftermath of stressful experience. Moreover, the most distinctive symptom of PTSD, flashbacks (Brewin, 2011), exemplify the prototypical failure of mentalizing, that is, the psychic equivalence-mode in which mental states (memories) are conflated with external reality (traumatic events). The need for mentalizing is implicit in the most fundamental antidote to intrusive memories, separating the present from the past. This antidote applies to mentalizing in current attachment relationships; a relatively ordinary rupture in a current relationship must be distinguished from a profoundly traumatic past betrayal. Capturing the phenomenon of stress sensitization (Post, Weiss & Smith, 1995), we use the metaphor of a "90–10" response as a prompt to mentalizing: we invite patients to distinguish the 10% of emotion appropriate to the present provocation from the 90% stemming from the past (Lewis, Kelly & Allen, 2004). Psychotherapy is one key relationship in which such 90–10 reactions can be identified, and these reactions typically are triggered by mentalizing failures in the present (i.e., the 10%), including such failures in psychotherapy.

Dissociative disorders

As described previously, dissociative disorders might be one exception to the rule that attachment trauma is a nonspecific risk factor for subsequent psychopathology. Some developmental continuity has been observed from dissociative behavior in the Strange Situation (i.e., consistent with disorganized attachment) and dissociative symptoms observed from school age to young adulthood (E. A. Carlson, Yates & Sroufe, 2009; Dutra, Bianchi, Siegel & Lyons-Ruth, 2009). To reiterate, I find it helpful to distinguish broadly between detachment and compartmentalization. Diagnostically, detachment is prominent in depersonalizaiton and derealization; compartmentalization is prominent in amnesia and dissociative identity disorder.

Dissociative detachment is evident in feelings of unreality (e.g., dreamlike experience) as well as in feeling "spacey" or even "gone," as if "in the void." To a degree, dissociative detachment is part and parcel of a high level of fear, evident in the freeze response. Dissociative detachment in the midst of trauma is common, and it is a significant risk factor for the subsequent development of PTSD (Ozer, Best, Lipsey & Weiss, 2003). Although it is a reflex-like aspect of the fear response, dissociative detachment also can be employed strategically as a defense against various painful emotions. Patients can learn to detach, for example, by narrowing their attention (e.g., concentrating on a spot on the wall) or by retreating into fantasy. Detachment exemplifies the nonmentalizing pretend mode; whereas, in the psychic-equivalence mode, mental states are experienced as all too real, in the pretend mode, mental states are too detached from reality. Dissociation in the midst of trauma and in its aftermath is conducive to the development of PTSD in part because it blocks mentalizing, that is, assimilating the experience into normal consciousness. Thus detachment precludes integrating the trauma into the autobiographical self. Just as important, detachment blocks emotional communication, thus robbing the patient of the benefit of restoring security in attachment relationships.

Dissociative identity disorder (DID) exemplifies compartmentalization at the extreme: dramatic switches in sense of self are associated with amnesia, and these switches often are associated with traumatic experiences that are blocked from ordinary consciousness. DID is exceptionally controversial among diagnoses, and many professionals simply do not believe it to be a valid diagnosis (Cormier & Thelen, 1998; Pope, Oliva, Hudson, Bodkin & Gruber, 1999). To me, seeing is believing; I have seen it often, and I believe it—which is not to say that I can give a convincing theoretical account of it. It is helpful to keep in mind the compartmentalized—flagrantly contradictory—behavior of disorganized infants in the Strange Situation. While feeling distressed in relation to a caregiver who is frightening or frightened, there is no satisfactory strategy to ameliorate that distress; the infant is torn between opposites, such as screaming and pounding on the door for mother to return when she leaves and then running to the far corner of the playroom when she returns.

With this developmental foundation of fragmented consciousness, subsequent trauma such as sexual abuse is liable to remain compartmentalized. For example, child cannot simultaneously hold in mind an ordinary attachment relationship and a sexual relationship (DePrince & Freyd, 2007; Freyd, 1996). In the face of a multiplicity of traumatic interactions, a cascading process can occur with proliferating dissociated states, each related to different ages, emotions, or traumatic relationships. Such compartmentalization is an extreme failure of mentalizing, which is an inherently integrative process through which a coherent autobiography is constructed. Compartmentalization, coupled with amnesia, is the antithesis of narrative coherence. In what is typically an arduous and lengthy treatment, the therapist must hold the patient's fragmented mind in mind while building a climate of stability and security that enables the patient gradually to expand the range of awareness of painful emotions, experiences, and relationships.

Depression

Whereas PTSD and dissociative disorders are closely linked to trauma, depression develops in a wide range of contexts, although varying degress of stress invariably play a key role in etiology. In educating patients (Allen, 2006a), I use a stress-pileup model in which adversity in childhood attachment relationships contributes substantially to vulnerability to depression in response to later stressors (Bifulco & Thomas, in press). Depression merits our attention, because depression is a more common trauma-related disorder than PTSD (Bryant, 2010). Patients typically come to our hospital doors because they are depressed—and often suicidal—far more often than seeking help with PTSD or dissociative disorders. Moreover, PTSD and dissociation often are intermingled with trauma-related depression.

Bowlby (1980) placed vulnerability to depression squarely in the territory of attachment in contending, "loss of a loved person is one of the most intensely painful experiences any human being can suffer" (p. 7). Consistent with the thesis of this book, research has shown that the quality of attachment relationships following the loss plays a major role in risk of subsequent depression (G. W. Brown, Bifulco, Veiel & Andrews, 1990). Moreover, the developmental pathway from childhood trauma to adulthood depression is complex: the risk of depression is heightened by insecure attachment in adulthood, and insecure adult attachment is associated with conflict and lack of support in close relationships in adulthood. Conversely, secure relationships in childhood, adolescence, and adulthood provide a buffer against the development of depression following childhood maltreatment (Bifulco & Thomas, in press).

In my view, depression is one of mentalizing's main enemies, as any psychotherapist who has worked with a profoundly depressed person can attest. I remember walking and sitting with such a patient in the sun; surely, the sun was doing him more good than I. At best, working with severely depressed patients, I assume the role of a supportive, encouraging coach; mentalizing in the form of psychotherapeutic reflection is beyond reach. Yet, in this context, attachment begins to develop and, thankfully, multimodal hospital treatment gradually helps; this treatment includes medication along with a daily routine, activity, and—most important—a social milieu that fosters engagement.

Yet mentalizing not only collapses with depression but also contributes to its development in a vicious circle (Luyten, Fonagy, Lemma & Target, 2012). As the history of cognitive therapy (Beck, 1991) attests, distorted working models of self and others play a significant role in the development of depression, as does rigidity in thinking exemplified by depressive rumination (Nolen-Hoeksema, 2000). Rumination not only fuels and maintains depression but also interferes with social problem solving and undermines social support (Nolen-Hoeksema & Davis, 1999). In an inevitably futile effort, patients attempt to think themselves out of depression; plainly, they need the help of another person who can hold their mind in mind and thereby help them consider other perspectives. Here the mindfulness and mentalizing approaches overlap (Segal, Teasdale & Williams, 2004): the first step is a move out of psychic equivalence, recognizing that depressive thinking is a reflection of a mental state, not an absolute truth. Maintaining the distinction between *feeling* hopeless and *being* hopeless is a prime example of needed mentalizing.

Substance abuse

When we educate patients about the relation between psychiatric disorders and impaired mentalizing, we start with substance abuse (Allen, O'Malley, Freeman & Bateman, 2012), a ubiquitous problem in conjunction with childhood trauma (Felitti & Anda, 2010). Nothing impairs mentalizing like intoxication. Moreover, withdrawal and preoccupation with obtaining substances also impair mentalizing. Secrecy is a blatant barrier to mentalizing in relationships. These points are all too obvious to patients when they are invited to think about them. Yet we also ask patients to consider how impared mentalizing might contribute to subtance abuse. No doubt, shame and self-hatred associated with distorted working models of the self play a key role in generating the stress that substance abuse is intended to assuage—while ultimately fueling a degraded sense of self.

Yet we place greatest emphasis on the role of impaired mentalizing in generating conflicts and breaches in relationships; then the addiction takes the place of a secure attachment relationship. We note the irony that addictive substances are employed to salve the wounds from tormenting relationships, but the relationship with the substance also becomes one of torment, adding fuel to the vicious cycle. With the confluence of insecure attachment, impaired mentalizing, and substance abuse, the evolution of mentalizing-enhanced substance abuse treatment is a promising development (Philips, Kahn & Bateman, 2012).

Eating disorders

Like substance abuse, eating disorders have a complex etiology that includes childhood trauma and insecure attachment (Fischer, Stojek & Hartzell, 2010; Mallinckrodt, McCreary & Robertson, 1995). Anorexia exemplifies the nonmentalizing teleological mode of functioning: the patient strives to attain emotional control by exerting control over something tangible, namely, what goes into the body. Somewhat akin to substance abuse, bingeing is a form of self-soothing as well as abetting dissociative detachment; yet, followed by shame, disgust, and self-loathing, binging can lead to purging, which provides transient relief from these emotions. Plainly, bingeing and purging operate in a vicious circle; each fuels emotional distress that prompts the other.

As prototypes of substituting action for reflection, eating disorders are fertile ground for a mentalizing approach to treatment. Finn Skärderud (Skärderud & Fonagy, 2012) has developed a mentalizing intervention, aptly named *Minding the Body*, aimed at enhancing awareness that the body is a symbolic representation of the self and fostering awareness of the relation between body sensations and emotional feelings. More broadly, the treatment promotes patients' capacities to address problems in attachment relationships directly, as contrasted with futile efforts to solve these problems concretely through the vehicles of food and the body.

Nonsuicidal self-injury

For many traumatized patients, nonsuicidal self-injury—like substance abuse, bingeing, and purging—is a potent means of providing relief from unbearably painful emotions. Defined by the absence of suicidal intent, nonsucidal self-injury includes self-cutting, banging, burning, inserting sharp objects into skin or ingesting them, interfering with wound healing, and the like (Nock, 2009). A history of childhood trauma, including disorganized attachment, is a predisposing factor for nonsuicidal self-injury (Yates, 2009), and a feeling of emotional neglect is a common precipitant for the behavior (Kaplan, 1991). While the predominant function of self-injury is tension relief, it also has a powerful communicative function (often interpreted unhelpfully as "manipulative" or "attention seeking"). In the teleological mode, actions speak louder than words: the patient enraged by the therapist's insensitivity displays her arms with recent wounds to express the depth of her pain.

I draw patients' attention to the likelihood that their self-injurious efforts to manage unbearable pain borne of insecurity generate similarly unbearable painful states in their partner—sometimes by conscious intent. Moreover, the behavior fuels the partner's insecurity in the relationship, which inevitably increases the patient's insecurity.

At worst, the partner also engages in destructive efforts to regulate distress; then vicious circles become intertwined with vicious circles. In the course of such spirals, the patient's conviction that the partner is fed up and the relationship is doomed are reinforced by the partner's behavior; sometimes in a counterphobic maneuver, the patient will precipitate the destruction of the relationship to take control of the dreaded outcome. Relationships with psychotherapists are hardly immune to this pattern. Mentalizing these processes, rather than enacting them, is a pathway to interrupting them.

Suicidal states

Karl Menninger (1938) construed self-injury as anti-suicidal behavior to the extent that it is a way of surviving emotional pain, albeit a temporary solution. In contrast, suicide is the ultimate—permanent—escape from pain. As with all other stopgap maneuvers I have considered, a history of attachment truama contributes significantly to suicidal behavior (Bifulco, Moran, Baines, Bunn & Stanford, 2002; Felitti & Anda, 2010). Suicidal despair seems the most poignant instantiation of reliving past trauma: feeling alone in pain and despair. This experience is consistent with two major contributors to suicidal states: lacking a sense of belonging and the feeling of being a burden to others upon whom the patient depends (Joiner, 2005). Accordingly, in no other clinical situation is establishing an empathic, mentalizing connection more urgent and crucial (Allen, 2011; Orbach, 2011).

Unfortunately, the therapist's anxiety is liable to impair mentalizing—an especially problematic instance of the principle that applies to therapists as it does to patients: you most need to mentalize when you are least capable of doing it. Understandably, therapists can bypass mentalizing by taking control; of course doing so (e.g., via involuntary hospitalization) might be necessary to save the patient's life. Yet, short of the most dire circumstances, efforts to take control while circmventing mentalizing may be counterproductive. No-suicide contracts are as ubiquitous as they are ineffective (Rudd, Mandrusiak & Joiner, 2006). The patient might sign such a contract in one state of mind that holds no force in another state of mind (Bateman & Fonagy, 2006).

Having been hospitalized after a suicide attempt, many patients understandably defend against their formerly suicidal state of mind (e.g., "Now that I realize how much it would hurt my children, I'll never do that again!"). Therapists should not be reassured easily; the enduring vulnerabilities to suicidal states, invariably embedded in attachment relationships, must be explored and mentalized (Allen, 2011; J. Holmes, 2011). Treating depression without addressing these vulnerabilities is likely to be insufficient for long-term prevention. David Jobes (2006, 2011) has developed and researched a structured approach to address psychological and interpersonal vulnerabilities in a collaborative (and mentalizing) fashion.

Complex traumatic stress disorders

Attesting to the nonspecific relation between attachment trauma and psychiatric disorder, not only does such trauma contribute to a range of clinical syndromes as just illustrated but also to diverse personality disorders (J. G. Johnson, Cohen, Brown, Smailes & Bernstein, 1999). Among these, borderline personality disorder (BPD) has garnered most attention in relation to attachment trauma and insecurity; BPD commonly is intermingled with the various disorders and problems I have just discussed (PTSD, dissociation, depression, substance abuse, eating disorders, nonsuicidal self-harm, and suicidality), and I have seen a number of patients with all these problems combined. Given its link to attachment disturbance, BPD is the disorder that evoked Peter Fonagy's interest in mentalizing (Fonagy, 1989, 1991) and thus the disorder for which Mentalization-Based Treatment initially was developed (Bateman & Fonagy, 2004, 2006). Most conspicuous in BPD are impairments in three facets of mentalizing: explicit, cognitive mentalizing of internal mental states is compromised as a result of automatic, implicit, emotion-driven mentalizing (Fonagy & Luyten, 2009). For example, feeling endangered, the unreflective patient does not consider the possibility that the therapist's frown is an expression of puzzlement but rather immediately becomes convinced that he is disgusted and fed up with her—ready to terminate the treatment.

Given the stigma associated with the diagnosis of BPD—even among mental health professionals—Judith Herman (1992a, 1992b) proposed instead that the amalgam of trauma-related problems be construed as "complex PTSD" and officially diagnosed as Disorders of Extreme Stress Not Otherwise Specified (Herman, 1993). More recently, Bessel van der Kolk and colleagues (van der Kolk, 2005; van der Kolk & d'Andrea, 2010) proposed a childhood counterpart to complex PTSD, "developmental trauma disorder." Given the complexity of PTSD and associated controversies about its criteria, I am dubious about lumping far more problems into a single diagnostic category. I am partial to Julian Ford and Christine Courtois's (2009) terms, complex psychological trauma (referring to prolonged and severe trauma in attachment relationships at developmentally vulnerable periods) and complex traumatic stress disorders, namely, "changes in mind, emotions, body, and relationships experienced following complex psychological trauama, including severe problems with dissociation, emotion dysregulation, somatic distress, or relational or spiritual alienation" (p. 13).

While the diagnostic lexicon and criteria are continually evolving, there will always be a place for disorder-specific treatments. Yet attachment trauma defies this approach, as I will continue to emphasize in the next section of this chapter. We cannot rely on a slew of diagnoses to achieve true diagnostic understanding; rather, while not ignoring psychiatric diagnoses, we must take the approach of developmental psychopathology, moving from a disorder-centered to a person-centered mindset. Sidney Blatt and colleagues (Blatt, 2008; Blatt & Luyten, 2010) advocate such a developmental approach, building on the two-polarities model (i.e., developmental intertwining of relatedness and self-definition). This approach aspires "to map the myriad complex pathways from early childhood to later adaptive or maladaptive development which can then form the basis of interventions for both preventing and treating disorders" (Luyten, Vliegen, van Houdenhove & Blatt, 2008, p. 29). Hence we must use existing treatments for trauma as stepping stones to a more developmentally informed, integrative treatment approach. Yet, rather than bypassing more specialized treatments, we must build upon them.

Existing trauma treatments

We are blessed with a set of specialized treatments for PTSD that have received a grade of "A" from the PTSD Treatment Guidelines Taskforce (Foa, Keane, Friedman & Cohen, 2009) based on replicated randomized, well-controlled trials. Prominent among these are prolonged exposure (Foa, Hembree & Rothbaum, 2007), cognitive therapies (Ehlers, Clark, Hackmann, McManus & Fennell, 2005; Resick, Monson & Rizvi, 2008), and Eye Movement Desensitization and Reprocessing (EMDR) (F. Shapiro, 1995). Yet, as is characteristic of the field of psychotherapy more generally, researchers are hard pressed to demonstrate that any one of these treatments is more effective than any other (Powers, Halpern, Ferenschak, Gillihan & Foa, 2010). To reiterate a common refrain, "we have not reached the point where we can predict which treatments are most suitable for which patients" (Friedman, Cohen, Foa & Keane, 2009, p. 617); in short, after a half-century of psychotherapy research, we continue to struggle to answer the fundamental question, What works for whom? (Roth & Fonagy, 2005).

Plainly, as Foa and colleagues (Foa & Kozak, 1986, 1991) have argued for decades, exposure is central to trauma treatments, including not only prolonged exposure but also cognitive therapies and EMDR. Albeit at a lower dose, cognitive therapy entails exposure (e.g., in talking or writing about tramatic experience). Conversely, exposure therapy includes cognitive processing: "In effect, we practice informal cognitive therapy during exposure, in that we help clients to examine ways in which they evaluate threat and to develop inferential processes that lead to more realistic conclusions" (Foa & Kozak, 1991, p. 45). EMDR is an amalgam of exposure and cognitive processing, although the exposure is relatively brief as the patient is encouraged to bring images of the trauma to mind and then to focus on a bilateral stimulus (e.g., the therapist's fingers moving back and forth in front of the face). Although EMDR is an effective treatment (Wilson, Becker & Tinker, 1995; Wilson, Becker & Tinker, 1997), there is no evidence for its superiority to prolonged exposure (Powers, Halpern, Ferenschak, Gillihan & Foa, 2010) or other cognitive-behavioral approaches (Seidler & Wagner, 2006). Ironically, there is no consistent evidence that the distinctive component for which it is named—eye movements or other bilateral stimuli—contributes to its effectiveness (Spates, Koch, Cusack, Pagoto & Waller, 2009). Exposure may be the common denominator in all these treatments (Powers, Halpern, Ferenschak, Gillihan & Foa, 2010) but, as Anthony Roth and Peter Fonagy (2005) contend, "Specialist knowledge of this population may … be more critical to outcome than the choice of any specific exposure-based treatment" (p. 235).

It is hard to envision any therapy that does not involve thinking and talking about painful emotional experience and memories; psychoanalysis paved the way for all that followed. I think it is profoundly misleading to liken exposure therapy to simple habituation, as if therapy were akin to habituating to a repeated sound. The mechanisms by which exposure treatments exert their effects are complex and matters of continuing investigation (Craske et al., 2008); developing increased tolerance for distressing emotions is among these mutative effects. I find it noteworthy that Foa's (Foa, Huppert & Cahill, 2006) account of the effectiveness of prolonged exposure includes three elements: emotional engagement with the trauma memory; modifying unrealistic beliefs that the world is extremely dangerous and the self is incompetent; and developing a coherent narrative of the traumatic experience. With minimal translation, this account is consistent with the need to mentalize emotion (Jurist, 2005), modify internal working models of self and others, and—most striking—achieve narrative coherence, which is a key criterion for attachment security in relation to trauma in the Adult Attachment Interview.

Although noted in treatment manuals (Foa, Hembree & Rothbaum, 2007), glaringly absent in theoretical accounts of cognitive-behavioral trauma treatments is the central importance of the patient-therapist relationship. David Barlow and colleagues' (Barlow, Allen & Choate, 2004) unified protocol for treating overlapping anxiety and depressive disorders brings this point home. These disorders have a common history and shared vulnerability. Important in both disorders is the biological vulnerability to anxiety proneness, the genetic basis of which is becoming increasingly evident. Crucially, this biological vulnerability interacts with adverse early life experience: "a generalized psychological vulnerability emerges from early childhood experience characterized by a stressful unpredictable environment and/or the influence of specific parenting styles described in detail in the *attachment theory* literature" (Wiliamoska et al., 2010, p. 884, emphasis added). Yet the patient-therapist relationship plays no part in the theory of treatment. Although not universal (McBride & Atkinson, 2009), this typical omission of relationship factors in cognitive-behavioral approaches is especially noteworthy; as noted in the introduction to this chapter, we have scant evidence for systematic differences in effectiveness among various specialized treatments, coupled with extensive evidence for the substantial contribution of the therapeutic relationship to treatment outcomes.

Given that attachment trauma is embedded in relationships, in its origins and its repetitions, failure to put the patient-therapist relationship center stage in the theory of treatment makes no sense. Yet, in my view, the primary value of the psychotherapy relationship is its potential to promote mentalizing and security in *other* relationships; in effect, psychotherapy serves as a *bridge* to other relationships. Why not bypass the bridge and work directly on other relationships? As one who concentrates on individual psychotherapy, I am continually humbled by the observation that many hospitalized patients value most their relationships with other patients as having been most helpful in their treatment. To a considerable extent, our job as clinicians is to foster and maintain a healing community (e.g., by promoting a mentalizing stance) and to help patients make optimal use of these other relationships. Consistent with this view, group psychotherapy has been a mainstay of trauma treatments (Ford, Fallot & Harris, 2009), although groups are extremely diverse in composition and focus. Given their ubiquity, the effectiveness of group treatments for trauma is insufficently researched (Welch & Rothbaum, 2007), notwithstanding some promising studies (Shea, McDevitt-Murphy, Ready & Schnurr, 2009). Given the fact that mentalizing approaches place a premium on cultivating multiple perspectives, group psychotherapy is central to Mentalization-Based Treatment in its partial-hospital and outpatient applications (Bateman & Fonagy, 2006; Karterud & Bateman, 2012).

Most compelling, in my view, is the rationale for intervening directly in current attachment relationships, that is, in couples, marital, and family therapy. Sue Johnson (S. M. Johnson, 2008, 2009), who has applied attachment theory and research to the development of Emotionally Focused Therapy for couples and families, rightly protests the "overuse of individual therapy at the expense of couple or family work" (S. M. Johnson & Courtois, 2009, p. 374). Family therapy affords a prime opportunity for cultivating mentalizing in the attachment relationships most central in the patient's life (Asen & Fonagy, 2012; Fearon et al., 2006). Unfortunately, as in group therapy, research on the effectiveness of couples and family therapy in trauma treatment is limited, in stark contrast for its compelling theoretical rationale (Riggs, Monson, Glynn & Canterino, 2009). Given Johnson's trenchant critique of the overuse of individual therapy, I take solace in the fact that, working in a hospital setting, my therapy patients also have the benefit of family work, which often plays a central role in treatment (as does group therapy). But Johnson's plea for greater focus on intervening directly in attachment relationships also has a solid basis in the emerging evidence for the effectiveness of parent-infant and parent-child therapies (Berlin, Zeanah & Lieberman, 2008), some of which include an explicit mentalizing focus (Sadler, Slade & Mayes, 2006; Slade, 2008b).

To return to my starting point, I have commented on the limited evidence for the effectiveness of group, couples, and family therapy for treating trauma. But this evidence base has been focused only on the most conspicuous (if not most prevalent) trauma-related disorder, PTSD. Yet Foa and colleagues (Foa, Hembree & Rothbaum, 2007) acknowledge that prolonged exposure is "a treatment for PTSD, not a treatment for trauma" (p. 21). Moreover, Foa makes the related point that the practice guidelines have limited applicability to the treatment of complex traumatic stress disorders: "relatively little is known about the successful treatment of patients with these trauma histories. There is a growing clinical consensus, with a degree of empirical support, that some patients with these histories require multimodal interventions, applied consistently over a longer time period" (Foa, Keane, Friedman & Cohen, 2009, p. 2).

With Herman's (1992b) pioneering work, we have a rich clinical literature pertinent to the treatment of complex traumatic stress disorders, founded on a stage-oriented model in which establishing safety and stabilization provides a foundation for processing traumatic memories and constructing a coherent narrative; this trauma focus is followed by a focus on social and vocational functioning, with a premium on developing trusting and intimate relationships as well as effective parenting practices. Plainly, complex disorders require complex—and often long-term—treatments. Interventions for complex trauma continue to evolve (Courtois, Ford & Cloitre, 2009), concomitant with accruing evidence for the effectiveness of cognitive-behavioral protocols (Jackson, Nissenson & Cloitre, 2009).

Following Herman's (1992a) lead, if not her preferred terminology, we might take BPD and its commonly comorbid psychiatric disorders as a prototype for complex traumatic stress disorders. Then we can take heart in the multiplicity of well-researched treatments for BPD. Based on its substantial research base, Marsha Linehan regards her Dialectical Behavior Therapy (DBT; Linehan, 1993) as the current standard of care for BPD (Linehan et al., 2006). With its central focus on emotion regulation, DBT is highly pertinent to trauma treatment, and clinicians have taken an interest in integrating DBT interventions with trauma-focused treatment (Follette, Iverson & Ford, 2009). Although it might have some credibility as the standard of care, there is no reason to believe that DBT is superior to other specialized approaches to treating BPD. For example, John Clarkin and colleagues (Clarkin, Levy, Lenzenweger & Kernberg,

2007) compared Transference-Focused Psychotherapy (TFP) directly with DBT and a manualized version of supportive therapy for BPD. Notably, TFP includes attention to mentalizing (Kernberg, Diamond, Yeomans, Clarkin & Levy, 2008). In Clarkin and colleagues' study, all treatments were generally equivalent in effectiveness; yet, pertinent to my interests, based on results of Adult Attachment Interviews administered before and after one year of treatment, TFP was superior to DBT and supportive psychotherapy in showing improvements in the proportions of patients showing secure attachment as well as in demonstrating improvements in narrative coherence and mentalizing (Levy et al., 2006).

The partial-hospital application of Mentalization-Based Treatment (MBT) for BPD has been shown to be effective in comparison with usual community treatment in a series of controlled trials (Bateman & Fonagy, 1999, 2001), culminating in an eight-year follow-up study (Bateman & Fonagy, 2008)—the longest follow-up study of BPD treatment to date. MBT diminished suicide attempts, emergency-room visits, inpatient admissions, medication and outpatient treatment utilization, and impulsivity. Compared to the control group, far fewer patients continued to meet criteria for BPD, and they showed substantially improved interpersonal and occupational functioning. These results prompted Ken Levy (Levy, 2008) to comment, "the findings clearly support the notion that developing behavioral control need not be skill based but can occur through the development of mental skills" (p. 557). The impressive follow-up results led Herman (2009) to propose, "this study may ultimately define a new standard of care for BPD. It leads me to wonder about developing similarly intensive, multimodal models for complex PTSD" (pp. xvi-xvii). The question about degree of intensiveness, however, must remain open; the more recent outpatient implementation of MBT, which combines individual and group psychotherapy, also has proven effective in the treatment of BPD (Bateman & Fonagy, 2009).

Research on attachment in psychotherapy

In his oft-quoted passage, Bowlby (1988) captured the essence of psychotherapy as an attachment relationship, the intent of which is

> to provide the patient with a secure base from which he can explore the various unhappy and painful aspects of his life, past and

present, many of which he finds it difficult or perhaps impossible to think about and reconsider without a trusted companion to provide support, encouragement, sympathy, and, on occasion, guidance. (p. 138)

A patient in a trauma-education group put it even more succinctly: when I commented that the mind can be a scary place, she quipped, "and you wouldn't want to go in there alone."

Research is consistent with Bowlby's view insofar as patients rely on the relationship as a safe haven and secure base; they are concerned about the therapist's availability; and they can be perturbed by separations (Eagle & Wolitzky, 2009). Yet the professional nature of the relationship, contingent on maintaining clear boundaries, sharply distinguishes psychotherapy from other attachment relationships. Hence Bowlby (1988) proposed that the therapist's role is *analogous* to that of the mother, and Holmes (J. Holmes, 2010) views the therapist as providing a *quasi*-secure base. Plainly, the strength of the attachment will be highly variable among patient-therapist pairs, depending on both members' attachment proclivities. Ambivalent patients might quickly form an emotionally intense relationship and depend heavily on the therapist; avoidant patients might approach the therapy as something akin to a buisness or consulting relationship; and fearful patients might be extremely hard to reach for long periods. Also significant will be the frequency of sessions, the duration of the relationship, and the therapeutic approach (e.g., the extent of emphasis on emotion versus cognition).

Research on the influence of attachment patterns in psychotherapy yields straightforward results (Obegi & Berant, 2009; Slade, 2008a). Patients who are securely attached fit Bowlby's ideal model of psychotherapy: they are more likely to seek treatment; they form a positive alliance; they are trusting and likely to view the therapist as available and sensitive; they are self-disclosing; and they are able to reveal their negative feelings so as to repair ruptures in the alliance. Patients who are avoidant are less likely to seek therapy and more likely to have difficulty forming a positive alliance. They are likely to be critical and to see the therapist as critical as well, and they are loath to show their vulnerability. Although patients who are ambivalent are likely to become emotionally engaged quickly, they are prone to disappointment and disillusionment, such that the alliance is unstable. In addition, they are likely to be averse to support for growth and autonomy, as such movement portends the loss of dependency on the therapist. Patients who are disorganized pose particular challenges, not only because of stark oscillations between closeness and distance but also owing to lapses in attunement to the present reality of the relationship. Some traumatized patients slip into profoundly dissociatively detached states in which they feel as if they are endangered or being abused in the present—or they are so detached as to be psychologically unreachable. They exemplify the experience of fright without solution, in the therapist's office as in the Strange Situation.

Like the parent-child attachment relationship, the therapist-patient relationship is an attachment partnership, to which both partners' attachment patterns make a contribution. More avoidant therapists will have difficulty with emotional closeness and expressiveness, whereas more ambivalent therapists will have difficulty with patients who are rejecting or inclined to maintain distance. Not surprisingly, therapists' attachment security is associated with more positive therapeutic alliances (Levy, Ellison, Scott & Bernecker, 2011) and better treatment outcomes (Beutler & Blatt, 2006). Attachment security also is consistent with flexibility in relating, enabling the therapist gently to counter the patient's insecure style. Thus secure therapists are adept at moving avoidant patients toward more emotional engagement while providing more structuring and containment for ambivalent patients (Mallinckrodt, Daly & Wang, 2009; Slade, 2008a).

Consistent with expectations, securely attached patients are likely to show higher levels of functioning at entry into therapy and at termination (Obegi & Berant, 2009), and they are more likely to show improvement over the course of therapy (Levy, Ellison, Scott & Bernecker, 2011). Of course, insecurely attached patients—especially those with a history of attachment truama—are more likely than their secure counterparts to *need* treatment. Although the number of studies on shifts in security associated with psychotherapy is few, results are encouraging. As noted earlier in this chapter, Levy and colleagues (Levy et al., 2006) found a significant increase in the proportion of patients with BPD showing attachment security after a year of Transference-Focused Psychotherapy. Notably, although they found a modest decrease in unresolved trauma in the AAI at the end of treatment, the difference was not statistically significant. On the other hand, Chase Stovall-McClough and colleagues (Stovall-McClough, Cloitre &

McClough, 2008) found a significant decrease in unresolved status over the course of treatment for a group of women with a history of child abuse who were diagnosed with PTSD. In a study of psychodynamic psychotherapy conducted with inpatients, Fonagy and colleagues (Fonagy et al., 1995) also found that, whereas none of the patients showed secure attachment at the beginning of treatment, 40% were secure at termination. In my view, mentalizing is the primary means by which such increases in security are brought about, but much further research is needed to firmly establish mentalizing as a mechanism of change in psychotherapy.

Mentalizing as a distinctive style of psychotherapy

I cannot imagine conducting psychotherapy without mentalizing. Even the most highly prescriptive treatments require mentalizing on the part of the patient and therapist, for example, in formulating a diagnosis and gauging the response to treatment. Accordingly, we have proposed that mentalizing is the *most fundamental* common factor in psychotherapies (Allen, Fonagy &Bateman, 2008) while also acknowledging that our focus on mentalizing in psychotherapy is the *least novel* approach imaginable (Allen & Fonagy, 2006). Hence we therapists invariably are mentalizing—unless, as John Oldham (2008) shrewdly commented—we are failing to do our job. As we often say to patients, we all mentalize naturally—we cannot help doing so. Yet we all can learn to mentalize more consistently and skillfully, therapists and patients alike. Psychotherapy is one emotionally charged context in which skillful mentalizing is necessary and difficult.

In proposing that mentalizing and its foundation of mindful attention are central to the conduct of psychotherapy, regardless of the therapist's theoretical orientation (J. G. Allen, 2008a), I have set the stage for significant confusion. If mentalizing is characteristic of *all* psychotherapy, what is the justification for a particular brand of therapy—Mentalization-Based Treatment? Is all psychotherapy MBT? I think this confusion comes about in part because there are no unique techniques or interventions in MBT—no couch, no free association, no thought records, no eye movements. Thus, if you were observing an MBT therapy session, you could not identify it as MBT (although you might discern a high level of mentalizing)—unless you recognized Anthony Bateman or Peter Fonagy conducting it.

Absent any uniqueness, I view the focus on mentalizing as a *distinctive style* of psychotherapy that Bateman and Fonagy developed as especially suitable for treating patients with BPD, many of whom show conspicuous impairments of mentalizing in emotionally charged interactions with persons to whom they are ambivalently attached. Thus, ubiquitous as mentalizing might be in psychotherapies of various persuasions, the development of MBT has contributed substantially to the refinement of mentalizing in clinical practice. As with other approaches to therapy—cognitive therapy being a prime example—what we learn in treating one disorder can be applied helpfully in treating others. As is evident from the discussion of trauma-related psychopathology earlier in this chapter, following this common developmental pathway in therapy applications, principles of MBT are now being applied to a wide range of disorders beyond BPD (Bateman & Fonagy, 2012b).

Yet, in advocating the mentalizing style of therapy as suited to patients with a history of attachment trauma, I do not want to equate adopting this style with conducting MBT. MBT entails meticulous and continual attention to stimulating mentalizing and to any interventions that inadvertently undermine mentalizing. This process sounds easy—until you try it. Accordingly, as in any other specialized approach, learning to conduct MBT requires specific training and ongoing supervision.

As burgeoning interest in mentalizing and eagerness to extend its applications attest, this style of therapy is highly appealing to many clinicians. To me, the mentalizing style is a breath of fresh air. I find this fresh air to be especially pertinent to supervising beginning therapists. They come with so many prohibitions and prescriptions in mind that they are practicing in a psychological straightjacket, often oppressed by their supervisory superego. I agree firmly with Paul Wachtel (2008): "there is no single right way to conduct psychotherapy" (p. 303). Putting a personal stamp on it, Wachtel proposes that his approach "reflects not just my theory but who I am as a person. This is *my* way of working with people" (p. 266, emphasis in original). While acknowledging the role of theory, as all of us should do, Wachtel states forthrightly that his way of working "is partly simply me" (p. 267). How could it be otherwise? With mentalizing being the skill that best distinguishes us from our animal kin, I believe that therapeutic skill is founded in *skill in being human*. Hence, in providing supervision, I counsel the obvious: be yourself; be natural. Furthermore, as one of my supervisors, Peter Novotny, once quipped, when you don't know what else to do, be kind.

Rigid rules and prescriptions—not to mention preoccupation about conducting therapy in just the right way—interfere with mentalizing, which requires mindful attentiveness to the patient as well as flexibility. Paradoxically, obsessing about whether you are mentalizing properly in psychotherapy blocks mentalizing. I remember a session I had with a patient just after meeting with Anthony Bateman. This was the final session before the patient's discharge from the hospital, and I simply wanted to know more about his plans. I was thinking I should be stimulating mentalizing instead of exploring his plans, and then I became irked. I remember saying to myself, "Screw mentalizing!" and proceeded with my inquiry. We must not substitute one straightjacket for another.

The principles of mentalizing therapy that I find appealing are elaborated elsewhere (Allen, Fonagy &Bateman, 2008; Bateman & Fonagy, 2006, 2012a). In brief, the style is conversational, collaborative, and commonsensical—natural. There is an egalitarian spirit to the approach: each member of the dyad brings an attachment history and mentalizing capacity to the encounter; in that sense, we are in the same boat. No doubt, we therapists have substantial professional knowledge and expertise to offer our patients; yet our patients are the experts regarding their experience and history. MBT eschews the idea that the therapist is the expert on the patient's mind. In my view, one difference in roles is this: we therapists are obligated to mentalize and our patients are not so obligated; yet we encourage them in this direction. Nor should we assume that we therapists are better mentalizers than our patients as a rule. We must count on our patients to help us mentalize when we are confused or off track. I find that when I am open to their help, patients provide it graciously.

In conducting educational groups on mentalizing (Allen, O'Malley, Freeman & Bateman, 2012; Groat & Allen, 2011), we professionals routinely are humbled by our patients' talents. We employ a number of exercises designed to stimulate mentalizing. For example, we ask patients in a group to provide a visual image symbolizing their current experience of treatment. They come up with images such as "climbing a slippery slope and sliding back down" or "being trapped at the bottom of a well and screaming for help, but only hearing the echo of my own voice." After writing down the array of images on a board, we ask group members to choose images they find intriguing and to speculate about the mental state of the image creator while the creator remains silent. After the group has had its say, the creator reflects on what comments fit and what did not, amplifying on the meaning of the image. Commonly, we group leaders are impressed by the group members' sensitivity and insightfulness regarding the meaning of the images, which often outstrips our own mentalizing ability. Sometimes the creator is surprised by interpretations that identify something of which the creator had not been aware. Not uncommonly, those who created the image are profoundly moved by the group members' insight and especially by their keen interest and attentiveness to their state of mind.

Of all the principles of MBT, the one I find most crucial is *transparency*. I make my mind (i.e., my mental perspective) available to my patients, and I hope they will do likewise. I am not stonefaced but rather quite expressive. Often, I comment on my facial expressions (when I am aware of them): "I was frowning because I fear that you're going down the path to another relapse." Anthony Bateman once said to me that the most distinctive feature of MBT is the therapist's use of "I" statements: "I'm concerned that I might have insulted you." "I'm thinking that you might be reluctant to voice your irritation." "I'm not sure what we should be working on at the moment." "I think I just slipped a gear and lost your train of thought." "I'm silent because I'm thinking." "It's striking that you say you feel like an 'idiot' right now, because I was thinking a few minutes ago how insightful you were." "You seem convinced that the staff is trying to provoke an angry outburst; I think it's quite unlikely—there's enough natural aggravation in this hospital that we don't need to go out of our way to create it." "If I were your parent, I'd have been scared out of my wits when you took off for a week." "Brace yourself for bluntness: I found your smiling when talking about humiliating him to be quite ruthless." As such comments indicate, I am not making declarations about the patient but rather offering my thoughts and feelings for the patient's consideration.

On the theme of transparency, I am especially partial to Bateman and Fonagy's (2006) statement, "The patient has to find himself in the mind of the therapist and, equally, the therapist has to understand himself in the mind of the patient if the two together are to develop a mentalizing process. *Both have to experience a mind being changed by a mind*" (p. 93, emphasis added). The inability to influence the mind of another person is a common source of profound helplessness, and it is utterly typical of traumatic attachment relationships. Conversely, the ability to have such an influence—through persuasion and negotiation, not coercion—provides a fundamental sense of power that lies at the core of personal agency.

I had a session with a patient who was angrily at odds with his hospital treatment team about his discharge plan—they wanted more structure and he wanted less. He complained that he was not being "heard." I was in agreement with his treatment team, but I expressed interest in his thoughts and plans. He conveyed that he understood their reasoning but also showed considerable excitement about the alternative scenario he had envisioned. Moreover, he said he felt "shut down" and "disrespected" by his treatment team, just as he had felt squelched by his parents regarding a number of painful matters that we had discussed previously in the therapy. At one point in this discussion as I was listening silently, he asked me what I was thinking. I told him the thought in my mind at that moment: "He's not being unreasonable, even though he's pissed off." I also pointed out that one can be "heard" without others agreeing. Indeed, I said I still had doubts about his plan, given how dangerous his previous behavior had been. He could understand my lingering disagreement, but he was aware by my responsiveness that I had opened my mind, and he felt considerably settled down by the end of the session—heard if not agreed with.

When indicated, I like to use assessments (questionnaires or structured interviews) to guide the therapy. On the whole, however, I am averse to highly structured approaches. I employ only one technique: conversation, often infused with emotion. Yet I am equally averse to free-wheeling processes that lack a focus or sense of direction. To provide a modicum of structure, and to share my mind with the patient, I like to provide a written formulation after the initial sessions to ensure that we are in accord about the main problems. I present the formulation at the beginning of the session and ask the patient to read it through. Then I inquire about its accuracy and comprehensiveness. I am eager to correct and revise it as needed, sometimes on the spot with the patient's help. If the formulation needs significant revision, I will work on it more and review the revised version in the next session. The following is an example:

> I thought it might be helpful to summarize my understanding of your problems and the work we need to do in psychotherapy. No doubt, this work will not be easy. You let me know up front that you

are coming to therapy only because you're feeling "desperate." You said you've never been "deeper in the pit," as evidenced by becoming suicidal for the first time in your lifetime. Although you've been suffering intensely for the past few years, you've "avoided therapy like the plague." You've assumed that you would be "beaten up" with all your failings and that you wouldn't be helped. My hope is that you might discover that you need not be so frightened of therapy and that you might benefit from it. This hope is based on the fact that, despite your describing yourself as "distrusting to the point of paranoia," you've been open with me even though we've met for a relatively short time. Admittedly, you don't see this openness as a result of trust but rather "driven by desperation."

From what you've told me about your childhood, you had much previous experience of feeling deep in the pit, especially in your home. Being the youngest of five children, by the time you were born, your mother was exhausted, stressed, depressed, and frequently "drank herself into a fog" by the late afternoon. You remember her as being attentive and concerned about you only when you were "deathly ill," which was very rare. The main emotion you saw displayed in your family was anger—your father's anger toward your mother for her drinking and the "shameless mess" the house was in; his anger toward your oldest brother for being a "wild, ungrateful son of a bitch;" and your brother's anger toward your father, which your brother took out on you. You learned very early in life what it was like to feel "beaten up." In addition, your mother didn't hide her resentment, telling you repeatedly that she should have stopped having children after one—your oldest sister, the family favorite who could "do no wrong." While you mainly observed anger, you said you mainly felt fear and despair. To me, the anchor point for the deep pit and your suicidal hopelessness is your statement that you grew up on an "emotional desert island" and that you were forced to survive on your own, often feeling "on the brink of emotional starvation."

While staying mindful of all that went wrong, I think we need to pay equal attention to all that went right. If you were merely distrusting to the point of paranoia, you would not have been able to convey to me the extent of your emotional pain or the reasons for it. You had some companionship on the island, that is, your brother next to you in age; shutting the door to your room and playing with him provided some refuge. You also had a best friend in the neighborhood for several years, although his moving away was a big setback, leading you to become more isolated. Fortunately, much of the time, school also was a refuge; you remember classes as a time when you felt safe and could concentrate. As you said, your schoolwork took your mind off the family chaos. School was something of an exception to the emotional desert island, as a few teachers were enthusiastic about your work, and their recognition was important to you. And your capacity for hard work has paid off throughout school and college and graduate school, as well as in the business world. In my mind, however, the biggest exception to the emotional desert island was your maternal grandfather. As you said, the two of you "clicked," and your time with him was precious, if only occasional. He seemed to have a good grasp of the family problems; although he could not do anything to change the situation, his encouragement for you to endure it and make the best of your abilities helped you keep going. Indeed, you followed his advice. His death two years ago coincides with your worsening depression.

I can see some early roots of your distrust and paranoia, but you also overcame the distrust to a considerable degree. Unfortunately, the distrusting side of you was fueled in recent years by two major betrayals that, coupled with the death of your grandfather, contributed to your "tailspin" into depression and alcohol abuse. Your self-confidence had been buoyed by your relationship with your supervisor, whose enthusiasm for your competence and productivity was evident. As earlier teachers had done in school and college, he served as a mentor. You were disillusioned by the "dog-eat-dog corporate world" when—apparently under pressure from his boss—your supervisor chose one of your co-workers to move with him to a new team in the corporation, leaving you "high and dry" in the hands of a new supervisor whom you described as a "nit-picking nitwit." This disillusionment at work had a cascading effect, because you became more irritable and began drinking too much; you worried that you were becoming some "twisted amalgam" of your father and mother.

Most troubling, your spiral drove a wedge between you and Tammy, whom you had hoped to marry. She had become your main companion on the island: as you stated, she was the first person in your life by whom you felt truly loved; she was the joy of your life. You shared much in the way of family background, and she had been steadfast in putting up with your moodiness. After things went south at work, however, she became increasingly frustrated with your remoteness. You had told her about your image of the "emotional desert island" and she responded by telling you that, especially with your drinking, you were leaving her stranded on the island, which resonated with her early family experience. As you said, she was sending up flares, but you were not paying attention to them—until she had a "romantic fling" with one of her co-workers that led to a major blow-up and then to your coming to the brink of suicide.

Where do we go from here? As you see, I am partial to your "island" metaphor. I like the metaphor of "islands of security" in the midst of childhood relationships that were fraught with insecurity. You have had a number of islands of security (or secure relationships on your island) that have led you to be trusting as well as distrusting. You have shown that trust in our initial work together, despite your reservations. Although in sheer desperation, you have reached out for help by coming to the hospital.

I think you're on the right course, and the hospital affords you lots of opportunities to obtain help. You've noticed that "the fog of depression has begun to lift," and you have just begun to open up in groups about your suicidal depression and some reasons for it. I encourage you to do more of the same and also to risk reaching out to members of the nursing staff with whom you feel comfortable when you find yourself diving into the pit of suicidal despair. You have no idea what to do about the crisis in your relationship with Tammy; I suggest that you talk about the possibility of couples' sessions with your social worker. I am inclined to focus our work on exploring further your vulnerability to becoming suicidal, with the hope that you will use this and subsequent therapy as a means to discover alternatives.

Patients generally are highly appreciative of such written formulations, which exemplify holding their mind in mind. Writing a formulation also helps me clarify my thinking about the treatment. Accordingly, sometimes I am prompted to write a formulation when the patient expresses confusion about the purpose of the therapy and I need to provide some direction. Once I wrote a formulation after a session that was a complete muddle; owing to a blunder on my part, the patient felt hopeless—quite certain that I had no idea what I was doing and fearful that he was beyond help. Articulating my understanding and sense of direction got us back in sync. In some cases, I write a final formulation for the patient in tandem with working on a discharge summary; upon discharge from the hospital, this formulation provides them with a platform for subsequent psychotherapy. There is only one obvious downside: writing these formulations takes a great deal of time and effort.

Mentalizing traumatic experience

If there is a particular context for the mentalizing approach to be the least novel imaginable, working with trauma qualifies. In my view, the essence of trauma treatment was invented when one person developed the capacity to communicate traumatic experience to another who listened empathically. Mind-minded parents routinely provide the gist of trauma treatment to their children who have undergone stressful experiences, minor and major—as do trusted confidants throughout life. We should not lose sight of the fact that professional psychotherapy is a recent invention. Our profession merely capitalizes on our basic human capacities, upon which varying degrees of technology (e.g., in the form of treatment manuals) are superimposed.

I do not deny the benefit of professional expertise; I merely strive to put it in perspective as subordinate to skill in being human. For all my complaints about the limitations of psychiatric diagnostic categories, I find knowledge of psychopathology to be indispensable. I embarked on my trauma-education project (Allen, 2005) as a result of bewilderment about dissociative disturbance, most notably, dissociative identity disorder but also severe dissociative detachment. When we began developing a specialized trauma treatment program (Allen, Coyne & Console, 2000) at The Menninger Clinic, we clinicians knew little more than our bewildered hospital patients, which included those who were diagnosed with dissociative identity disorder and those who were not. Nonsuicidal self-injury also ranked high as a problem that required specialized knowledge. Commonplace as it may be among traumatized patients, depression also warrants thorough understanding. I originally thought that, simply by virtue of working with depressed patients for decades, I knew a lot about depression. I learned otherwise when I dove into the literature for the sake of educating patients more knowledgeably (Allen, 2006a). For example, I have found a simple principle to be enormously helpful to depressed patients who berate themselves for the seemingly glacial speed of their recovery, namely, the catch-22: everything you need to do to recover (e.g., be active, sleep well, engage in enjoyable activities, think realistically) is made difficult by the symptoms of depression (e.g., lethargy, insomnia, loss of interest and pleasure, negative thinking and rumination). To state the obvious, educating traumatized patients and family members about trauma-related disorders and treatment can help contain their anxiety and feelings of helplessness in the face of their confusion. Understanding psychopathology is a form of mentalizing, and we clinicians can be grateful for decades of research that helps with this endeavor.

If I am right, exposure therapy equals mentalizing in being the least novel approach to trauma imaginable. Who invented *in vivo* exposure, that is, going back into a situation that has been frightening (i.e., while safe)? Who invented imaginal exposure (i.e., thinking, feeling, and talking about frightening experience)? As implied earlier in this chapter, I find Foa's account of the effectiveness of exposure to be utterly reasonable as it entails emotional engagement with the traumatic experience, altering unrealistic views of self and others, and achieving narrative coherence. As already stated, from an attachment perspective, I find the relative neglect of the patient-therapist relationship (in theory if not in practice) to be disconcerting. All the standard treatments that entail processing of traumatic experience involve mentalizing in the context of an attachment relationship (albeit varying as all therapies do in the strength of the attachment).

Commonsensical as it may be, exposure commonly goes against the grain of the patient's understandable desire to be rid of painfully and bewilderingly intrusive memories of trauma. Recognizing the futility of avoidance, while sympathizing with their wishes, I counsel patients with PTSD that they cannot avoid being blindsided by traumatic memories and emotions, given the ever-present exposure to reminders. You do not need to go to movies, turn on the television, or read a newspaper to be exposed to reminders. You merely need to feel helpless, out of control, or invisible to someone you depend on when you are in emotional pain. Accordingly, the goal of trauma treatment—exposure or mentalizing—is to be able to have traumatic memories and emotions in mind and to feel that you are not entirely alone in this experience.

This experience of psychological connection renders such memories bearable and manageable, thereby diminishing anxiety and thus the intensity and frequency of the intrusive experiences.

Averse to highly structured procedures as I may be, I think there is a significant advantage to the evidence-based treatments for PTSD, such as prolonged exposure, cognitive processing therapy, and EMDR: these treatments prevent the therapist and the patient from avoiding dreaded traumatic experiences, which is all too easy to do in an unstructured approach. Such avoidance by both parties can go unnoticed in the flurry of innumerable pressing daily concerns that can easily take precedence. Moreover, avoiding traumatic experience can be abetted by beliefs that the patient's functioning or psychological capacity is too precarious to permit exposure. These concerns are entirely legitimate: undaunted processing of traumatic memories without adequate support can lead to deteriorating functioning and undermine therapy (Allen, 2001; Chu, 1992). Yet, just as we should not overestimate the patient's capacity, neither should we underestimate it in the service of avoidance. To take an especially noteworthy instance, Chris Frueh and colleagues (Frueh et al., 2009) showed that exposure therapy could be employed effectively in the treatment of patients with PTSD in the context of psychotic disorders—provided that the exposure procedures were preceded by and embedded in a high degree of support.

I already have mentioned the irony that securely attached patients benefit most from treatment and insecurely attached patients most need it. Similarly, processing trauma requires containment in the form of supportive attachment relationships and self-regulation capacities. As I hope to have made abundantly clear throughout this book, this capacity for containment is precisely what attachment trauma undermines. Hence it is just as reasonable to assert that containment is the optimal *outcome* of trauma therapy as it is a *precondition* for trauma therapy. We made a parallel case for the therapeutic alliance in treating patients with BPD (Horwitz et al., 1996): a stable alliance is a *result* of effective treatment—as I now understand it, likely as a consequence of increased attachment security and mentalizing capacity. Plainly, as carefully staged trauma treatment approaches attest (Courtois, Ford & Cloitre, 2009; Herman, 1992b), we might envision a ratcheting-up process in which a modicum of containment is required for mentalizing traumatic experience, and the process of doing so further enhances containment. Indeed, I believe that the primary reason for processing trauma is to enhance containment through attachment, mentalizing, and self-regulation. I am an avowed fan of the principle, let sleeping dogs lie. But patients would not come to our doors if the dogs were not awake and barking.

Practicing in an inpatient setting, I believe both sides of the following contradiction to be true: if a patient has the support of the hospital, this is the best time to be processing trauma; conversely, if the patient's functioning is so impaired as to require hospitalization, this is the worst time to be processing trauma. Deciding how to proceed must be done on an individual basis and must be done conjointly. No amount of experience, expertise, and judicious planning prevents trauma therapy from being a potentially harrowing endeavor.

In her mid-forties, Sabrina sought hospitalization after she felt she was "going insane." She had become so distraught that she bought a gun, not sure if she was going to kill herself or someone else. She said she had been going "steadily downhill" for several months but she "fell off the cliff" when her housemate, Natalie, left for an extended period to look after Natalie's ageing mother who had suffered a stroke. By sheer good fortune—divine intervention, in Sabrina's view—Natalie returned unannounced not long after Sabrina had acquired the gun. Alarmed at Sabrina's disheveled condition, and downright terrified when she learned of the gun, Natalie contacted the police, who helped with an emergency hospitalization. After she was stabilized, Sabrina was transferred for longer-term inpatient treatment.

Distraught as she remained, Sabrina was highly collaborative from the outset of therapy. She said it had been totally out of character—contrary to her "peace-loving nature"—for her to buy a gun. She was horrified by her thought of shooting strangers—particularly "middle-aged hags"—on the street, although she said she would have done so in "self-defense." She said she had lots of "disturbing" thoughts that she believed she needed to talk about. Yet merely touching on her aggressive thoughts and feelings led her to become so agitated that she had trouble staying seated. I asked her if she was feeling safe with me, and she assured me that she did. She said it helped that I was "calm" in comparison with a previous therapist who seemed "bent out of shape" when she talked about what was on her mind. Nonetheless, I let Sabrina know that she was free to leave the office whenever she chose to do so. I pointed out in the first session that we were "walking a tightrope" in the sense that, while she felt a need to talk about her disturbing thoughts (and I agreed), doing so was obviously creating more distress. I let her know one of my favorite maxims: "The slower you go, the faster you get there" (Kluft, 1993, p. 42). She liked it.

Going slowly is an aspiration not easily achieved. Sabrina was plagued by intrusive images of brutal beatings, some of which she described in detail. Sometimes she was doing the beating; sometimes she was being beaten. She said she was "losing it," for example, as she imagined being assaulted by a nurse who had gently redirected her when she was becoming agitated in a mild confrontation with one of her peers. Her experience of being beaten felt so real she described it as akin to "dreaming while you're awake." She let me know that she had been trying to get the images out of her head by painting bloody scenes and writing about them in her journal. While sympathizing with her intentions, I suggested that she was inadvertently "fanning the flames" and advised her to stay grounded in the present to the extent possible. Sabrina had some familiarity with mindfulness in the context of Yoga, so she was able to redirect her attention to present external reality to some degree when she sensed she was starting to "lose it."

Bit by bit, over the course of therapy, Sabrina talked about a history of exposure to aggression and violence that put her otherwise inexplicable intrusive images into context. She said her mother was a "certifiable manic-depressive" who was repeatedly hospitalized, but "never long enough." She said her mother was an "incorrigible rage-aholic" until she suicided by gunshot when Sabrina was in her mid-adolescence. Sabrina felt compassion for her "peace-loving" father who bore the brunt of her mother's continual emotional "harangues" and occasional physical attacks. She remembered being terrorized on one occasion when her mother wielded a butcher knife at her father, only to be distracted by the raucous barking of their german shepherd, whom she kicked in disgust. Sabrina felt guilty about wishing her mother dead, and she was especially horrified by fleeting images of stabbing her mother in the back with a knife when they were together in the kitchen.

As Sabrina's functioning had deteriorated in the months prior to her hospitalization, so did her appearance. As she approached her mother's age at the time of her mother's suicide, she was shocked by some similarities in their appearance, particularly her "witchy-looking, scraggly dirty-blond hair." Hence, fueled by her increasingly violent inner world, Sabrina saw her "worst nightmare" coming true: she was becoming more like her mother. Reflecting on this dreaded transformation in the psychotherapy, Sabrina realized that, in buying the gun, she was not only following in her mother's footsteps but also—in effect—wanting to kill her mother in herself.

Sabrina was right that she needed to talk about all that had been on her mind, and she did indeed benefit from the fact that I listened fairly calmly, although I expressed reflexively my shock and horror about the events of her childhood. I also resonated with Sabrina's inherent benevolence, which was evident in her relationships in the hospital as well as in her friendships. I think she was reassured by my lack of fear and appreciation for her good will, which were at great variance with her violent fantasies. It did not hurt that I reminded her of her father in some respects.

Nonetheless, this therapy process did not go smoothly. In the middle of the process, as we were tangled up in some amalgam of violent intrusive images in the present and frightening memories from the past, Sabrina became more paranoid. She said she was feeling less safe in the hospital at times and she expressed some fear that she might attack the nurse by whom she had felt reprimanded and whom she saw as "stern." In collaboration with the hospital treatment team, I suggested that we stop talking about Sabrina's traumatic past in therapy, and she agreed. We had understood, in broad outlines, some reasons for the violent images that had led her to the brink of suicide.

We had plenty else to talk about besides trauma. We discussed her relationship with her father who was still living. She said her father had been her "lifeline" growing up, but his episodic alcohol abuse and increasing ill health had made for significant insecurity. We also talked about her relationships outside the family, not only her friendships but also a long-term romantic relationship in which she had felt loved and valued. Tragically, this relationship ended with her partner's early death from cancer, and this loss had played a role in the depression that preceded her deteriorating functioning. She was buoyed by strong religious faith, which included a sense of her partner's ongoing presence in her life as well as a feeling of connection with God. I let Sabrina know about my fondness for the idea of "islands of security," and she agreed that she had them. I concurred, however, with her point that as she became more depressed and isolated—culminating in Natalie's departure—she had "plunged into the sea."

Declaring talk about trauma to be off limits in therapy seems downright draconian, and it is hardly a plausible general strategy. It proved effective in this treatment process in part because we *had* addressed the trauma in a manner that was containing—at least in the therapy sessions. But encouragement to focus her attention on present reality was feasible in large part because Sabrina was hospitalized. She was not only occupied fully with activity but also ensconced in supportive relationships with her peers and staff members. By no means did her intrusive violent images come to an abrupt halt. Rather, she experienced them as more fleeting and clearly at variance with her strengthened sense of herself as benevolent. She no longer lost mentalizing—experiencing the past as if it were in the present. Often, but by no means always, she could identify some event that evoked a violent image. Moreover, after our agreed hiatus and her increasing feeling of stability, we were able to revisit some of the key points we had discussed when we were in the thick of trauma, particularly noting the basis for seemingly inexplicable (i.e., "insane") violent images in actual past experience. As Sabrina concluded, as her illness evolved, she had "turned one nightmare into another." She gradually felt she was "living by the light of day," and she worked on a plan for continued treatment outside the hopsital in a supportive community living program.

I presume that the psychotherapy process I described with Sabrina qualifies as the least novel approach to trauma treatment imaginable. Perhaps it also qualifies as reflecting adequate skill in being human, a skill that Sabrina certainly exemplified.

Concluding reflections

I can imagine (mentalize) readers' pique in arriving at the end of a long book only to encounter the disclaimer that they have been presented with the least novel approach to trauma treatment imaginable.

I know from attending and conducting numerous workshops that many clinicians come seeking new and more effective ways of conducting their practice. I am always concerned with effectiveness, but I am more invested in soundness than newness. And I am more interested in understanding than technique. I am well acquainted with the feeling of not knowing what I am doing, despite decades of clinical experience buttressed by researching and writing about trauma. Yet, general as the aspiration might be, I anchor myself in the effort to promote mentalizing in a climate of safety. Figuring out *how* to implement this broad aspiration on a moment-to-moment basis is frequently challenging; I am short on concrete prescriptions.

No doubt, I am bucking the tide in downplaying specialized, evidence-based treatments. I am happy to enlist the help of specialists when needed. I am grateful to be working in a multidisciplinary hospital setting that provides group and family therapy as well as a therapeutic community. And I am mindful that traumatized patients benefit substantially from learning practical coping techniques afforded by Dialectial Behavior Therapy skills groups that are offered throughout the clinic. Frequently, our patients want "tools" to cope. I view mentalizing as the foundational tool for making use of other more specific tools (e.g., thought records in cognitive-behavioral therapy or emotion-regulation strategies in Dialectical Behavior Therapy). But I take a broad view of what constitutes an "evidence base." To a substantial extent, I have endeavored to base treatment on evidence, relying heavily on attachment research. Coupled with decades of research on the general effectiveness of diverse psychotherapies and the extensive evidence for the paramount contribution of the patient-therapist relationship to treatment outcomes, I believe the developmental research I have reviewed puts us generalist therapists on solid empirical ground.

My enthusiasm for the therapeutic benefits of understanding gleaned from knowledge of attachment theory and research is tempered by the humbling awareness of the sheer severity and chronicity of disorders related to attachment trauma and the associated limitations in effectiveness of our current treatment approaches. Randomized-controlled trials quite consistently show various treatment methods to be more effective than control groups, but treatments are generally more effective in ameliorating symptoms of disorders—the original purpose for which they were developed—than in improving patients' quality of life (Levy, 2008). Despite the substantial long-term benefits of MBT in not only ameliorating symptoms of BPD but also improving social and vocational functioning, slightly over half the patients continued to show at least moderate impairment of functioning (Bateman & Fonagy, 2008). Of equally great concern, patients' access to our most effective treatments is limited by availability of treatments, coupled with financial constraints.

I have come to believe that we hear the word, trauma, so frequently that we have become desensitized to it, no longer appreciating its sheer gravity. In my view, it makes no sense to aspire to "get over" trauma as if it had not happened. Trauma not only contributes to psychiatrc disorders but also has a lasting existential impact (Allen, 2007, 2013)— profoundly affecting your sense of meaning and purpose. To varying degrees, patients must live with the enduring effects of trauma at physiological, psychological, and existential-spiritual levels. We now have abundant evidence that our treatment efforts help, and we will continue to improve the effectiveness of these efforts. But I am convinced that, at every stage of the lifelong effort to recover from trauma and to live as well as possible with its legacy, there is no better support than attachment relationships, our best resource for feeling safe and secure in the world. We psychotherapists have an important role to play in providing this resource, but we are new to the endeavor, and—thankfully—we are hardly alone in it.

REFERENCES

Adolphs, R. (2003). Cognitive neuroscience of human social behavior. *Nature Reviews Neuroscience, 4*: 165–178.

Aggleton, J. P. & Young, A. W. (2000). The enigma of the amygdala: On its contribution to human emotion. In: R. D. Lane & L. Nadel (Eds.), *Cognitive Neuroscience of Emotion* (pp. 106–128). New York: Oxford University Press.

Ainsworth, M. D. (1963). The development of infant-mother interaction among the Ganda. In: M. B. Foss (Ed.), *Determinants of Infant Behaviour II* (pp. 67–104). New York: Wiley.

Ainsworth, M. D. (1989). Attachments beyond infancy. *American Psychologist, 44*: 709–716.

Ainsworth, M. D., Blehar, M. C., Waters, E. & Wall, S. (1978). *Patterns of Attachment: A Psychological Study of the Strange Situation*. Hillsdale, NJ: Erlbaum.

Allen, J. G. (2001). *Traumatic Relationships and Serious Mental Disorders*. Chichester, UK: Wiley.

Allen, J. G. (2003). Mentalizing. *Bulletin of the Menninger Clinic, 67*: 87–108.

Allen, J. G. (2005). *Coping with Trauma: Hope through Understanding* (2nd edn). Washington, DC: American Psychiatric Publishing.

Allen, J. G. (2006a). *Coping with Depression: From Catch-22 to Hope*. Washington, DC: American Psychiatric Publishing.

Allen, J. G. (2006b). Mentalizing in practice. In J. G. Allen & P. Fonagy (Eds.), *Handbook of Mentalization-Based Treatment* (pp. 3–30). Chichester, UK: Wiley.

Allen, J. G. (2007). Evil, mindblindness, and trauma: Challenges to hope. *Smith College Studies in Social Work, 77*: 9–31.

Allen, J. G. (2008a). Mentalizing as a conceptual bridge from psychodynamic to cognitive-behavioral therapy. *European Psychotherapy, 8*: 103–121.

Allen, J. G. (2008b). Psychotherapy: The artful use of science. *Smith College Studies in Social Work, 78*: 159–187.

Allen, J. G. (2011). Mentalizing suicidal states. In K. Michel & D. A. Jobes (Eds.), *Building a Therapeutic Alliance with the Suicidal Patient* (pp. 81–91). Washington, DC: American Psychological Association.

Allen, J. G. (2013). *Restoring Mentalizing in Attachment Relationships: Treating Trauma with Plain Old Therapy*. Washington, DC: American Psychiatric Publishing.

Allen, J. G., Coyne, L. & Console, D. A. (2000). Course of illness following specialized inpatient treatment for women with trauma-related psychopathology. *Bulletin of the Menninger Clinic, 64*: 235–256.

Allen, J. G. & Fonagy, P. (2006). Preface. In J. G. Allen & P. Fonagy (Eds.), *Handbook of Mentalization-Based Treatment* (pp. ix–xxi). Chichester, UK: Wiley.

Allen, J. G., Fonagy, P. & Bateman, A. (2008). *Mentalizing in Clinical Practice*. Washington, DC: American Psychiatric Publishing.

Allen, J. G., O'Malley, F., Freeman, C. & Bateman, A. W. (2012). Brief treatment. In P. Fonagy & A. W. Bateman (Eds.), *Handbook of Mentalizing in Mental Health Practice* (pp. 159–196). Washington, DC: American Psychiatric Publishing.

Allen, J. P. (2008). The attachment system in adolescence. In J. Cassidy & P. R. Shaver (Eds.), *Handbook of Attachment: Theory, Research, and Clinical Applications* (2nd edn, pp. 419–435). New York: The Guilford Press.

Alter, M. D. & Hen, R. (2009). Serotonin, sensitive periods, and anxiety. In G. Andrews, D. S. Charney, P. J. Sirovatka & D. A. Reiger (Eds.), *Stress-Induced and Fear Circuitry Disorders: Refining the Research Agenda for DSM-V* (pp. 159–173). Arlington, VA: American Psychiatric Publishing.

Amodio, D. M. & Frith, C. D. (2006). Meeting of minds: The medial frontal cortex and social cognition. *Nature Reviews Neuroscience, 7*: 268–277.

APA. (2000). *Diagnostic and Statistical Manual of Mental Disorders, Fourth Edition, Text Revision (DSM-IV-TR)*. Washington, DC: American Psychiatric Association.

Armstrong, K. (2010). *Twelves Steps to a Compassionate Life*. New York: Knopf.

Arnott, B. & Meins, E. (2007). Links between antenatal attachment representations, postnatal mind-mindedness, and infant attachment security: A preliminary study of mothers and fathers. *Bulletin of the Menninger Clinic, 71*: 132–149.

Arnsten, A. F. T. (1998). The biology of being frazzled. *Science, 280*: 1711–1712.

Aronson, H. (2004). *Buddhist Practice on Western ground: Reconciling Eastern Ideals and Western Psychology*. Boston, MA: Shambhala.

Asen, E. & Fonagy, P. (2012). Mentalization-Based Family Therapy. In A. Bateman & P. Fonagy (Eds.), *Handbook of Mentalizing in Mental Health Practice* (pp. 107–128). Washington, DC: American Psychiatric Publishing.

Barlow, D. H., Allen, L. B. & Choate, M. L. (2004). Toward a unified treatment for emotional disorders. *Behavior Therapy, 35*: 205–230.

Barnett, D., Manly, J. T. & Cicchetti, D. (1993). Defining child maltreatment: The interface between policy and research. In D. Cicchetti & S. L. Toth (Eds.), *Child Abuse, Child Development, and Social Policy. Advances in Applied Developmental Psychology* (Vol. 8, pp. 7–73). Norwood, NJ: Ablex Publishing Corporation.

Baron-Cohen, S. (1995). *Mindblindness: An Essay on Autism and Theory of Mind*. Cambridge, MA: MIT Press.

Baron-Cohen, S., Wheelwright, S., Hill, J., Raste, Y. & Plumb, I. (2001). The "Reading the Mind in the Eyes" test revised version: A study with normal adults, and adults with Asperger Syndrome or high-functioning autism. *Journal of Child Psychology and Psychiatry, 42*: 241–251.

Bartles, A. & Zeki, S. (2000). The neural basis of romantic love. *NeuroReport, 11*: 3829–3834.

Bartles, A. & Zeki, S. (2004). The neural correlates of romantic love. *NeuroImage, 21*: 1155–1166.

Bartlett, R. C. & Collins, S. D. (2011). *Aristotle's Nicomachean Ethics*. Chicago: University of Chicago Press.

Bartz, J. A., Simeon, D., Hamilton, H., Kim, S., Crystal, S., Braun, A. & Vicens, V. (2011). Oxytocin can hinder trust and cooperation in borderline personality disorder. *Social Cognitive and Affective Neuroscience, 6*: 556–563.

Bartz, J. A., Zaki, J., Ochsner, K. N., Bolger, N., Kolevzon, A. & Ludwig, N. (2010). Effects of oxytocin on recollections of maternal care and closeness. *PNAS, 107*: 21371–21375.

Bateman, A. & Fonagy, P. (1999). Effectiveness of partial hospitalization in the treatment of borderline personality disorder: A randomized controlled trial. *American Journal of Psychiatry, 156*: 1563–1569.

Bateman, A. & Fonagy, P. (2001). Treatment of borderline personality disorder with psychoanalytically oriented partial hospitalizaiton: An 18-month follow-up. *American Journal of Psychiatry, 158*: 36–42.

Bateman, A. & Fonagy, P. (2004). *Psychotherapy for Borderline Personality Disorder: Mentalization-Based Treatment*. New York: Oxford University Press.

Bateman, A. & Fonagy, P. (2006). *Mentalization-Based Treatment for Borderline Personality Disorder: A Practical Guide*. New York: Oxford University Press.

Bateman, A. & Fonagy, P. (2008). 8-year follow-up of patients treated for borderline personality disorder: Mentalization-based treatment versus treatment as usual. *American Journal of Psychiatry, 165*: 631–638.

Bateman, A. & Fonagy, P. (2009). Randomized controlled trial of outpatient Mentalization-Based Treatment versus structured clinical management for borderline personality disorder. *American Journal of Psychiatry, 166*: 1355–1364.

Bateman, A. & Fonagy, P. (2012a). Individual techniques of the basic model. In A. Bateman & P. Fonagy (Eds.), *Handbook of Mentalizing in Mental Health Practice* (pp. 67–80). Washington, DC: American Psychiatric Publishing.

Bateman, A. & Fonagy, P. (Eds.) (2012b). *Handbook of Mentalizing in Mental Health Practice*. Washington, DC: American Psychiatric Publishing.

Baumeister, R. F. (1990). Suicide as escape from self. *Psychological Review, 97*: 90–113.

Baumeister, R. F. & Masicampo, E. J. (2010). Conscious thought is for facilitating social and cultural interactions: How mental simulations serve the animal-culture interface. *Psychological Review, 117*: 945–971.

Baumeister, R. F., Masicampo, E. J. & Vohs, K. D. (2011). Do conscious thoughts cause behavior? *Annual Review of Psychology, 62*: 331–361.

Baumeister, R. F., Vohs, K. D., DeWall, C. N. & Zhang, L. (2007). How emotion shapes behavior: Feedback, anticipation, and reflection, rather than direct causation. *Personality and Social Psychology Review, 11*: 167–203.

Beck, A. T. (1991). Cognitive therapy: A 30-year retrospective. *American Psychologist, 46*: 368–375.

Beck, A. T., Rush, A. J., Shaw, B. F. & Emery, G. (1979). *Cognitive Therapy of Depression*. New York: The Guilford Press.

Beebe, B., Jaffe, J., Markese, S., Buck, K., Chen, H., Cohen, P., Bahrick, L., Andrews, H. & Feldstein, S. (2010). The origins of 12-month attachment: A microanalysis of 4-month mother-infant interaction. *Attachment and Human Development, 12*: 3–141.

Belsky, J. (2005). Attachment theory and research in ecological perspective: Insights from the Pennsylvania Infant and Familly Development Project and the NICHD Study of Early Child Care. In K. E. Grossman, K. Grossman & E. Waters (Eds.), *Attachment from Infancy to Adulthood: The Major Longitudinal Studies* (pp. 71–97). New York: The Guilford Press.

Belsky, J. & Fearon, R. M. P. (2008). Precursors of attachment security. In J. Cassidy & P. R. Shaver (Eds.), *Handbook of Attachment: Theory, Research, and Clinical Applications* (2nd edn, pp. 295–316). New York: The Guilford Press.

Berlin, L. J., Cassidy, J. & Appleyard, K. (2008). The influence of early attachments on other relationships. In J. Cassidy & P. R. Shaver (Eds.), *Handbook of Attachment: Theory, Research, and Clinical Applications (Second Edition)* (pp. 333–347). New York: The Guilford Press.

Berlin, L. J., Zeanah, C. H. & Lieberman, A. F. (2008). Prevention and intervention programs for supporting early attachment security. In J. Cassidy & P. R. Shaver (Eds.), *Handbook of Attachment: Theory, Research, and Clinical Applications (Second Edition)* (pp. 745–761). New York: The Guilford Press.

Beutler, L. E. & Blatt, S. J. (2006). Participant factors in treating dysphoric disorders. In L. G. Castonguay & L. E. Beutler (Eds.), *Principles of Therapeutic Change that Work* (pp. 13–63). New York: Oxford University Press.

Bifulco, A., Brown, G. W. & Harris, T. O. (1994). Childhood Experience of Care and Abuse (CECA): A retrospective interview measure. *Journal of Child Psychology and Psychiatry, 35*: 1419–1435.

Bifulco, A., Brown, G. W., Neubauer, A., Moran, P. M. & Harris, T. O. (1994). *Childhood Experience of Care and Abuse (CECA) Training Manual*. London: Royal Holloway, University of London.

Bifulco, A., Jacobs, C., Bunn, A., Thomas, G. & Irving, K. (2008). The Adult Attachment Style Interview (ASI): A support-based adult assessment tool for adoption and fostering practice. *Adoption and Fostering, 32*: 33–45.

Bifulco, A. & Moran, P. (1998). *Wednesday's Child: Research into Women's Experience of Neglect and Abuse in Childhood, and Adult Depression*. London: Routledge.

Bifulco, A., Moran, P., Jacobs, C. & Bunn, A. (2009). Problem partnersw and parenting: Exploring linkages with maternal insecure attachment style and adolescent offspring internalizing disorder. *Attachment and Human Development, 11*: 69–85.

Bifulco, A., Moran, P. M., Baines, R., Bunn, A. & Stanford, K. (2002). Exploring psychological abuse in childhood II: Association with other abuse and adult clinical depression. *Bulletin of the Menninger Clinic, 66*: 241–258.

Bifulco, A., Moran, P. M., Ball, C. & Bernazzani, O. (2002). Adult attachment style. I: Its relaitonship to clinical depression. *Social Psychiatry and Psychiatric Epidemiology, 37*: 50–59.

Bifulco, A. & Thomas, G. (in press). *Understanding Adult Attachment in Family Relationships: Assessment and Intervention*. London: Routledge.

Bishop, S. R., Lau, M. A., Shapiro, S. L., Carlson, L., Anderson, N. D., Carmody, J., Segal, Z. V., Abbey, S., Speca, M., Velting, D. & Devins, G. (2004). Mindfulness: A proposed operational definition. *Clinical Psychology: Science and Practice, 11*: 230–241.

Blatt, S. J. (2008). *Polarities of Experience: Relatedness and Self-Definition in Personality Development, Psychopathology, and the Therapeutic Process*. Washington, DC: American Psychological Association.

Blatt, S. J. & Luyten, P. (2010). Reactivating the psychodynamic approach to the classification of psychopathology. In T. Millon, R. F. Krueger & E. Simonson (Eds.), *Contemporary Directions in Psychopathology: Scientific Foundations of the DSM-V and ICD-11* (pp. 483–514). New York: The Guilford Press.

Block-Lerner, J., Wulfert, E. & Moses, E. (2009). ACT in context: An exploration of experiential acceptance. *Cognitive and Behavioral Practice, 16*: 443–456.

Bogdan, R. J. (1997). *Interpreting Minds: The Evolution of a Practice*. Cambridge, MA: MIT Press.

Bowlby, J. (1944). Forty-four juvenile thieves: Their characters and home-life. *International Journal of Psycho-Analysis, 25*: 19–53, 107–128.

Bowlby, J. (1951). *Maternal Care and Mental Health*. Geneva: World Health Organization Monograph Series.

Bowlby, J. (1958). The nature of the child's tie to his mother. *International Journal of Psycho-Analysis, 39*: 350–373.

Bowlby, J. (1973). *Attachment and Loss, Volume II: Separation*. New York: Basic Books.

Bowlby, J. (1980). *Attachment and Loss, Volume III: Loss, Sadness and Depression*. New York: Basic Books.

Bowlby, J. (1982). *Attachment and Loss, Volume I: Attachment* (2nd edn). New York: Basic Books.

Bowlby, J. (1988). *A Secure Base: Parent-Child Attachment and Healthy Human Development*. New York: Basic Books.

Brennan, K. A., Clark, C. L. & Shaver, P. R. (1998). Self-report measurement of adult attachment: An integrative overview. In J. A. Simpson & W. S. Rholes (Eds.), *Attachment Theory and Close Relationships* (pp. 46–75). New York: The Guilford Press.

Bretherton, I. (2005). In pursuit of the internal working model construct and its relevance to attachment relationships. In K. E. Grossman, K. Grossman & E. Waters (Eds.), *Attachment from Infancy to Adulthood: The Major Longitudinal Studies* (pp. 13–47). New York: The Guilford Press.

Bretherton, I. & Munholland, K. A. (2008). Internal working models in attachment relationships: Elaborating a central construct in attachment theory. In J. Cassidy & P. R. Shaver (Eds.), *Handbook of Attachment: Theory, Research, and Clinical Applications* (2nd edn, pp. 102–127). New York: The Guilford Press.

Brewin, C. R. (2003). *Posttraumatic Stress Disorder: Malady or Myth?* New Haven, CT: Yale University Press.

Brewin, C. R. (2011). The nature and significance of memory disturbance in posttraumatic stress disorder. *Annual Review of Clinical Psychology,* 7: 203–227.

Brewin, C. R., Reynolds, M. & Tata, P. (1999). Autobiographical memory processes and the course of depression. *Journal of Abnormal Psychology,* 108: 511–517.

Brothers, L. (1997). *Friday's Footprint: How Society Shapes the Human Mind.* New York: Oxford University Press.

Brown, G. W., Bifulco, A., Veiel, H. O. F. & Andrews, B. (1990). Self-esteem and depression. II. Social correlates of self-esteem. *Social Psychiatry and Psychiatric Epidemiology, 25:* 225–234.

Brown, G. W. & Harris, T. O. (1978). *Social Origins of Depression: A Study of Psychiatric Disorder in Women.* New York: Free Press.

Brown, K. W., Ryan, R. M. & Creswell, J. D. (2007). Mindfulness: Theoretical foundations and evidence for its salutary effects. *Psychological Inquiry,* 18: 211–237.

Bryant, R. A. (2010). Treating the full range of posttraumatic reactions. In G. M. Rosen & B. C. Frueh (Eds.), *Clinician's Guide to Posttraumatic Stress Disorder* (pp. 205–234). New York: Wiley.

Burgess, P. W., Gonen-Yaacovi, G. & Volle, E. (2012). Rostral prefronatl cortex: What neuroimaging can learn from human neuropsychology. In B. Levine & F. I. M. Craik (Eds.), *Mind and the Frontal Lobes: Cognition, Behavior, and Brain Imaging* (pp. 47–92). New York: Oxford University Press.

Burgess, P. W., Simons, J. S., Dumontheil, I. & Gilbert, S. J. (2005). The gateway hypothesis of rostral prefrontal cortex (area 10) function. In J. Duncan, L. Phillips & P. McLeod (Eds.), *Measuring the Mind: Speed, Control and Age* (pp. 217–248). New York: Oxford University Press.

Buss, A. H. (1992). Personality: Primate heritage and human distinctiveness. In R. A. Zucker, A. I. Rabin & J. Aronoff (Eds.), *Personality Structure in the Life Course: Essays on Personology in the Murray Tradition* (pp. 57–100). New York: Springer.

Carlson, E. A. (1998). A prospective longitudinal study of attachment disorganization/disorientation. *Child Development, 69:* 1107–1128.

Carlson, E. A., Egeland, B. & Sroufe, L. A. (2009). A prospective investigation of the development of borderline personality symptoms. *Development and Psychopathology, 21:* 1311–1334.

Carlson, E. A., Yates, T. M. & Sroufe, L. A. (2009). Dissociation and the development of the self. In P. F. Dell & J. A. O'Neil (Eds.), *Dissociation and the Dissociative Disorders: DSM-V and Beyond* (pp. 39–52). New York: Routledge.

Carlson, E. B. & Putnam, F. W. (1993). An update on the Dissociative Experiences Scale. *Dissociation, 6*: 16–27.

Carson, J. W., Carson, K. M., Gil, K. M. & Baucom, D. H. (2004). Mindfulness-based relationship enhancement. *Behavior Therapy, 35*: 471–494.

Carter, C. S. (1998). Neuroendocrine perspectives on social attachment and love. *Psychoneuroendocrinology, 23*: 779–818.

Carter, C. S., DeVries, A. C., Taymans, S. E., Roberts, R. L., Williams, J. R. & Getz, L. L. (1999). Peptides, steroids, and pair bonding. In C. S. Carter, I. I. Lederhendler & B. Kirkpatrick (Eds.), *The Integrative Neurobiology of Affiliation* (pp. 169–181). Cambridge, MA: MIT Press.

Cassidy, J. (2008). The nature of the child's ties. In J. Cassidy & P. R. Shaver (Eds.), *Handbook of Attachment: Theory, Research, and Clinical Applications* (2nd edn, pp. 3–22). New York: The Guilford Press.

Cassidy, J. & Shaver, P. R. (Eds.) (2008). *Handbook of Attachment: Theory, Research, and Clinical Applications* (2nd edn). New York: The Guilford Press.

Cassidy, J., Shaver, P. R., Mikulincer, M. & Lavy, S. (2009). Experimentally induced security influences responses to psychological pain. *Journal of Social and Clinical Psychology, 28*: 463–478.

Castonguay, L. G. & Beutler, L. E. (Eds.) (2006). *Principles of Therapeutic Change that Work.* New York: Oxford University Press.

Choi-Kain, L. W. & Gunderson, J. G. (2008). Mentalization: Ontongeny, assessment, and application in the treatment of borderline personality disorder. *American Journal of Psychiatry, 165*: 1127–1135.

Christian, C. W., Scribano, P., Seidl, T. & Pinto-Martin, J. A. (1997). Pediatric injury resulting from family violence. *Pediatrics, 99*: 1–4.

Chu, J. A. (1992). The therapeutic roller coaster: Dilemmas in the treatment of childhood abuse survivors. *Journal of Psychotherapy: Practice and Research, 1*: 351–370.

Churchland, P. S. (2011). *Braintrust: What Neuroscience Tells us about Morality.* Princeton, NJ: Princeton University Press.

Clarkin, J. F., Levy, K. N., Lenzenweger, M. F. & Kernberg, O. F. (2007). Evaluating three treatments for borderline personality disorder: A multiwave study. *American Journal of Psychiatry, 164*: 922–928.

Coan, J. A. (2008). Toward a neuroscience of attachment. In J. Cassidy & P. R. Shaver (Eds.), *Handbook of Attachment: Theory, Research, and Clinical Applications* (2nd edn, pp. 241–265). New York: The Guilford Press.

Coan, J. A., Schaefer, H. S. & Davidson, R. J. (2006). Lending a hand: Social regulation of the neural response to threat. *Psychological Science, 17*: 1032–1039.

Cormier, J. F. & Thelen, M. H. (1998). Professional skepticism of multiple personality disorder. *Professional Psychology: Research and Practice, 29*: 163–167.

Courtois, C. A., Ford, J. D. & Cloitre, M. (2009). Best practices in psychotherapy for adults. In C. A. Courtois & J. D. Ford (Eds.), *Treating Complex Traumatic Stress Disorders: An Evidence-Based Guide* (pp. 82–103). New York: The Guilford Press.

Cozolino, L. (2010). *The Neuroscience of Psychotherapy: Healing the Social Brain.* New York: Norton.

Craig, A. D. (2009). How do you feel—now? The anterior insula and human awareness. *Nature Reviews Neuroscience, 10*: 59–70.

Craske, M. G. & Barlow, D. H. (2008). Panic disorder and agoraphobia. In D. H. Barlow (Ed.), *Clinical Handbook of Psychological Disorders: A Step-by-Step Treatment Manual* (pp. 1–64). New York: The Guilford Press.

Craske, M. G., Kircanski, K., Zelikowsky, M., Mystkowski, J., Chowdhury, N. & Baker, A. (2008). Optimizing inhibitory learning during exposure therapy. *Behaviour Research and Therapy, 46*: 5–27.

Crowell, J. A., Fraley, R. C. & Shaver, P. R. (2008). Measurement of individual differences in adolescent and adult attachment. In J. Cassidy & P. R. Shaver (Eds.), *Handbook of Attachment: Theory, Research, and Clinical Applications* (2nd edn, pp. 599–634). New York: The Guilford Press.

Crowell, J. A. & Hauser, S. T. (2008). AAIs in a high-risk sample: Stability and relation to functioning from adolescence to 39 years. In H. Steele & M. Steele (Eds.), *Clinical Applications of the Adult Attachment Interview* (pp. 341–370). New York: The Guilford Press.

Crowell, J. A. & Waters, E. (2005). Attachment representations, secure-base behavior, and the evolution of adult relationships: The Stony Brook Adult Relationship Project. In K. E. Grossman, K. Grossman & E. Waters (Eds.), *Attachment from Infancy to Adulthood: The Major Longitudinal Studies* (pp. 223–244). New York: The Guilford Press.

Csibra, G. & Gergely, G. (1998). The teleological origins of mentalistic action explanations: A developmental hypothesis. *Developmental Science, 1*: 255–259.

Damasio, A. (2010). *Self comes to Mind: Constructing the Conscious Brain.* New York: Pantheon.

Davidson, R. J., Kabat-Zinn, J., Schumacher, J., Rosenkranz, M., Muller, D., Santorelli, S. F., Urbanowski, F., Harrington, A., Bonus, K. & Sheridan, J. F. (2003). Alterations in brain and immune function produced by mindfulness meditation. *Psychosomatic Medicine, 65*: 564–570.

Davis, D. M. & Hayes, J. A. (2011). What are the benefits of mindfulness? A practice review of psychotherapy-related research. *Psychotherapy, 48*: 198–208.

De Bellis, M. D., Hooper, S. & Sapia, J. L. (2005). Early trauma exposure and the brain. In J. J. Vasterling & C. R. Brewin (Eds.), *Neuropsychology of PTSD: Biological, Cognitive, and Clinical Perspectives* (pp. 153–177). New York: The Guilford Press.

Dehaene, S., Changeux, J. -P., Naccache, L., Sackur, J. & Sergent, C. (2006). Conscious, preconscious, and subliminal processing: A testable taxonomy. *Trends in Cognitive Sciences, 10*: 204–211.

Dehaene, S. & Naccache, L. (2001). Towards a cognitive neuroscience of consciousness: Basic evidence and a workspace framework. In S. Dehaene (Ed.), *The Cognitive Neuroscience of Consciousness* (pp. 1–37). Cambridge, MA: MIT Press.

Deklyen, M. & Greenberg, M. T. (2008). Attachment and psychopathology in childhood. In J. Cassidy & P. R. Shaver (Eds.), *Handbook of Attachment: Theory, Research, and Clinical Applications* (2nd edn, pp. 637–665). New York: The Guilford Press.

DePrince, A. P. & Freyd, J. J. (2007). Trauma-induced dissociation. In M. J. Friedman, T. M. Keane & P. A. Resick (Eds.), *Handbook of PTSD: Science and Practice* (pp. 135–150). New York: The Guilford Press.

Diamond, D., Stovall-McClough, C., Clarkin, J. F. & Levy, K. N. (2003). Patient-therapist attachment in the treatment of borderline personality disorder. *Bulletin of the Menninger Clinic, 67*: 227–259.

Diamond, L. (2003). What does sexual orientation orient? A biobehavioral model distingishing romantic love and sexual desire. *Psychological Review, 110*: 173–192.

Domes, G., Heinrichs, M., Glascher, J., Buchel, C., Braus, D. F. & Herpertz, S. C. (2007). Oxytocin attenuates amygdala responses to emotional faces regardless of valence. *Biological Psychiatry, 62*: 1187–1190.

Domes, G., Heinrichs, M. & Michel, A. (2007). Oxytocin improves "mind-reading" in humans. *Biological Psychiatry, 61*: 731–733.

Dorahy, M., van der Hart, O. & Middleton, W. (2010). The history of early life trauma and abuse from the 1850s to the current time: How the past influences the present. In R. A. Lanius, E. Vermetten & C. Pain (Eds.), *The Impact of Early Life Trauma on Health and Disease: The Hidden Epidemic* (pp. 3–12). New York: Cambridge University Press.

Dozier, M., Stovall-McClough, K. C. & Albus, K. E. (2008). Attachment and psychopathology in adulthood. In J. Cassidy & P. R. Shaver (Eds.), *Handbook of Attachment: Theory, Research, and Clinical Applications* (2nd edn, pp. 718–744). New York: The Guilford Press.

Dutra, L., Bianchi, I., Siegel, D. J. & Lyons-Ruth, K. (2009). The relational context of dissociative phenomena. In P. F. Dell & J. A. O'Neil (Eds.), *Dissociation and the Dissociative Disorders: DSM-V and Beyond* (pp. 83–92). New York: Routledge.

Dutton, D. & Painter, S. L. (1981). Traumatic bonding: The development of emotional attachments in battered women and other relationships of intermittent abuse. *Victimology, 6*: 139–155.

Eagle, M. N. & Wolitzky, D. L. (2009). Adult psychotherapy from the perspectives of attachment theory and psychoanalysis. In J. H. Obegi & E. Berant (Eds.), *Attachment Theory and Research in Clinical Work with Adults* (pp. 351–378). New York: The Guilford Press.

Egeland, B. (1997). Mediators of the effects of child maltreatment on developmental adaptation in adolescence. In D. Cicchetti & S. L. Toth (Eds.), *Developmental Perspectives on Trauma: Theory, Research, and Intervention* (Vol. 8, pp. 403–434). Rochester, NY: University of Rochester Press.

Ehlers, A., Clark, D. M., Hackmann, A., McManus, F. & Fennell, M. (2005). Cognitive therapy for post-traumatic stress disorder: Development and evaluation. *Behaviour Research and Therapy, 43*: 413–431.

Erickson, M. F. & Egeland, B. (1996). Child neglect. In J. Briere, L. Berliner, J. A. Bulkley, C. Jenny & T. Reid (Eds.), *The APSAC Handbook on Child Maltreatment* (pp. 4–20). Thousand Oaks, CA: Sage.

Erickson, M. T. (1993). Rethinking Oedipus: An evolutionary perspective of incest avoidance. *American Journal of Psychiatry, 150*: 411–416.

Farb, N., Anderson, A. K., Mayberg, H. S., Bean, J., McKeon, D. & Segal, Z. V. (2010). Minding one's emotions: Mindfulness training alters the neural expression of sadness. *Emotion, 10*: 25–33.

Farb, N., Segal, Z. V., Mayberg, H. S., Bean, J., McKeon, D., Fatima, Z. & Anderson, A. K. (2007). Attending to the present: Mindfulness meditation reveals distinct neural modes of self-reference. *Social Cognitive and Affective Neuroscience, 2*: 313–322.

Fearon, P., Target, M., Sargent, J., Williams, L., McGregor, J., Bleiberg, E. & Fonagy, P. (2006). Short-Term Mentalization and Relational Therapy (SMART): An integrative family therapy for children and adolescents. In J. G. Allen & P. Fonagy (Eds.), *Handbook of Mentalization-Based Treatment* (pp. 201–222). Chichester, UK: Wiley.

Feeney, J. A. (2008). Adult romantic attachment: Developments in the study of couple relationships. In J. Cassidy & P. R. Shaver (Eds.), *Handbook of Attachment: Theory, Research, and Clinical Applications* (2nd edn, pp. 456–481). New York: The Guilford Press.

Feldman, R., Gordon, I., Schneiderman, I., Weisman, O. & Zagoory-Sharon, O. (2010). Natural variations in maternal and paternal care are associated with systematic changes in oxytocin following parent-infant contact. *Psychoneuroendocrinology, 35*: 1133–1141.

Feldman, R., Gordon, I. & Zagoory-Sharon, O. (2011). Maternal and paternal plasma, salivary, and urinary oxytocin and parent-infant synchrony: Considering stress and affiliation components of human bonding. *Developmental Science, 14*: 752–761.

Feldman, R., Weller, A., Zagoory-Sharon, O. & Levine, A. (2007). Evidence for a neuroendocrinological foundation of human affiliation: Plasma oxytocin levels across pregnancy and the postpartum period predict mother-infant bonding. *Psychological Science, 18*: 965–970.

Felitti, V. J. & Anda, R. F. (2010). The relationship of aderse childhood experiences to adult medical disease, psychiatric disorders and sexual behavior: Implications for healthcare. In R. A. Lanius, E. Vermetten & C. Pain (Eds.), *The Impact of Early Life Trauma on Health and Disease: The Hidden Epidemic* (pp. 77–87). New York: Cambridge University Press.

Finkelhor, D. (1984). *Child Sexual Abuse: New Theory and Research.* New York: Free Press.

Firestone, L. (2006). Suicide and the inner voice. In T. E. Ellis (Ed.), *Cognition and Suicide: Theory, Research, and Therapy* (pp. 119–147). Washington, DC: American Psychological Association.

Fischer, S., Stojek, M. & Hartzell, E. (2010). Effects of multiple forms of child abuse and sexual assault on current eating disorder symptoms. *Eating Behaviors, 11*: 190–192.

Flint, J., Greenspan, R. J. & Kendler, K. S. (2010). *How Genes Influence Behavior.* New York: Oxford University Press.

Foa, E. B., Hembree, E. A. & Rothbaum, B. O. (2007). *Prolonged Exposure Therapy for PTSD: Emotional Processing of Traumatic Experiences.* New York: Oxford University Press.

Foa, E. B., Huppert, J. D. & Cahill, S. P. (2006). Emotional processing theory: An update. In B. O. Rothbaum (Ed.), *Pathological Anxiety: Emotional Processing in Etiology and Treatment.* New York: The Guilford Press.

Foa, E. B., Keane, T. M., Friedman, M. J. & Cohen, J. A. (2009). Introduction. In E. B. Foa, T. M. Keane, M. J. Friedman & J. A. Cohen (Eds.), *Effective Treatments for PTSD: Practice Guidelines from the International Society for Traumatic Stress Studies* (2nd edn, pp. 1–20). New York: The Guilford Press.

Foa, E. B. & Kozak, M. J. (1986). Emotional processing of fear: Exposure to corrective information. *Psychological Bulletin, 99*: 20–35.

Foa, E. B. & Kozak, M. J. (1991). Emotional processing: Theory, research, and clinical implications for anxiety disorders. In J. D. Safran & L. S. Greenberg (Eds.), *Emotion, Psychotherapy, and Change* (pp. 21–49). New York: The Guilford Press.

Foa, E. B., Zinbarg, R. & Rothbaum, B. O. (1992). Uncontrollability and unpredictability in post-traumatic stress disorder: An animal model. *Psychological Bulletin, 112*: 218–238.

Follan, M. & Minnis, H. (2010). Forty-four juvenile thieves revisited: From Bowlby to reactive attachment disorder. *Child: Care, Health and Development, 36*: 639–645.

Follette, V. M., Iverson, K. M. & Ford, J. D. (2009). Contextual behavior trauma therapy. In C. A. Courtois & J. D. Ford (Eds.), *Treating Complex Traumatic Stress Disorders: An Evidence-Based Guide* (pp. 264–285). New York: The Guilford Press.

Fonagy, P. (1989). A child's understanding of others. *Bulletin of the Anna Freud Centre, 12*: 91–115.

Fonagy, P. (1991). Thinking about thinking: Some clinical and theoretical considerations in the treatment of a borderline patient. *International Journal of Psycho-Analysis, 72*: 639–656.

Fonagy, P. (2001). *Attachment Theory and Psychoanalysis.* New York: Other Press.

Fonagy, P. (2006). The mentalization-focused approach to social development. In J. G. Allen & P. Fonagy (Eds.), *Handbook of Mentalization-Based Treatment* (pp. 53–99). Chichester, UK: Wiley.

Fonagy, P., Bateman, A. & Luyten, P. (2012). Introduction and overview. In P. Fonagy & A. Bateman (Eds.), *Handbook of Mentalizing in Mental Health Practice* (pp. 3–42). Washington, DC: American Psychiatric Publishing.

Fonagy, P., Gergely, G., Jurist, E. L. & Target, M. (2002). *Affect Regulation, Mentalization, and the Development of the Self.* New York: Other Press.

Fonagy, P., Gergely, G. & Target, M. (2007). The parent-infant dyad and the construction of the subjective self. *Journal of Child Psychology and Psychiatry, 48*: 288–328.

Fonagy, P., Gergely, G. & Target, M. (2008). Psychoanalytic constructs and attachment theory and research. In J. Cassidy & P. R. Shaver (Eds.), *Handbook of Attachment: Theory, Research, and Clinical Applications* (2nd edn, pp. 783–810). New York: The Guilford Press.

Fonagy, P. & Luyten, P. (2009). A developmental, mentalization-based approach to the understanding and treatment of borderline personality disorder. *Development and Psychopathology, 21*: 1355–1381.

Fonagy, P., Steele, H. & Steele, M. (1991). Maternal representations of attachment during pregnancy predict the organization of infant-mother attachment at one year of age. *Child Development, 62*: 891–905.

Fonagy, P., Steele, M., Steele, H., Leigh, T., Kennedy, R., Mattoon, G. & Target, M. (1995). Attachment, the reflective self, and borderline states: The predictive specificity of the Adult Attachment Interview and pathological emotional development. In S. Goldberg, R. Muir & J. Kerr (Eds.), *Attachment Theory: Social, Developmental, and Clinical Perspectives* (pp. 233–278). New York: Analytic Press.

Fonagy, P., Steele, M., Steele, H., Moran, G. S. & Higgitt, A. C. (1991). The capacity for understanding mental states: The reflective self in parent and child and its significance for security of attachment. *Infant Mental Health Journal, 12*: 201–218.

Fonagy, P. & Target, M. (1997). Attachment and reflective function: Their role in self-organization. *Development and Psychopathology, 9*: 679–700.

Fonagy, P. & Target, M. (2005). Bridging the transmission gap: An end to an important mystery of attachment research? *Attachment and Human Development, 7*: 333–343.

Fonagy, P., Target, M., Steele, H. & Steele, M. (1998). *Reflective-Functioning Manual, Version 5, for Application to Adult Attachment Interviews*. University College London, London.

Ford, J. D. (2009). Neurobiological and developmental research: Clinical implications. In C. A. Courtois & J. D. Ford (Eds.), *Treating Complex Traumatic Stress Disorders: An Evidence-Based Guide* (pp. 31–58). New York: The Guilford Press.

Ford, J. D. & Courtois, C. A. (2009). Defining and understanding complex trauma and complex traumatic stress disorders. In C. A. Courtois & J. D. Ford (Eds.), *Treating Complex Traumatic Stress Disorders: An Evidence-Based Guide* (pp. 13–30). New York: The Guilford Press.

Ford, J. D., Fallot, R. D. & Harris, M. (2009). Group therapy. In C. A. Courtois & J. D. Ford (Eds.), *Treating Complex Traumatic Stress Disorders: An Evidence-Based Guide* (pp. 415–440). New York: The Guilford Presss.

Fraiberg, S., Adelson, E. & Shapiro, V. (1975). Ghosts in the nursery: A psychoanalytic approach ot the problems of impaired infant-mother relationships. *Journal of the American Academy of Child Psychiatry, 14*: 387–421.

Frank, J. D. (1961). *Persuasion and Healing*. New York: Schocken Books.

Freud, S. (1896/1962). The aetiology of hysteria (J. Strachey, Trans.). In J. Strachey (Ed.), *The Standard Edition of the Complete Psychological Works of Sigmund Freud* (Vol. 3, pp. 187–221). London: Hogarth Press.

Freud, S. (1929/1961). *Civilization and its Discontents* (J. Strachey, Trans.). New York: Norton.

Freud, S. (1936). *The Problem of Anxiety*. New York: Norton.

Freud, S. (1954). *The Origins of Psycho-Analysis: Letters to Wilhelm Fliess, Drafts and Notes: 1887–1902*. New York: Basic Books.

Freud, S. (1964). New introductory lectures on psycho-analysis (1933). In J. Strachey (Ed.), *The Standard Edition of the Complete Psychological Works of Sigmund Freud,* (Vol. 22, pp. 1–182). London: Hogarth Press.

Freyd, J. J. (1996). *Betrayal Trauma: The Logic of Forgetting Childhood Abuse.* Cambridge, MA: Harvard University Press.

Friedman, M. J., Cohen, J. A., Foa, E. B. & Keane, T. M. (2009). Integration and summary. In E. B. Foa, T. M. Keane, M. J. Friedman & J. A. Cohen (Eds.), *Effective Treatments for PTSD: Practice Guidelines from the International Society for Traumatic Stress Studies* (2nd edn, pp. 617–642). New York: The Guilford Press.

Frith, C. D. & Frith, U. (1999). Interacting minds: A biological basis. *Science, 286:* 1692–1695.

Frith, C. D. & Frith, U. (2006). The neural basis of mentalizing. *Neuron, 50:* 531–534.

Frith, U. & Frith, C. D. (2003). Development and neurophysiology of mentalizing. *Philosophical Transactions of the Royal Society of London, Series B, Biological Sciences, 358:* 459–473.

Frueh, B. C., Grubaugh, A. L., Cusack, K. J., Kimble, M. O., Elhai, J. D. & Knapp, R. G. (2009). Exposure-based cognitive-behavioral treatment of PTSD in adults with schizophrenia or schizoaffective disorder: A pilot study. *Journal of Anxiety Disorders, 23:* 665–675.

Gallagher, H. L., Jack, A. I., Roepstorff, A. & Frith, C. D. (2002). Imaging the intentional stance in a competitive game. *NeuroImage, 16:* 814–821.

Gallese, V. (2001). The "shared manifold" hypothesis: From mirror neurons to empathy. *Journal of Consciousness Studies, 8:* 33–50.

Garland, E. L., Gaylord, S. A. & Fredrickson, B. L. (2011). Positive reappraisal mediates stress-reductive effects of mindfulness: An upward spiral process. *Mindfulness, 2:* 59–67.

George, C. & Solomon, J. (2008). The caregiving system: A behavioral systems approach to parenting. In J. Cassidy & P. R. Shaver (Eds.), *Handbook of Attachment: Theory, Research, and Clinical Applications* (2nd edn, pp. 833–856). New York: The Guilford Press.

George, C. & Solomon, J. (2011). Caregiving helplessness: The development of a screening measure for disorganized maternal caregiving. In J. Solomon & C. George (Eds.), *Disorganized Attachment and Caregiving* (pp. 133–166). New York: The Guilford Press.

Gergely, G. (2007). The social construction of the subjective self: The role of affect mirroring, markedness, and ostensive communication in self development. In L. C. Mayes, P. Fonagy & M. Target (Eds.), *Developmental Science and Psychoanalysis.* London: Karnac.

Gergely, G., Egyed, K. & Kiraly, I. (2007). On pedagogy. *Developmental Science, 10:* 139–146.

Gergely, G., Nadasdy, Z., Csibra, G. & Biro, S. (1995). Taking the intentional stance at 12 months of age. *Cognition, 56*: 165–193.

Gergely, G. & Unoka, Z. (2008). Attachment and mentalization in humans: The development of the affective self. In E. L. Jurist, A. Slade & S. Bergner (Eds.), *Mind to Mind: Infant Research, Neuroscience, and Psychoanalysis* (pp. 50–87). New York: Other Press.

Gergely, G. & Watson, J. S. (1996). The social biofeedback theory of parental affect-mirroring: The development of emotional self-awareness and self-control in infancy. *International Journal of Psycho-Analysis, 77*: 1181–1212.

Giedd, J. N. (2003). The anatomy of mentalization: A view from neuroimaging. *Bulletin of the Menninger Clinic, 67*: 132–142.

Gilbert, P. (2010). *Compassion Focused Therapy.* New York: Routledge.

Gilbert, S. J., Williamson, I. D. M., Dumontheil, I., Simons, J. S., Frith, C. D. & Burgess, P. W. (2007). Distinct regions of medial rostral prefrontal cortex supporting social and nonsocial functions. *Social Cognitive and Affective Neuroscience, 2*: 217–226.

Goldman, A. I. (2006). *Simulating Minds: The Philosophy, Psychology, and Neuroscience of Mindreading.* New York: Oxford University Press.

Goldstein, J. & Kornfield, J. (1987). *Seeking the Heart of Wisdom: The Path of Insight Meditation.* Boston: Shambhala.

Goodwin, J. M. (1993). Sadistic abuse: Definition, recognition, and treatment. *Dissociation, 6*: 181–187.

Green, E. E. & Green, A. M. (1986). Biofeedback and states of consciousness. In B. B. Wolman & M. Ullman (Eds.), *Handbook of States of Consciousness* (pp. 553–589). New York: Van Nostrand Reinhold.

Greicius, M. D., Supekar, K., Menon, V. & Dougherty, R. F. (2009). Resting-state functional connectivity reflects structural connectivity in the default mode network. *Cerebral Cortex, 19*: 72–78.

Grey, N. & Holmes, E. A. (2008). "Hotspots" in trauma memories in the treatment of post-traumatic stress disorder: A replication. *Memory, 16*: 788–796.

Grienenberger, J., Kelly, K. & Slade, A. (2005). Maternal reflective functioning, mother-infant affective communication, and infant attachment: Exploring the link between mental states and observed caregiving behaviour in the intergenerational transmission of attachment. *Attachment and Human Development, 7*: 299–311.

Groat, M. & Allen, J. G. (2011). Promoting mentalizing in experiential psychoeducational groups: From agency and authority to authorship. *Bulletin of the Menninger Clinic, 75*: 315–343.

Grossman, K., Grossman, K. E., Kindler, H. & Zimmerman, P. (2008). A wider view of attachment and exploration: The influence of mothers and fathers on the development of psychological security from infancy to young adulthood. In J. Cassidy & P. R. Shaver (Eds.), *Handbook of Attachment: Theory, Research, and Clinical Applications* (2nd edn, pp. 857–879). New York: The Guilford Press.

Grossman, K. E., Grossman, K. & Waters, E. (Eds.) (2005). *Attachment from Infancy to Adulthood: The Major Longitudinal Studies*. New York: The Guilford Press.

Guastella, A. J. & Mitchell, P. B. (2008). Oxytocin enhances the encoding of positive social memories in humans. *Biological Psychiatry, 64*: 256–258.

Guastella, A. J., Mitchell, P. B. & Dadds, M. R. (2008). Oxytocin increases gaze to the eye region of human faces. *Biological Psychiatry, 63*: 3–5.

Gusnard, D. A. (2005). Being a self: Considerations from functional imaging. *Consciousness and Cognition, 14*: 679–697.

Gusnard, D. A., Akbudak, E., Shulman, G. L. & Raichle, M. E. (2001). Medial prefrontal cortex and self-referential mental activity: Relation to a default mode of brain function. *PNAS, 98*: 4259–4264.

Gusnard, D. A. & Raichle, M. E. (2001). Searching for a baseline: Functional imaging and the resting human brain. *Nature Reviews Neuroscience, 2*: 685–694.

Hahn, T. N. (1991). *Peace is Every Step: The Path of Mindfulness in Everyday Life*. New York: Bantam Books.

Hatfield, E., Cacioppo, J. T. & Rapson, R. L. (1994). *Emotional Contagion*. Paris: Cambridge University Press.

Hayes, S. C. (2004). Acceptance and Commitment Therapy and the new behavior therapies. In S. C. Hayes, V. M. Follette & M. M. Linehan (Eds.), *Mindfulness and Acceptance: Expanding the Cognitive-Behavioral Tradition* (pp. 1–29). New York: The Guilford Press.

Hayes, S. C. (2008). Climbing our hills: A beginning conversation on the comparison and Acceptance and Commitment Therapy and traditional cognitive behavioral therapy. *Clinical Psychology: Science and Practice, 15*: 286–295.

Hayes, S. C. & Strosahl, K. D. (Eds.) (2004). *A Practical Guide to Acceptance and Commitment Therapy*. New York: Springer.

Hayes, S. C., Strosahl, K. D., Bunting, K., Twohig, M. & Wilson, K. G. (2004). What is Acceptance and Commitment Therapy? In S. C. Hayes & K. D. Strosahl (Eds.), *A Practical Guide to Acceptance and Commitment Therapy* (pp. 3–29). New York: Springer.

Hayes, S. C., Strosahl, K. D. & Wilson, K. G. (1999). *Acceptance and Commitment Therapy: An Experiential Approach to Behavior Change*. New York: The Guilford Press.

Hazan, C. & Shaver, P. (1987). Romantic love conceptualized as an attachment processes. *Journal of Personality and Social Psychology, 52*: 511–524.

Hazan, C. & Shaver, P. R. (1994). Attachment as an organizational framework for research on close relationships. *Psychological Inquiry, 5*: 1–22.

Heinrichs, M., Baumgartner, T., Kirschbaum, C. & Ehlert, U. (2003). Social support and oxytocin interact to suppress cortisol and subjective responses to psychosocial stress. *Biological Psychiatry, 54*: 1389–1398.

Herman, J. L. (1981). *Father-Daughter Incest.* Cambridge, MA: Harvard University Press.

Herman, J. L. (1992a). Complex PTSD: A syndrome in survivors of prolonged and repeated trauma. *Journal of Traumatic Stress, 5*: 377–391.

Herman, J. L. (1992b). *Trauma and Recovery.* New York: BasicBooks.

Herman, J. L. (1993). Sequelae of prolonged and repeated trauma: Evidence for a complex posttraumatic syndrome (DESNOS). In J. R. T. Davidson & E. B. Foa (Eds.), *Posttraumatic Stress Disorder: DSM-IV and Beyond* (pp. 213–228). Washington, DC: American Psychiatric Press.

Herman, J. L. (2009). Foreword. In C. A. Courtois & J. D. Ford (Eds.), *Treating Complex Traumatic Stress Disorders* (pp. xiii-xvii). New York: The Guilford Press.

Hesse, E. (2008). The Adult Attachment Interview: Protocol, method of analysis, and empirical studies. In J. Cassidy & P. R. Shaver (Eds.), *Handbook of Attachment: Theory, Research, and Clinical Applications (Second Edition)* (pp. 552–598). New York: The Guilford Press.

Hobson, P. (2002). *The Cradle of Thought: Exploring the Origins of Thinking.* New York: Oxford University Press.

Hoffmann, S. G., Sawyer, A. T., Witt, A. A. & Oh, D. (2010). The effect of mindfulness-based therapy on anxiety and depression: A meta-analytic review. *Journal of Consulting and Clinical Psychology, 78*: 169–183.

Holmes, E. A., Brown, R. J., Mansell, W., Fearon, R. P., Hunter, E. C. M., Frasquilho, F. & Oakley, D. A. (2005). Are there two qualitatively distinct forms of dissociation? A review and some clinical implications. *Clinical Psychology Review, 25*: 1–23.

Holmes, E. A., Grey, N. & Young, K. A. D. (2005). Intrusive images and "hotspots" of trauma memories in posttraumatic stress disorder: An exploratory investigation of emotions and cognitive themes. *Journal of Behavior Therapy and Experimental Psychiatry, 36*: 3–17.

Holmes, J. (1999). Defensive and creative uses of narrative in psychotherapy: An attachment perspective. In G. Roberts & J. Holmes (Eds.), *Healing Stories: Narrative in Psychiatry and Psychotherapy* (pp. 49–66). London: Oxford University Press.

Holmes, J. (2001). *The Search for the Secure Base: Attachment Theory and Psychotherapy.* London: Routledge.

Holmes, J. (2010). *Exploring in Security: Towards an Attachment-Informed Psychoanalytic Psychotherapy.* New York: Routledge.

Holmes, J. (2011). Attachment theory and the suicidal patient. In K. Michel & D. A. Jobes (Eds.), *Building a Therapeutic Alliance with the Suicidal Patient* (pp. 149–167). Washington, DC: American Psychological Association.

Holzel, B. K., Carmody, J., Vangel, M., Congelton, C., Yerramsetti, S. M., Gard, T. & Lazar, S. W. (2011). Mindfulness practice leads to increases in regional brain gray matter density. *Psychiatry Research: Neuroimaging, 191*: 36–43.

Horwitz, L., Gabbard, G. O., Allen, J. G., Frieswyk, S. H., Colson, D. B., Newsom, G. E. & Coyne, L. (1996). *Borderline Personality Disorder: Tailoring the Therapy to the Patient.* Washington, DC: American Psychiatric Press.

Hrdy, S. B. (2009). *Mothers and others: The Evolutionary Origins of Mutual Understanding.* Cambridge, MA: Harvard University Press.

Humphrey, N. K. (1988). The social function of intellect. In R. W. Byrne & A. Whiten (Eds.), *Machiavellian Intelligence: Social Expertise and the Evolution of Intellect in Monkeys, Apes, and Humans* (pp. 13–26). New York: Oxford University Press.

Iacoboni, M. (2008). *Mirroring People: The New Science of How we Connect with Others.* New York: Farrar, Straus and Giroux.

Insel, T. R. (2003). Is social attachment an addictive disorder? *Physiology and Behavior, 79*: 351–357.

Insel, T. R. & Young, L. J. (2001). The neurobiology of attachment. *Nature Reviews Neuroscience, 2*: 129–136.

Jackson, C., Nissenson, K. & Cloitre, M. (2009). Cognitive-behavioral therapy. In C. A. Courtois & J. D. Ford (Eds.), *Treating Complex Traumatic Stress Disorders: An Evidence-Based Guide* (pp. 243–263). New York: The Guilford Press.

Jacobvitz, D. (2008). Afterword: Reflections on clinical applications of the Adult Attachment Interview. In H. Steele & M. Steele (Eds.), *Clinical Applications of the Adult Attachment Interview* (pp. 471–486). New York: The Guilford Press.

Jaffe, P. G., Sudermann, M. & Reitzel, D. (1992). Child witnesses of marital violence. In R. T. Ammerman & M. Hersen (Eds.), *Assessment of Family Violence: A Clinical and Legal Sourcebook* (pp. 313–331). New York: Wiley.

Jobes, D. A. (2006). *Managing Suicidal Risk: A Collaborative Approach.* New York: The Guilford Press.

Jobes, D. A. (2011). Suicidal patients, the therapeutic alliance, and the Collaborative Assessment and Management of Suicidality. In K. Michel & D. A. Jobes (Eds.), *Building a Therapeutic Alliance with the Suicidal Patient* (pp. 205–229). Washington, DC: American Psychological Association.

Johnson, J. G., Cohen, P., Brown, J., Smailes, E. M. & Bernstein, D. P. (1999). Childhood maltreatment increases risk for personality disorders during early adulthood. *Archives of General Psychiatry, 56*: 600–606.

Johnson, S. M. (2008). Couple and family therapy: An attachment perspective. In J. Cassidy & P. R. Shaver (Eds.), *Handbook of Attachment: Theory, Research, and Clinical Applications* (2nd edn, pp. 811–829). New York: The Guilford Press.

Johnson, S. M. (2009). Attachment theory and emotionally focused therapy for individuals and couples. In J. H. Obegi & E. Berant (Eds.), *Attachment Theory and Research in Clinical Work with Adults* (pp. 410–433). New York: The Guilford Press.

Johnson, S. M. & Courtois, C. A. (2009). Couple therapy. In C. A. Courtois & J. D. Ford (Eds.), *Treating Complex Traumatic Stress Disorders: An Evidence-Based Guide* (pp. 371–390). New York: The Guilford Press.

Johnson, S. M., Dweck, C. S. & Chen, F. S. (2007). Evidence for infants' internal working models of attachment. *Psychological Science, 18*: 501–502.

Joiner, T. E. (2005). *Why People Die by Suicide*. Cambridge, MA: Harvard University Press.

Jones, A. (2008). The AAI as a clinical tool. In H. Steele & M. Steele (Eds.), *Clinical Applications of the Adult Attachment Interview* (pp. 175–194). New York: The Guilford Press.

Jurist, E. L. (2005). Mentalized affectivity. *Psychoanalytic Psychology, 22*: 426–444.

Kabat-Zinn, J. (1990). *Full Catastrophe Living: Using the Wisdom of your Body and Mind to Face Stress, Pain, and Illness*. New York: Delta.

Kabat-Zinn, J. (1994). *Wherever You Go, There You Are: Mindfulness Meditation in Everyday Life*. New York: Hyperion.

Kabat-Zinn, J. (2003). Mindfulness-based interventions in context: Past, present, and future. *Clinical Psychology: Science and Practice, 10*: 144–156.

Kabat-Zinn, J., Massion, A. O., Kristeller, J., Peterson, L. G., Fletcher, K. E., Pbert, L., Lenderking, W. R. & Santorelli, S. F. (1992). Effectiveness of a meditation-based stress reduction program in the treatment of anxiety disorders. *American Journal of Psychiatry, 149*: 936–943.

Kagan, J. (2003). Behavioral inhibition as a temperamental category. In R. J. Davidson, K. R. Scherer & H. H. Goldsmith (Eds.), *Handbook of Affective Sciences* (pp. 320–331). New York: Oxford University Press.

Kandel, E. R. (2005). *Psychiatry, Psychoanalysis, and the New Biology of Mind*. Washington, DC: American Psychiatric Publishing.

Kandel, E. R. (2006). *In Search of Memory: The Emergence of a Science of Mind*. New York: Norton.

Kaplan, L. J. (1991). *Female Perversions: The Temptations of Emma Bovary*. New York: Doubleday.

Karen, R. (1998). *Becoming Attached: First Relationships and How they Shape our Capacity to Love*. New York: Oxford University Press.

Karterud, S. & Bateman, A. (2012). Group therapy techniques. In A. Bateman & P. Fonagy (Eds.), *Handbook of Mentalizing in Mental Health Practice* (pp. 81–105). Washington, DC: American Psychiatric Publishing.

Kempe, C. H., Silverman, F. N., Steele, B. F., Droegemueller, W. & Silver, H. K. (1962). The battered-child syndrome. *Journal of the American Medical Association, 181*: 105–112.

Kernberg, O. F., Diamond, D., Yeomans, F. E., Clarkin, J. F. & Levy, K. N. (2008). Mentalization and attachment in borderline patients in Transference Focused Psychotherapy. In E. L. Jurist, A. Slade & S. Bergner (Eds.), *Mind to Mind: Infant Research, Neuroscience, and Psychoanalysis* (pp. 167–201). New York: Other Press.

Keysers, C., Wicker, B., Gazzola, V., Anton, J. -L., Fogassi, L. & Gallese, V. (2004). A touching sight: SII/PV activation during the observation and experience of touch. *Neuron, 42*: 335–346.

Kim, P., Leckman, J. F., Mayes, L. C., Newman, M. -A., Feldman, R. & Swain, J. E. (2010). Perceived quality of maternal care in childhood and structure and function of mothers' brain. *Developmental Science, 13*: 662–673.

Kirsch, P., Esslinger, C., Chen, Q., Mier, D., Lis, S., Siddhanti, S., Gruppe, H., Mattay, V. S., Gallhofer, B. & Meyer-Lindenberg, A. (2005). Oxytocin modulates neural circuitry for social cognition and fear in humans. *Journal of Neuroscience, 25*: 11489–11493.

Kluft, R. P. (1992). Discussion: A specialist's perspective on multiple personality disorder. *Psychoanalytic Inquiry, 12*: 139–171.

Kluft, R. P. (1993). Basic principles in conducting the psychotherapy of multiple personality disorder. In R. P. Kluft & C. G. Fine (Eds.), *Current Perspectives on Multiple Personality Disorder* (pp. 19–50). Washington, DC: American Psychiatric Press.

Koenen, K. C., Fu, Q. J., Ertel, K., Lyons, M., True, W. R., Goldberg, J. & Tsuang, M. T. (2008). Common genetic liability to major depression and posttraumatic stress disorder in men. *Journal of Affective Disorders, 105*: 109–115.

Koenen, K. C., Moffitt, T. E., Poulton, R., Martin, J. & Caspi, A. (2007). Early childhood factors associated with the development of post-traumatic stress disorder: Results from a longitudinal birth cohort. *Psychological Medicine, 37*: 181–192.

Koos, O. & Gergely, G. (2001). A contingency-based approach to the etiology of "disorganized" attachment: The "flickering switch" hypothesis. *Bulletin of the Menninger Clinic, 65*: 397–410.

Kornfield, J. (2009). *The Wise Heart: A Guide to the Universal Teachings of Buddhist Psychology*. New York: Random House.

Kosfeld, M., Heinrichs, M., Zak, P. J., Fischbacher, U. & Fehr, E. (2005). Oxytocin increases trust in humans. *Nature, 435*: 673–676.

Kuyken, W., Watkins, E., Holden, E., White, K., Taylor, R. S., Byford, S., Evans, A., Radford, S., Teasdale, J. D. & Dalgleish, T. (2010). How does mindfulness-based cognitive therapy work? *Behaviour Research and Therapy, 48*: 1105–1112.

Labuschagne, I., Phan, K. L., Wood, A., Angstadt, M., Chua, P., Heinrichs, M., Stout, J. C. & Nathan, P. (2010). Oxytocin attenuates amygdala reactivity to fear in generalized social anxiety disorder. *Neuropsychopharmacology, 35*: 2403–2413.

Lanius, R. A., Vermetten, E. & Pain, C. (Eds.) (2010). *The Impact of Early Life Trauma on Health and Disease: The Hidden Epidemic*. New York: Cambridge University Press.

Lazar, S. W., Kerr, C. E., Wasserman, R. H., Gray, J. R., Greve, D. N., Treadway, M. T., McGarvey, M., Quinn, B. T., Dusek, J. A., Benson, H., Rauch, S. L., Moore, C. I. & Fischl, B. (2005). Meditation experience is associated with increased cortical thickness. *NeuroReport, 16*: 1893–1897.

Lecours, S. & Bouchard, M. -A. (1997). Dimensions of mentalisation: Outlining levels of psychic transformation. *International Journal of Psycho-Analysis, 78*: 855–875.

Lenzi, D., Trentini, C., Pantano, P., Macaluso, E., Iacoboni, M., Lenzi, G. L. & Ammaniti, M. (2009). Neural basis of maternal communication and emotional expression processing during infant preverbal stage. *Cerebral Cortex, 19*: 1124–1133.

Levy, K. N. (2008). Psychotherapies and lasting change. *American Journal of Psychiatry, 165*: 556–559.

Levy, K. N., Ellison, W. D., Scott, L. N. & Bernecker, S. L. (2011). Attachment style. In J. C. Norcross (Ed.), *Psychotherapy Relationships that Work: Evidence-Based Responsiveness* (2nd edn, pp. 377–401). New York: Oxford University Press.

Levy, K. N., Meehan, K. B., Kelly, K. M., Reynoso, J. S., Weber, M., Clarkin, J. F. & Kernberg, O. F. (2006). Change in attachment patterns and reflective function in a randomized control trial of Transference-Focused Psychotherapy for borderline personality disorder. *Journal of Consulting and Clinical Psychology, 74*: 1027–1040.

Lewis, L., Kelly, K. A. & Allen, J. G. (2004). *Restoring Hope and Trust: An Illustrated Guide to Mastering Trauma*. Baltimore, MD: Sidran Press.

Lieberman, A. F., Padron, E., Van Horn, P. & Harris, W. W. (2005). Angels in the nursery: The intergenerational transmission of benevolent parental influences. *Infant Mental Health Journal, 26*: 504–520.

Lieberman, A. F. & Zeanah, C. H. (1999). Contributions of attachment theory to infant-parent psychotherapy and other interventions with infants and young children. In J. Cassidy & P. R. Shaver (Eds.), *Handbook of Attachment: Theory, Research, and Clinical Applications* (pp. 555–574). New York: The Guilford Press.

Linehan, M. M. (1993). *Cognitive-Behavioral Treatment of Borderline Personality Disorder*. New York: The Guilford Press.

Linehan, M. M., Comtois, K. A., Murray, A. M., Brown, M. Z., Gallop, R. J., Heard, H. L., Korslund, K. E., Tutek, D. A., Reynolds, S. K. & Lindenboim, N. (2006). Two-year randomized controlled trail and follow-up of dialectical behavior therapy vs therapy by experts for suicidal behaviors and borderline personality disorder. *Archives of General Psychiatry, 63*: 757–766.

Liotti, G. (1999). Disorganization of attachment as a model for understanding dissociative psychopathology. In J. Solomon & C. George (Eds.), *Attachment Disorganization* (pp. 291–317). New York: The Guilford Press.

Lombardo, M. V., Chakrabarti, B., Bullmore, E. T., Wheelwright, S. J., Sadek, S. A., Suckling, J. & Baron-Cohen, S. (2010). Shared neural circuits for mentalizing about the self and others. *Journal of Cognitive Neuroscience, 22*: 1623–1635.

Long, M. E., Elhai, J. D., Schweinle, A., Gray, M. J., Grubaugh, A. L. & Frueh, B. C. (2008). Differences in posttraumatic stress disorder diagnostic rates and symptom severity between Criterion A1 and non-Criterion A1 stressors. *Journal of Anxiety Disorders, 22*: 1255–1263.

Luborsky, L., Singer, B. & Luborsky, L. (1975). Comparative studies of psychotherapies: Is it true that "Everyone Has Won and All Must Have Prizes"? *Archives of General Psychiatry, 32*: 995–1008.

Luyten, P., Fonagy, P., Lemma, A. & Target, M. (2012). Depression. In P. Fonagy & A. Bateman (Eds.), *Handbook of Mentalizing in Mental Health Practice* (pp. 385–417). Washington, DC: American Psychiatric Publishing.

Luyten, P., Mayes, L. C., Fonagy, P. & Van Houdenhove, B. (submitted). Attachment and the interpersonal nature of stress regulation: A developmental framework.

Luyten, P., Vliegen, N., van Houdenhove, B. & Blatt, S. J. (2008). Equifinality, multifinality, and the rediscovery of the importance of early experiences: Pathways from early adversity to psychiatric and (functional) somatic disorders. *Psychoanalytic Study of the Child, 63*: 27–60.

Lyons-Ruth, K., Bronfman, E. & Atwood, G. (1999). A relational diathesis model of hostile-helpless states of mind: Expressions in mother-infant interaction. In J. Solomon & C. George (Eds.), *Attachment Disorganization* (pp. 33–70). New York: Guilford.

Lyons-Ruth, K. & Jacobvitz, D. (2008). Attachment disorganization: Genetic factors, parenting contexts, and developmental transformation from infancy to adulthood. In J. Cassidy & P. R. Shaver (Eds.), *Handbook of Attachment: Theory, Research, and Clinical Applications* (2nd edn, pp. 666–697). New York: The Guilford Press.

MacDonald, H. Z., Beeghly, M., Grant-Knight, W., Augustyn, M., Woods, R. W., Cabral, H., Rose-Jacobs, R., Saxe, G. N. & Frank, D. A. (2008). Longitudinal association between infant disorganized attachment and childhood posttraumatic stress symptoms. *Development and Psychopathology, 20*: 493–508.

Mace, C. (2008). *Mindfulness and Mental Health: Therapy, Theory and Science.* London: Routledge.

MacLean, P. D. (1985). Brain evolution relating to family, play, and the separation call. *Archives of General Psychiatry, 42*: 405–417.

MacLean, P. D. (1990). *The Triune Brain in Evolution: Role in Paleocerebral Functions.* New York: Plenum.

Magai, C. (2008). Attachment in middle and later life. In J. Cassidy & P. R. Shaver (Eds.), *Handbook of Attachment: Theory, Research, and Clinical Applications* (2nd edn, pp. 532–551). New York: The Guilford Press.

Main, M. (1991). Metacognitive knowledge, metacognitive monitoring, and singular (coherent) vs. multiple (incoherent) model of attachment. In C. M. Parkes, J. Stevenson-Hinde & P. Marris (Eds.), *Attachment Across the Life Cycle* (pp. 127–159). London: Routledge.

Main, M. & Goldwyn, R. (1994). *Adult Attachment Scoring and Classification Systems (Unpublished Scoring Manual).* Berkeley, CA: Department of Psychology, University of California, Berkeley.

Main, M. & Hesse, E. (1990). Parents' unresolved traumatic experiences are related to infant disorganized attachment status: Is frightened and/or frightening parental behavior the linking mechanism? In M. T. Greenberg, D. Cicchetti & E. M. Cummings (Eds.), *Attachment in the Preschool Years: Theory, Research, and Intervention* (pp. 161–182). Chicago: University of Chicago Press.

Main, M., Hesse, E. & Goldwyn, R. (2008). Studying differences in language usage in recounting attachment history: An introduction to the AAI. In H. Steele & M. Steele (Eds.), *Clinical Applications of the Adult Attachment Interview* (pp. 31–68). New York: The Guilford Press.

Main, M., Hesse, E. & Kaplan, N. (2005). Predictability of attachment behavior and representational processes at 1, 6, and 19 years of age. In K. E. Grossman, K. Grossman & E. Waters (Eds.), *Attachment from Infancy to Adulthood: The Major Longitudinal Studies* (pp. 245–304). New York: The Guilford Press.

Main, M., Kaplan, N. & Cassidy, J. (1985). Security in infancy, chldhood, and adulthood: A move to the level of representation. In I. Bretherton & E. Waters (Eds.), *Growing Points of Attachment Theory and Research (Monographs of the Society for Research in Child Development)* (Vol. 50, 1–2, Serial No. 209, pp. 66–104). Chicago: University of Chicago Press.

Main, M. & Solomon, J. (1990). Procedures for identifying infants as disorganized/disoriented during the Ainsworth Strange Situation. In M. T. Greenberg, D. Cicchetti & E. M. Cummings (Eds.), *Attachment in the Preschool Years: Theory, Research, and Intervention* (pp. 121–160). Chicago: University of Chicago Press.

Maker, A. H., Kemmelmeier, M. & Peterson, C. (1998). Long-term psychological consequences in women of witnessing parental physical conflict and experiencing abuse in childhood. *Journal of Interpersonal Violence, 13*: 574–589.

Mallinckrodt, B., Daly, K. & Wang, C. -C. D. C. (2009). An attachment approach to adult psychotherapy. In J. H. Obegi & E. Berant (Eds.), *Attachment Theory and Research in Clinical Work with Adults* (pp. 234–268). New York: The Guilford Press.

Mallinckrodt, B., McCreary, B. A. & Robertson, A. K. (1995). Co-occurrence of eating disorders and incest: The role of attachment, family environment, and social competencies. *Journal of Counseling Psychology, 42*: 178–186.

March, J. S. (1993). What constitutes a stressor? The "Criterion A" issue. In J. R. T. Davidson & E. B. Foa (Eds.), *Posttraumatic Stress Disorder: DSM-IV and Beyond* (pp. 37–54). Washington, DC: American Psychiatric Press.

Martin, J. R. (1997). Mindfulness: A proposed common factor. *Journal of Psychotherapy Integration, 7*: 291–312.

Marvin, R. S. & Britner, P. A. (2008). Normative development: The ontogeny of attachment. In J. Cassidy & P. R. Shaver (Eds.), *Handbook of Attachment: Theory, Research, and Clinical Applications* (2nd edn, pp. 269–294). New York: The Guilford Press.

Marvin, R. S., Cooper, G., Hoffman, K. & Powell, B. (2002). The Circle of Security project: Attachment-based intervention with caregiver-pre-school child dyads. *Attachment and Human Development, 4*: 107–124.

Mayes, L. C. (2000). A developmental perspective on the regulation of arousal states. *Seminars in Perinatology, 24*: 267–279.

McBride, C. & Atkinson, L. (2009). Attachment theory and cognitive-behavioral therapy. In J. H. Obegi & E. Berant (Eds.), *Attachment Theory and Research in Clinical Work with Adults* (pp. 434–458). New York: The Guilford Press.

McIntosh, W. D. (1997). East meets west: Parallels between Zen Buddhism and social psychology. *The International Journal for the Psychology of Religion, 7*: 37–52.

Meins, E. (1997). *Security of Attachment and the Social Development of Cognition*. East Sussex, UK: Psychology Press.

Meins, E., Fernyhough, C., Fradley, E. & Tuckey, M. (2001). Rethinking maternal sensitivity: Mothers' commments on infants' mental processes predict security of attachment at 12 months. *Journal of Child Psychology and Psychiatry, 42*: 637–648.

Meins, E., Fernyhough, C., Russell, J. & Clark-Carter, D. (1998). Security of attachment as a predictor of symbolic and mentalising abilities: A longitudinal study. *Social Development, 7*: 1–24.

Melnick, S., Finger, B., Hans, S., Patrick, M. & Lyons-Ruth, K. (2008). Hostile-helpless states of mind in the AAI: A proposed additional AAI category with implications for identifying disorganized infant attachment in high-risk samples. In H. Steele & M. Steele (Eds.), *Clinical Applications of the Adult Attachment Interview* (pp. 399–423). New York: The Guilford Press.

Menninger, K. A. (1938). *Man Against Himself*. New York: Harcourt, Brace and Company.

Menninger, K. A. (1983). The suicidal intention of nuclear armament. *Bulletin of the Menninger Clinic, 47*: 325–353.

Mikulas, W. L. (2011). Mindfulness: Significant common confusions. *Mindfulness, 2*: 1–7.

Mikulincer, M. & Shaver, P. R. (2004). Security-based self-representations in adulthood: Contents and processes. In W. S. Rholes & J. A. Simpson (Eds.), *Adult Attachment: Theory, Research, and Clinical Implications* (pp. 159–195). New York: The Guilford Press.

Mikulincer, M. & Shaver, P. R. (2007a). *Attachment in Adulthood: Structure, Dynamics, and Change*. New York: The Guilford Press.

Mikulincer, M. & Shaver, P. R. (2007b). Reflections on security dynamics: Core constructs, psychological mechanisms, relational contexts, and the need for an integrative theory. *Psychological Inquiry, 18*: 197–209.

Mikulincer, M. & Shaver, P. R. (2008). Adult attachment and affect regulation. In J. Cassidy & P. R. Shaver (Eds.), *Handbook of Attachment: Theory, Research, and Clinical Applications* (2nd edn, pp. 503–531). New York: The Guilford Press.

Mohr, J. J. (2008). Same-sex romantic attachment. In J. Cassidy & P. R. Shaver (Eds.), *Handbook of Attachment: Theory, Research, and Clinical Applications* (2nd edn, pp. 482–502). New York: The Guilford Press.

Moran, P. M., Bifulco, A., Ball, C., Jacobs, C. & Benaim, K. (2002). Exploring psychological abuse in childhood: I. Developing a new interview scale. *Bulletin of the Menninger Clinic, 66*: 213–240.

Morton, J. (1989). The origins of autism. *New Scientist, 1694*: 44–47.

Moss, E., Bureau, J. -F., St-Laurent, D. & Tarabulsy, G. M. (2011). Understanding disorganized attachment at preschool and school age: Examining divergent pathways of disorgnaized and controlling children. In J. Solomon & C. George (Eds.), *Disorganized Attachment and Caregiving* (pp. 52–79). New York: The Guilford Press.

Munafo, M. R., Brown, S. M. & Hariri, A. R. (2008). Serotonin transporter (5-HTTLPR) genotype and amygdala activation: A meta-analysis. *Biological Psychiatry, 63*: 852–857.

Murdoch, I. (1971). *The Sovereignty of Good.* London: Routledge.

Murdoch, I. (1992). *Metaphysics as a Guide to Morals.* London: Penguin.

Naber, F., van Ijzendoorn, M. H., Deschamps, P., van Engeland, H. & Bakermans-Kranenburg, M. J. (2010). Intranasal oxytocin increases fathers' observed responsiveness during play with their children: A double-blind within-subject experiement. *Psychoneuroendocrinology, 35*: 1583–1586.

Neff, K. D. (2009). The role of self-compassion in development: A healthier way to relate to oneself. *Human Development, 52*: 211–214.

Neff, K. D. (2011). *Self-Compassion.* New York: HarperCollins.

Nemeroff, C. B., Bremner, J. D., Foa, E. B., Mayberg, H. S., North, C. S. & Stein, M. B. (2006). Posttraumatic stress disorder: A state-of-the-science review. *Journal of Psychiatric Research, 40*: 1–21.

Neumann, I. D. (2008). Brain oxytocin: A key regulator of emotional and social behaviors in both females and males. *NeuroImage, 20*: 858–865.

Nock, M. K. (Ed.) (2009). *Understanding Nonsuicidal Self-Injury.* Washington, DC: American Psychological Association.

Nolen-Hoeksema, S. (2000). The role of rumination in depressive disorders and mixed anxiety/depressive symptoms. *Journal of Abnormal Psychology, 109*: 504–511.

Nolen-Hoeksema, S. & Davis, C. G. (1999). "Thanks for sharing that": Ruminators and their social support networks. *Journal of Personality and Social Psychology, 77*: 801–814.

Norcross, J. C. (Ed.). (2011). *Psychotherapy Relationships that Work: Evidence-Based Responsiveness* (2nd edn). New York: Oxford University Press.

Nussbaum, M. C. (2001). *Upheavals of Thought: The Intelligence of the Emotions.* Cambridge: Cambridge University Press.

Obegi, J. H. & Berant, E. (Eds.) (2009). *Attachment Theory and Research in Clinical Work.* New York: The Guilford Press.

Oldham, J. M. (2008). Epilogue. In J. G. Allen & P. Fonagy (Eds.), *Mentalizing in Clinical Practice* (pp. 341–346). Washington, DC: American Psychiatric Publishing.

Oliver, J. E. (1993). Intergenerational transmission of child abuse: Rates, research, and clinical implications. *American Journal of Psychiatry, 150*: 1315–1324.

Onishi, K. H. & Baillargeon, R. (2005). Do 15-month-old infants understand false beliefs? *Science, 308*: 255–258.

Orbach, I. (2011). Taking an inside view: Stories of pain. In K. Michel & D. A. Jobes (Eds.), *Building a Therapeutic Alliance with the Suicidal Patient* (pp. 111–128). Washington, DC: American Psychological Association.

Osofsky, J. D. (1995). Children who witness domestic violence: The invisible victims. *Social Policy Report, Society for Research in Child Development, 9*: 1–16.

Ozer, E. J., Best, S. R., Lipsey, T. L. & Weiss, D. S. (2003). Predictors of posttraumatic stress disorder and symptoms in adults: A meta-analysis. *Psychological Bulletin, 129*: 52–73.

Panksepp, J. (1998). *Affective Neuroscience: The Foundations of Human and Animal Emotions.* New York: Oxford University Press.

Panksepp, J. (2009). Brain emotional systems and qualities of mental life: From animal models of affect to implications for psychotherapeutics. In D. Fosha, D. J. Siegal & M. F. Solomon (Eds.), *The Healing Power of Emotion: Affective Neuroscience, Development and Clinical Practice* (pp. 1–26). New York: Norton.

Panksepp, J., Nelson, E. & Bekkedal, M. (1999). Brain systems for the mediation of social separation-distress and social-reward: Evolutionary antecedents and neuropeptide intermediaries. In C. S. Carter, I. I. Lederhendler & B. Kirkpatrick (Eds.), *The Integrative Neurobiology of Affiliation* (pp. 221–243). Cambridge, MA: MIT Press.

Perner, J. (1991). *Understanding the Representational Mind.* Cambridge, MA: MIT Press.

Philips, B., Kahn, U. & Bateman, A. (2012). Drug addiction. In P. Fonagy & A. Bateman (Eds.), *Handbook of Mentalizing in Mental Health Practice* (pp. 445–461). Washington, DC: American Psychiatric Publishing.

Pincus, D., Kose, S., Arana, A., Johnson, K., Morgan, P. S., Borckardt, J., Herbsman, T., Hardaway, F., George, M. S., Panksepp, J. & Nahas, Z. (2010). Inverse effects of oxytocin on attributing mental activity to others in depressed nd healthy subjects: A double-blind placebo controlled fMRI study. *Frontiers in Psychiatry, 1*: 1–10.

Polan, H. J. & Hofer, M. A. (2008). Psychobiological origins of infant attachment and its role in development. In J. Cassidy & P. R. Shaver (Eds.), *Handbook of Attachment: Theory, Research, and Clinical Applications* (2nd edn, pp. 158–172). New York: The Guilford Press.

Pope, H. G., Oliva, P. S., Hudson, J. I., Bodkin, J. A. & Gruber, A. J. (1999). Attitudes toward DSM-IV dissociative disorder diagnoses among board-certified American psychiatrists. *American Journal of Psychiatry, 156*: 321–323.

Post, R. M., Weiss, S. R. B. & Smith, M. A. (1995). Sensitization and kindling: Implications for the evolving neural substrates of post-traumatic stress disorder. In M. J. Friedman, D. S. Charney & A. Y. Deutch (Eds.), *Neurobiological and Clinical Consequences of Stress: From Normal Adaptation to Post-Traumatic Stress Disorder* (pp. 203–224). Philadelphia: Lippincott-Raven.

Powers, M. B., Halpern, J. M., Ferenschak, M. P., Gillihan, S. J. & Foa, E. B. (2010). A meta-analytic review of prolonged exposure for posttraumatic stress disorder. *Clinical Psychology Review, 30*: 635–641.

Raichle, M. E. & Snyder, A. Z. (2007). A default mode of brain function: A brief history of an evolving idea. *NeuroImage, 37*: 1083–1090.

Redclay, E., Dodell-Feder, D., Pearrow, M. J., Mavros, P. L., Kleiner, M., Gabrieli, J. D. E., Saxe, R. (2010). Live face-to-face interaction during fMRI: A new tool for social cognitive neuroscience. *NeuroImage, 50*: 1639–1647.

Resick, P. A., Monson, C. M. & Rizvi, S. L. (2008). Posttraumatic stress disorder. In D. H. Barlow (Ed.), *Clinical Handbook of Psychological Disorders: A Step-by-Step Treatment Manual* (pp. 65–122). New York: The Guilford Press.

Richardson, R. (2010). *The Heart of William James*. Cambridge, MA: Harvard University Press.

Riem, M. M. E., Bakermans-Kranenburg, M. J., Pieper, S., Tops, M., Boksem, M. A. S., Vermeiren, R. R. J. M., van Ijzendoorn, M. H. & Rombouts, S. A. R. B. (2011). Oxytocin modulates amygdala, insula, and inferior frontal gyrus responses to infant crying: A randomized controlled trial. *Biological Psychiatry, 70*: 291–297.

Riggs, D. S., Monson, C. M., Glynn, S. M. & Canterino, J. (2009). Couple and family therapy for adults. In E. B. Foa, T. M. Keane, M. J. Friedman & J. A. Cohen (Eds.), *Effective Treatments for PTSD: Practice Guidelines from the International Society for Traumatic Stress Studies* (2nd edn, pp. 458–478). New York: The Guilford Press.

Robins, C. J., Schmidt, H. I. & Linehan, M. M. (2004). Dialectical Behavior Therapy: Synthesizing radical acceptance with skillful means. In S. C. Hayes, V. M. Follette & M. M. Linehan (Eds.), *Mindfulness and Acceptance: Expanding the Cognitive-Behavioral Tradition* (pp. 30–44). New York: The Guilford Press.

Roemer, L. & Orsillo, S. M. (2009). *Mindfulness- and Acceptance-Based Behavioral Therapies in Practice*. New York: The Guilford Press.

Rolls, E. T. (1999). *The Brain and Emotion*. New York: Oxford University Press.

Rosen, G. M. & Lilienfeld, S. O. (2008). Posttraumatic stress disorder: An empirical evaluation of core assumptions. *Clinical Psychology Review, 28*: 837–868.

Ross, S. M. (1996). Risk of physical abuse to children of spouse abusing parents. *Child Abuse and Neglect, 20*: 589–598.

Roth, A. & Fonagy, P. (2005). *What Works for Whom? A Critical Review of Psychotherapy Research* (2nd edn). New York: The Guilford Press.

Rudd, M. D., Mandrusiak, M. & Joiner, T. E. (2006). The case against no-suicide contracts: The commitment to treatment statement as a practice alternative. *Journal of Clinical Psychology, 62*: 243–251.

Sadler, L. S., Slade, A. & Mayes, L. C. (2006). Minding the Baby: A mentalization-based parenting program. In J. G. Allen & P. Fonagy (Eds.), *Handbook of Mentalization-Based Treatment* (pp. 271–288). Chichester, UK: Wiley.

Sahdra, B. K., Shaver, P. R. & Brown, K. W. (2010). A scale to measure nonattachment: A Buddhist complement to western research on attachment and adaptive functioning. *Journal of Personality Assessment, 92*: 116–127.

Saxe, R. & Powell, L. J. (2006). It's the thought that counts: Specific brain regions for one component of theory of mind. *Psychological Science, 17*: 692–699.

Saxe, R. & Wexler, A. (2005). Making sense of another mind: The role of the right temporo-parietal junction. *Neuropsychologia, 43*: 1391–1399.

Schafer, J., Caetano, R. & Clark, C. L. (1998). Rates of intimate partner violence in the United States. *American Journal of Public Health, 88*: 1702–1704.

Schardt, D. M., Erk, S., Nusser, C., Nothen, M. M., Cichon, S., Rietschel, M., Treutlein, J., Goschke, T. & Walter, H. (2010). Volition dimishes genetically mediated amygdala hyperreactivity. *NeuroImage, 53*: 943–951.

Schore, A. N. (2001). Effects of a secure attachment relationship on right brain development, affect regulation, and infant mental health. *Infant Mental Health Journal, 22*: 7–66.

Schuengel, C., Bakermans-Kranenburg, M. J. & van IJzendoorn, M. H. (1999). Frightening maternal behavior linking unresolved loss and disorganized infant attachment. *Journal of Consulting and Clinical Psychology, 67*: 54–63.

Segal, Z. V., Bieling, P., Young, T., MacQueen, G., Cooke, R., Martin, L., Bloch, R. & Levitan, R. D. (2010). Antidepressant monotherapy vs sequential pharmacotherapy and mindfulness-based cognitive therapy, or placebo, for relapse prophylaxis in recurrent depression. *Archives of General Psychiatry, 67*: 1256–1264.

Segal, Z. V., Ma, S. H., Teasdale, J. D. & Williams, J. M. G. (2007). Initial psychometric properties of the Experiences Questionnaire; Validation of a self-report measure of decentering. *Behavior Therapy, 38*: 234–246.

Segal, Z. V., Teasdale, J. D. & Williams, J. M. G. (2004). Mindfulness-Based Cognitive Therapy: Theoretical rationale and empirical status. In S. C. Hayes, V. M. Follette & M. M. Linehan (Eds.), *Mindfulness and Acceptance: Expanding the Cognitive-Behavioral Tradition* (pp. 45–65). New York: The Guilford Press.

Segal, Z. V., Williams, J. M. G. & Teasdale, J. D. (2002). *Mindfulness-Based Cognitive Therapy for Depression: A New Approach to Preventing Relapse.* New York: The Guilford Press.

Seidler, G. H. & Wagner, F. E. (2006). Comparing the efficacy of EMDR and trauma-focused cognitive-behavioral therapy in the treatment of PTSD: A meta-analytic study. *Psychological Medicine, 36*: 1515–1522.

Shallice, T. & Cooper, R. P. (2011). *The Organisation of Mind.* New York: Oxford University Press.

Shapiro, F. (1995). *Eye Movement Desensitization and Reprocessing: Basic Principles, Protocols, and Procedures.* New York: The Guilford Press.

Shapiro, S. L., Carlson, L. E., Astin, J. A. & Freedman, B. (2006). Mechanisms of mindfulness. *Journal of Clinical Psychology, 62*: 373–386.

Shaver, P. R., Lavy, S., Saron, C. D. & Mikulincer, M. (2007). Social foundations of the capacity for mindfulness: An attachment perspective. *Psychological Inquiry, 18*: 264–271.

Shaver, P. R. & Mikulincer, M. (2011). Clinical implications of attachment theory, *Creating Connections: International Conference on Attachment, Neuroscience, Mentalization-Based Treatment, and Emotionally Focused Therapy.* Kaatsheuvel, The Netherlands.

Shea, M. T., McDevitt-Murphy, M., Ready, D. J. & Schnurr, P. P. (2009). Group therapy. In E. B. Foa, T. M. Keane, M. J. Friedman & J. A. Cohen (Eds.), *Effective Treatments for PTSD: Practice Guidelines from the International Society for Traumatic Stress Studies* (2nd edn, pp. 306–326). New York: The Guilford Press.

Shohat-Ophir, G., Kaun, K. R., Azanchi, R. & Heberlein, U. (2012). Sexual deprivation increases ethanol intake in drosophila. *Science, 335*: 1351–1355.

Siegel, D. J. (1999). *The Developing Mind: Toward a Neurobiology of Interpersonal Experience.* New York: The Guilford Press.

Siegal, D. J. (2007). *The Mindful Brain: Reflection and Attunement in the Cultivation of Well-Being.* New York: Norton.

Siegal, D. J. (2010). *The Mindful Therapist: A Clinician's Guide to Mindsight and Neural Integration.* New York: Norton.

Simpson, J. A. & Belsky, J. (2008). Attachment theory within a modern evolutionary framework. In J. Cassidy & P. R. Shaver (Eds.), *Handbook of Attachment: Theory, Research, and Clinical Applications* (2nd edn, pp. 131–157). New York: The Guilford Press.

Singer, T., Seymour, B., O'Doherty, J., Kaube, H., Dolan, R. J. & Frith, C. D. (2004). Empathy for pain involves the affective but not sensory components of pain. *Science, 303*: 1157–1162.

Skärderud, F. & Fonagy, P. (2012). Eating disorders. In P. Fonagy & A. Bateman (Eds.), *Mentalizing in Mental Health Practice* (pp. 347–383). Washington, DC: American Psychiatric Publishing.

Slade, A. (2005). Parental reflective functioning: An introduction. *Attachment and Human Development, 7*: 269–281.

Slade, A. (2006). Reflective parenting program: Theory and development. *Psychoanalytic Inquiry, 26*: 640–657.

Slade, A. (2008a). The implications of attachment theory and research for adult psychotherapy: Research and clinical perspectives. In J. Cassidy & P. R. Shaver (Eds.), *Handbook of Attachment: Theory, Research, and Clinical Applications* (2nd edn, pp. 762–782). New York: The Guilford Press.

Slade, A. (2008b). Mentalization as a frame for working with parents in child psychotherapy. In E. L. Jurist, A. Slade & S. Bergner (Eds.), *Mind to Mind: Infant Research, Neuroscience, and Psychoanalysis* (pp. 307–334). New York: Other Press.

Slade, A., Grienenberger, J., Bernbach, E., Levy, D. & Locker, A. (2005). Maternal reflective functioning, attachment, and the transmission gap: A preliminary study. *Attachment and Human Development, 7*: 283–298.

Slade, A., Sadler, L. S., Currier, J., Webb, D., Dedios-Kenn, C. & Mayes, L. C. (2004). *Minding the Baby: A Manual.* New Haven, CT: Yale Child Study Center.

Smith, J. D., Shields, W. E. & Washburn, D. A. (2003). The comparative psychology of uncertainty monitoring and metacognition. *Behavior and Brain Sciences, 26*: 317–373.

Solomon, J. & George, C. (2008). The measurement of attachment security and related constructs in infancy and early childhood. In J. Cassidy & P. R. Shaver (Eds.), *Handbook of Attachment: Theory, Research, and Clinical Applications* (2nd edn, pp. 383–416). New York: The Guilford Press.

Solomon, J. & George, C. (2011). Disorganization of maternal caregiving across two generations: The origins of caregiving helplessness. In J. Solomon & C. George (Eds.), *Disorganized Attachment and Caregiving* (pp. 25–51). New York: The Guilford Press.

Sonuga-Barke, E. J. S. & Castellanos, F. X. (2007). Spontaneous fluctuations in impaired states and pathological conditions: A neurobiological hypothesis. *Neuroscience and Biobehavioral Reviews, 31*: 977–986.

Spates, C. R., Koch, E., Cusack, K. J., Pagoto, S. & Waller, S. (2009). Eye Movement Desensitization and Reprocessing. In E. B. Foa, T. M. Keane, M. J. Friedman & J. A. Cohen (Eds.), *Effective Treatments for PTSD: Practice Guidelines from the International Society for Traumatic Stress Studies* (2nd edn, pp. 279–305). New York: The Guilford Press.

Spitzer, R. L., First, M. B. & Wakefield, J. C. (2007). Saving PTSD from itself in DSM-V. *Journal of Anxiety Disorders, 21*: 233–241.

Sroufe, L. A., Egeland, B., Carlson, E. A. & Collins, W. A. (2005). *The Development of the Person: The Minnesota Study of Risk and Adaptation from Birth to Adulthood.* New York: The Guilford Press.

Sroufe, L. A. & Waters, E. (1977). Attachment as an organizational construct. *Child Development, 48*: 1184–1199.

Steele, H. & Steele, M. (2008). Ten clinical uses of the Adult Attachment Interview. In H. Steele & M. Steele (Eds.), *Clinical Applications of the Adult Attachment Interview* (pp. 3–30). New York: The Guilford Press.

Steele, H., Steele, M. & Fonagy, P. (1996). Associations among attachment classificaitons of mothers, fathers, and their infants. *Child Development, 67*: 541–555.

Stern, D. N. (1985). *The Interpersonal World of the Infant: A View from Psychoanalysis and Developmental Psychology.* New York: Basic Books.

Stevenson-Hinde, J. (2005). The interplay between attachment, temperament, and maternal style: A Madingley perspective. In K. E. Grossman, K. Grossman & E. Waters (Eds.), *Attachment from Infancy to Adulthood: The Major Longitudinal Studies* (pp. 198–222). New York: The Guilford Press.

Stovall-McClough, K. C., Cloitre, M. & McClough, J. F. (2008). Adult attachment and posttraumatic stress disorder in women with histories of childhood abuse. In H. Steele & M. Steele (Eds.), *Clinical Applications of the Adult Attachment Interview* (pp. 320–340). New York: The Guilford Press.

Strathearn, L. (2011). Maternal neglect: Oxytocin, dopamine and the neurobiology of attachment. *Journal of Neuroendocrinology, 23*: 1054–1065.

Strathearn, L., Fonagy, P., Amico, J. & Montague, P. R. (2009). Adult attachment predicts maternal brain and oxytocin response to infant cues. *Neuropsychopharmacology, 34*: 2655–2666.

Strathearn, L., Iyengar, U., Fonagy, P. & Kim, S. (2012). Maternal oxytocin response during mother-infant interaction: Associations with adult temperament. *Hormones and Behavior, 61*: 429–435.

Strathearn, L., Li, J., Fonagy, P. & Montague, P. R. (2008). What's in a smile? Maternal brain responses to infant facial cues. *Pediatrics, 122*: 40–51.

Striepens, N., Kendrick, K. M., Maier, W. & Hurlemann, R. (2011). Prosocial effects of oxytocin and clinical evidence for its therapeutic potential. *Frontiers in Neuroendocrinology, 32*: 426–450.

Suomi, S. J. (2008). Attachment in rhesus monkeys. In J. Cassidy & P. R. Shaver (Eds.), *Handbook of Attachment: Theory, Research, and Clinical Applications* (2nd edn, pp. 173–191). New York: The Guilford Press.

Swain, J. E. (2011). The human parental brain: In vivo neuroimaging. *Progress in Neuro-Psychopharmacology and Biological Psychiatry, 35*: 1242–1254.

Swain, J. E., Thomas, P., Leckman, J. F. & Mayes, L. C. (2008a). Parent-infant attachment systems. In E. L. Jurist, A. Slade & S. Bergner (Eds.), *Mind to Mind: Infant Research, Neuroscience, and Psychoanalysis* (pp. 264 303). New York: Other Press.

Swain, J. E., Thomas, P., Leckman, J. F. & Mayes, L. C. (2008b). Parent-infant attachment systems: Neural circuits and early-life programming. In E. L. Jurist, A. Slade & S. Bergner (Eds.), *Mind to Mind: Infant Research, Neuroscience, and Psychoanalysis* (pp. 264–303). New York: Other Press.

Swanton, C. (2003). *Virtue Ethics: A Pluralistic View*. New York: Oxford.

Taylor, S. E., Saphire-Bernstein, S. & Seeman, T. E. (2010). Are plasma oxytocin in women and plasma vasopressin in men biomarkers of distressed pair-bond relationships? *Psychological Science, 21*: 3–7.

Thompson, R. (2008). Early attachment and later relationships: Familiar questions, new answers. In J. Cassidy & P. R. Shaver (Eds.), *Handbook of Attachment: Theory, Research, and Clinical Applications* (2nd edn, pp. 348–365). New York: The Guilford Press.

Trickett, P. K., Reiffman, A., Horowitz, L. A. & Putnam, F. W. (1997). Characteristics of sexual abuse trauma and the prediction of developmental outcomes. In D. Cicchetti & S. L. Toth (Eds.), *Developmental Perspectives on Trauma: Theory, Research, and Intervention* (Vol. 8, pp. 289–311). Rochester, NY: University of Rochester Press.

van der Kolk, B. A. (2005). Developmental trauma disorder. *Psychiatric Annals, 35*: 401–408.

van der Kolk, B. A. (2007). The history of trauma in psychiatry. In M. J. Friedman, T. M. Keane & P. A. Resick (Eds.), *Handbook of PTSD: Science and Practice* (pp. 19–36). New York: The Guilford Press.

van der Kolk, B. A. & d'Andrea, W. (2010). Towards a developmental trauma disorder diagnosis for childhood interpersonal trauma. In R. A. Lanius, E. Vermetten & C. Pain (Eds.), *The Impact of Early Life Trauma on Health and Disease: The Hidden Epidemic* (pp. 57–68). New York: Cambridge University Press.

van IJzendoorn, M. H. (1995). Adult attachment representations, parental responsiveness, and infant attachment: A meta-analysis on the predictive validity of the Adult Attachment Interview. *Psychological Bulletin, 117*: 387–403.

van Ijzendoorn, M. H. & Bakermans-Kranenburg, M. J. (2008). The distribution of adult attachment representations in clinical groups: A meta-analytic search for patterns of attachment in 105 AAI studies. In H. Steele & M. Steele (Eds.), *Clinical Applications of the Adult Attachment Interview* (pp. 69–96). New York: The Guilford Press.

van Ijzendoorn, M. H. & Sagi-Schwartz, A. (2008). Cross-cultural patterns of attachment: Universal and contextual dimensions. In J. Cassidy & P. R. Shaver (Eds.), *Handbook of Attachment: Theory, Research, and Clinical Applications* (2nd edn, pp. 880–905). New York: The Guilford Press.

van IJzendoorn, M. H., Schuengel, C. & Bakermans-Kranenburg, M. J. (1999). Disorganized attachment in early childhood: Meta-analysis of precursors, concomitants, and sequelae. *Development and Psychopathology, 11*: 225–249.

Vanderwal, T., Hunyadi, E., Grupe, D. W., Connors, C. M. & Schulz, R. T. (2008). Self, mother and abstract other: An fMRI study of reflective social processing. *NeuroImage, 41*: 1437–1446.

Vaughn, B. E., Bost, K. K. & van Ijzendoorn, M. H. (2008). Attachment and temperament: Additive and interactive influences on behavior, affect, and cognition during infancy and childhood. In J. Cassidy & P. R. Shaver (Eds.), *Handbook of Attachment: Theory, Research, and Clinical Applications* (2nd edn, pp. 192–216). New York: The Guilford Press.

Vygotsky, L. S. (1978). *Mind in Society: The Development of Higher Psychological Processes.* Cambridge, MA: Harvard University Press.

Wachtel, P. L. (2008). *Relational Theory and the Practice of Psychotherapy.* New York: The Guilford Press.

Walker, L. E. (1979). *The Battered Woman.* New York: Harper & Row.

Walker, L. E. (1999). Psychology and domestic violence around the world. *American Psychologist, 54*: 21–29.

Wallace, B. A. (2009). *Mind in the Balance: Meditation in Science, Buddhism and Christianity.* New York: Columbia University Press.

Wallin, D. J. (2007). *Attachment in Psychotherapy.* New York: The Guilford Press.

Weaver, I. C. G., Cervoni, N., Champagne, F. A., D'Alessio, A. C., Sharma, S., Seckl, J. R., Dymov, S., Szyf, M. & Meaney, M. J. (2004). Epigenetic programming by maternal behavior. *Nature Neuroscience, 7*: 847–854.

Wegner, D. M. (1994). Ironic processes of mental control. *Psychological Review, 101*: 34–52.

Weinfield, N. S., Sroufe, L. A., Egeland, B. & Carlson, E. (2008). Individual differences in infant-caregiver attachment. In J. Cassidy & P. R. Shaver (Eds.), *Handbook of Attachment: Theory, Research, and Clinical Applications* (2nd edn, pp. 78–101). New York: The Guilford Press.

Welch, S. S. & Rothbaum, B. O. (2007). Emerging treatments for PTSD. In M. J. Friedman, T. M. Keane & P. A. Resick (Eds.), *Handbook of PTSD: Science and Practice* (pp. 469–496). New York: The Guilford Press.

Wellman, H. M. & Lagattuta, K. H. (2000). Developing understandings of mind. In S. Baron-Cohen, H. Tager-Flusberg & D. J. Cohen (Eds.), *Understanding other Minds: Perspectives from Developmental Cognitive Neuroscience* (pp. 21–49). New York: Oxford University Press.

Wells, A. (2009). *Metacognitive Therapy for Anxiety and Depression*. New York: The Guilford Press.

Whalen, P. J., Rauch, S. L., Etcoff, N. L., McInerney, S. C., Lee, M. B. & Jenike, M. A. (1998). Masked presentations of emotional facial expressions modulate amygdala activity without explicit knowledge. *Journal of Neuroscience, 18*: 411–418.

Wicker, B., Keysers, C., Plailly, J., Royet, J. -P., Gallese, V. & Rizzolatti, G. (2003). Both of us disgusted in my insula: The common neural basis of seeing and feeling disgust. *Neuron, 40*: 655–664.

Widom, C. S. (1989). The cycle of violence. *Science, 244*: 160–166.

Wiliamoska, Z. A., Thompson-Hollands, J., Fairholme, C. P., Ellard, K. K., Farchione, T. J. & Barlow, D. H. (2010). Conceptual background, development, and preliminary data from the unified protocol for transdiagnostic treatment of emotional disorders. *Depression and Anxiety, 27*: 882–890.

Williams, J. C. & Lynn, S. J. (2010). Acceptance: An historical and conceptual review. *Imagination, Cognition and Personality, 30*: 5–56.

Wilson, S. A., Becker, L. A. & Tinker, R. H. (1995). Eye Movement Desensitization and Reprocessing (EMDR) treatment for psychologically traumatized individuals. *Journal of Consulting and Clinical Psychology, 63*: 928–937.

Wilson, S. A., Becker, L. A. & Tinker, R. H. (1997). Fifteen-month follow-up of Eye Movement Desensitization and Reprocessing (EMDR) treatment for posttraumatic stress disorder and psychological trauma. *Journal of Consulting and Clinical Psychology, 65*: 1047–1056.

Wimmer, H. & Perner, J. (1983). Beliefs about beliefs: Representation and constraining function of wrong beliefs in young children's understanding of deception. *Cognition, 13*: 103–128.

Winnicott, D. W. (1971). *Playing and Reality*. London: Routledge.

Wolock, I. & Horowitz, B. (1984). Child maltreatment as a social problem: The neglect of neglect. *American Journal of Orthopsychiatry, 54*: 530–542.

Yates, T. M. (2009). Developmental pathways from child maltreatment to nonsuicidal self-injury. In M. K. Nock (Ed.), *Nonsuicidal Self-Injury: Origins, Assessment, and Treatment* (pp. 117–137). Washington, DC: American Psychological Association.

Young, L. J. & Wang, Z. (2004). The neurobiology of pair bonding. *Nature Neuroscience, 7*: 1048–1054.

Zahn, R., Moll, J., Krueger, F., Huey, E. D., Garrido, G. & Grafman, J. (2007). Social concepts are represented in the superior anterior temporal cortex. *PNAS, 104*: 6430–6435.

Zanarini, M. C., Williams, A. A., Lewis, R. E., Reich, R. B., Soledad, C. V., Marino, M. F., Levin, A., Yong, L. & Frankenburg, F. R. (1997). Reported pathological childhood experiences associated with the development of borderline personality disorder. *American Journal of Psychiatry, 154*: 1101–1106.

Zanetti, C. A., Powell, B., Cooper, G. & Hoffman, K. (2011). The Circle of Security intervention: Using the therapeutic relationship to amelioratee attachment security in disorganized dyads. In J. Solomon & C. George (Eds.), *Disorganized Attachment and Caregiving* (pp. 318–342). New York: The Guilford Press.

Zeifman, D. & Hazan, C. (2008). Pair bonds as attachments: Reevaluating the evidence. In J. Cassidy & P. R. Shaver (Eds.), *Handbook of Attachment: Theory, Research, and Clinical Applications* (2nd edn, pp. 436–455). New York: The Guilford Press.

Zeki, S. (2009). *Splendors and Miseries of the Brain: Love, Creativity, and the Quest for Human Happiness.* Chichester, UK: Wiley.

INDEX

327